The Act of Writing

Canadian Essays for Composition
Second Edition

The Act of Writing

Canadian Essays for Composition

Second Edition

Ronald Conrad

Ryerson Polytechnical Institute

McGraw-Hill Ryerson Limited

Toronto   Montreal   New York   Auckland   Bogotá
Cairo   Hamburg   Lisbon   London   Madrid   Mexico
Milan   New Delhi   Panama   Paris   San Juan
São Paulo   Singapore   Sydney   Tokyo

The Act of
Writing
Canadian Essays for Composition
Second Edition

Copyright© McGraw-Hill Ryerson Limited, 1987, 1983. All rights reserved. No part of this publication may be reproduced, stored in a retrieval system, or transmitted, in any form or by any means, electronic, mechanical, photocopying, recording, or otherwise, without prior written permission of McGraw-Hill Ryerson Limited.

ISBN 0-07-549302-0

1 2 3 4 5 6 7 8 9 0 AP 6 5 4 3 2 1 0 9 8 7

Printed and bound in Canada

Cover illustration by David Chang

Art Direction by Daniel Kewley

Cover photography: Zipper Studios

Care has been taken to trace ownership of copyright material contained in this text. The publishers will gladly take any information that will enable them to rectify any reference or credit in subsequent editions.

Canadian Cataloguing in Publication Data

Conrad, Ronald, date -
The act of writing : Canadian essays for composition

ISBN 0-07-549302-0

1. English language — Rhetoric.   2. Canadian essays (English).*   I. Title.

PE1429.C66 1987   808'.0427   C86-094209-0

TABLE OF CONTENTS

AND THEN. . . .

WRITING ABOUT MYSELF

"There were cheers and laughter as Tivadar hit me in the nose
before I got my jacket off. It was not the first time I had tasted my
own blood, but it was the first time a Christian had made it flow."

i

WRITING ABOUT OTHERS

FOR EXAMPLE. . . .

four histories of Ontario counties, five books on how to diet, two authorized biographies of Teilhard de Chardin, and one book by a man who lived six months with a colony of apes and didn't find out anything."

IT'S LARGE AND YELLOW AND. . . .

HERE'S WHY. . . .

IT'S JUST THE OPPOSITE OF. . . .

IN A WAY, IT'S LIKE. . . .
Chapter 6: ANALOGY and related devices 203

THERE ARE THREE KINDS OF THEM. . . .
CHAPTER 7: CLASSIFICATION 231

HERE'S HOW IT'S DONE. . . .

HERE'S EXACTLY WHAT IT IS. . . .

Chapter 9: EXTENDED DEFINITION 313

TABLE OF CONTENTS BY SUBJECT

CHILDHOOD AND OLD AGE

ix

PEOPLES AND PLACES

MAINLY CANADIAN

ACKNOWLEDGEMENTS

Ian Adams: "Living with Automation in Winnipeg" from *The Poverty Wall* by Ian Adams. Reprinted by permission of the Canadian Publishers, McClelland and Stewart Limited, Toronto.

Doris Anderson: "The 51-Per-Cent Minority," Doris Anderson, *Maclean's*, January 1980. Reprinted by permission of Doris Anderson.

Margaret Atwood: "Canadians: What Do They Want?" by Margaret Atwood from *Mother Jones*, January 1982. Used by permission of *Mother Jones*.

Pierre Berton: "The Dirtiest Job in the World" from *The Smug Minority* by Pierre Berton. Reprinted by permission of The Canadian Publishers, McClelland and Stewart Limited, Toronto.

Harry Bruce: "Johnny Canuck is a Yuk" by Harry Bruce. Reprinted from *Each Moment as It Flies*, Methuen Publications, 1984.

Gregory Clark: "The Cat" by Gregory Clark. Used by permission of the Montreal Standard (1973) Limited.

Austin Clarke: Excerpt from *Growing Up Stupid Under the Union Jack* by Austin Clarke. Reprinted by permission of The Canadian Publishers, McClelland and Stewart Limited, Toronto.

Mary Conrad and Jean-Paul Chavy: Translation of letter by Edgar Roussel to The Honourable Mark MacGuigan in *Le Devoir*. Permission granted by the translators, by *Le Devoir* and by The Honourable Mr. Justice Mark R. MacGuigan, Federal Court of Appeal, Ottawa K1A 0M9.

Donald Creighton: Excerpt from *Canada: The Heroic Beginnings*, 1974. Reproduced by permission of the Minister, Supply and Services Canada, from the publication *Canada: The Heroic Beginnings*, published by Macmillan of Canada in cooperation with Indian and Northern Affairs Canada, Parks Canada and the Canadian Government Publishing Centre, Supply and Services Canada.

Jill Davey: "Pumping Iron — à la Femme" by Jill Davey. Printed by permission of the author.

Robertson Davies: "The Decorums of Stupidity" from *A Voice from the Attic* by Robertson Davies. Reprinted by permission of The Canadian Publishers, McClelland and Stewart Limited, Toronto.

Wendy Dennis: "A Tongue-Lashing for Deaf Ears" by Wendy Dennis, *Maclean's*, November 1981. Used by permission of the author.

Allan Fotheringham: "When the Natives Surrender" by Allan Fotheringham, *Maclean's*, October 17, 1983. Reprinted by permission of Allan Fotheringham.

Robert Fulford: From *Crisis at the Victory Burlesk: Culture, Politics & Other Diversions* by Robert Fulford © copyright 1968 Oxford University Press Canada. Reprinted by permission.

George Gabori: "Coming of Age in Putnok" from *When Evils Were Most Free*, George Gabori, Deneau Publishers. Used by permission of the publishers.

John Kenneth Galbraith: From *The Scotch* by John Kenneth Galbraith. Copyright © 1974 by John Kenneth Galbraith. Reprinted by permission of Houghton Mifflin Company.

David Godfrey: "No More Teacher's Dirty Looks" by David Godfrey, from *Gutenberg Two*, 1st Edition (Press Porcépic, 1979), reprinted by permission of the author.

Richard Gossage and Melvin J. Gunton: Copyright © Richard Gossage and Melvin Gunton, 1981. Reprinted with permission from Seal Books.

Martin Allerdale Grainger: "In Vancouver" from *Woodsmen of the West* by Martin Allerdale Grainger, 1908. Courtesy of Daryl Duke and Norman Klenman, The Canadian Kinetoscope Company Limited.

Ray Guy: "Outharbor Menu" from *That Far Greater Bay* by Ray Guy. Reprinted by permission of Breakwater Books.

Terry Hackenberger: "Michelle" by Terry Hackenberger. Printed by permission of the author.

Roderick Haig-Brown: "Articles of Faith for Good Anglers" from *The Master and His Fish* by Roderick Haig-Brown. Reprinted by permission of The Canadian Publishers, McClelland and Stewart Limited, Toronto.

Charles Yale Harrison: From *Generals Die in Bed* by Charles Yale Harrison (Potlatch Publications Limited, Hamilton, Ontario).

Pauline Harvey: From "Si tu n'as pas fait ta rhetorique chez Satan" by Pauline Harvey (translated by Mary Conrad), *Le Devoir*, November 16, 1985, in the supplement "Salon du Livre de Montreal." Used by permission of *Le Devoir*.

Bruce Hutchison: "Cowboy from Holland" from *Canada: Tomorrow's Giant*, Bruce Hutchison, 1957. Permission granted by the author.

Claude Jasmin: From *La Petite Patrie* by Claude Jasmin. Copyright © 1972 Les Editions la Presse Ltée.

Joanne Kates: "Real Foods and Cold Comfort" by Joanne Kates. From the *Globe and Mail*, April 13, 1985. Used by permission of the author.

W.P. Kinsella: "How to Write Fiction" by W.P. Kinsella. From the *Globe and Mail*, April 27, 1985. Used by permission of the author.

Joy Kogawa: From *Obasan* by Joy Kogawa, © 1981. Reprinted by permission of Lester & Orpen Dennys Publishers Ltd., Canada.

Myrna Kostash: "Profile of the Rapist as an Ordinary Man" by Myrna Kostash. From *Maclean's*, April 1975. Used by permission of the author.

Gary Lautens: "Man, You're a Great Player!" from *Laughing with Lautens* by Gary Lautens. Reprinted by permission of McGraw-Hill Ryerson Limited.

Stephen Leacock: "How to Live to be 200" from *Literary Lapses* by Stephen Leacock. Reprinted by permission of The Canadian Publishers, McClelland and Stewart Limited, Toronto.

Félix Leclerc: Excerpt from *Pieds nus dans l'aube*. Coll. "Bibliothèque canadienne-française." Montreal, Fidès 1978. Permission to reprint Philip Stratford's English translation of the excerpt granted by Nelson Canada Limited.

Christie McLaren: "Suitcase Lady Holds a Package of Dreams" by Christie McLaren in the *Globe and Mail*, January 24, 1981. Permission granted by the *Globe and Mail*.

Hugh MacLennan: Selection from *Barometer Rising* by Hugh MacLennan. Reprinted by permission of the author and his agent, Blanche C. Gregory, Inc. Copyright © 1941 by Hugh MacLennan.

Thierry Mallet: Extract from "Glimpses of the Barren Lands" by Captain Thierry Mallet, one of Canada's fur-trading post settlers of REVILLON FRÈRES, pioneer fur company since 1723. Copyright © 1930 by The Atlantic Monthly Company, Boston. Reprinted with permission.

Philip Marchand: "Learning to Love the Big City" from *Just Looking, Thank You* by Philip Marchand. Copyright © 1976 by Philip Marchand.

John Metcalf: "What Happened to CanLit?" by John Metcalf in the *Globe and Mail*, November 19, 1983. Permission granted by John Metcalf.

Farley Mowat: Excerpt from *People of the Deer* by Farley Mowat. Copyright © 1952, Farley Mowat Limited. Used by permission of the author.

Richard Needham: "A Sound of Deviltry by Night" from *The Hypodermic Needham*, 1970. Used by permission of Richard J. Needham and the *Globe and Mail*, Toronto.

Michael Ondaatje: Copyright © Michael Ondaatje, from RUNNING IN THE FAMILY (McClelland and Stewart, 1982). Used by permission of the author.

Al Purdy: "The Iron Road" from *No Other Country* by Al Purdy. Reprinted by permission of The Canadian Publishers, McClelland and Stewart Limited, Toronto.

Bill Reno: "Supermarket Technology" by Bill Reno in *The Canadian Forum*, March 1982. Used by permission of Bill Reno, Director of Research and Education, United Food and Commercial Workers.

Mordecai Richler: Excerpt from *Home Sweet Home: My Canadian Album* by Mordecai Richler (McClelland and Stewart, 1984). Used by permission of the author.

Erika Ritter: Excerpt from URBAN SCRAWL © 1984 Erika Ritter. Reprinted by permission of Macmillan of Canada, A Division of Canada Publishing Corporation.

Paul Rush: Column by Paul Rush that appeared in *The Financial Post Magazine* on July 1, 1985. Permission of THE FINANCIAL POST MAGAZINE.

Franklin Russell: From *The Hunting Animal* by Franklin Russell. Used by permission of The Canadian Publishers, McClelland and Stewart Limited, Toronto.

Alan Stewart: "Cars Make the Man a Boy" by Alan Stewart, *Globe and Mail*, May 9, 1981. Used by permission of the author.

Judy Stoffman: "The Way of All Flesh" by Judy Stoffman, *Weekend Magazine*, September 15, 1979. Reprinted by permission of the author.

David Suzuki: "Don't Count on 'Futurists' to Know What the Future Holds." Reprinted with permission — The Toronto Star Syndicate.

To the Student

This book is designed to help you develop a skill: your writing. But it is designed for you on another level as well: If you love or hate computers, if the small town bores you or the big city excites you, if you like being young and fear growing old, if you work with factory machines and feel like one yourself, if you think Americans help us or harm us, if you have suffered because of your race or language or religion or sex, if you like hockey because it's a rough game, if you love or hate work — then read the essays in this book. Hear what some of our most provocative Canadian writers say about life. You will agree sometimes and disagree other times. But since most of these writers discuss things that in some way you have experienced or will experience, let them make their argument. You may learn something. And if you sometimes disagree, you may still learn something as your reaction helps you to realize what you believe.

The essays in this book vary greatly. Some are short and some are long; some are easy and some are challenging; some are funny and some are serious. But they all have two things in common:

1. They are models of good writing — writing that is entertaining, graceful in style, and clearly focussed on a message. Just as hearing good models of speech helps us to speak, reading good models of writing helps us to write.

2. They illustrate the most common ways of organizing information. Each chapter contains several essays that all use the same underlying pattern of development. As you begin a chapter you will read some of the essays, then discuss their message and their underlying form in class. (Key terms that appear in SMALL CAPITALS in the discussion questions are explained in a glossary at the end of the book.) Finally, in an essay of your own, you will practise the form that you have discussed.

The essay topics are carefully chosen for their significance. Writing about things that matter increases our interest in the writing. And research has demonstrated what many students and teachers have experienced: it is motivation, more than any other factor, that leads to improvement in writing. It is my hope, then, that you will enjoy not only these readings but also the act of writing that follows them.

R.C.

To the Teacher

The warm reception that students and teachers have given *The Act of Writing* since its publication in 1983 has been gratifying. As revision time approached, it also posed a challenge: how can a text be renewed while preserving the qualities that readers liked in the first edition?

We began with a survey of teachers. Almost all respondents who had used the first edition wanted "little" to "moderate" overall change, especially in the general character and main features of the book. Yet they suggested an average of about one-third new essays and agreed to a remarkable extent on which selections to keep and which to replace. We have followed their advice: just over a third of the selections are new, yet we have kept every one of the dozen essays rated most highly in the survey and have dropped most of those toward the bottom of the list. (We kept three or four that did not rate high but which we view as exceptional in quality or significance.)

Respondents were also nearly unanimous that "clarity of organization" is their main criterion in choosing essays for class discussion. We have respected this priority, adding a good number of selections that are more clearly structured than those they replace (many are also shorter, to facilitate analysis and to provide models closer in length to student essays).

In other respects the second edition has evolved while keeping its basic character: we have added two essays from the world of business, two more from French Canada (for a total of four), one more by a student (for a total of three), and have kept roughly the same proportion of humorous pieces. The total number of essays has risen slightly from 48 to 52, and many of the 19 new selections are by nationally known authors: Allan Fotheringham, John Kenneth Galbraith, Claude Jasmin, John Metcalf, Michael Ondaatje, Mordecai Richler, Erika Ritter, David Suzuki and more.

Finally, the pedagogical apparatus has been fine-tuned but not changed in character. The introductory essay, "The Act of Writing," has two new sections: "Prewriting" and "How Many Drafts?" Some of the chapter introductions have been revised lightly, biographical introductions have been updated where necessary, discussion questions have been improved here and there, some of the end-of-chapter essay topics have been replaced, and a few definitions have been added to the glossary. (The instructor's manual has of course been revised and is available gratis upon request.)

How to Use This Book

The Act of Writing offers flexibility and encourages individualization. It deliberately presents more selections than you will use (seven chapters with six selections each and two chapters with five selections each). Thus you can choose the essays that best suit the level and subject matter of your course and the interests of your students. This book also offers a range of difficulty, from essays that are easily accessible to almost all students to essays that are frankly challenging. (NOTE: The beginning of your instructor's manual ranks all selections by level of difficulty, so that if you are new to this book you can more easily plan a syllabus to fit the needs of your class.)

Note also the two tables of contents. The first lists all selections in their chapters arranged by *form of organization* (you can choose from six essays, for example, that all demonstrate organization through comparison and contrast). The second table of contents lists all essays by general *subject,* to help you choose selections of interest to your particular students.

An introductory essay, "The Act of Writing," starts the book off by putting to rest a number of widespread misconceptions about writing that plague students in the classroom, then attempts to describe what it is that an essayist actually does. It emphasizes the individuality of the writer, the importance of motivation, the usefulness of intuition as well as logic, and a balance of spontaneity and craftsmanship.

The essays are all by Canadians or by persons with Canadian experience, but the scope ranges widely: some essays are about Canada, some are about other countries, and most are concerned with such universal themes as childhood, aging, work, technology, sport and war. The use of Canadian essays is not a statement of nationalism. In fact, it is an attempt to bring to Canada the kind of anthology that is taken for granted in other countries: a collection of works that are mostly universal in theme but that, naturally, draw a good part of their content from the country in which the book will be used.

The selections are chosen first of all for clarity of organization and quality of style, so that they will serve as enjoyable reading and as models of good writing. Other main considerations are variety and significance of subject matter; variety of style, tone, length and difficulty; and representation of women and minorities. Most of this book's 52 selections are essays. A few are carefully crafted examples of popular journalism, and a few are self-contained passages of fiction or autobiography.

As we have seen, the essays are arranged in chapters that each demonstrate a fundamental and useful pattern of organization. Narration starts the book off because no approach is easier or more motivating for a first assignment than writing a story, in chronological order, about oneself. Example and Description follow, because these methods of development are used to some degree in almost all writing. Cause and Effect and the following chapter, Comparison and Contrast, are the heart of the book: these are probably the most effective patterns to know. Analogy and Classification follow Comparison and Contrast, for they are both varieties of comparison. Process Analysis and Extended Definition end the book. Although they are well-used devices of organization, one or both might be omitted from a busy course without doing major damage.

Each essay is prefaced with an introduction to the author and his or her work, and each essay is followed by a number of discussion questions arranged in three groups: STRUCTURE, STYLE and IDEAS. Note that different questions serve different purposes. Some are directive, calling attention to major features of the essay. Some are technical, for example focussing on a specific point of language that illustrates a technique. And still others are exploratory, encouraging open-ended response. The instructor's manual offers answers to those questions that are not open-ended and suggests responses to some that are. Read the manual's introduction: it gives more suggestions for using *The Act of Writing* in class. For each essay, the manual also lists vocabulary that may need attention.

Each of the nine chapters begins with a discussion of how and why to use the form at hand, and ends with a selection of 25 to 30 essay topics chosen to fit that form. Some of these topics came from a survey that asked students what they would most like to write about; others were originated by students in journal writing or in open-ended class essays; still others have been newly devised to tap some of the students' deepest concerns and channel them into motivation for writing. The reason for this attention to topics is that no one problem is more destructive to the performance of both student and teacher than dull or superficial subject matter. How can writing be important if its content is not? And how can a teacher enjoy or even tolerate marking without an interest in *what* the students are saying? Further topics for writing appear *within* the chapter, one or more at the end of each selection. If class members have had a good discussion about the selection, their motivation and writing performance may be greatest if they explore these topics, which draw upon both the subject and the underlying form of the essay that precedes them.

Finally, a glossary at the end defines literary terms often used in the discussion questions; when one of these terms is a key part of a passage, it appears in SMALL CAPITALS.

I would like to thank those who helped me in planning and writing this edition: students, colleagues, teachers who gave their opinions in our survey, writers, and editors. I appreciate the help given me by faculty members of Université Laval: Aurélien Boivin, John Stockdale, and Melaine and Philippe Duchâstel. I would also like to thank John Miller and Dorothy O'Brien, both of St. Lawrence CEGEP, as well as Sue Brown, J. J. Gingras, Richard and Cathy Brown and Monique Dorval. Sincere thanks to my wife, Mary, for her good advice. I am grateful to Norma Christensen for her sustained help in securing permissions for this edition. Finally and especially, I thank Ryerson Polytechnical Institute for the sabbatical leave that made this edition possible.

R.C.

The Act of Writing

Writing is one of the most widely misunderstood of human activities. It is odd that after all the years we have spent in school, after all the hours we have spent reading other people's writing and producing our own, most of us cannot say what really happens when we write. We can describe other complicated tasks — driving a car, baking bread, building a radio or programming a computer. But to most people the act of writing is a mystery. Not that we don't have theories, either those told us in school or those we have arrived at ourselves. But many of these theories are misconceptions that actually hinder our efforts to write. Let's look at some of them.

MISCONCEPTION: Writing is like following a blueprint: I figure it all out in advance and then just fill in the details.
Of course an outline, used sensibly, will help. But too many of us were taught in school that our best thinking goes into a logical and detailed outline — and that the writing itself is secondary. Thus we are reduced to carpenters or plumbers of the written word, who merely saw, cut and fit the pieces in place once the master plan has been established. The problem with this reassuringly logical approach is that it views writing as a science, not as the art that all our practical experience tells us it is. How many of us have given up on a required outline, done our thinking mostly as we wrote the essay itself, then produced an outline by seeing what we just wrote? Or how many of us have painfully constructed a detailed outline in advance, only to find while writing the essay that our real message does not fit the plan?

Writing is exploring! We know the direction in which we will go and the main landmarks we hope to pass, but not every twist and turn of the path. What a dull trip it would be if we did! Let's leave room for discovery, because some of our best ideas occur in the act of writing. But while avoiding the rigor mortis of overplanning, let's not go to the opposite extreme, like Stephen Leacock's famous horseman who "rode madly off in all directions." We do work best with an outline, five or ten or fifteen lines that define the main point and how we will support it. But our outline should be a brief one — a compass on a journey, not a blueprint for a construction project.

MISCONCEPTION: If I don't hit it right the first time, I've failed.
It's not hard to see where this idea came from: in school we write so many essays and tests within the limits of one class period that writing in a hurry begins to seem normal. But merely completing

such an assignment is difficult; seriously revising it is impossible. Few people, under these circumstances, can "hit it right the first time." Professional writers know this; most of them take longer to write than do the rest of us. They tinker with words and sentences, they cross out and replace sections, they go through two or three or even five or ten drafts — and sometimes they throw the whole thing out and start over. These writers know by experience that writing is not a hit-or-miss affair with only one try allowed, but a *process.* They know that careful polishing can yield astonishing results.

Unfortunately, little can be done to polish an in-class essay. Your other writing, though, deserves better. Scrutinize it. Hear it read aloud. Replace weak words with strong ones and vague words with exact ones. Revise awkward sentences. Make sure that what you mean is what you say. Of course the process is work, but that work brings with it the pleasure of craftsmanship.

MISCONCEPTION: When I write, I am speaking on paper.
If you have heard yourself speaking on tape, you were no doubt surprised at the number of filler words you used. "Uh," "um," "well" and "hmmm" are good to fill in the gaps between your thoughts but hardly help to carry the message. And if you listened closely, you may have been surprised at the number of incomplete statements — fragments that by themselves made little or no sense. Fillers and fragments are tolerated in speech because, after all, we are making up our message on the spot. There is no chance to plan, revise, proofread or polish.

But in writing there is, and this fact increases the expectations of your reader far beyond those of your listener. Language in written form is planned. It is complete. It is precise and concise. It uses standard words. It is punctuated. It follows all the rules. In short, it is a product of the time that its written form allows you to give it, not a spur-of-the-moment hope-for-the-best effort like the speech that comes so easily from your mouth.

MISCONCEPTION: The best words are the biggest words.
Variations on this theme are *If my writing looks scholarly it will impress the reader,* and even *If I make my essay so difficult that no one knows what I'm saying, everyone will believe me.* At the roots of these widespread ideas is a notion that writing is a kind of competition between writer and reader. If the writer is obscure enough he will make the reader feel like a dummy and will thus win the game.

Avoiding the game altogether is difficult when so many leaders in business, education and government play it. The first step toward open communication, though, is to think of your reader not as an opponent but as an ally. You are both working toward the same goal, which is the reader's clear understanding of your ideas. Another step is to admit that words small in size can be large in meaning. The best-loved writings in our language show a strong preference for short words. Writing made of them is more concise, more vivid and usually more understandable than writing made of the elephantine words that some of us ransack the dictionary for. When a long word conveys your meaning best — perhaps like "elephantine" above — by all means use it. But all too often the writer, like the architect, finds that *more is less*.

MISCONCEPTION: I don't like to write.
For some unfortunate people this statement is true. For most who say it, though, the truth is really "I don't like to *begin* writing." Who does? Staring at that blank page is like staring from a diving board at the cold water below. But a swimmer and a writer both work up their courage to plunge in, and soon they both experience a new sensation: they don't want to come out. Teachers whose students write journals in class see the process at work every day. As class begins, the writers are filled with stress: they chew their pens and frown as they stare at the page to be filled. But a few minutes later they are scribbling furiously away, recording in an almost trance-like state their latest experiences, feelings and insights. And when the teacher asks them to stop, in order to begin the next activity, they are annoyed: they sigh and *keep on writing* until asked a second or third time to stop.

Let's admit that most writers — and that includes professionals — dread the beginning. Let's also admit that most writers enjoy the rest of it, hard work though it may be.

With some of the most widespread misconceptions behind us, let's take a fresh look at the act of writing. First, let's allow for personal differences. *Know yourself!* If you are the kind of person whose desk is piled a foot high with papers and books, whose closet is an avalanche waiting to happen and whose shoes have not been shined in two years, you may write best by planning little and emphasizing your spontaneity. If you are the kind of person who plans an August holiday in January, who keeps a budget right down to the penny, and who washes the car every Wednesday and Saturday whether it needs it or not, you may write best by planning extensively. On the other hand, your natural tendencies may have caused you problems and may therefore need to be fought. If your spontaneity has produced writings that can't stay on topic, plan more: make a careful outline. If overorganizing has sucked the life out of your writing, free yourself up: leave more room for discovery as you write. Whatever the case, use the approach that works for *you*.

Let's allow also for differences in assignments. If you are dashing off a short personal sketch, your planning may be no more than an idea and a few moments of thought. If you are writing a 30-page research essay, the product of weeks in the library, you may need an outline two pages long. No one approach works for every person and for every assignment. Keep in mind, then, that the process we are about to examine is a *starting point,* a basis but not a blueprint for your own writing.

THE BEGINNINGS OF AN ESSAY CAN BE FOUND IN THE ANSWERING OF SEVERAL QUESTIONS:

1. *Why am I writing?* This most basic of questions too often goes unasked. If the answer is "to fill up five pages," "to impress" or "to get an 'A'," you are beginning with a severe handicap. The immediate reason to write may be a class assignment, but the real reason must be to communicate something of value. Otherwise your motivation is lost and so is your performance. Therefore, choose from a list of topics the one that is most significant to you. If no topic seems significant, devise a way to *make* one significant. Look at it from a new viewpoint or approach it in some unusual way. If that fails, and if your teacher is approachable, voice your concern and suggest an alternative topic. One teacher always made his first-year university students analyze the relative merits of chocolate and vanilla ice cream, on the theory that a dull subject will not distract a writer from the real goals: grammar and style. He was wrong. Research demonstrates that motivation is the prime cause of improvement in writing — and motivation comes largely from writing about things that matter.

When you write on your own, as in a private journal, you may still need to answer the question *Why am I writing?* Simply recording events can be dull. Record also your feelings, your perceptions and your conclusions about those events. If you have personal problems, as most people do, confront them on the page. The more you discover yourself and your world through writing, the more important the writing becomes.

2. *How big is my topic?* Classroom essays are shorter than most people realize. A book may contain 100,000 words; a magazine article 2000 or 5000; a classroom essay as few as 500 or even 250.

Therefore narrowing the essay topic is more important than most people realize.

One student, who had been a political prisoner, decided to write about economic systems. He knew the subject well and was committed to it. But what he attempted was an analysis of communism, socialism and capitalism — all in two pages! A lack of focus spread his very short essay so thin that it approached the state of saying nothing about everything. It was the barest scratching of the surface, a summary of basic facts that everyone already knows.

If the same person had described his arrest and imprisonment — or even one day in his cell — he might have said far more about the system he had fought against. It is in specifics that we best learn generalities. Think of writing as photography. Putting aside the wide-angle lens that includes too much at a distance, look through the telephoto lens that brings you up close to a small part of the subject. Select the part most meaningful to you, perhaps the part most characteristic of the whole, and then take the picture.

Nearly all of the essays in this book are closeups: they tend to explore one situation, one incident, one person or one process. Yet most of them are longer than the essays you will write, especially in class. Therefore when you choose a topic, judge its size before you write. And if you have to, *change* its size.

3. *What message am I sending?* You may know your topic well. But unless you send a message concerning it, your reader will think *what's the point?* A message is often a value judgment: are robots dangerous? Will they take away our jobs or someday even rule over us? Or do they help us? Will they free us at last from the dehumanizing tyranny of manual labour? Most of the essays in this book take such a stance, either pro or con, toward their subjects. Some avoid judging their subjects directly, but send other messages: one shows what it's like to be down and out; one shows how a childhood event can shape us as adults; another shows how aging is a continual, life-long process.

If you have chosen a topic because it seems meaningful, you will no doubt have a message to send. What do you most feel like saying about the topic? Once you know, get it down in writing. This THESIS STATEMENT, as it is often called, normally comes at or near the beginning of an essay. It is an introductory sentence or passage that does more than just tell what the topic is; it clearly states, as well, what you are saying *about* the topic. It lets your reader know what is coming — and, in the process, it commits you to a purpose that all the rest of the essay must in one way or another support. It is your guide as you write.

4. *Who is my reader?* Do you talk the same way to a friend and a stranger? To an old person and a child? To a hockey coach and a professor? Probably not. Neither would you write the same way to all readers. In a private journal you can write as freely as you think, for you are the reader: omissions and excesses of all kinds will be understood and forgiven. In letters to a close friend you are nearly as free, for the reader knows you well enough to supply missing explanations or interpret remarks in the light of your personality. But your freedom shrinks when you write for others: a business person, a public official, a teacher. Now you must fight a misconception shared by many people: *everyone is like me.*

This idea is seldom articulated but may lurk as a natural assumption in the backs of our minds. It is a form of egotism. If you assume that everyone is like you, many readers will not accept or even understand your message — because they are *not* like you. They did not grow up in your family, neighbourhood or even country. They are older or younger, or of the opposite sex. They have had different life experiences and as a result have different knowledge and temperaments and values.

Keep these differences in mind as you write. You will not prove your point by quoting Marx to a capitalist, the Bible to an atheist, or Germaine Greer to a male supremicist. Any argument built on a partisan foundation will collapse if the reader does not accept that foundation. Instead, build from facts or ideas that your reader probably does accept: killing is bad, government is necessary, women are human beings and so on. Is your topic controversial? Then avoid an open display of bias. Calling intellectuals "Commies" or abortionists "hired killers" will appeal only to those who shared your view in the first place.

Does the reader know what you know? If you write about statistics for a statistics teacher, use any technical terms customary to the field, and avoid the insult of explaining elementary points. But if you write on the same subject for a class exercise in English or a letter to the editor, your reader will be very different: avoid most technical terms, define those you do use, and explain more fully each step of your argument.

The more open you become to the individuality of your reader, the more open your reader becomes to your message. It is a matter of mutual respect.

Prewriting

How do we begin the act of writing: by putting those first words on a page? The philosopher Lao-Tze said, "A journey of a thousand miles begins with the first step." In a way he was right: if we never take that official first step, we will certainly never arrive at our destination. But how much day-dreaming, planning and scheming do we do beforehand? Do we set out on a journey without consulting the map or the calendar or the tourist brochure or the travel guide — not to mention our bankbook? And do we write an essay without in some way resolving the questions we have just asked:

Why am I writing?
How big is my topic?
What message am I sending?
Who is my reader?

The act of writing, then, begins in thought. But thoughts do not come on command. Like the diver, we look down at the cold water and dread the plunge. Some writers try to "break the ice" by manipulating their environment: finding a quiet spot in front of a blank wall, a particularly soft or hard chair, good lighting or a favourite pen. Others fortify themselves with a good night's sleep, food or a cup of coffee. Still others loosen up through exercise or music. Any of these tricks may help, but they all avoid the real issue: how do we begin to *think?*

One very direct approach, a variation on the traditional technique of outlining, is *brainstorming:* once you have roughly identified your subject, simply write down words or phrases that relate in any way to it. Cover a page with these fragments. Put down anything that comes, letting one thought lead to another. Some entries will seem off topic, trivial or even loony, but others may be just what you need: the keys to your essay. Circle them. Put them in order. As crude as this primitive outline may seem, it has served a purpose: your thoughts have begun to arrive. You are now ready for the first "step" of your journey.

A similar but much more powerful "icebreaker" is *freewriting.* Put a blank piece of paper on the desk with your watch beside it. Think of your topic. Now *write!* Put down anything that comes: sentences, phrases, words — logical thoughts, hasty impressions, even pure garbage. Do not cease the physical act of writing, do not even lift the pen from the page, for at least five minutes. If your next thought doesn't come, write the last one over and over until the next one does come. What you produce may surprise you.

Like brainstorming, freewriting is an exercise in free association: the flow of your thoughts, the unpredictable leaps of your intuition, will "break the ice," priming you to write. They may also do much more: as in brainstorming, you may end up with a page of scribbling that contains the main points of your essay. Try to find them. Circle them. Put them in order. See if your intuition has led the way in answering the questions: *Why am I writing? How big is my topic? What message am I sending? Who is my reader?* If all goes well, you are now both emotionally and logically prepared to begin your journey.

The First Words

Once your thoughts are flowing, you perform the official first step of Lao-Tze's thousand-mile journey, the opening passage of your essay. In a very short composition your THESIS STATEMENT may serve also as the first words. In many longer essays it comes at the end of an introduction. Only about one-fourth of the selections in this book start right off with what could be called a thesis statement. What do the others start with?

Background information: About half the essays in this book lead off by relating the circumstances in which the topic is set. For examples, see the beginnings of our essays by Berton (p. 168), Dobbs (p. 31), Gabori (p. 4), Jasmin (p. 100) and Roussel (p. 245).

Anecdote: A brief story, usually of a humorous or dramatic incident, can lead into the topic. See Atwood (p. 121), Hutchison (p. 63), Kostash (p. 335) and Leacock (p. 277).

Quotation or allusion: The words of a philosopher, of a news report, of a recognized specialist in the subject or of anyone with close experience of it can be used to break the ice. See Bruce (p. 319), Godfrey (p. 259) and Kogawa (p. 66).

Sense images: Vivid description can attract a reader's interest to the topic. See Adams (p. 81), Clarke (p. 163), Grainger (p. 303) and Mallet (p. 85).

A striking comparison or contrast: Showing how things are like or unlike each other is a dramatic way to introduce a topic. See Atwood (p. 121), Fotheringham (p. 116), Haig-Brown (p. 233) and Marchand (p. 175).

A poem: See Purdy (p. 7).

Narrative: Several selections in this book begin by telling a story upon which the essay is based. See Dennis (p. 141), Harrison (p. 15) and MacLennan (p. 104).

Unusual or puzzling statement: Such an opening appeals to the reader's curiosity. See Fotheringham (p. 116), Fulford (p. 51) and Kinsella (p. 252).

Figures of speech: A striking METAPHOR, SIMILE or PERSONIFICA-TION can spark the opening. See Leclerc (p. 223), Metcalf (p. 55), Stewart (p. 208) and Stoffman (p. 282).

Most of these introductions are short: a couple of sentences or a paragraph or two at the most. And almost all of them are designed to *interest* the reader, for an apathetic reader may not even finish the essay, let alone like or understand it. Writing is fishing. You throw in the line. Your reader tastes the bait (your introduction), bites, is pulled through the waters of your argument, and — if the line of thought doesn't break — lands in your net.

You, the writer, may also be "hooked." Once you have hit upon a strong introduction, one that shows off the drama or importance of your topic, the beginning may carry you along with it. And once you get going, the idea embodied in your thesis statement may pull you through the essay, enabling you to write freely as one passage leads to another. You may become less and less aware of your surroundings as you become more and more immersed in your subject. With a good beginning, you may experience the act of writing the way one student described it: "At first I couldn't start, but then I couldn't stop."

The Body

By itself, an introduction is a head without a body. A head gives direction, but without a body it goes nowhere. The "body" of your essay has the main work to do: following the direction set by your introduction, and especially by your thesis statement, it explains, illustrates, and sometimes attempts to prove your point. But if it ever ignores the direction set by the head, it ceases to do its job. Even the best of explanations, without a sense of direction, is like one of those unfortunate football players we sometimes hear about who complete a ninety-yard run to the wrong goal.

The most obvious way to keep a direction is to base your essay on a particular form — and that is what most of this book is about. As you read and discuss the essays that follow, and as you write your own essays using the forms upon which other writers have based their organization, you will develop a range of choices:

Narration: In simple time order, from the first event to the last event, tell a story that illustrates the point.

Example: Give one in-depth example or a number of shorter examples that explain the point.

Description: Recreate for your reader, through the most vivid language possible, your own or someone else's experience with the subject.

Cause and effect: Explain by showing how one situation or event causes another.

Comparison and contrast: Explain by showing how two things are like or unlike each other.

Analogy: In comparing two things, use the one to explain the other.

Classification: Make a point by fitting the parts of your subject into categories.

Process analysis: Show how something happens or how something is done.

Extended definition: Explain your subject by showing in detail what it is.

Seldom does one of these forms appear alone. A *process analysis,* for example, is usually told as a *narrative.* Here and there it may use *examples, description* or any of the other patterns to help make its point. But these combinations occur naturally, often without the writer's knowing it. In most cases the only form deliberately chosen by a writer is the main one upon which the whole essay is structured.

How do you choose the right form? Let the subject be your guide. In architecture, form follows function. Rather than cram an office into a pre-selected structure, a designer likes to begin with the *function* of that office. How much space best serves its needs? What shape? What barriers and passageways between one section and another? What front to present to the world?

An essay is much the same: the needs of its subject, if you are sensitive to them, will in most cases suggest a form. If the main point is to show your reader what something is like, you may naturally use examples and description. If the subject is unusual or little known, you may use a comparison or contrast, or an analogy to something that the reader does know. If its parts seem important, you may discuss them one by one in a classification. And when some other need is greater, you may use still another form. If you stay open to the subject, whatever it is, this process can be so natural that you *recognize* rather than *choose* a form.

If the process is natural, then why study the forms in this book? Think of the architect again: why does he or she study design in school? For one thing, knowing how each form is constructed assures that the building will not collapse. For another, in those cases when the choice is *not* easy, a conscious knowledge of all the possibilities will help.

Consider the longer essay — perhaps a report or research paper. A stack of notes sits on your desk. They are in chaos. Even knowing your purpose, having the facts and completing a thesis statement, you can't think of how to coordinate all those facts. First give the natural process its best chance: sort all your notes into groups of related material, using a pair of scissors if necessary to divide unrelated points. When everything is in two stacks, or five stacks or ten, let your mind work freely. How do these groups relate to each other? Does one come before another in time? Does one cause another? Does one contradict another? Are they all steps in a process or parts of a whole? Now add your conscious knowledge of the forms: do you see narration, example, description, cause and effect, comparison and contrast, analogy, classification, process analysis or extended definition? It is the rare case when one of these forms cannot supply the basic structure to support your argument.

If you use the essay topics at the end of each chapter in this book, your choice of form will already be made. This process may seem to bypass the ideal method of letting form follow function. The topics, though, are selected to go well with the form studied in their chapter. And just as the architect practises the standard designs in school to learn their forms and functions, so can the writer deliberately practise the standard essay designs to learn *their* forms and functions. Both architect and writer will then be ready when the choice is truly open.

Transitions

We have mentioned the passageways inside a building. Without them an office would be useless: no one could move from one room to another or pass business from one stage to another. Yet some essays are built without passageways. One point ends where another begins, without even a "then" or "therefore" or "however" or "finally" to join them. Readers have to spend a great deal of effort breaking through the walls in order to follow the writer's train of thought from one room to the next.

Help your readers. *You* know why one point follows another, but do *they?* Make sure by supplying transitions: say "although" or "but" or "on the other hand"; say "because" or "as a result" or "since"; say "first" or "next" or "last"; say "for example" or "in conclusion." And when moving readers from one major division of your essay to the next, devote a full sentence or even a paragraph to the job (one good example is paragraph 10 of Doris Anderson's essay).

Your plan may be the right one, setting your points in their most logical order. But let that logic show: give your readers a door between every room.

The Closing

We've discussed the beginning, the middle and transitions between parts. What remains is of course the ending. Every essay has one — the point at which the words stop. But not all endings are closings. A closing is deliberate. In some clear way it tells the reader that you have not just run out of time, ink or ideas, but that you have *chosen* to stop here. If you end at just any convenient spot, without engineering an effect to fit your ending, the essay may trail off or even fall flat. But as preachers, composers, playwrights and film directors know, a good closing can be even stronger than a good opening. How do the essays in this book come to a close? They use a variety of devices:

Reference to the opening: Repeating or restating something from the opening gives a sense of culmination, of having come full circle. See the openings and closings by Atwood (pp. 121 and 124), Berton (pp. 168 and 173), Kogawa (pp. 66 and 69) and Stoffman (pp. 282 and 289).

Contrast or reversal: This ironic device exploits the dramatic potential of the closing. See the openings and closings by Fulford (pp. 51 and 53), Purdy (pp. 7 and 12) and Stoffman (pp. 282 and 289).

Question: A question and its answer, or a question calling for the reader's answer, is a common means of closing. See Bruce (p. 319), Davies (p. 205), Dennis (p. 141), Leacock (p. 277), Reno (p. 132), and Stewart (p. 208).

Quotation: A good quotation, either of prose or poetry, can add authority and interest to a closing. See Haig-Brown (p. 233) and Harvey (p. 326).

Transition signals: Words, phrases or sentences of transition commonly signal the closing. See Fotheringham (p. 116), Gabori (p. 4), Galbraith (p. 94) and Marchand (p. 175).

Revealing the significance: Showing the implications or importance of the subject makes for a strong closing. See Bruce (p. 319), Clark (p. 127), Gabori (p. 4) and Reno (p. 132).

Summary: About a fourth of the essays in this book give a summary, either alone or in combination with other closing techniques, but one that is always *short*. See Berton (p. 168), Haig-Brown (p. 233) and Mallet (p. 85).

Conclusion: Although "conclusion" is often a label for the closing in general, more accurately it is only one of many closing techniques — the drawing of a conclusion from the discussion in the essay. See Fotheringham (p. 116), Kostash (p. 335) and Reno (p. 132).

Prediction: A short look at the subject's future can very logically close a discussion of that subject's past or present. See Godfrey (p. 259), Marchand (p. 175), Reno (p. 132) and Rush (p. 315). Sometimes discussing the future takes the form of a call to action (see Dennis, p. 141).

You have probably noticed that some authors are named more than once; like openings, closings can exploit more than one technique. In fact, the more, the better. Stay open to techniques that appear while you write, even as you construct a closing on the one technique you have deliberately chosen. Any of these choices will be stronger, though, when used with the most fundamental technique of all: building your whole essay toward a high point or climax. Put your points in order from least important to most important, from least useful to most useful or from least dramatic to most dramatic. Then you will have made possible a closing that applies all the dramatic power of the final position.

When you get there, apply the force of that closing to a real message. Techniques used just for their own sake are cheap tricks. Do not waste them. Instead, use them to underline your basic message, to impress upon your reader one last and most convincing time that what you have to say is significant. Your closing, more than any other part of your essay, can send the reader away disappointed — or moved.

How Many Drafts?

We have discussed the fact that some essays are crammed into one class period. We have also labelled as a misconception the idea that a writer will "hit it right the first time." How do we reconcile these opposites? Basically we cannot. Few people benefit from writing more than one draft in a single class period: the sheer act of recopying takes so long that virtually no time is left for the actual revising. Yet a single draft is often more of an exploration than a finished product — closer to freewriting than to most of the carefully written and rewritten essays in this book.

A few small steps can help to reduce the damage when you must write fast in class. If you know the topic beforehand, prewrite before arriving (see "Prewriting"). If you do not, as in an essay exam, think your topic out briefly and get a few notes on paper before you start. Then watch the time, finishing a few minutes before the period ends, so you can fix up at least a few of the minor flaws.

Let's leave this emergency situation now and look at better circumstances. Most of the important writing you will do in your lifetime — major essays, essential letters, reports and proposals — will be the products of more thought and more time.

First you think. You prewrite. You find your thesis statement. Then you write the first draft, fairly fast, postponing major revisions that will choke off the flow of your thought. If you type, the speed of a first draft done right on the machine may help your thought to flow freely. (Double- or triple-space, to make later revision easier.) And if you use a word processor, do not correct all the errors now — there will be plenty of time later, when your thoughts are safely out in the open.

As you finish this "discovery draft," you may experience a sense of exultation that we could call the "writer's high." Enjoy it. But don't believe it, because first drafts have a way of looking worse the next day. When that next day arrives, read over what you wrote. It seems like a good beginning. But in a while you reach for the pen or pencil to improve a little point, then another and another — until in an hour or so your draft is covered with revisions. The word "revision" literally means "seeing again." As you see again, you will find inexact thoughts. Make them exact. You will find long and flabby words. Replace them with short and strong ones. You will find abstractions. Bring them alive with examples. You will find barriers between thoughts. Bridge them with transitions. And you may find errors of grammar, punctuation and spelling. These may seem minor, but they are all worth your attention: correct them.

How many times must we "see again" to reach our best writing performance? In most cases two or three drafts will heighten the force of your thoughts to a level far beyond that of the first draft. Sometimes another draft or two will take you even farther. It is in these final stages that the act of writing provides its greatest reward: your response to a significant topic becomes so direct, so exact, so forceful, that at last you know exactly what you think. It is clear that you were writing for others, but at this moment it is even clearer that you were writing for yourself.

In Memoriam
Nellie A. Bailey
1887-1986

Canapress Photo Service (Chuck Stoody)

" 'You're selling tickets,' I said. 'You're a gate attraction now — not some bum
who only can skate and shoot and the rest of it. Your profanity is beautiful.' "
Gary Lautens, "Man, You're a Great Player!"

And then....

NARRATION

Telling a story, or narrating, is one of the most appealing and natural ways to convey information. Every time you tell a joke, trade gossip, invent a ghost story or tell a friend what you did on the weekend, you are narrating. In both speech and writing, telling a story can be the most direct way to make a point. If your idea or opinion was formed by your experience, a clear account of that experience will often help people to understand and even to accept your point.

How could a soldier explain the terrors of a shelling attack better than by narrating his own experience of it? Charles Yale Harrison narrates the third selection of this chapter, "In the Trenches." He might have constructed a logical argument to make his point. But instead he tells us how the blast threw him into the air, how the ground heaved, how he breathed the smoke and tasted his own blood. As his readers, we tend to identify with him, share his experience and, most important of all, understand his point.

In some ways narrating is easy. The only research Harrison required was his own experience. And his basic plan of organization was no more complicated than the chronological order in which the events occurred. (A flashback to the past or a glance at the future may intervene, but basically a narrative is the easiest of all writing to organize.) Yet a narrative, like any other form of writing, is built on choices:

Scope: Time stretches infinitely toward both the past and future — but where does your narrative most logically begin and end? In "The Iron Road" Al Purdy narrates a journey, telling how at age seventeen he rode the rails to Vancouver. He also rode the rails back, but does *not* include that part: instead he chooses to end on a high point, the sudden self-perception that made him start back the very day he arrived. Include only the section of your story that best illustrates your point. If facts about the past or future are needed sketch them in, as Purdy does, with a few words of explanation.

Details: Which details will contribute to the main point? Reject the trivial ones and seek those that represent your dominant impression or idea. Which details are most vivid? Reject the weak ones and select those that help the reader to see, hear, feel, smell or taste — in other words, those that most encourage the reader to *experience* the events.

Connections: Readers like to be "swept along" by a narrative. How is this effect achieved? Partly by an economical use of words, and partly by the use of time signals. Like road signs for the motorist, the words "at first," "next," "then," "immediately," "suddenly," "later," "finally" and "at last" show the way and encourage progress. Use these words, and others like them, wherever they fit. Choose carefully, making the right signals help to build your effect.

So far we have discussed only the first-person narrative. There are many advantages to writing about yourself. You know your subject well (in fact, is there any subject that you know better?), yet in writing about yourself you may come to new understandings of your ideas and actions. You are vitally interested in your subject and thus will be motivated to do your best in writing about it. And finally, your reader may appreciate the authenticity of a story told by the very person who experienced the event.

But it is not always possible or even desirable to limit the subject to oneself. In choosing the third-person narrative, which tells the actions of others, the writer opens up a vast area of possibilities. Only through writing about others can one discuss past eras, places one has never visited and events one has never experienced. In the second half of this chapter, Donald Creighton uses archaeological and historical evidence to write about the Vikings, Kildare Dobbs uses an interview to write about the first victims of nuclear war and Gary Lautens consults his imagination to produce a narrative in its freest form, fiction.

George Gabori

Coming of Age in Putnok

Translated from the Hungarian by Eric Johnson with George
Faludy

*George Gabori (pronounced Gábori) is a taxi driver in Toronto. But like
many immigrants to Canada, he has a past that he will not soon forget.
Gabori was born in 1924 to a Jewish family in the village of Putnok,
Hungary. His childhood was happy but short, for when the Germans
occupied Hungary and threatened the existence of the Jews, he joined the
resistance. He led daring sabotage raids on railyards and docks until the
Gestapo sent him, still a teenager, to a concentration camp. Things did not
improve when the Russians drove out the Germans; soon after his release
from a Nazi camp, he found himself breaking rocks in a notorious Soviet
labour camp. Always outspoken, Gabori played a part in the 1955 revolution,
then escaped from Hungary and eventually wrote his memoirs in Hungarian.
Eric Johnson condensed and translated the work. When it appeared in 1981,
the critics were moved. Our selection, "Coming of Age in Putnok," is the
opening passage of George Gabori's story in* When Evils Were Most Free.*

1   When I was nine years old my father, victorious after a long
argument with my grandfather, took me out of our town's
only *cheder* and enrolled me in its only public school.
Overnight I was transported from the world of Hebrew letters and
monotonously repeated texts to the still stranger world of Hungarian letters, patriotic slogans and walls covered with maps.

2   Grandfather rolled his eyes and predicted trouble, but it seemed
he was wrong. I sat beside a boy my own age named Tivadar, a
gentile — everybody was a gentile in that school except me. Tivadar
and I got along famously until, after two or three weeks, he
approached me in the schoolyard one day and asked me if it was true
what the others were saying, that "we" had murdered Jesus.

3   Strange to tell — for this was 1933 and we were in Hungary — I
had never heard about this historical episode, and I left Tivadar
amicably enough, promising to ask my father about it. We met
again the next morning and I told him what I had learned: that the
Romans had killed Jesus, and that anyway Jesus had been a Jew,
like me, so what did it matter to the Christians?

4   "That's not true," said Tivadar menacingly.

5   "My father does not lie," I replied.

4

By now a crowd had gathered around us and there was nothing for 6
it but to fight it out. There were cheers and laughter as Tivadar hit
me in the nose before I got my jacket off. It was not the first time I
had tasted my own blood, but it was the first time a Christian had
made it flow. Tivadar was flushed with pleasure and excitement at
the applause and not at all expecting it when I lashed out with my
fist and sent him sprawling backward on the cobbles. The crowd of
boys groaned and shouted to Tivadar to get up and kill the Jew, but
poor Tivadar did not move. Frightened, I grabbed my jacket and
shoved my way through the crowd stunned into silence by this
overturning of the laws of nature.

They were silent at home too when I told them what had 7
happened. My father sent for me from his office in the afternoon, and
I entered cap in hand. He always wore a braided Slovak jacket at
work and looked more like a peasant than a Jewish wine merchant.

"Well, who started it?" asked my father, wearing an expression I 8
had never seen on his face before. I was not at all frightened.

"He did. I told him what you said about Jesus and he challenged 9
me."

My father clamped his teeth on his cigar and nodded, looking 10
right through me.

"Jews don't fight," he finally said. 11

"Then why did you put me in a Christian school?" I asked in a 12
loud, outraged whine.

"That's why I put you there, my son," he said at last, then swept 13
me up and kissed me on the forehead. "You're learning fast; only
next time don't hit him quite so hard."

Then he sent me out quickly and I stopped on the landing, startled 14
to hear loud, whooping, solitary laughter coming out of my father's
office.

Structure:

1. What is the most basic pattern by which this selection is
   organized?
2. Point out at least ten words or phrases that signal the flow of
   time in this narrative.
3. Reread the first paragraph carefully. Has Gabori given us a good
   background to the selection? Name every fact that this
   introduction reveals about the setting and about the author.

Style:

1. How economical or wasteful of words is this opening passage of George Gabori's autobiography? After reading it, how well do you think you know the author and his times? Could you predict with confidence anything of his character or fate as an adult? Does this opening selection make you feel like reading the rest of the book? Why or why not?
2. Gabori's book, *When Evils Were Most Free,* is a translated and condensed version of the Hungarian original. To what extent does this fact separate us from the author's thoughts? How exact can a translation be? If you yourself speak two languages, how precisely can you express sayings from one in the other? To what extent can Gabori's translator, Eric Johnson, be thought of as the author of this selection?
3. Gabori states in paragraph 6, "It was not the first time I had tasted my own blood. . . ." Is this image effective? If so, why?
4. When Gabori refers to "poor Tivadar" (par. 6), is the word "poor" used in a special sense? What is Gabori really saying?

Ideas:

1. What is the "overturning of the laws of nature" to which Gabori refers at the end of paragraph 6?
2. Was Gabori's father right in moving the boy from a Hebrew *cheder* to a public school? In disproving the idea that "Jews don't fight" (par. 11), has the boy learned a worthwhile lesson? Or has he merely imitated the worst traits of his opponents, thereby becoming like them?
3. Every ethnic group in Canada — including the English Canadians — is a minority. Has your minority suffered any form of persecution in Canada? If you have been a victim, narrate an actual incident and your reaction to it. Give plentiful details, as Gabori does.
4. What are autobiographies for? What do you think writing your own life story would do for you? What might it do for others?
5. Write a chapter of your own autobiography. Select *one* incident that taught you something about yourself or about life in general, and *narrate* it in chronological order. Following the example of Gabori, use words economically and vividly.

(NOTE: See also the Topics for Writing at the end of this chapter.)

Al Purdy

The Iron Road

Al Purdy is one of Canada's most prolific and best-known poets. Born in 1918 in Wooler, Ontario, Purdy has had a wide range of experiences that have been reflected in the unusual variety of his writings. He rode the rails during the Depression, spent six years with the RCAF during World War II, ran a taxi business, helped organize a union in a Vancouver mattress factory and has travelled widely both in Canada and abroad. He now lives in Ameliasburg, Ontario. Purdy has written more than a hundred plays for radio and television and since 1944 has published and edited over twenty-five books, mostly of poetry. Among his best known are The Cariboo Horses *(winner of the Governor-General's Award, 1965),* Wild Grape Wine *(1968),* Love in a Burning Building *(1970),* Sex and Death *(1973),* In Search of Owen Roblin *(1974) and* The Stone Bird *(1981). He has also written many articles for magazines. Our selection was first published in* Canada Month *in 1963, then in 1977 was collected in a book of Purdy's essays,* No Other Country. *It illustrates both Purdy's love of concrete experience and his ability to convey that experience in words.*

> Riding the boxcars out of Winnipeg in a
> morning after rain so close to
> the violent sway of fields it's
> like running and running
> naked with summer in your mouth
> being a boy scarcely a moment and you
> hear the rumbling iron roadbed singing
> under the wheels at night and a door jerking open
> mile after dusty mile riding into Regina with
> the dust storm crowding behind you
> night and morning over the clicking rails

The year was 1937, and I was seventeen. I rode the freight 1
trains to Vancouver, along with thousands of other Canadians during the Great Depression. In the Hungry Thirties it seemed that half the population was on the move. The unemployed workmen of Toronto and Montreal and all the other big cities swarmed over the boxcars, moving west to the Prairies, west to Vancouver, wherever there might be hope of finding work.

There were also the professional hoboes, who always went in the 2
opposite direction from where there was any rumour of employment.

They lived in hobo jungles beside rivers and near the towns, never far from the railway yards. There they lit campfires, cooked food, washed clothing — if it was absolutely necessary — and told tales of the steel highways while standing over the fires at night. Of towns where housewives always invited you inside for dinner when you asked for a handout, and never handed you an axe while pointing sternly at the woodpile. Of towns where you never had to work, there was always plenty of beer. . . . But after a day or two in the jungle they got restless again, and boarded the train to Anywhere.

3   It was a dark night in early June when I caught my first train at the railway yards in Trenton, Ontario. It had chuffed in from the east an hour earlier, and was about to pull out for Toronto. The yards were full of shunting switch engines bustling back and forth in the night, red and green signal lights gleaming like the eyes of stationary cats, and every now and then you heard a hoarse, impatient scream from the whistles of the westbound train.

4   I'll never know how I had the nerve to board that train, for I was scared to death of it. I'd quit school a couple of years before, and there was no work at all in Trenton. But that wasn't the reason why I was heading west. The reason was boredom. I wanted adventure. That was why I crouched in some bushes beside the tracks, almost too nervous to breathe, wondering how I'd ever manage to climb onto that boxcar. Was it something like getting on a bicycle or a horse? And where were the railway police hiding?

5   Suddenly the westbound train made a peculiar "toot-toot" that signaled departure — a sound I've heard many times since. Hoboes call it "the highball." Then a great metallic crash came from the couplings, and the train grunted away into the night. I broke from cover and ran alongside, grabbing at the steel ladder of a passing boxcar, and climbed up onto the roof — collapsing on the swaying catwalk while all the vertebrae of the wriggling wooden serpent beneath me thundered west.

6   A few days later and miles from home, I received my first instructions from a professional bum about the proper method of boarding a moving train. A lean little man with a dark stubble of beard, he'd seen me swing onto a train by the rear ladder of a boxcar.

7   "That's the way guys get killed," he said. "Ya gotta do it the right way." He spat tobacco on the boxcar floor and gestured. "I seen guys lose a leg or arm falling under them wheels. Ya always go for the ladder at the front end of the car, never the one at the back end. If ya miss yer hold on the rear ladder ya fall between the cars and yer a gone goose. Always the front ladder. An remember that, kid."

8   There were other famous bums who wrote their names and deeds on boxcar walls or on the supports of watertanks with knife and

pencil — Regina Sam Jones, Montana Slim, Midnight Frank. I've often wondered: why should a man call himself "Midnight Frank"? There was also the immortal Kilroy, who wrote "Kilroy was here" the length and breadth of the continent.

Farther west, at Broadview, Saskatchewan, the Mounties had a reputation for being very tough on bums. The stories about their toughness alarmed me so much that I crawled down the trap door of a threshing machine mounted on a flatcar before going through town. I crouched in the darkness of that monster, nervously waiting to be discovered and hauled off to jail. I heard the police tramping around outside, making a tremendous racket, but they didn't find me. When the train pulled out on its way west, I was the only illicit passenger left of the three score or so who had ridden with me into Broadview.

When I first started out for Vancouver I had some money in my pockets. But it was soon spent. I had to forsake the aristocratic habit of eating in restaurants and join the other bums knocking on doors to ask for handouts. It was embarrassing, but I got used to it. You nerved yourself, knocked on a door, and waited, wondering what might happen. The dignity of man was, of course, a lesser consideration than being hungry.

You might get a sandwich from a housewife, perhaps even a full meal, a "sitdown" we used to call it; but you might also be given an axe and directed to the woodpile; or a man in shirtsleeves might come to the door and tell you to "Beat it, bum!" It was all part of the game, and you didn't really hold any grudges for a harsh reception. You just kept on trying.

Sometimes you went to the bakery of whatever small town you happened to be passing through, asking the baker if he had any stale bread or buns. Most of the time you got something to eat, but occasionally there were long stretches on the train where it wasn't possible to ask for a handout. At such times you stayed hungry.

On my first trip west I hitchhiked north from Sault Ste. Marie, and was disheartened to find that the road ended at a little village called Searchmont (at that time the Trans-Canada Highway was not yet completed through Northern Ontario). Near midnight I boarded a freight travelling north and west, riding in an open-air gondola used to transport coal. After an hour it began to rain, and the coaldust made things worse. My face and hands were streaked with it. We stopped around 5 AM and it was still dark. I had no idea where I was, but the rain and coaldust were too miserable to be borne. I ripped the seal off a boxcar with my hunting knife and tried to get inside. But the door was too big and heavy for me to move, so I went back to my gondola and huddled under the rain in silent misery.

14   A railway cop materialized out of the greyness not long after I got settled. He'd seen the broken seal, and knew I was responsible. He told me that the settlement was named Hawk Junction, then locked me up in a caboose with barred windows and padlocked door. And I thought: how would my mother feel now about her darling boy? At noon the railway cop took me to his house for dinner with his wife and children, gave me some *Ladies Home Journals* to read, and casually mentioned that I could get two years for breaking the boxcar seal.

15   When returned to my prison-on-wheels I felt panicstricken. I was only seventeen, and this was the first time I'd ventured far away from home. I examined the caboose-prison closely, thinking: two years! Why, I'd be nineteen when I got out, an old man! And of course it was hopeless to think of escape. Other prisoners had tried without success, and windows were broken where they'd tried to wrench out the bars. And the door: it was wood, locked on the outside with a padlock, opening inward. It was a very springy door though: I could squeeze my fingertips between sill and door, one hand at the top and the other a foot below. That gave me hope, blessed hope, for the first time. My six-foot-three body was suspended in air by my hands, doubled up like a coiled spring, and I pulled. Lord, how I pulled! The door bent inward until I could see a couple of daylight inches between door and sill. Then, Snap! and screws pulled out of the steel hasp outside. I fell flat on my back.

16   Peering cautiously outside, right and left, I jumped to the ground, walking as slowly and sedately as I could make myself — toward freedom. The urge to run was hard to resist, especially when crossing a bridge over a wide river along the tracks, and continuing steadily in the direction of Sault Ste. Marie, 165 miles south of the railway divisional point. But that cop would be looking for me, and so would other blue uniforms! Two years! Walking the tracks would make me far too obvious, much too easy to find. So how about making the journey twenty or thirty feet into the heavy forest lining both sides of the right of way? That way I could see if anyone came after me, and duck back among the trees. Brilliant, positively brilliant.

17   But the trees went uphill and down, turned leftways and rightways, without landmarks or anything to orient me with the tracks. I began to feel uneasy: better stay close to the railway. Too late. I was deep into the woods, not knowing in which direction to turn. I was lost — and didn't even feel stupid, just terrified. My heart began to pump hard, and I ran, with branches and leaves slapping my face, blundering into trees, splashing through little streams.

Finally I stopped, knowing panic was useless but feeling it   18
anyway. The possibility of dangerous animals occurred to me: what
about bears? — bears must live in these woods. I had no defense
against them; the railway cop had confiscated my hunting knife.
Besides, what good would such a feeble weapon be against an angry
black bear? And the brown shape that flitted between the trees, not
so much seen as realized, what was that?

I slept on the side of a hill, huddled around a mother-tree, and it   19
was cold, cold. Morning was grey with a light rain falling, more mist
than rain. By this time I'd thought of the sun as some kind of
directional reference, but there was no sun. And just a couple of
miles away I could hear engines shunting and butting back and
forth in the railway yard, the sound seeming to come from all
directions among the trees. Old logging trails meandered through
the forest, but they were so old that when I tried to follow them they
vanished in the vague greyness. Once I stumbled on an old hunting
camp, so ancient that the lean-to logs were rotten. Later in the day,
during my stumbling, lurching progress, I came on that hunting
camp twice more, each time increasingly terrified about walking in
circles.

At age seventeen I didn't believe in God, at least I told myself I   20
didn't. But this was no time to take chances one way or the other. I
prayed. Fervently, passionately, and with no reservations, I prayed
to get out of that forest. And remembered the forty-some Sundays
I'd attended church two years before, without listening to the
preacher's sermon but in order to receive a prize for attendance.
Since then I'd become a non-believer in that fire-and-brimstone God,
but now for reasons of expediency I pretended to myself and to a
possible Him that my backsliding was over — at least for as long as I
was lost in this northern forest.

And maybe it worked: I still don't know. That railway bridge   21
I'd crossed when leaving Hawk Junction popped into my head.
Adolescent high school logic took over. The river and railway tracks
would make two sides of a very large isosceles triangle. And carry it
a step farther: if I could finally walk in something close to a straight
line, which hadn't happened thus far, then I must finally locate
either river or tracks. And the sun, now becoming a pale spot in the
overhead grey, gave me some small direction. I walked and walked,
and two hours later nearly fell head-first down an embankment into
that blessed blessed river.

That same evening I boarded a passenger train just behind the   22
engine, and rode south to the Soo in style, careless of legal
consequences. But no cops appeared on the smoky, cindered horizon
of fear. At the steel town I dived into a Scandinavian steambath to

stop the shivering chill that I'd picked up from two days in the woods. And sleeping that night in a cheap flophouse, I was still shuddering a little, in slow motion.

23   I think my first sight of the mountains was worth all the hardships — waking early in the morning inside an empty boxcar and gazing down into a lake surrounded by forest stretching for miles and miles — cupped and cradled by the white peaks. And myself crawling round the side of a mountain like a fly on a sugar bowl. For the first time I realized how big this country was. And, naively, because I was only seventeen years old, I felt a tremendous exaltation at the sight. How marvelous to be alive and to ride a barebacked train through such a country. And, naively, forty years later, I've not changed my mind.

24   Vancouver was a sprawling, dingy, beautiful giant of a waterfront city even in 1937. I walked down Water Street, over the puddles and wet grey concrete in the early morning. An old Indian woman on an iron balcony called down for me to come up and see her daughter, mentioning explicitly certain delights that could be expected. Rather prudishly, I declined. I spent the afternoon at a movie, paying fifteen cents for the privilege of watching Dorothy Lamour disport herself in a sarong. But I'm not sure if the Indian girl wouldn't have been a better bargain.

25   After the movie I was seized with a realization of the immense distance I had come from home. Originally I had meant to get a job fishing on a purse seiner at Vancouver, but the smelly old harbour depressed me. The Lions Gate Bridge, stretching spider-like across First Narrows, seemed alien; the streets themselves were unfriendly and peopled by strangers. I was homesick.

26   On the same day that I had arrived I slipped under the barrier at a level crossing and boarded a freight train moving east. And all the immense width of a continent was before me again, all the lakes and rivers and mountains — and the green country of childhood lay behind.

> Riding into the Crowsnest mountains with
> your first beard itching and a
> hundred hungry guys fanning out thru
> the shabby whistlestops for handouts and
> not even a sandwich for two hundred miles
> only the high mountains and knowing
> what it's like to be not quite a child
> any more and listening to the tough men

talk of women and talk of the way things are
in 1937 —

Structure:

1. What do the lines of poetry at the beginning and end contribute to this essay?
2. What do paragraphs 1 and 2 achieve?
3. Which paragraph begins the actual narrative and which paragraph ends it?
4. Does the narrative move steadily in chronological order or does it stop for explanations or flashbacks?
5. In addition to chronological order, what other order helps to organize this essay?
6. If you think paragraph 26 is effective, explain why.

Style:

1. Apart from the actual poems at beginning and end, a number of passages in this essay seem to reflect the fact that Al Purdy is a poet. Point out some especially poetic passages that are rich in SENSE IMAGES or in FIGURES OF SPEECH.
2. In paragraph 3 Purdy writes, ". . . and every now and then you heard a hoarse, impatient scream from the whistles of the westbound train." What is the effect of the word "you," which Purdy uses here and elsewhere in the essay?
3. Is "The Iron Road" a good title for this essay? What feelings do the words convey and how do they fit what follows?

Ideas:

1. Like this selection, a great many novels are stories of growing up. Why do you think this theme has been popular in literature?
2. The journey is another of this selection's themes that commonly appears in literature. Why do you think it does?
3. In what ways do you think Purdy's journey would be different if it were undertaken today instead of in 1937?
4. In what ways is poverty presented in this selection?
5. How is Purdy's poverty different from that of the others?
6. Write a vivid *narrative* of a journey that you have taken, and —

like Purdy — include your *interior* journey: what you learned along the way.

_____

(NOTE: See also the Topics for Writing at the end of this chapter.)

Charles Yale Harrison

In the Trenches

Charles Yale Harrison (1898-1954) was born in Philadelphia and grew up in Montreal. His independent spirit revealed itself early: in grade four he condemned Shakespeare's The Merchant of Venice *as anti-Semitic, and when his teacher beat him he quit school. At sixteen he went to work for* The Montreal Star *and at eighteen joined the Canadian army. As a machine gunner in France and Belgium during 1917 and 1918, Harrison witnessed the gruesome front-line scenes he was later to describe in fiction. He was wounded at Amiens and decorated for bravery in action. After the war Harrison returned to Montreal but soon left for New York, where he began a career in public relations for the labour movement and for numerous humanitarian causes. He also wrote several books, both nonfiction and fiction. By far the best is* Generals Die in Bed, *an account of trench warfare that shocked the public and became the best seller of 1930. Spare in style, biting and vivid, this autobiographical novel was described by the* New York Evening Post *as "the best of the war books." From it comes our selection, "In the Trenches."*

We leave the piles of rubble that was once a little Flemish 1 peasant town and wind our way, in Indian file, up through the muddy communication trench. In the dark we stumble against the sides of the trench and tear our hands and clothing on the bits of embedded barbed wire that runs through the earth here as though it were a geological deposit.

Fry, who is suffering with his feet, keeps slipping into holes and 2 crawling out, all the way up. I can hear him coughing and panting behind me.

I hear him slither into a water-filled hole. It has a green scum on 3 it. Brown and I fish him out.

"I can't go any farther," he wheezes. "Let me lie here, I'll come on 4 later."

We block the narrow trench and the oncoming men stumble on us, 5 banging their equipment and mess tins on the sides of the ditch. Some trip over us. They curse under their breaths.

Our captain, Clark, pushes his way through the mess. He is an 6 Imperial, an Englishman, and glories in his authority.

"So it's you again," he shouts. "Come on, get up. Cold feet, eh, 7 getting near the line?"

Fry mumbles something indistinctly. I, too, offer an explanation. 8 Clark ignores me.

15

9   "Get up, you're holding up the line," he says to Fry.

10 Fry does not move.

11 "No wonder we're losing the bloody war," Clark says loudly. The men standing near-by laugh. Encouraged by his success, the captain continues:

12 "Here, sergeant, stick a bayonet up his behind — that'll make him move." A few of us help Fry to his feet, and somehow we manage to keep him going.

13 We proceed cautiously, heeding the warnings of those ahead of us. At last we reach our positions.

● ● ● ● ● ● ●

14 It is midnight when we arrive at our positions. The men we are relieving give us a few instructions and leave quickly, glad to get out.

15 It is September and the night is warm. Not a sound disturbs the quiet. Somewhere away far to our right we hear the faint sound of continuous thunder. The exertion of the trip up the line has made us sweaty and tired. We slip most of our accouterments off and lean against the parados. We have been warned that the enemy is but a few hundred yards off, so we speak in whispers. It is perfectly still. I remember nights like this in the Laurentians. The harvest moon rides overhead.

16 Our sergeant, Johnson, appears around the corner of the bay, stealthily like a ghost. He gives us instructions:

17 "One man up on sentry duty! Keep your gun covered with the rubber sheet! No smoking!"

18 He hurries on to the next bay. Fry mounts the step and peers into No Man's Land. He is rested now and says that if he can only get a good pair of boots he will be happy. He has taken his boots off and stands in his stockinged feet. He shows us where his heel is cut. His boots do not fit. The sock is wet with blood. He wants to take his turn at sentry duty first so that he can rest later on. We agree.

19 Cleary and I sit on the firing-step and talk quietly.

20 "So this is war."

21 "Quiet."

22 "Yes, just like the country back home, eh?"

23 We talk of the trench; how we can make it more comfortable.

24 We light cigarettes against orders and cup our hands around them to hide the glow. We sit thinking. Fry stands motionless with his steel helmet shoved down almost over his eyes. He leans against the parapet motionless. There is a quiet dignity about his posture. I

remember what we were told at the base about falling asleep on
sentry duty. I nudge his leg. He grunts.

"Asleep?" I whisper.   25

"No," he answers, "I'm all right."   26

"What do you see?"   27

"Nothing. Wire and posts."   28

"Tired?"   29

"I'm all right."   30

The sergeant reappears after a while. We squinch our cigarettes.   31

"Everything O.K. here?"   32

I nod.   33

"Look out over there. They got the range on us. Watch out."   34

We light another cigarette. We continue our aimless talk.   35

"I wonder what St. Catherine Street looks like—"   36

"Same old thing, I suppose — stores, whores, theaters —"   37

"Like to be there just the same —"   38

"Me too."   39

We sit and puff our fags for half a minute or so.   40

I try to imagine what Montreal looks like. The images are murky.   41
All that is unreality. The trench, Cleary, Fry, the moon overhead —
this is real.

In his corner of the bay Fry is beginning to move from one foot to   42
another. It is time to relieve him. He steps down and I take his place.
I look into the wilderness of posts and wire in front of me.

After a while my eyes begin to water. I see the whole army of wire   43
posts begin to move like a silent host towards me.

I blink my eyes and they halt.   44

I doze a little and come to with a jerk.   45

So this is war, I say to myself again for the hundredth time. Down   46
on the firing-step the boys are sitting like dead men. The thunder to
the right has died down. There is absolutely no sound.

I try to imagine how an action would start. I try to fancy the   47
preliminary bombardment. I remember all the precautions one has
to take to protect one's life. Fall flat on your belly, we had been told
time and time again. The shriek of the shell, the instructor in trench
warfare said, was no warning because the shell traveled faster than
its sound. First, he had said, came the explosion of the shell — then
came the shriek and then you hear the firing of the gun. . . .

From the stories I heard from veterans and from newspaper   48
reports I conjure up a picture of an imaginary action. I see myself
getting the Lewis gun in position. I see it spurting darts of flame
into the night. I hear the roar of battle. I feel elated. Then I try to
fancy the horrors of the battle. I see Cleary, Fry and Brown

stretched out on the firing-step. They are stiff and their faces are white and set in the stillness of death. Only I remain alive.

49   An inaudible movement in front of me pulls me out of the dream. I look down and see Fry massaging his feet. All is still. The moon sets slowly and everything becomes dark.

50   The sergeant comes into the bay again and whispers to me:

51   "Keep your eyes open now — they might come over on a raid now that it's dark. The wire's cut over there —" He points a little to my right.

52   I stand staring into the darkness. Everything moves rapidly again as I stare. I look away for a moment and the illusion ceases.

53   Something leaps towards my face.

54   I jerk back, afraid.

55   Instinctively I feel for my rifle in the corner of the bay.

56   It is a rat.

57   It is as large as a tom-cat. It is three feet away from my face and it looks steadily at me with its two staring, beady eyes. It is fat. Its long tapering tail curves away from its padded hindquarters. There is still a little light from the stars and this light shines faintly on its sleek skin. With a darting movement it disappears. I remember with a cold feeling that it was fat, and why.

58   Cleary taps my shoulder. It is time to be relieved.

• • • • • • •

59   Over in the German lines I hear quick, sharp reports. Then the red-tailed comets of the *minenwerfer** sail high in the air, making parabolas of red light as they come towards us. They look pretty, like the fireworks when we left Montreal. The sergeant rushes into the bay of the trench, breathless. "Minnies," he shouts, and dashes on.

60   In that instant there is a terrific roar directly behind us.

61   The night whistles and flashes red.

62   The trench rocks and sways.

63   Mud and earth leap into the air, come down upon us in heaps.

64   We throw ourselves upon our faces, clawing our nails into the soft earth in the bottom of the trench.

65   Another!

66   This one crashes to splinters about twenty feet in front of the bay.

67   Part of the parapet caves in.

68   We try to burrow into the ground like frightened rats.

69   The shattering explosions splinter the air in a million fragments.

---

minenwerfer: mine-throwing trench mortars

I taste salty liquid on my lips. My nose is bleeding from the force of the detonations.

SOS flares go up along our front calling for help from our artillery. 70
The signals sail into the air and explode, giving forth showers of red, white and blue lights held aloft by a silken parachute.

The sky is lit by hundreds of fancy fireworks like a night carnival. 71

The air shrieks and cat-calls. 72

Still they come. 73

I am terrified. I hug the earth, digging my fingers into every 74
crevice, every hole.

A blinding flash and an exploding howl a few feet in front of the 75
trench.

My bowels liquefy. 76

Acrid smoke bites the throat, parches the mouth. I am beyond 77
mere fright. I am frozen with an insane fear that keeps me cowering in the bottom of the trench. I lie flat on my belly, waiting. . . .

Suddenly it stops. 78

The fire lifts and passes over us to the trenches in the rear. 79

We lie still, unable to move. Fear has robbed us of the power to 80
act. I hear Fry whimpering near me. I crawl over to him with great effort. He is half covered with earth and débris. We begin to dig him out.

To our right they have started to shell the front lines. It is about 81
half a mile away. We do not care. *We* are safe.

Without warning it starts again. 82

The air screams and howls like an insane woman. 83

We are getting it in earnest now. Again we throw ourselves face 84
downward on the bottom of the trench and grovel like savages before this demoniac frenzy.

The concussion of the explosions batters against us. 85

I am knocked breathless. 86

I recover and hear the roar of the bombardment. 87

It screams and rages and boils like an angry sea. I feel a prickly 88
sensation behind my eyeballs.

A shell lands with a monster shriek in the next bay. The 89
concussion rolls me over on my back. I see the stars shining serenely above us. Another lands in the same place. Suddenly the stars revolve. I land on my shoulder. I have been tossed into the air.

I begin to pray. 90

"God — God — please. . ." 91

I remember that I do not believe in God. Insane thoughts race 92
through my brain. I want to catch hold of something, something that will explain this mad fury, this maniacal congealed hatred that pours down on our heads. I can find nothing to console me, nothing

to appease my terror. I know that hundreds of men are standing a mile or two from me pulling gun-lanyards, blowing us to smithereens. I know that and nothing else.

93   I begin to cough. The smoke is thick. It rolls in heavy clouds over the trench, blurring the stabbing lights of the explosions.

94   A shell bursts near the parapet.

95   Fragments smack the sandbags like a merciless shower of steel hail.

96   A piece of mud flies into my mouth. It is cool and refreshing. It tastes earthy.

97   Suddenly it stops again.

98   I bury my face in the cool, damp earth. I want to weep. But I am too weak and shaken for tears.

99   We lie still, waiting. . . .

Structure:

1. Does this narrative ever deviate from chronological order? If so, where and how?
2. This selection contains a great many short paragraphs, some only a word or two long. Examine paragraphs 25-30, 53-56 and 60-68, determining in each passage why the paragraphs are so short.
3. This account of an artillery attack ends with the words "We lie still, waiting. . . ." Is the ending effective, and if so, how?

Style:

1. What degree of CONCISENESS has Harrison achieved in this selection?
2. Discuss the horror of this statement about the rat and how Harrison achieves such horror in so few words: "I remember with a cold feeling that it was fat, and why" (par. 57).
3. An apparently simple account of events can sometimes carry great power. Discuss the sources of power in paragraph 89: "A shell lands with a monster shriek in the next bay. The concussion rolls me over on my back. I see the stars shining serenely above us. Another lands in the same place. Suddenly the stars revolve. I land on my shoulder. I have been tossed into the air."
4. One way in which Harrison makes war come alive for us is by attacking our five senses. Find at least one example each of a strong appeal to our senses of sight, hearing, touch, taste and smell.

5. This narrative is filled with FIGURES OF SPEECH. Point out at least one good SIMILE and one good METAPHOR.
6. All the other narratives in this chapter are in the past tense. Why is "In the Trenches" in the present tense, even though the book in which it appeared was published years after the war?

Ideas:

1. Our narrator relates his first experience of war. Has it taught him anything?
2. Have you read books or seen films that show war in a positive light? Name them. In what ways does "In the Trenches" differ from those accounts?
3. "In the Trenches" is part of a book entitled *Generals Die in Bed.* Discuss the implications of this title.
4. In paragraph 48, our narrator imagines what the attack will be like: "I see Cleary, Fry and Brown stretched out on the firing-step. They are stiff and their faces are white and set in the stillness of death. Only I remain alive." Do many people think this way, expecting to survive though others may not? Do we secretly feel immortal, despite knowing intellectually that we are not? If so, can you think of reasons why?
5. If you have read "Coming of Age in Putnok," compare the conflict described by George Gabori with that described by Harrison. Does hostility between individuals in any way contribute to hostility between nations?
6. If you have not been to war, as our narrator has, have you been through another dangerous or frightening experience that taught you something? Tell the story in a *narrative,* using chronological order, the present tense and vivid details, as Harrison does.

(NOTE: See also the Topics for Writing at the end of this chapter.)

Donald Creighton

*The Western Way**

Donald Creighton (1902-1979) has been one of Canada's most widely read historians. He was born in Toronto, held numerous degrees both earned and honorary, had a distinguished career as history professor at the University of Toronto from 1927 to 1970 and wrote numerous and varied works of history that brought him both scholarly and popular acclaim. The most important of these are The Commercial Empire of the St. Lawrence *(1937); his massive biography in two volumes,* John A. Macdonald: the Young Politician *(1952) and* John A. Macdonald: the Old Chieftain *(1955); and* The Forked Road: Canada 1939-1957 *(1976). In his later years Creighton was seen by some as overly conservative, writing history that favoured the powerful and slighted the weak, while he was seen by others as anti-American, anti-Quebec and overly nationalistic. But if his interpretation was at times controversial, his research was massive and solid. Others criticized him for his style, often so vivid and dramatic that it seemed more typical of fiction than of history. But it is this very style that enabled the general public, as well as specialists, to read and appreciate his work. Creighton's colourful and at times even racy prose is nowhere better displayed than in our selection, "The Western Way," which appeared in a book aimed at the general public,* Canada: The Heroic Beginnings *(1974).*

1   It was the Norsemen who first fought their way westward across the North Atlantic and gained the earliest footholds on the shore of what is now Canada. Their precarious lodgement at the edge of the New World was the ultimate achievement of a vast expansion of the Scandinavian peoples. Driven forth by the pressure of over-population and the hope of spacious lands and easy riches, the Vikings of Norway and Denmark first burst out of their restricted homelands towards the end of the eighth century. Their assault on western Europe and the islands beyond, maintained for more than 200 years of raids, pillage, conquest, and colonization, was the greatest movement of people that the West had known since the Germanic barbarians had overwhelmed the Roman Empire five centuries earlier. The Franks and the Goths had travelled westward by land; but the Vikings, "the dark red seabirds", came by sea, and a large part of the surprise and terror of their coming lay in the swift mobility of their ships.

2   Their typical warship, the Viking "long-ship", was a long, low, graceful vessel, clinker-built with overlapping planks of oak, a

*Editor's title

single, square, brightly coloured sail, and carved and ornamented dragon prows. Sixty or seventy warriors, their shields hung on the bulwarks of the vessels, their barbaric costumes adorned with brooches and bracelets, would man the long-ship, sail or row it across the North Sea or down the Channel, beach it on some shore or drive it up an estuary or river, and then, with bow and sword and battle-axe, descend upon the countryside and its helpless villages.

These savage pirates and marauders followed two main routes. 3 One ran north-westward to Scotland, to the Orkney, Shetland, and Faroe Islands, and beyond to Iceland. The other led south-westward towards England, the Netherlands, France, Spain, and Portugal and into the Mediterranean. The second route, which was soon distinguished by such Viking triumphs as the founding of the Danelaw in England and the conquest of Normandy in France, became the more frequented and the more famous of the two; but the north-west route, the "western way" as it was called, which swept in a great arc across the North Atlantic and ended in North America, had its own special interest and importance.

Although almost everything the Vikings did was marred by 4 violence and stained with blood, the advance along the "western way" was marked, not so much by warfare and conquest, as by discovery and colonization. The Norwegians had found and peacefully settled the Orkney, Shetland, and Faroe Islands before the violent Viking onslaught on western Europe began; and during the latter part of the ninth century, they discovered and occupied Iceland, a volcanic island, much of it a desolate wilderness of lava and glacier. Like the long-ships, the ships of these Norwegian colonists were clinker-built, but in other respects they differed radically from the Viking war vessels; they were cargo boats, decked fore and aft, with a wide beam and a deep draft, and roomy enough to carry passengers, animals, and cargo, as well as crew. Unlike the ornately garbed warriors who terrorized England and Europe, the mariners of the "western way" wore plain hooded gowns made of a coarse woollen cloth called wadmal, and carried sleeping bags of sheepskin or cowhide.

On good days, as one looked out from the west coast of Iceland, a 5 faint line of mountains could be seen in the remote distance; and to Eric the Red, the violent son of a savage father, they offered both a way of escape and a promise of adventure. Thorwaldr, the father, outlawed from Norway for manslaughter, had fled to Iceland; Eric, outlawed in his turn for homicide, determined to find his refuge in the unknown country to the west. In 982 he sailed west, discovered a huge ice-covered island, and wintered on its farther coast. He could not return home for good, nor did he want to: instead, he decided to found a colony on the land of his discovery. He called it Greenland, a boldly fraudulent advertisement intended to attract prospective immigrants; and in 986, triumphantly leading a fleet of twenty-four ships, he set sail again, reached the west coast of his island once more in safety, and laid the bases of two settlements.

6   Even yet the westward urge had not spent itself. The drive that had brought Thorwaldr to Iceland and Eric to Greenland was still strong and insistent enough to carry Leif, Eric's son, to the end of the "western way" and to the New World. About 1000, he captained a planned expedition to the west and south. He found first a barren land of flat rock and glacier, which he called Helluland (Flagstone Land), and then a very different country, heavily forested, with white sandy beaches, which he named Markland (Forestland). A strong north-east wind drove the ship on for two days; and finally, on the bright morning of the third, it brought the voyagers to a beautiful land, with ample pasture, and grape vines, and the biggest salmon they had ever seen. Leif called their discovery Vinland (Wineland), and there he and his men built houses and started a permanent settlement. The good reports they brought home stimulated the interest of the Greenlanders, and during the next fifteen years, there were several voyages to Vinland, two by Leif's brothers and one by his illegitimate daughter, Freydis, as ferocious a murderess as any in Viking history. There was at least an attempt at large-scale colonization, but in fact the settlement did not endure.

7   Helluland was probably the southern shore of Baffin Island, and there can be little doubt that Markland formed part of the Labrador coast. The location of Vinland is much more uncertain. The topographical indications in the Norse Sagas are confused and at times seemingly contradictory. Vinland, the beautiful land of the Greenlanders, has been located all the way from Newfoundland to New England; but until 1960, no archaeological evidence had been found to prove the truth of any of these conjectures. In that year, a Norwegian, Helge Ingstad, discovered the buried foundations of a number of pre-Columbian houses at L'Anse aux Meadows, on Epaves Bay, part of Sacred Bay, a much larger body of water, at the northern tip of Newfoundland.

8   Epaves Bay is a broad, gently curving bay facing the entrance to the Strait of Belle Isle and so shallow that at low tide it is dry a long way out from the shore. A wide, green, grassy plain, level or slightly undulating, springy to the step with peat turf, stretches away inland on every side. A rich variety of small bushes, plants, and grasses — mountain ash, prostrate juniper, iris, angelica, Labrador tea, blueberries, and partridge and bakeapple berries — covers the plain with a dense shaggy coat; and through it, ending in the bay, winds a

tumultuous little river, picturesquely named the Black Duck Brook. A little way in from the shore, the land rises slightly in an ancient marine terrace; and along it, in a straggling line, lie the foundations, made of layers of turf, of eight houses of different sizes, and the remnants of boat sheds and of cooking and charcoal pits. Most of these sites, including the largest, where a structure of six rooms once stood, are north of Black Duck Brook; but one, which was evidently a smithy, is situated on the south side of the little river; and since bog iron is available near by, a Norse smith may have smelted ore here as well as worked iron. A Norse woman must have sat spinning in one of the rooms in the largest house, for a soapstone spindle whorl, of characteristic Norse design, was found there, as well as a bronze pin with a ring in its head and several iron rivets.

The Norse sagas date the discovery and occupation of Vinland at   9
the beginning of the eleventh century, and radio carbon tests place the ruins at L'Anse aux Meadows in approximately the same period. The L'Anse aux Meadows site may not be Vinland; but there can be no doubt that the Norse men and women who built and inhabited these houses were among the first Europeans who ever lived in North America.

Structure:

1. Why does Creighton discuss the violence of Viking expansion to the east before he describes in detail Viking expansion to the west?
2. To what extent does this selection analyze the *causes* of Norse exploration and settlement along the "western way"? Name all the major causes identified by Creighton.
3. In what sense are paragraphs 1-4 a narrative? What is the story being narrated?
4. What is the main difference between the opening narrative and the narrative found in paragraphs 5 and 6?
5. In what sense do paragraphs 7-9 form a narrative?
6. What similarity do you find between the opening and closing of this selection?

Style:

1. Our selection is typical of historical writing in its narrative form, but certainly not in its STYLE. Point out at least five passages

which, in their vivid or even racy style, seem more typical of
FICTION than of history.

2. Reread carefully the opening paragraph of this selection, then
point out all the ways in which it appeals to the reader's interest.

3. In what way does the beginning of paragraph 5 appeal to the
reader?

4. What effect is sought in the words "Leif, Eric's son" (par. 6)?

5. How long would Creighton's paragraphs be if you wrote them
out? Do you ever write paragraphs as long as his? Should his be
shorter? Why or why not?

Ideas:

1. Name as many reasons as you can for the study of history.

2. Napoleon defined history as "a set of lies agreed upon." Oscar
Wilde defined it as "gossip" and Henry Ford as "bunk." What
motives do you think might lead some historians to falsify
history? If falsification occurs, is it deliberate or unconscious?
Can you think of an example of history as "bunk"?

3. Why do historians pay more attention to the "discovery" of the
New World by Europeans than to the original discovery of the
New World by Asians who crossed the Bering Strait to Alaska?

4. Both the Scandinavians and the French had colonized what is
now Canada long before the British arrived. In what major ways
can you imagine your present life would be different if the
Vikings had established the dominant culture of our country? If
the French had established it?

5. Write a *narrative* about one branch of your family, beginning
with your earliest known ancestor. Show, as fully as you can, how
the actions of these ancestors resulted in your being where you
are and in your being what you are.

(NOTE: See also the Topics for Writing at the end of this chapter.)

Gary Lautens

Man, You're a Great Player!

*"An old English teacher of mine," writes Gary Lautens, "once said she'd drop
dead if I ever made a living as a writer. Now, if she's a good sport, she'll keep
her end of the bargain." In fact Lautens did go on to make his living by
writing. Born in 1928 in Fort William, Ontario, he graduated from
McMaster University in 1950 with a B.A. in history — then spent the next
thirteen years as a sports columnist with the* Hamilton Spectator. *Moving to*
The Toronto Star *in 1962, he wrote a column of zany humour which became
so popular that selections from it were reprinted in books:* Laughing with
Lautens *(1964),* Take My Family — Please! *(1980) and* No Sex Please . . .
We're Married *(1983). In 1981 Lautens won the Leacock Medal for Humour.
The high point of his journalistic career, though, came in 1982 to 1984, when
he served as executive managing editor of* The Toronto Star. *Our selection,
"Man, You're a Great Player!", reflects Lautens' experience both as a sports
writer and a humorist. It is from* Laughing with Lautens.

O
ccasionally I run into sports figures at cocktail parties, on the   1
street, or on their way to the bank.

"Nice game the other night," I said to an old hockey-player   2
pal.

"Think so?" he replied.   3

"You've come a long way since I knew you as a junior."   4

"How's that?"   5

"Well, you high-stick better for one thing — and I think the way   6
you clutch sweaters is really superb. You may be the best in the
league."

He blushed modestly. "For a time," I confessed, "I never thought   7
you'd get the hang of it."

"It wasn't easy," he confided. "It took practice and encouragement.   8
You know something like spearing doesn't come naturally. It has to
be developed."

"I'm not inclined to flattery but, in my book, you've got it made.   9
You're a dirty player."

"Stop kidding."   10

"No, no," I insisted. "I'm not trying to butter you up. I mean it.   11
When you broke in there were flashes of dirty play — but you
weren't consistent. That's the difference between a dirty player and
merely a colourful one."

"I wish my father were alive to hear you say that," he said quietly.   12
"He would have been proud."

13   "Well, it's true. There isn't a player in the league who knows as many obscene gestures."

14   "I admit I have been given a few increases in pay in recent years. Management seems to be treating me with new respect."

15   "You're selling tickets," I said. "You're a gate attraction now — not some bum who only can skate and shoot and the rest of it. Your profanity is beautiful."

16   "C'mon."

17   "No, I'm serious. I don't think anyone in the league can incite a riot the way you can."

18   "I've had a lot of help along the way. You can't make it alone," he stated generously.

19   "No one does," I said.

20   "Take that play where I skate up to the referee and stand nose-to-nose with my face turning red. It was my old junior coach who taught me that. He was the one who used to toss all the sticks on the ice and throw his hat into the stands and pound his fist on the boards."

21   "You were lucky to get that sort of training. A lot of players never learn the fundamentals."

22   "I think there are a few boys in the league who can spit better than me."

23   "Farther, perhaps, but not more accurately," I corrected.

24   "Well, thanks anyway. I've always considered it one of my weaknesses."

25   "That last brawl of yours was perfectly executed. Your sweater was torn off, you taunted the crowd, you smashed your stick across the goal posts. Really a picture Donnybrook."

26   "The papers gave me a break. The coverage was outstanding."

27   "Do you ever look back to the days when you couldn't cut a forehead or puff a lip or insult an official?"

28   "Everyone gets nostalgic," he confessed. "It's a good thing I got away from home by the time I was fifteen. I might never have been any more than a ham-and-egger, you know, a twenty-goal man who drifts through life unnoticed."

29   "What was the turning point?"

30   "I had heard prominent sportsmen say that nice guys finish last, and that you have to beat them in the alley if you hope to beat them in the rink. But it didn't sink in."

31   "Nobody learns overnight."

32   "I wasted a few years learning to play my wing and to check without using the butt of the stick. But I noticed I was being passed by. I skated summers to keep in shape, exercised, kept curfew."

"Don't tell me. They said you were dull." 33

"Worse than that. They said I was clean. It's tough to live down 34
that sort of reputation."

I nodded. 35

"Anyway, during a game in the sticks, I was skating off the ice — 36
we had won five-one and I had scored three goals. The home crowd
was pretty listless and there was some booing. Then it happened."

"What?" 37

"My big break. My mother was in the stands and she shouted to 38
me. I turned to wave at her with my hockey stick and I accidentally
caught the referee across the face. He bled a lot — took ten stitches
later."

"Is that all?" 39

"Well someone pushed me and I lost my balance and fell on the 40
poor man. A real brawl started. Luckily, I got credit for the whole
thing — went to jail overnight, got a suspension. And, talk about
fate! A big league scout was in the arena. He offered me a contract
right away."

"It's quite a success story," I said. 41

"You've got to get the breaks," he replied, humbly. 42

Structure:

1. What proportion of this selection do you estimate is DIALOGUE?
   And what function is served by the parts that are not dialogue?
2. What is the most basic way in which the dialogue is organized?
   Are there major divisions within it? If so, where, and how do the
   parts differ?
3. Should this selection be labelled ESSAY or FICTION? In what
   senses might it be both?

Style:

1. Why are there so many paragraph breaks in this short selection?
2. In paragraph 9 the narrator tells his friend, " 'I'm not inclined to
   flattery but, in my book, you've got it made. You're a dirty
   player.' " Discuss the IRONY that underlies this comment. How
   important is Lautens' ironic TONE to the humour and the
   message of this selection as a whole? In particular, examine the
   use of irony in the title and in paragraphs 1, 8, 12, 15, 20, 21, 34
   and 40.

3. Do you think the humorous approach chosen by Lautens has made the point strongly? Would a serious approach, like that of the other narratives in this chapter, have worked as well?
4. Point out at least five COLLOQUIAL or SLANG terms that seem more at home in the dialogue of this selection than they would in a typical essay.

Ideas:

1. As the saying puts it, "I went to the fights and a hockey game broke out." To what extent do people watch hockey for the fights and to what extent do they watch it for the traditional skills of the game? Is violence necessary to attract fans? How could hockey be made more interesting without resorting to fights?
2. In this selection that criticizes violence in hockey, where does Lautens blame parents? Fans? Coaches? Management? Sports writers?
3. It is said that soccer originated in warfare: villagers would kick the severed head of an enemy, like a ball, from one end of the village to the other. Think of the sports you play. What resemblances, if any, do you see between competition on the playing field and competition on the battlefield?
4. Must a sport be based on conflict, as in two teams each moving a puck or ball in the opposite direction? Name or devise a sport that is free of conflict. Can such a sport be interesting?
5. Compare the conflict examined in "Man, You're a Great Player!" with that examined in Gabori's "Coming of Age in Putnok," Harrison's "In the Trenches" or Dobbs' "The Scar."
6. Write a detailed *narrative* of a violent incident that you witnessed at a sports event.

(NOTE: See also the Topics for Writing at the end of this chapter.)

Kildare Dobbs

The Scar[*]

Kildare Dobbs was born in Meerut, India, in 1923, was educated in Ireland, then during World War II spent five years in the Royal Navy. After the war he worked in the British Colonial Service in Tanganyika and, after earning an M.A. at Cambridge, came in 1952 to Canada. Dobbs has been a teacher, editor for Macmillan, managing editor of Saturday Night *and book editor of* The Toronto Star. *He was one of the founders, in 1956, of* The Tamarack Review. *He is also the author of several books:* Running to Paradise *(essays, 1962, winner of the Governor-General's Award);* Canada *(an illustrated travel book, 1964);* Reading the Time *(essays, 1968);* The Great Fur Opera *(a comic history of the Hudson's Bay Company, 1970);* Pride and Fall *(short fiction, 1981) and* Historic Canada *(1984). Our selection is from* Reading the Time: *"The Scar" is about an event that Dobbs did not witness, yet its vivid style recreates all too clearly what that event must have been like.*

This is the story I was told in 1963 by Emiko Okamoto, a young Japanese woman who had come to live in Toronto. She spoke through an interpreter, since at that time she knew no English. It is Emiko's story, although I have had to complete it from other sources.

But why am I telling it? Everyone knows how terrible this story is. Everyone knows the truth of what von Clausewitz said: "Force to meet force arms itself with the inventions of art and science." First the bow-and-arrow, then Greek fire, gunpowder, poison-gas — and so on up the lethal scale. These things, we're told, should be considered calmly. No sweat — we should think about the unthinkable, or so Herman Kahn suggests, dispassionately. And he writes: "We do not expect illustrations in a book of surgery to be captioned 'Good health is preferable to this kind of cancer'. Excessive comments such as 'And now there is a lot of blood' or 'This particular cut really hurts' are out of place. . . . To dwell on such things is morbid." Perhaps the answer to Herman Kahn is that if surgeons hadn't dwelt on those things we wouldn't now have anaesthetics, or artery forceps either, for that matter.

To think about thermonuclear war in the abstract is obscene. To think about any kind of warfare with less than the whole of our mind and imagination is obscene. This is the worst treason.

---

[*]Editor's title

4   Before that morning in 1945 only a few conventional bombs, none of which did any great damage, had fallen on the city. Fleets of U.S. bombers had, however, devastated many cities round about, and Hiroshima had begun a program of evacuation which had reduced its population from 380,000 to some 245,000. Among the evacuees were Emiko and her family.

5   "We were moved out to Otake, a town about an hour's train-ride out of the city," Emiko told me. She had been a fifteen-year-old student in 1945. Fragile and vivacious, versed in the gentle traditions of the tea ceremony and flower arrangement, Emiko still had an air of the frail school-child when I talked with her. Every day, she and her sister Hideko used to commute into Hiroshima to school. Hideko was thirteen. Their father was an antique-dealer and he owned a house in the city, although it was empty now. Tetsuro, Emiko's thirteen-year-old brother, was at the Manchurian front with the Imperial Army. Her mother was kept busy looking after the children, for her youngest daughter Eiko was sick with heart trouble, and rations were scarce. All of them were undernourished.

6   The night of August 5, 1945, little Eiko was dangerously ill. She was not expected to live. Everybody took turns watching by her bed, soothing her by massaging her arms and legs. Emiko retired at 8.30 (most Japanese people go to bed early) and at midnight was roused to take her turn with the sick girl. At 2 a.m. she went back to sleep.

7   While Emiko slept, the *Enola Gay,* a U.S. B-29 carrying the world's first operational atom bomb, was already in the air. She had taken off from the Pacific island of Iwo Jima at 1.45 a.m., and now Captain William Parsons, U.S.N. ordnance expert, was busy in her bomb-hold with the final assembly of Little Boy. Little Boy looked much like an outsize T.N.T. block-buster but the crew knew there was something different about him. Only Parsons and the pilot, Colonel Paul Tibbets, knew exactly in what manner Little Boy was different. Course was set for Hiroshima.

8   Emiko slept.

9   On board the *Enola Gay* co-pilot Captain Robert Lewis was writing up his personal log. "After leaving Iwo," he recorded, "we began to pick up some low stratus and before very long we were flying on top of an under-cast. Outside of a thin, high cirrus and the low stuff, it's a very beautiful day."

10 Emiko and Hideko were up at six in the morning. They dressed in the uniform of their women's college — white blouse, quilted hat, and black skirt — breakfasted and packed their aluminum lunch-boxes with white rice and eggs. These they stuffed into their shoulder bags as they hurried for the seven-o'clock train to Hiroshima. Today there would be no classes. Along with many women's groups, high school students, and others, the sisters were

going to work on demolition. The city had begun a project of clearance to make fire-breaks in its downtown huddle of wood and paper buildings.

It was a lovely morning.   11

While the two young girls were at breakfast, Captain Lewis, over   12
the Pacific, had made an entry in his log. "We are loaded. The bomb is now alive, and it's a funny feeling knowing it's right in back of you. Knock wood!"

In the train Hideko suddenly said she was hungry. She wanted to   13
eat her lunch. Emiko dissuaded her: she'd be much hungrier later on. The two sisters argued, but Hideko at last agreed to keep her lunch till later. They decided to meet at the main station that afternoon and catch the five-o'clock train home. By now they had arrived at the first of Hiroshima's three stations. This was where Hideko got off, for she was to work in a different area from her sister. "Sayonara!" she called. "Goodbye." Emiko never saw her again.

There had been an air-raid at 7 a.m., but before Emiko arrived at   14
Hiroshima's main station, two stops farther on, the sirens had sounded the all-clear. Just after eight, Emiko stepped off the train, walked through the station, and waited in the morning sunshine for her streetcar.

At about the same moment Lewis was writing in his log. "There'll   15
be a short intermission while we bomb our target."

It was hot in the sun. Emiko saw a class-mate and greeted her.   16
Together they moved back into the shade of a high concrete wall to chat. Emiko looked up at the sky and saw, far up in the cloudless blue, a single B-29.

It was exactly 8.10 a.m. The other people waiting for the streetcar 17
saw it too and began to discuss it anxiously. Emiko felt scared. She felt that at all costs she must go on talking to her friend. Just as she was thinking this, there was a tremendous greenish-white flash in the sky. It was far brighter than the sun. Emiko afterwards remembered vaguely that there was a roaring or a rushing sound as well, but she was not sure, for just at that moment she lost consciousness.

"About 15 seconds after the flash," noted Lewis, 30,000 feet high   18
and several miles away, "there were two very distinct slaps on the ship from the blast and the shock wave. That was all the physical effect we felt. We turned the ship so that we could observe the results."

When Emiko came to, she was lying on her face about forty feet   19
away from where she had been standing. She was not aware of any pain. Her first thought was: "I'm alive!" She lifted her head slowly and looked about her. It was growing dark. The air was seething

with dust and black smoke. There was a smell of burning. Emiko felt
something trickle into her eyes, tasted it in her mouth. Gingerly she
put a hand to her head, then looked at it. She saw with a shock that
it was covered with blood.

20   She did not give a thought to Hideko. It did not occur to her that
her sister who was in another part of the city could possibly have
been in danger. Like most of the survivors, Emiko assumed she had
been close to a direct hit by a conventional bomb. She thought it had
fallen on the post-office next to the station. With a hurt child's panic,
Emiko, streaming with blood from gashes in her scalp, ran blindly
in search of her mother and father.

21   The people standing in front of the station had been burned to
death instantly (a shadow had saved Emiko from the flash). The
people inside the station had been crushed by falling masonry.
Emiko heard their faint cries, saw hands scrabbling weakly from
under the collapsed platform. All around her the maimed survivors
were running and stumbling away from the roaring furnace that
had been a city. She ran with them toward the mountains that ring
the landward side of Hiroshima.

22   From the *Enola Gay,* the strangers from North America looked
down at their handiwork. "There, in front of our eyes," wrote Lewis,
"was without a doubt the greatest explosion man had ever
witnessed. The city was nine-tenths covered with smoke of a boiling
nature, which seemed to indicate buildings blowing up, and a large
white cloud which in less than three minutes reached 30,000 feet,
then went to at least 50,000 feet."

23   Far below, on the edge of this cauldron of smoke, at a distance of
some 2,500 yards from the blast's epicentre, Emiko ran with the rest
of the living. Some who could not run limped or dragged themselves
along. Others were carried. Many, hideously burned, were screaming with pain; when they tripped they lay where they had fallen.
There was a man whose face had been ripped open from mouth to
ear, another whose forehead was a gaping wound. A young soldier
was running with a foot-long splinter of bamboo protruding from
one eye. But these, like Emiko, were the lightly wounded.

24   Some of the burned people had been literally roasted. Skin hung
from their flesh like sodden tissue paper. They did not bleed but
plasma dripped from their seared limbs.

25   The *Enola Gay,* mission completed, was returning to base. Lewis
sought words to express his feelings, the feelings of all the crew. "I
might say," he wrote, "I might say 'My God! What have we done?' "

26   Emiko ran. When she had reached the safety of the mountain she
remembered that she still had her shoulder bag. There was a small

first-aid kit in it and she applied ointment to her wounds and to a small cut in her left hand. She bandaged her head.

Emiko looked back at the city. It was a lake of fire. All around her the burned fugitives cried out in pain. Some were scorched on one side only. Others, naked and flayed, were burned all over. They were too many to help and most of them were dying. Emiko followed the walking wounded along a back road, still delirious, expecting suddenly to meet her father and mother. 27

The thousands dying by the roadside called feebly for help or water. Some of the more lightly injured were already walking in the other direction, back towards the flames. Others, with hardly any visible wounds, stopped, turned ashy pale, and died within minutes. No one knew then that they were victims of radiation. 28

Emiko reached the suburb of Nakayama. 29

Far off in the *Enola Gay*, Lewis, who had seen none of this, had been writing, "If I live a hundred years, I'll never get those few minutes out of my mind. Looking at Captain Parsons, why he is as confounded as the rest, and he is supposed to have known everything and expected this to happen. . . ." 30

At Nakayama, Emiko stood in line at a depot where riceballs were being distributed. Though it distressed her that the badly maimed could hardly feed themselves, the child found she was hungry. It was about 6 p.m. now. A little farther on, at Gion, a farmer called her by name. She did not recognize him, but it seemed he came monthly to her home to collect manure. The farmer took Emiko by the hand, led her to his own house, where his wife bathed her and fed her a meal of white rice. Then the child continued on her way. She passed another town where there were hundreds of injured. The dead were being hauled away in trucks. Among the injured a woman of about forty-five was waving frantically and muttering to herself. Emiko brought this woman a little water in a pumpkin leaf. She felt guilty about it; the schoolgirls had been warned not to give water to the seriously wounded. Emiko comforted herself with the thought that the woman would die soon anyway. 31

At Koi, she found standing-room in a train. It was heading for Otake with a full load of wounded. Many were put off at Ono, where there was a hospital; and two hours later the train rolled into Otake station. It was around 10 p.m. 32

A great crowd had gathered to look for their relations. It was a nightmare, Emiko remembered years afterwards; people were calling their dear kinfolk by name, searching frantically. It was necessary to call them by name, since most were so disfigured as to be unrecognizable. Doctors in the town council offices stitched 33

Emiko's head-wounds. The place was crowded with casualties lying on the floor. Many died as Emiko watched.

34 The town council authorities made a strange announcement. They said a new and mysterious kind of bomb had fallen in Hiroshima. People were advised to stay away from the ruins.

35 Home at midnight, Emiko found her parents so happy to see her that they could not even cry. They could only give thanks that she was safe. Then they asked, "Where is your sister?"

36 For ten long days, while Emiko walked daily one and a half miles to have her wounds dressed with fresh gauze, her father searched the rubble of Hiroshima for his lost child. He could not have hoped to find her alive. All, as far as the eye could see, was a desolation of charred ashes and wreckage, relieved only by a few jagged ruins and by the seven estuarial rivers that flowed through the waste delta. The banks of these rivers were covered with the dead and in the rising tidal waters floated thousands of corpses. On one broad street in the Hakushima district the crowds who had been thronging there were all naked and scorched cadavers. Of thousands of others there was no trace at all. A fire several times hotter than the surface of the sun had turned them instantly to vapour.

37 On August 11 came the news that Nagasaki had suffered the same fate as Hiroshima; it was whispered that Japan had attacked the United States mainland with similar mysterious weapons. With the lavish circumstantiality of rumour, it was said that two out of a fleet of six-engined trans-Pacific bombers had failed to return. But on August 15, speaking for the first time over the radio to his people, the Emperor Hirohito announced his country's surrender. Emiko heard him. No more bombs! she thought. No more fear! The family did not learn till June the following year that this very day young Tetsuro had been killed in action in Manchuria.

38 Emiko's wounds healed slowly. In mid-September they had closed with a thin layer of pinkish skin. There had been a shortage of antiseptics and Emiko was happy to be getting well. Her satisfaction was short-lived. Mysteriously she came down with diarrhoea and high fever. The fever continued for a month. Then one day she started to bleed from the gums, her mouth and throat became acutely inflamed, and her hair started to fall out. Through her delirium the child heard the doctors whisper by her pillow that she could not live. By now the doctors must have known that ionizing radiation caused such destruction of the blood's white cells that victims were left with little or no resistance against infection.

39 Yet Emiko recovered.

The wound on her hand, however, was particularly troublesome 40
and did not heal for a long time.

As she got better, Emiko began to acquire some notion of the 41
fearful scale of the disaster. Few of her friends and acquaintances
were still alive. But no one knew precisely how many had died in
Hiroshima. To this day the claims of various agencies conflict.

According to General Douglas MacArthur's headquarters, there 42
were 78,150 dead and 13,083 missing. The United States Atomic
Bomb Casualty Commission claims there were 79,000 dead. Both
sets of figures are probably far too low. There's reason to believe that
at the time of the surrender Japanese authorities lied about the
number of survivors, exaggerating it to get extra medical supplies.
The Japanese welfare ministry's figures of 260,000 dead and
163,263 missing may well be too high. But the very order of such
discrepancies speaks volumes about the scale of the catastrophe.
The dead were literally uncountable.

This appalling toll of human life had been exacted from a city that 43
had been prepared for air attack in a state of full wartime readiness.
All civil-defence services had been overwhelmed from the first
moment and it was many hours before any sort of organized rescue
and relief could be put into effect.

It's true that single raids using so-called conventional weapons on 44
other cities such as Tokyo and Dresden inflicted far greater
casualties. And that it could not matter much to a victim whether he
was burnt alive by a fire-storm caused by phosphorus, or by napalm
or by nuclear fission. Yet in the whole of human history so savage a
massacre had never before been inflicted with a single blow. And
modern thermonuclear weapons are upwards of 1,000 times more
powerful and deadly than the Hiroshima bomb.

The white scar I saw on Emiko's small, fine-boned hand was a tiny 45
metaphor, a faint but eloquent reminder of the scar on humanity's
conscience.

Structure:

1. What is Dobbs' THESIS STATEMENT? And what is the most
   important way in which his narrative supports it?
2. In "The Scar," two narratives are combined. Compare and
   contrast them. How does each help to explain nuclear war? And
   in the process, how does the one complement the other?

3. Kildare Dobbs did not witness the nuclear blast that, on August 6, 1945, levelled Hiroshima — yet he wrote an account of the event that may seem only too real. How did he know what it was like? Name the sources of information which he mentions. What other kinds of sources do you think he may have used? Do you think any of this narrative is the product of his imagination? If so, would that be a weakness or a strength?

Style:

1. In his log, Captain Lewis writes ". . . it's a very beautiful day" (par. 9), and in paragraph 11 Dobbs writes "It was a lovely morning." What effect do these pleasant words have in the context of the situation? What literary device underlies their power?
2. Captain Lewis writes in his log, "There'll be a short intermission while we bomb our target" (par. 15). Do these words seem peculiar? If so, why?
3. In referring to the first operational nuclear bomb as "Little Boy" (par. 7), what does Dobbs add to the force of his narrative?
4. Paragraphs 23, 24, 27 and 36 are filled with gruesome details that illustrate the effects of "Little Boy." Do these details help or hurt the purpose of the narrative? Do they encourage in the reader an opposition to nuclear weapons? Or, in their dreadfulness, do they encourage the reader merely to drop the subject and think of other things?
5. In paragraphs 42-44, why does Dobbs leave the narrative and turn instead to statistics and generalizations?
6. In what sense is the scar on Emiko's hand a METAPHOR, and what qualifies this metaphor to end our selection?

Ideas:

1. According to the estimates quoted by Dobbs, between 78,150 and 260,000 people were killed by the one bomb that hit Hiroshima. And according to Jonathan Schell, 1,600,000 times the firepower of that bomb now exists in the nuclear arsenals of the world (*The Fate of the Earth*, Knopf, 1982). What is your response to these statistics?
2. According to the Washington, D.C., research group World Priorities (quoted by Michele Landsberg in the *Globe and Mail*, February 1, 1986), the world now spends an average of $162 per person per year on the military; it spends 6¢ per person per year on peacekeeping. What is your response to these figures?

3. It has been estimated that the Soviet Union has enough nuclear warheads to destroy the United States twenty-five times over, and that the United States has enough nuclear warheads to destroy the Soviet Union fifty times over. In view of these figures, how do you interpret the fact that in recent years both East and West have greatly increased the production of nuclear warheads and their delivery systems?

4. Robert Falls, the Canadian head of NATO's military committee in Europe, said, "NATO strategy is to use nuclear weapons *first* if we are faced with overwhelming conventional odds and if retreat or surrender are the only alternatives" (*Maclean's,* February 15, 1982). Do you believe that NATO's concept of a "limited" nuclear war such as this is valid? Or do you believe that any nuclear first strike would result in a global conflict?

5. Do you think that civilians around the world should be trained in civil defence against a nuclear attack? Would it save lives? Or on the other hand, would it make such an attack more acceptable to military leaders and thus more likely?

6. What do you believe Canada's role should be in limiting or contributing to the arms race? For example, Litton Systems, Ltd., of Toronto, makes the guidance system that leads the American Cruise missile to its target. Do you approve or disapprove? Explain your reasons.

7. In a letter to the prime minister, the minister of national defence, your M.P. or the editor of your local newspaper, argue for or against Canada's participation in the arms race. Explain your reasons clearly. If this is a required assignment let your teacher see your letter, then mail it.

8. Write, in either first person or third person, a vivid *narrative* telling in detail what you imagine one of the following events would be like:

> The council of war at which a national leader decides to launch or not to launch a nuclear attack
>
> A nuclear attack on your own city
>
> A nuclear attack on your own country, experienced from the relative safety of a bomb shelter or a remote location
>
> A day in the life of a survivor ten years after a global nuclear war
>
> The visit of a Martian, one thousand years from now, and his report to his chief about what he sees on earth

---

(NOTE: See also the Topics for Writing at the end of this chapter.)

Topics for Writing

Chapter 1: Narration
Writing About Myself

(Note also the topics for writing that appear after each selection in this chapter.)

Choose one of these topics as the basis of a narrative about yourself. Tell a good story: give colourful details and all the facts needed to help your reader understand and appreciate the event.

1. The day I was born (interview one or both parents first)
2. My earliest memory
3. The most important event of my childhood
4. The day I learned to know myself
5. The day I learned to appreciate my parents
6. The day I first met my husband, wife or friend
7. An event that changed my life
8. The day I began my first job
9. The day I conquered a fear
10. The day I broke the law
11. My most serious accident or illness
12. The best day of my life
13. My most frightening moment
14. My proudest moment
15. My most heroic moment

Narration:
Writing About Others

From this list of events, choose one that you witnessed in person (or, in the case of numbers 9 and 10, that you learned about by interviewing). Narrate it, giving colourful details and all the facts needed to help your reader understand and appreciate the event.

1. The birth of a brother, sister, son or daughter
2. The wedding of a friend or relative
3. The death of a family member or friend
4. The day a friend or relative suddenly became rich or poor
5. The day a friend or relative experienced a religious conversion or a loss of faith
6. The day a friend or relative surprised everyone by revealing his or her true self

7. An event that was a major success or failure in the life of a friend or relative
8. The day that a friend or relative experienced a major change of attitude about life
9. The most important event in the life of an elderly relative (interview the person before writing the narrative)
10. The day your parents first met (interview one or both before writing the narrative)
11. An accident in the neighbourhood
12. A fire in the neighbourhood
13. A crime in the neighbourhood
14. A major confrontation between two or more people
15. An event that symbolizes the spirit of the town, city, province or country in which it occurred

"What feeds we used to have. Not way back in the pod auger days, mind you.
That was before my time. I mean not long ago, just before the tinned stuff and
the packages and the baker's bread started to trickle into the outports."

Ray Guy, "Outharbor Menu"

For example . . . .

EXAMPLE

Many an audience, after trying in vain to understand a speaker's message, has been saved from boredom or even sleep by those powerful words, "FOR EXAMPLE. . . ." Heads lift up, eyes return to the front and suddenly the message is clear to everyone. Writers, as well as speakers, need to use examples. Pages of abstract reasoning, of generalizations, of theory without application, will only confuse, bore and finally alienate your reader. But the same ideas supported by well-chosen examples will much more easily interest and even convince your reader. Examples take many forms:

Personal experience: To illustrate your point, narrate an incident that you experienced. Did an earthquake or tornado or flood show you the power of nature? Did an accident illustrate the dangers of drinking and driving, or did a fire illustrate the dangers of smoking in bed? Did a major success or failure demonstrate the importance of work or planning or persistence?

The experience of others: To illustrate your point, narrate an incident that you have seen yourself or heard about from other sources. Did your neighbour's unloved child run away from home or rob a milk store or get married at age sixteen? Did your uncle lose his job because of automation or recession or imports? Did a famous person succeed despite a physical handicap or a deprived childhood?

Hypothetical examples: In a future-oriented society like ours, many arguments speculate about what might happen *if.* . . . Since the event or situation has not yet come to pass, use your best judgment to imagine the results. What would happen if children had the vote? If street drugs were legalized? If shopping were done by computer? If gasoline were five dollars a litre? If a woman became prime minister? If a world government were adopted?

Quotations: If the words of a poet, politician, scientist or other prominent person illustrate your point clearly and authoritatively, quote them and of course state who said them. What did Aristotle, Shakespeare, Machiavelli, Freud, Marx or John Diefenbaker say about love or power or sex or money or old age or war? Start with the index of *Bartlett's Quotations* or *Colombo's Canadian Quotations* to find an apt statement on almost any important topic.

Statistics: These numerical examples lend a scientific, objective quality to your argument. Tell what percentage of marriages will end in divorce or how many minutes each cigarette takes off your life or how much energy a person consumes travelling by car as opposed to train, bus or airplane. Five good sources of statistics are *Information Please Almanac, The World Almanac and Book of Facts, The Corpus Almanac of Canada, Canada Year Book* and any good atlas. Be scrupulously honest, because almost everyone knows how statistics are sometimes made to lie (remember the statistician who drowned in the river that averaged two feet deep!).

Other devices: Later chapters in this book discuss cause and effect, comparison and contrast, and analogy. These devices may be used not only to plan the structure of an entire essay, but also to construct short and vivid examples within the essay.

Almost all good writing contains examples, but some writing contains so many that it uses examples as a means of organizing as well as a means of illustrating. Ray Guy's essay "Outharbor Menu" has a brief introduction, a one-sentence closing and a body made of nothing but examples. Such a collection could be a mere list of trivia, but Ray Guy — like anyone who writes well — has chosen his examples carefully for their colour and for the support which they give to his point.

EXAMPLE   45

Another technique is to use one long, well-developed example —
in effect, a narrative. Bruce Hutchison does so in "Cowboy from
Holland": focussing almost totally on the little Dutch boy, he gives
us one long example to represent the millions of other immigrants
who have become Canadians. Of course one example — or twenty —
will prove nothing. Statistics come close to proof, especially when
based on a large and carefully designed study. But in general an
example is not a device of proof; it is a device of illustration and
therefore an aid to both understanding and enjoyment.

Ray Guy

Outharbor Menu

Although Ray Guy has been Newfoundland's favourite writer for some years, he is only now being discovered by the rest of Canada. Guy was born in 1939 at Arnold's Cove, an outport on Placentia Bay, and as a child learned to value the self-reliance of traditional Newfoundland life. After two years at Memorial University he went to Toronto, where in 1963 he earned a diploma in journalism at Ryerson Polytechnical Institute. Upon his return to Newfoundland he began reporting for the St. John's Evening Telegram *but found that reporting was not enough. His distaste for the Liberal government of Joey Smallwood, and especially for its policy of closing down the outports where for centuries Newfoundlanders had lived as fishermen, led Guy to become a political columnist. His satirical attacks on Smallwood were so devastating that some people credit him with Smallwood's defeat in the provincial election of 1971. Guy no longer works for the* Evening Telegram, *but he writes a column that appears in several newspapers. His humorous essays about many aspects of life in Newfoundland have been collected in* You May Know Them as Sea Urchins, Ma'am *(1975) and in* That Far Greater Bay *(1976), which won the Leacock Medal for Humour. Our selection first appeared in the latter.*

1   What feeds we used to have. Not way back in the pod auger days,* mind you. That was before my time. I mean not long ago, just before the tinned stuff and the packages and the baker's bread started to trickle into the outports.

2   Out where I come from the trickle started when I was about six or seven years old. One day I went next door to Aunt Winnie's (that's Uncle John's Aunt Winnie) and she had a package of puffed rice someone sent down from Canada.*

3   She gave us youngsters a small handful each. We spent a long time admiring this new exotic stuff and remarking on how much it looked like emmets' eggs. We ate it one grain at a time as if it were candy, and because of the novelty didn't notice the remarkable lack of taste.

4   "Now here's a five cent piece and don't spend it all in sweets, mind." You never got a nickel without this caution attached.

---

*the pod auger days: a common Newfoundland expression meaning "the old days"
A pod auger is an auger with a lengthwise groove.
*from Canada: Newfoundland did not join Confederation until 1949, after the time Ray Guy describes.

46

EXAMPLE *47*

Peppermint knobs. White capsules ringed around with flannelette   5
pink stripes. Strong! You'd think you were breathing icewater.
They're not near as strong today.

Chocolate mice shaped like a crouching rat, chocolate on the   6
outside and tough pink sponge inside. Goodbye teeth. Bullseyes
made from molasses. And union squares — pastel blocks of
marshmallow.

Those mysterious black balls that were harder than forged steel,   7
had about 2,537 different layers of color and a funny tasting seed at
the centre of the mini-universe.

Soft drinks came packed in barrels of straw in bottles of different   8
sizes and shapes and no labels. Birch beer, root beer, chocolate,
lemonade, and orange.

Spruce beer, which I could never stomach, but the twigs boiling on   9
the stove smelled good. Home brew made from "Blue Ribbon" malt
and which always exploded like hand grenades in the bottles behind
the stove.

Rum puncheons. Empty barrels purchased from the liquor control   10
in St. John's. You poured in a few gallons of water, rolled the barrel
around, and the result was a stronger product than you put down
$7.50 a bottle for today.

Ice cream made in a hand-cranked freezer, the milk and sugar and   11
vanilla in the can in the middle surrounded by ice and coarse salt. I
won't say it was better than the store-bought stuff today but it
tasted different and I like the difference.

Rounders (dried tom cods) for Sunday breakfast without fail. Cods   12
heads, boiled sometimes, but mostly stewed with onions and bits of
salt pork.

Fried cod tongues with pork scruncheons.* Outport soul food. Salt   13
codfish, fish cakes, boiled codfish and drawn butter, baked cod with
savoury stuffing, stewed cod, fried cod.

Lobsters. We always got the bodies and the thumbs from the   14
canning factories. When eating lobster bodies you must be careful to
stay away from the "old woman," a lump of bitter black stuff up near
the head which is said to be poisonous.

I was always partial to that bit of red stuff in lobster bodies but   15
never went much on the pea green stuff although some did.

We ate turrs* (impaled on a sharpened broomstick and held over   16
the damper hole to singe off the fuzz), some people ate tickleaces*
and gulls but I never saw it done.

---

*pork scruncheons: crisp slices of fried pork fat
*turr: a term applied to both the razor-billed auk and the murre, in this case probably
the auk
*tickleace: the kittiwake, a kind of gull

17   We ate "a meal of trouts," seal, rabbits that were skinned out like a sock, puffin' pig (a sort of porpoise that had black meat), mussels and cocks and hens, otherwise known as clams, that squirt at you through air holes in the mud flats.

18   Potatoes and turnips were the most commonly grown vegetables although there was some cabbage and carrot. The potatoes were kept in cellars made of mounds of earth lined with sawdust or goosegrass. With the hay growing on them they looked like hairy green igloos.

19   A lot was got from a cow. Milk, certainly, and cream and butter made into pats and stamped with a wooden print of a cow or a clover leaf, and buttermilk, cream cheese. And I seem to remember a sort of jellied sour milk. I forget the name but perhaps the stuff was equivalent to yogurt.

20   There was no fresh meat in summer because it wouldn't keep. If you asked for a piece of meat at the store you got salt beef. If you wanted fresh beef you had to ask for "fresh meat."

21   Biscuits came packed in three-foot long wooden boxes and were weighed out by the pound in paper bags. Sultanas, Dad's cookies, jam jams, lemon creams with caraway seeds, and soda biscuits.

22   Molasses was a big thing. It was used to sweeten tea, in gingerbread, on rolled oats porridge, with sulphur in the spring to clean the blood (eeeccchhhh), in bread, in baked beans, in 'lassie bread.

23   It came in barrels and when the molasses was gone, there was a layer of molasses sugar at the bottom.

24   Glasses of lemon crystals or strawberry syrup or limejuice. Rolled oats, farina, Indian meal. Home-made bread, pork buns, figgy duff,* partridgeberry tarts, blanc mange, ginger wine, damper cakes.*

25   Cold mutton, salt beef, peas pudding, boiled cabbage, tinned bully beef for lunch on Sunday, tinned peaches, brown eggs, corned caplin.*

26   And thank God I was twelve years old before ever a slice of baker's bread passed my lips.

Structure:

1. Point out everything that Ray Guy's first sentence tells us about the essay which will follow.

---

*figgy duff: boiled raisin pudding
*damper cakes: a kind of bannock made on the damper (upper surface) of a cookstove
*caplin: a small and edible ocean fish often used by cod fishermen as bait

EXAMPLE *49*

2. In his last sentence Ray Guy exclaims, "And thank God I was twelve years old before ever a slice of baker's bread passed my lips." What does this sentence achieve that qualifies it to conclude the essay?
3. What percentage of this essay do you estimate consists of examples? Are there enough to illustrate the point? Are there too many?
4. Why does Ray Guy relate the incident of the puffed wheat (pars. 2 and 3)?

Style:

1. How wastefully or economically does Ray Guy use words in this essay?
2. Point out sentence fragments in this essay. Why do you think Guy uses them?
3. Point out the expressions that most strongly give "Outharbor Menu" a TONE that is folksy and COLLOQUIAL. Is this tone appropriate to the topic?
4. In paragraph 18 Guy describes the root cellars: "With the hay growing on them they looked like hairy green igloos." Where else has he used SIMILES — comparisons that describe one thing in terms of another?

Ideas:

1. How nostalgic is Ray Guy about his topic? To what extent do you think he exaggerates or presents a one-sided picture because he is writing about his childhood? Is nostalgia desirable in our lives? Can it ever work against us?
2. In his newspaper columns, Ray Guy strongly opposed governmental measures to move people from Newfoundland's outports — such as the one described in this essay — to centralized locations where they would work in factories instead of fish. To what extent do you think the traditional life of a culture should be preserved? Is a government ever justified in deliberately changing it? If so, under what conditions?
3. In the last decade or two, fast-food chains such as McDonald's have been standardizing the eating habits not only of North America but also of many other parts of the world. What are we gaining in this process? What are we losing in this process?
4. Describe the worst or best meal you have ever had in a fast-food restaurant, using numerous examples to support your main idea.

5. In paragraph 13, Guy uses the expression "outport soul food." What does "soul food" usually refer to? Do we all prefer a kind of "soul food" that we experienced while growing up? In an essay, describe the "soul food" of your own childhood. Give plentiful *examples,* as Ray Guy does in "Outharbor Menu."

(NOTE: See also the Topics for Writing at the end of this chapter.)

Robert Fulford

Where, Exactly, Are This Book's Readers?

A self-educated man, Robert Fulford is one of Canada's most respected journalists, editors and critics. Born in Ottawa in 1932, he grew up in Toronto where in 1949 he began his career in journalism as a copy boy for the Globe and Mail. *Soon after, he became a reporter. In 1957 Fulford was named editor of* Canadian Homes and Gardens, *and since then he has held editorial positions at* Maclean's, Mayfair, The Canadian Forum *and, since 1968,* Saturday Night. *Fulford's greatest achievement, through his editorial abilities and his own penetrating and well-written columns, has been to secure the position of* Saturday Night *as English Canada's best magazine of culture and public affairs. Since 1960 Fulford has also been a columnist for* The Toronto Star, *a radio and television broadcaster, and the author of several books.* "Where, Exactly, Are This Book's Readers?" *appeared first in* The Toronto Star, *then in a 1968 collection of Fulford's essays,* Crisis at the Victory Burlesk: Culture, Politics & Other Diversions.

There's always the possibility, of course, that the world already has enough books; may, in fact, have *too many* books. This thought has never occurred to a publisher; it has probably occurred to only a minority of authors; but certainly it has occurred at one time or another to every book reviewer in the world.

For the fact is that book reviewers spend their lives surrounded by piles of books they will never read and they can't imagine anyone else reading. Every morning a young man comes into my office with a pile of half a dozen books, and on the average three of them fall into this category.

Take one that turned up yesterday: *They Gave Royal Assent,* subtitled *The Lieutenant-Governors of British Columbia.* Imagine it. Not just a book on lieutenant-governors — a subject with truly monumental possibilities for producing boredom — but a book on *British Columbia* lieutenant-governors.

Now the thing about lieutenant-governors is that, in general, they don't do anything. They just sort of *preside.* Their lives lack, not to put too fine a point on it, drama. So who will read this book? If you were lieutenant-governor of British Columbia you might well want to read it, and if you aspired to that office you would almost certainly be anxious to obtain a copy. But surely that makes a limited market. In addition there are descendants and other connections of lieutenant-governors; but this, too, must be a comparatively small group. Will the author, D.A. McGregor ('veteran journalist, editor and history-researcher', the jacket says) meet friends who have read his book and who will congratulate him on it? 'Nice job on the lieutenant-governors, old man,' one imagines them saying. But who would they be?

5   The publishers, Mitchell Press of Vancouver, have dutifully sent out review copies. Why? Because publishers do this — they operate automatically on the I-shot-an-arrow-into-the-air theory of publicity. They just send out books at random, whether anybody wants them or not. It gives them some queer sense of satisfaction. They feel they are playing their part.

6   So here are all these books floating around in the mails and then ending up on the desks of people who view them with apathy if not distaste. Any book reviewer can at any moment, and to his horror, look around his office and instantly spot three books on the Quebec crisis, four histories of Ontario counties, five books on how to diet, two authorized biographies of Teilhard de Chardin, and one book by a man who lived six months with a colony of apes and didn't find out anything.

7   Right now I have here, in front of me: *The Bahamas Handbook* (547 pages, would you believe it?); *One of Our Brains is Draining,* a novel by someone named Max Wilk; *The Nation Keepers,* a book of essays by the likes of Wallace McCutcheon and John Robarts; *Brant County, A History, 1784-1945; Success at the Harness Races,* by Barry Meadow, 'a practical guide for handicapping winners'; *Churchill, His Paintings,* a gift book priced at only $12.50 and worth, anyway, a nickel; *Vigor for Men Over 30,* as depressing a title as any I've encountered this season, by Warren Guild, M.D., Stuart D. Cowan, and Samm Sinclair Baker (a slim book, but it took three men to write it); *A History of Peel County, 1867-1967; Nineteenth Century Pottery and Porcelain in Canada;* and *Great True Hunts,* a $17.95 picture book all about how various famous men — such as the Shah of Iran, Tito, and Roy Rogers — go out and kill beautiful animals for fun.

8   I can't get a copy of the new John O'Hara novel, no matter how hard I try, but I have all these other books around me, and they're piling up, piling up. A man came to my office yesterday and claimed he couldn't find me. I was there all the time, but hidden. The situation, as it often does in December, is reaching a critical phase.

9   But what about those Vancouver publishers? What exactly did they have in mind when they sent out those review copies of their lieutenant-governor book? Did they think people would *read* it, and

EXAMPLE *53*

then *write* something about it? Did they anticipate that soon they would begin receiving clippings, full of praise for their courage, imagination, and resourcefulness in publishing this significant volume? One can imagine the quotes:

'*A stimulating and indeed an engrossing account of . . . in places* 10 *thrilling, in others richly analytical . . . abrasive, tough, probing . . . profound and moving in its depiction of . . . a very badly needed contribution to the history of . . . . full of those insights we have come to expect from . . .*"

Or did they, retaining some grasp on reality, know all the time 11 what would happen — that one book editor after another across the country would silently pass the book along to his paper's library, hoping that someday someone on the staff — for some unthinkable reason — would want to know something about the lieutenant-governors of British Columbia?

The notion that perhaps there may be too many books in the 12 world, that perhaps it is more creative *not* to write a book than to write one, occurred to me when I returned the other day from two weeks of leave and began wading through a pile of books on Christian revival, books on space exploration, and books on nineteenth-century Canada. . . . But I immediately set that whole subversive idea aside. Because after all I'd just spent the previous two weeks, uh, writing a book.

Structure:

1. Where is Fulford's main point first stated?
2. What effect is achieved in the final sentence where Fulford confesses that he himself has just written a book?
3. Why do you think Fulford devotes six paragraphs to *They Gave Royal Assent: The Lieutenant-Governors of British Columbia,* but only a few words to each of the many other books he names?
4. How convincing are Fulford's examples? Would you want to read any of the books that he makes fun of?

Style:

1. When did you first realize that this is a humorous essay?
2. People say "uh" but hardly ever write it. Why does Fulford use it in his final sentence? Point out other places where he uses INFORMAL, conversational language and discuss the effects he achieves in doing so.

3. In paragraph 7, Fulford tells us that *Vigor for Men over 30* is "a slim book, but it took three men to write it." Point out other examples of IRONY, in which we hear the opposite of what we might have expected.
4. Why do you think Fulford wrote paragraph 7 as one long sentence?
5. What do Fulford's imagined book review quotations in paragraph 10 make fun of?

Ideas:

1. Fulford begins his essay by stating, "There's always the possibility, of course, that the world already has enough books; may, in fact, have *too many* books." Do you agree? How do you feel in a large library with thousands of books around you? Can you think of reasons why a library might collect the books Fulford criticizes?
2. What kinds of books do you own? Name your favourites. How do you choose a book to buy?
3. Why do people write books? What are some bad reasons? What are some good reasons?
4. If you have read "What Happened to CanLit?," compare John Metcalf's view of Canadian publishing with that of Robert Fulford.
5. Suppose you decide to become an author. Write an essay describing your first book: its subject, its approach to that subject, the most important points or scenes it would contain and the identity of its intended readers. Do you think a reviewer like Robert Fulford would consider it a book to read or avoid? Use frequent *examples* to explain all these points.

(NOTE: See also the Topics for Writing at the end of this chapter.)

John Metcalf

What Happened to CanLit?

Born in England in 1938, John Metcalf earned an Honours B.A. and a certificate in education before moving to Canada in 1962. First he taught in high schools, then at Loyola College, Montreal, and since 1971 has divided his time between writing, editing, part-time teaching and serving as writer in residence at several universities. Metcalf is at home with many forms of writing. He has published collections of his short stories, The Lady Who Sold Furniture *(1970),* The Teeth of My Father *(1975) and* Selected Stories *(1982); a book of two novellas,* Girl in Gingham *(1978); novels,* Going Down Slow *(1972) and* General Ludd *(1980); and essays,* Kicking Against the Pricks *(1982). He has also edited many collections of short stories by other writers. Metcalf derives his power as a writer from the combination of a polished style with a satirical tone. "Writing is very hard work but at the same time it is delightful play," he states in his book* Making It New *(1982). Both the "work" and the "play" are evident in our selection, which appeared in 1983 in the Toronto* Globe and Mail.

Think of CanLit as a pyramid. 1

Inverted. And kept upright by the power of subsidy. 2

The point of precarious balance is composed of writers. 3
Just above them are two or three narrow courses of readers. The mass of the inverted pyramid is made up of publishers, reviewers, critics, teachers, anthologizers, librarians, compilers of tomes of reference, arts organizations and cultural agencies both federal and provincial.

The base of the pyramid, were it in its normal position, should, of 4
course, be composed of readers, but there are so few readers in Canada that "public" response to a book is more or less irrelevant. A sale of 1,000 copies of a novel is considered respectable enough; probably half that figure will end up in public libraries, possibly to be read.

All aspects of writing, publishing, and critical study are 5
subsidized and the books will keep on appearing, whether they are bought or not. Books are not actually published to be sold; they're published to ensure the publisher an even larger subvention from the Secretary of State in the following year.

Many of the books unsold will be purchased by the Canada 6
Council itself (their commissioner, in effect) in the first place, and

will be made up into crates called Book Kits Canada to be sent, as I wrote elsewhere, "as compulsory gifts to underdeveloped countries, hospitals, institutions for the blind, prisons and lunatic asylums."

7 CanLit, in one sense, does not exist; it is a dream, a folly, a vast bureaucratic phantasmagoria fueled by government gold.

8 Apart from readers, just about the only literary component so far unsubsidized is professional critics outside the academy, critics who interpret, judge, and popularize the work of contemporary artists, critics who might be ideally typified by such figures as Cyril Connolly and Kenneth Clark.

9 The reason they remain unsubsidized is because we haven't got any.

10 How can one judge a dream?

11 Nathan Cohen tried to be such a critic and this so excited Toronto, in retrospect, that books and a play were written about him. Which somehow reminds me of Lady Whatsit, who said that she'd only ever read one book but it was so good that she had never felt the need to read another.

12 Judgments about contemporary literature are made in Canada, then, not as they are in most other countries by readers and professional critics, but by subsidized academics, blurb-writers, and newspaper reviewers.

13 It is sobering to have read the book review pages from papers all across the country. Book page editors who dictate what shall and shall not be reviewed sometimes seem to lack a sense of the grand design. On the same page one can find reviewed a collection of exquisite stories by Alice Munro, How to Build Your Own Garage, a historical romance involving bosoms and claymores, *Fifty Winning Ways With Brown Rice,* a pamphlet of poesie from Fiddlehead Books, and the latest disaster from Richard Rohmer. But why not? In Canada, a book is a book.

14 Reviews of an appalling standard are not confined to papers from backwaters; shame mantles the cheek whenever I think of literate foreign visitors in the Nation's Capital scanning the book reviews in the Ottawa Citizen.

15 Reviewing is usually a freelance activity left to writers, aspiring writers, failed writers and academics who specialize in CanLit with varying degrees of brilliance. Some reviewers have credentials even more tangential. Many have a rough-and-ready way with the English language. Some are simply content to regurgitate the hype of blurbwriters (a word I have heard translated for the benefit of a unilingual French Canadian as "le bulls—"), which may explain why so many Canadian books are hailed as "great," "hilarious," and "major."

EXAMPLE 57

The academic critics are beavering away publishing "explications   16
de textes" of such figures as Hugh Garner, author of Violation of the
Virgins and Death in Don Mills. Others are exhuming Isabella
Valancy Crawford. Hordes more profess themselves fascinated by
Frederick Philip Grove — and I believe them.

Academics are important in molding a sense of our literature, but   17
unfortunately they can't seem to agree on much. There is little
consensus about what constitutes the Canadian canon. Making
judgments about good and bad is, however, a novel idea for many of
them. Inspired by Margaret Atwood's very wrong-headed book,
Survival, our brighter intellectual lights have busied themselves for
the last decade describing and cataloguing themes, a grown-up
version of the Grade 7 book report.

They are, however, becoming sensible of this wandering-in-the-   18
desert and are trying hard to rectify matters. In 1978, stage-
managed by McClelland and Stewart, they lined up at Calgary
University like shampooed sheep and cast ballots to select the 100
Best Canadian Novels. McClelland and Stewart subsequently
struck a committee of obscure authority to certify certain books as
"Canadian Classics."

Such mildly sad buffooneries can be acted out only because there   19
is no audience and no readership to blow a collective raspberry.

While in the academic night Professor Burke mumbles to   20
Professor Hare, the media continue their endless quest for new
stars. Being a literary star in Canada tends to entail having
photographs of your bathroom in Chatelaine. Margaret Laurence
was a star; Margaret Atwood is still a star. Is the candlepower of
Jack Hodgins dimming? Is Robert Kroetsch beginning to flicker? Is
Leon Rooke rising? Is the Art Deco revival finished?

It was typical that CBC's Sunday Morning's piece on the   21
Tutankhamen exhibition concentrated not on the history of
archeology, not on Egyptian funerary rites, not on Egyptian art, but
on the vast sums raised by the sale of King Tut T-shirts. For all our
new and vaunted sophistication, a glance at Beverley Slopen's
column and an earful of Sunday Morning confirm that there is a
gross confusion in the minds of our cultural commentators between
art and cash.

And then there are readers.   22

What readers there are positively embrace boredom.   23

Robertson Davies seems a quintessential product of the CanLit   24
dream. Publishers and reviewers, magazines, low-wattage academics, apathetic readers — all seem to have conspired, if that is not too
active a verb, to create a climate in which Davies can be promoted as
Grade-A Certified CanLit.

25   His latest florid booming, Rebel Angels, is even more stunningly boring than its prototypes by Thomas Love Peacock, yet it was purchased by Penguin Books for infliction on an even wider section of the populace.

26   Readers seem compliant to the point of masochism.

27   It does not seem to matter to readers *or* critics that all the characters speaking in Rebel Angels speak in the same voice, that Mordecai Richler's Joshua Then and Now, though thick, was painfully thin in characterization and motive and desperate in humor, that Mavis Gallant was *finally* honored with the Governor-General's Award *for the wrong book* . . . . It does not seem to matter to readers *or* critics that Morley Callaghan's prose is pedestrian and plonking, that the word "purple" is inadequate to describe the prose of Ernest Buckler, that far too many of Rudy Wiebe's sentences are, well, *kind of weird.* . . .

28   But anyway, say those who are made uncomfortable by such a display of bad manners, isn't this just a question of style?

29   This defensive question is always put by those who seem to believe that "style" is a decorative afterthought, an additive, fancy icing on the honest business of the cake.

30   When one advances the literary commonplace that the *way* a writer writes is *what* he writes, bafflement is palpable. Readers are going to continue missing all the fun until they learn that the search for "le mot juste" is not some quaint, writerly eccentricity. Mangled rhetoric, purple prose, slapdash vocabulary, the odd patch of total incomprehensibility — these are not mere facial blemishes, as it were, but mortal wounds.

31   So what can be salvaged from the dream?

32   About some of our writers there is widespread agreement: Alice Munro, Michael Ondaatje and, belatedly, Mavis Gallant. But other writers of quality have not been widely celebrated.

33   What follows is a list of books I like to share, books of quality that have been undervalued or ignored. All are modern. From the "classical" period of CanLit, that period most beloved by the CanLit Dream Machine and such crankers of its handle as Robin Matthews, the period from petroglyphs to the first books of Margaret Laurence and Hugh Hood, the only writer who holds my interest is Ethel Wilson. There are more story writers on my short shelf than novelists simply because our story writers are more sophisticated.

34   The passage of another decade will doubtless shorten even this short list. But that is as it should be.

35   Novels.

36   How *could* our academic brethren select — *select* — 100? I have difficulty thinking of 25. And some of *them* are not really . . . .

EXAMPLE *59*

Laurence, Richler, Moore, Hood, David Adams Richards 37
I really can't go further. 38
Can I dare say, publicly, that one good 12-page story is worth more 39
than 10 competent novels? Worth more than another writer's whole
career?
Yes. Without qualms. 40
Stories and short fiction, then. Alice Munro and Mavis Gallant. 41
No great need to mention *them*. Curious, Munro's most recent work.
It's becoming increasingly powerful, dreamlike. I'm thinking of a
story like "Visitors," from The Moons of Jupiter. I'm content not to
understand it; I just wander about inside; it's a marvellous place to
be.
And here's Hugh Hood again: Flying a Red Kite and Around the 42
Mountain. Grossly ill-read and misunderstood. Subtle books,
challenging, full of complex delights.
Beside them are A North American Education (out of print) and 43
Tribal Justice (out of print). Both marked by Clark Blaise's
gorgeous, poetic texturing. Both full of formal innovation.
Almost hidden (it's so thin a book) is The Truth and Other Stories 44
by Terrence Heath. House of Anansi, 1972, 69 pages (out of print).
This is the sort of book that writers talk about when they get
together — and refuse to lend.
And here's Leon Rooke hailed by the media as post-modernist, 45
surrealist, magic realist, fabulist etc. But don't worry. He's actually
a warm-hearted, old-fashioned moralist, thank God, and about as
surreal as an old settee. Try the ones that were largely ignored: The
Love Parlor (out of print) and Cry Evil (out of print).
Margaret Laurence's The Tomorrow Tamer, a book much richer 46
than the better-known A Bird in the House. The CanLit Brigade has
taken to its bosom, of course, the latter. If one wishes to appeal to
CanLitters, it must be "about" Canada. This "about" business is, of
course, the centre of the problem. When will they learn that it's the
"how" that matters?
And here's my favorite Audrey Thomas book, Ten Green Bottles 47
— though not hers. "About" Africa again (out of print).
Norman Levine's seemingly simple stories next. Perhaps only 48
another writer can know how hard-won that "simplicity" is. There is
an austerity and chastity about Levine's best work which is
extremely sophisticated; his elegance is a durable pleasure. Try
One-Way Ticket, I Don't Want to Know Anyone Too Well, and
Selected Stories (out of print).
Here's Ray Smith's Cape Breton Is the Thought-Control Centre of 49
Canada (out of print). Bizarre, challenging and containing, among
many good things, the entrancing story "Peril."

50   Beside him stands Mavis Gallant's From the Fifteenth District —
the book which *should* have won the Governor-General's Award but
which wasn't "about" Canada.

51   And here at the end of the shelf is a first book of stories by Keath
Fraser called Taking Cover. Fraser has a marvellous literary
intelligence and Taking Cover contains some dazzling rhetorical
performances. What a pleasure to know there's more to come! This
book is already a year old; get it quickly before it's remaindered or
made up into a Book Kit Canada or becomes . . .

52   (out of print).

Structure:

1. Is Metcalf's opening IMAGE effective? In what way does the
   inverted pyramid prepare us for the argument that follows?
2. Metcalf's investigation is divided into four main parts: the
   introduction, an examination of critics, an examination of
   readers and, finally, Metcalf's version of what little is good in
   Canadian literature. Where does each part begin and end? Does
   this progression of parts make sense?
3. Does Metcalf use good strategy in placing his criticism first and
   his praise last? Or does putting the praise last give a positive
   impression, which diminishes the main point of the essay —
   that "CanLit" is in a sorry state?
4. What proportion of this essay would you say consists of
   examples? How effective would Metcalf's argument be without
   them?

Style:

1. Is Metcalf angry? If so, how do you react to his anger? Is the
   expression of anger effective in an essay? Are there times when
   it is ineffective?
2. In paragraph 16 Metcalf reports the "exhuming" of author
   Isabella Valancy Crawford (1850-1887), whose once little-read
   works are increasingly being studied and publicized by critics.
   Explain the power of Metcalf's IMAGE. Does its SATIRE seem
   directed mainly at Crawford or at her critics?
3. Examine Metcalf's IMAGES of "shampooed sheep" (par. 18),
   "Grade-A Certified CanLit" (par. 24) and of "purple" prose
   (par. 27). What does each imply about the object of its SATIRE?

EXAMPLE *61*

4. Why are some of Metcalf's paragraphs long while others are as short as one word? Why are some of his sentences long and formal while others are literally sentence fragments?
5. The phrase "out of print" is repeated nine times from paragraph 43 to the end. What is the effect? What are the uses of repetition in an essay? What are the pitfalls?

Ideas:

1. Does Metcalf's harsh condemnation do a disservice to Canadian literature, discouraging writers, publishers and readers? Or, in exposing abuses, does it pave the way for improvement?
2. In criticizing our system of publishing based on governmental subsidy, is Metcalf implying that subsidies should be stopped? Do you think that aid such as Canada Council grants to writers helps or harms our literature and its ultimate consumer, the reader?
3. In Metcalf's view, few Canadians read books. Do you agree? Give evidence, perhaps examples, to support your opinion. If few of us read books, what are the reasons? Are books important or necessary in our time? Will we read books in the future?
4. If you have taken a Canadian literature course, were most of the books or selections "about" Canada? If so, did you find this good or bad? Give examples. Is Metcalf right in saying "This 'about' business is, of course, the centre of the problem" (par. 46)?
5. Metcalf states that at least one work of Robertson Davies is "stunningly boring" (pars. 24-27), that "Morley Callaghan's prose is pedestrian and plonking" (par. 27), and that "far too many of Rudy Wiebe's sentences are, well, *kind of weird. . .*" (par. 27). If you are familiar with one or more of these authors, tell whether you agree or disagree, and why.
6. Starting at paragraph 32, Metcalf gives numerous *examples* of Canadian writers he does admire. Have you read one or more of these authors? If so, do you agree or disagree with his verdict?
7. Why do you suppose Metcalf, in his examination of "CanLit," never once mentions the literature of French Canada? Is he merely restricting and focussing his topic? Can you think of other possible reasons? What barriers exist between us and writers who use Canada's other official language? Are those barriers worth crossing? If so, how can the crossing be done?
8. Metcalf states in paragraphs 39 and 40 that a good 12-page story by one writer may be worth more than another writer's

whole career. Do you agree or disagree? If possible give examples.

9. If you have read "Where, Exactly, Are This Book's Readers?" compare Robert Fulford's view of Canadian publishing with that of John Metcalf.

10. Write an essay about the worst or best works you have studied in a previous literature class. Like Metcalf, use numerous *examples*.

———

(NOTE: See also the Topics for Writing at the end of this chapter.)

Bruce Hutchison

Cowboy from Holland

Bruce Hutchison, born in 1901 in Prescott, Ontario, has had a very long and full career as a journalist. Considered the dean of political commentators in Canada, Hutchison has written over a dozen books, won three National Newspaper Awards and three Governor-General's literary awards. He began reporting in Ottawa, was associate editor of the Winnipeg Free Press *from 1944 to 1950, editor of the Victoria* Daily Times *from 1950 to 1963, and from 1963 until his retirement in 1979 was editorial director of* The Vancouver Sun. *With a writing schedule that at times has reached 10,000 words a day, Hutchison has not stopped at newspaper work: he has also produced books of history, fiction, biography, geography and politics. His best-known are* The Unknown Country: Canada and Her People *(1942) and* Canada: Tomorrow's Giant *(1957). "Cowboy from Holland," our selection from the latter book, exemplifies the colourful and even impassioned nature of Hutchison's prose.*

The great myth of Canada and the essential ingredient of the 1
nation recently hurtled into my garden on a tricycle. It was ridden by a golden-haired boy of five years just out from Holland. I do not know his name. He has yet to master the English language. But he has learned the first word of the myth. The word, of course, is "cowboy." He shouted it through my gate, brandished two toy pistols, and whipped his three-wheeled horse over my flower beds.

Though my young friend knows little about Canada, he has hit 2
unerringly on its true content and oldest instinct. He has joined that long procession which started out of Europe in the first days of the seventeenth century, crossed an ocean and a continent, and marched westward to another ocean. He has grasped, by the deep wisdom of childhood, the primal force forever driving the Canadian westward against the wilderness. After the trim postage stamp of Holland he has seen the limitless space of a new land. He has breathed the west and become a cowboy. We are witnessing in our neighborhood the birth of a Canadian.

The other day the carefree cowboy got down to the serious 3
business of Canada. He became, by hereditary impulse, a farmer. His father, who had long cultivated the soil of Holland and acquired a Canadian farm only a month ago, gave the boy a set of tools, a little tin spade, rake, and hoe. Immediately the horse and pistols were laid aside.

63

4   As I drove down our country lane, the boy was digging up the roadside, smoothing it with his rake, and preparing to sow his first crop. There, in that small figure, was the genius of an ancient farm people transplanted across ocean and continent.

5   He shouted at me, in his own tongue, to observe his labors. They didn't amount to much beside his father's long spring furrows near by, but they were a beginning. The seeds of Holland would germinate in the Canadian soil, and the seeds of Canada in the boy.

6   Soon, I suppose, he will forget his native land and his father's language. Within a year or so of entering a Canadian school he will be indistinguishable from other young Canadians in appearance, speech, and mind. Yes, but he, and other boys from foreign lands, carry with them certain invisible baggage that no customs inspector will discern. They carry, like the first French Canadians, the English, the Scots, the Irish, and the rest of us, a fraction of the old world. It is of such fractions, mixed together and smoothed by environment, that Canada is made.

7   Yesterday some boys born in Canada jeered at the Dutch immigrant and trampled his new seed bed. When he sought refuge in my garden, I tried to tell him that the Canadians were only demonstrating, by a perverse method, their pride in Canada. They acted, I said, like boys everywhere and much like the world's statesmen.

8   I tried to tell the immigrant about another boy of his own age who reached Upper Canada in 1820, the son of a Scots storekeeper with a habit of unprofitable speculation and an addiction to strong drink. That boy seemed to have less chance in life than the boy from Holland. Yet he died as the first prime minister of Canada and the idol of his people.

9   John Alexander Macdonald, as I attempted to explain, was an immigrant. So were the French before him and the Indians before them. All Canadians were immigrants a few generations back, and so diverse in blood that no racial stock could now claim to be a national majority. We are a nation of immigrants and minorities, slowly combining and issuing in what we call the Canadian breed.

10   The Dutch boy listened, but he didn't understand. Repeating the only Canadian word in his vocabulary, he said he was a cowboy. Well, that would serve well enough for a start. He had begun to get to the root of the matter. And today I observed the next chapter in an old story — the native Canadian boys were teaching an immigrant the art of baseball, the secret of a robin's nest in an apple tree, the green mysteries of a swamp.

EXAMPLE *65*

Structure:

1. In what ways and to what degree does this extended example of one immigrant develop the topic of immigration to Canada?
2. To what extent does this essay use short examples, in addition to the one long example of the Dutch boy?
3. Is the last sentence effective as a conclusion? What does it accomplish?

Style:

1. The "three-wheeled horse" mentioned in paragraph 1 is of course not a horse but a tricycle. Point out at least three more METAPHORS, figures of speech that are literally false but poetically true.
2. Is Hutchison's approach to his topic mainly OBJECTIVE or SUBJECTIVE? Give reasons for your answer. In what ways might his essay be different if he had used the opposite approach?

Ideas:

1. In 1957 this selection first appeared as a part of Bruce Hutchison's book *Canada: Tomorrow's Giant.* Has the author's prophecy come true? In the years since 1957 has Canada become a "giant"? Might it be a "giant" in some ways but not in others? Give examples to support your answer.
2. Hutchison states in paragraph 3 that farming is "the serious business of Canada." If he had written his essay today, what do you think the immigrant boy would learn as "the serious business of Canada"?
3. To what extent is the myth of the cowboy still with us in Canada? Does it affect our lives in any concrete way? Do you view its influence, if any, as positive or negative? Give examples to support your answers.
4. If you have read "Grinning and Happy," compare the treatment given by Canada to Joy Kogawa's minority group with that given by the Canadian boys to the "cowboy from Holland."
5. If you have immigrated to Canada, write the story of your own first days in the country, illustrating the opportunities and/or pitfalls of the process. If you are a native-born Canadian, write a similar essay about moving to a new neighbourhood, school, town, city or province. Develop your story through *examples.*

(NOTE: See also the Topics for Writing at the end of this chapter.)

Joy Kogawa

*Grinning and Happy**

With three published books of poetry to her credit — The Splintered Moon
(1967), A Choice of Dreams (1974) and Jericho Road (1977) — Joy Kogawa
had become a respected minor poet. But in 1981 she created a sensation with
her first novel. Obasan represents a new step for Kogawa as a writer and as a
person: in it she explores her own past and one of the most dubious events of
Canadian history. Born in Vancouver in 1935, Kogawa was a child during
World War II when the federal government classified Japanese Canadians as
"enemy aliens." Her parents' house in Vancouver was seized, and the family
was moved first to a relocation camp in Slocan, B.C., then to the sugar-beet
fields of southern Alberta, which are the setting of our selection from the
novel. Our narrator is modelled after Kogawa herself, Stephen is the
narrator's brother, Obasan is the narrator's silent and suffering aunt, and
"Aunt Emily" is modelled after Muriel Kitagawa, a Japanese-Canadian
activist whose letters Kogawa studied in the National Archives in Ottawa.
Kogawa now lives in Toronto.

1   There is a folder in Aunt Emily's package containing only one
     newspaper clipping and an index card with the words "Facts
     about evacuees in Alberta." The newspaper clipping has a
photograph of one family, all smiles, standing around a pile of beets.
The caption reads: "Grinning and Happy."

2   Find Jap Evacuees Best Beet Workers
        Lethbridge, Alberta, Jan. 22.

3   Japanese evacuees from British Columbia supplied the
        labour for 65% of Alberta's sugar beet acreage last year, Phil
        Baker, of Lethbridge, president of the Alberta Sugar Beet
        Growers' Association, stated today.

4   "They played an important part in producing our all-time
        record crop of 363,000 tons of beets in 1945," he added.

5   Mr. Baker explained Japanese evacuees worked 19,500 acres
        of beets and German prisoners of war worked 5,000 acres. The
        labour for the remaining 5,500 acres of Alberta's 30,000 acres
        of sugar beets was provided by farmers and their families.
        Some of the heaviest beet yields last year came from farms
        employing Japanese evacuees.

6   Generally speaking, Japanese evacuees have developed into
        most efficient beet workers, many of them being better than

---

*Editor's title

66

EXAMPLE **67**

the transient workers who cared for beets in southern Alberta
before Pearl Harbor. . . .

Facts about evacuees in Alberta? The fact is I never got used to it   7
and I cannot, I cannot bear the memory. There are some nightmares
from which there is no waking, only deeper and deeper sleep.

There is a word for it. Hardship. The hardship is so pervasive, so   8
inescapable, so thorough it's a noose around my chest and I cannot
move any more. All the oil in my joints has drained out and I have
been invaded by dust and grit from the fields and mud is in my bone
marrow. I can't move any more. My fingernails are black from
scratching the scorching day and there is no escape.

Aunt Emily, are you a surgeon cutting at my scalp with your   9
folders and your filing cards and your insistence on knowing all?
The memory drains down the sides of my face, but it isn't enough, is
it? It's your hands in my abdomen, pulling the growth from the
lining of my walls, but bring back the anaesthetist turn on the ether
clamp down the gas mask bring on the chloroform when will this
operation be over Aunt Em?

Is it so bad?   10

Yes.   11

Do I really mind?   12

Yes, I mind. I mind everything. Even the flies. The flies and flies   13
and flies from the cows in the barn and the manure pile — all the
black flies that curtain the windows, and Obasan with a wad of
toilet paper, spish, then with her bare hands as well, grabbing them
and their shocking white eggs and the mosquitoes mixed there with
the other insect corpses around the base of the gas lamp.

It's the chicken coop "house" we live in that I mind. The   14
uninsulated unbelievable thin-as-a-cotton-dress hovel never before
inhabited in winter by human beings. In summer it's a heat trap, an
incubator, a dry sauna from which there is no relief. In winter the
icicles drip down the inside of the windows and the ice is thicker
than bricks at the ledge. The only place that is warm is by the coal
stove where we rotate like chickens on a spit and the feet are so cold
they stop registering. We eat cloves of roasted garlic on winter
nights to warm up.

It's the bedbugs and my having to sleep on the table to escape the   15
nightly attack, and the welts over our bodies. And all the swamp
bugs and the dust. It's Obasan uselessly packing all the cracks with
rags. And the muddy water from the irrigation ditch which we
strain and settle and boil, and the tiny carcasses of water creatures
at the bottom of the cup. It's walking in winter to the reservoir and
keeping the hole open with the axe and dragging up the water in
pails and lugging it back and sometimes the water spills down your

boots and your feet are red and itchy for days. And it's everybody taking a bath in the round galvanized tub, then Obasan washing clothes in the water after and standing outside hanging the clothes in the freezing weather where everything instantly stiffens on the line.

16 Or it's standing in the beet field under the maddening sun, standing with my black head a sun-trap even though it's covered, and lying down in the ditch, faint, and the nausea in waves and the cold sweat, and getting up and tackling the next row. The whole field is an oven and there's not a tree within walking distance. We are tiny as insects crawling along the grill and there is no protection anywhere. The eyes are lidded against the dust and the air cracks the skin, the lips crack, Stephen's flutes crack and there is no energy to sing any more anyway.

17 It's standing in the field and staring out at the heat waves that waver and shimmer like see-through curtains over the brown clods and over the tiny distant bodies of Stephen and Uncle and Obasan miles away across the field day after day and not even wondering how this has come about.

18 There she is, Obasan, wearing Uncle's shirt over a pair of dark baggy trousers, her head covered by a straw hat that is held on by a white cloth tied under her chin. She is moving like a tiny earth cloud over the hard clay clods. Her hoe moves rhythmically up down up down, tiny as a toothpick. And over there, Uncle pauses to straighten his back, his hands on his hips. And Stephen farther behind, so tiny I can barely see him.

19 It's hard, Aunt Emily, with my hoe, the blade getting dull and mud-caked as I slash out the Canada thistle, dandelions, crab grass, and other nameless non-beet plants, then on my knees, pulling out the extra beets from the cluster, leaving just one to mature, then three hand spans to the next plant, whack whack, and down on my knees again, pull, flick flick, and on to the end of the long long row and the next and the next and it will never be done thinning and weeding and weeding and weeding. It's so hard and so hot that my tear glands burn out.

20 And then it's cold. The lumps of clay mud stick on my gumboots and weight my legs and the skin under the boots beneath the knees at the level of the calves grows red and hard and itchy from the flap flap of the boots and the fine hairs on my legs grow coarse there and ugly.

21 I mind growing ugly.

22 I mind the harvest time and the hands and the wrists bound in rags to keep the wrists from breaking open. I lift the heavy mud-clotted beets out of the ground with the hook like an eagle's

EXAMPLE *69*

beak, thick and heavy as a nail attached to the top of the sugar-beet knife. Thwack. Into the beet and yank from the shoulder till it's out of the ground dragging the surrounding mud with it. Then crack two beets together till most of the mud drops off and splat, the knife slices into the beet scalp and the green top is tossed into one pile, the beet heaved onto another, one more one more one more down the icy line. I cannot tell about this time, Aunt Emily. The body will not tell.

We are surrounded by a horizon of denim-blue sky with clouds 23 clear as spilled milk that turn pink at sunset. Pink I hear is the colour of llama's milk. I wouldn't know. The clouds are the shape of our new prison walls — untouchable, impersonal, random.

There are no other people in the entire world. We work together 24 all day. At night we eat and sleep. We hardly talk anymore. The boxes we brought from Slocan are not unpacked. The King George/Queen Elizabeth mugs stay muffled in the *Vancouver Daily Province*. The camera phone does not sing. Obasan wraps layers of cloth around her feet and her torn sweater hangs unmended over her sagging dress.

Down the miles we are obedient as machines in this odd ballet 25 without accompaniment of flute or song.

"Grinning and happy" and all smiles standing around a pile of 26 beets? That is one telling. It's not how it was.

Structure:

1. Where is the main point of this selection first stated?
2. What percentage of this selection would you estimate consists of examples that illustrate the main point?
3. In what way does "Grinning and Happy" use contrast as a structural device?
4. To what extent is this selection based on description?
5. What qualifies paragraph 26 to end this selection?

Style:

1. Until the publication of *Obasan,* Joy Kogawa was best known as a poet. What poetical qualities do you find in this selection of her PROSE?
2. To what extent has Kogawa used SENSE IMAGES to make this selection vivid? Give one example each of appeals to sight, hearing, touch, taste and smell.

3. A SIMILE states that one thing is like another, while a METAPHOR states poetically that one thing is another. Which of the following are similes and which are metaphors?
    A. "The hardship is so pervasive, so inescapable, so thorough it's a noose around my chest . . . ." (par. 8)
    B. ". . . all the black flies that curtain the windows . . . ." (par. 13)
    C. "In summer it's a heat trap, an incubator, a dry sauna from which there is no relief." (par. 14)
    D. "The only place that is warm is by the coal stove where we rotate like chickens on a spit . . . ." (par. 14)
    E. "The whole field is an oven . . . ." (par. 16)
    F. "We are tiny as insects crawling along the grill . . . ." (par. 16)
    G. ". . . heat waves that waver and shimmer like see-through curtains . . . ." (par. 17)
    H. ". . . the hook like an eagle's beak, thick and heavy as a nail attached to the top of the sugar-beet knife." (par. 22)
    I. ". . . the knife slices into the beet scalp . . . ." (par. 22)
    J. "The clouds are the shape of our new prison walls — untouchable, impersonal, random." (par. 23)
4. In paragraphs 14 through 17, how many times do you find the contraction "it's" at or near the beginning of a sentence? Is this repetition accidental or deliberate? What is its effect?
5. How many words long is the first sentence of paragraph 19? How many times does it use the word "and"? Is this run-on sentence accidental or deliberate? What is its effect?

Ideas:

1. The narrator of "Grinning and Happy" and her immediate family are Canadian citizens of Japanese descent, removed by the federal government from the coast of British Columbia during World War II for fear they would betray Canada to enemy Japan. They were separated from other family members and their property was taken, never to be returned. Discuss the wisdom of our government's action against the Japanese-Canadians, who are accurately represented by this fictitious family. Did anything like it happen before World War II? Has anything like it happened since? Under what circumstances can you imagine it happening again and to what group or groups?
2. Have you personally or have any of your ancestors faced persecution based on race, nationality or religion? If so explain how and why, giving examples.

EXAMPLE *71*

3. How much racial prejudice, if any, do you see in the area where you live? What do you think may be its causes? Against whom is it directed? Give examples that you have personally witnessed.

4. If you have read "Coming of Age in Putnok," compare prejudice and its effects as they are described by George Gabori and by Kogawa.

5. The black American comedian Dick Gregory once said, "A lot of people tell me: 'We just have a small racial problem in Canada.' What I want to know is how do you say that a woman is a little bit pregnant?" He added, "I think the acid test to the problem here in Canada will be if every white person would go to bed and imagine waking up tomorrow morning black. I think then they would be aware that there are problems" (*Scan*, November 1965). Following Gregory's suggestion, imagine that you wake up one morning as a member of another race. Write an essay that describes that day in your life, showing through numerous *examples* how your life might have changed.

(NOTE: See also the Topics for Writing at the end of this chapter.)

Richard Needham

A Sound of Deviltry by Night

Richard Needham is a newspaperman who since 1964 has written a column of aphorisms, puzzles, riddles and satire for the Toronto Globe and Mail. *He has been described as one of our few genuine cynics, a writer who delights in attacking sacred cows — and who, for this reason, tends to provoke either love or hatred among his readers. Needham was born in 1912 in Gibraltar, grew up in India, Ireland and England, and at age sixteen left home to come to Canada. After working as a farm hand, he found his first writing job at* The Toronto Star. *Through the years he has worked also at the Hamilton* Herald, *the Sudbury* Star, The Calgary Herald *and — for most of the time since 1951 — the* Globe and Mail. *His short satires have been collected in* Needham's Inferno *(1966), which won the Stephen Leacock Medal for Humour,* The Garden of Needham *(1968),* A Friend in Needham *(1969),* The Wit & Wisdom of Richard Needham *(1977) and* You and All the Rest *(1982). Our selection typifies Needham's ironical tone, his love of puns and his extraordinarily concise style. It appears in* The Hypodermic Needham *(1970) in slightly different form.*

1   In the city, you can go broke on $20,000 a year; but in the suburbs, you can do it on $30,000. Suburbanites accomplish this in some measure by staging lavish cocktail parties at which matrons gobble pizza as they discuss their weight problem, and men get smashed out of their skulls while they boast how they gave up smoking.

2   What function these parties serve (outside of plunging the host and hostess further into debt) has long baffled sociologists. My theory — true for myself, at least — is that the cocktail party is a form of shock treatment comparable to the snake pit of earlier times. So great is the horror of it, so keen the sense of relief at escaping, that all one's other sufferings and problems are reduced to triviality.

3   Finding myself beset by fortune's slings and arrows not long ago, I subjected myself to the ordeal by guzzle, gabble and gorge at a home so far north of the city that several of the guests greeted each other by rubbing noses. The usual cocktail-party types were on hand — languid immigrants, inferior decorators, insulting engineers, gloomy dames, misplaced trustees, impractical nurses, a dean of women who had been fired for having men in her room at all hours

EXAMPLE 73

of the day and night, a marriage counsellor who announced that his third wife had just left him for the fifth time, and a psychiatrist who kept getting down on his hands and knees and frisking about the place, nipping at the women's heels.

It is customary at these gatherings to have the phonograph on at 4 full blast; this forces people to shout and scream at each other, which in turn dries out their throats, which in turn causes them to get bagged more quickly, which is why they went to the party in the first place. Having no opinions or information worth bellowing, I customarily listen to those of others. Standing near a group of women, I caught the following fragments:

'The only thing I have against men is me . . . *The Naked Ape* is 5 disgusting, I stayed up all night reading it . . . I don't know how old she is exactly, but she does enjoy a nice hot cup of tea . . . Even a newspaperman is better than no man at all . . . We eventually had to leave Picton; the pace was too fast . . . I keep having this awful nightmare; a big brute of a man is chasing me, and I escape . . . I found out early on Bay Street that all men are married, but some are less married than others . . . I didn't mind Jack's cruelty and extravagance; what finished it off was the way he kept clearing his throat every five minutes.'

Going out in the garden, I found a young man who told me, 'I hate 6 university but I have to stay there so I can graduate and get a good job, and pay back the money I borrowed to go to university.' The young woman with him said she had a different problem. 'It's my parents. They're so good and kind and trusting, and I'm so rotten. When I come home drunk at two in the morning with my clothes torn, and tell them I was in a car accident, they believe me. This makes me feel guilty, and so I become twice as rotten. I wish I had parents like Jill; her father drinks his pay, and her mother runs around with every man on the block, so she doesn't have to feel guilty about being even more rotten than I am.'

Going back into the house, I listened in on a group of men: 'I've 7 always thought of Highway 7 as the square route . . . When the postal strike ends, how will people be able to tell? . . . I've at last figured it out, Doris Day is her own grandmother . . . I know beer's the drink of moderation, that's why I hate it . . . When your plane lands in Toronto, you have to set your watch back thirty years . . . Liquor at the C.N.E.? It's enough to make Judge Robb turn over in his grave . . . I'm still looking for a woman who measures down to my standards . . . I didn't mind Marge's boozing and infidelity; what drove me out was that she never changed the blade after shaving her legs with my razor.'

8   It seemed at this point I'd had enough, so I finished the Scotch-and-tonic someone had pressed on me, said farewell to the hostess, and made an inglorious exit by tripping over the dachshund. Still, I was safely out; I wouldn't need to do it again for a long time; and I walked steadily south until the crumbling tenements, polluted air, garbage-littered streets, and screams of hold-up victims informed me I was back in civilization.

Structure:

1. Which paragraph states the main point of this essay?
2. Does the fact that the main point is satirical (see SATIRE) detract from its importance as the focus of this essay?
3. Where does the introduction end and what does it accomplish?
4. Which paragraphs are devoted to examples that illustrate the main point, and how are these paragraphs developed?
5. What effect is achieved by the use of a great many very short examples?
6. Paragraph 5 consists of comments by women, paragraph 6 of comments by one couple and paragraph 7 of comments by men. Do these groupings serve any purpose?
7. What basic form of development, other than example, helps to structure this essay?

Style:

1. Richard Needham is a journalist. Do you see ways in which this essay resembles or differs from a news article?
2. Needham uses words playfully. In paragraph 3, what is he doing when he refers to "languid immigrants," "inferior decorators" and "insulting engineers"?
3. Pick out examples of COLLOQUIAL or SLANG words used by Needham, and discuss the effects of this very informal language. What kinds of writing would you not use such words in?
4. Needham is known for his ability to condense an idea or a characterization into a one-sentence EPIGRAM. In paragraph 7, a guest says, "I know beer's the drink of moderation, that's why I hate it." How many more epigrams do you find?
5. When in paragraph 7 a guest says, "I've always thought of Highway 7 as the square route," what device of humour is Needham using?

EXAMPLE   75

6. Do you think that Needham's devices of light humour trivialize the argument? Or do they enhance the argument by making it entertaining?

7. In the phrase "beset by fortune's slings and arrows" (par. 3), Needham is alluding to Hamlet's famous speech:

> To be, or not to be: that is the question:
> Whether 'tis nobler in the mind to suffer
> The slings and arrows of outrageous fortune,
> Or to take arms against a sea of troubles,
> And by opposing end them?

Is the ALLUSION appropriate? Should we be thinking of Hamlet's serious problems and his contemplation of suicide in a sentence that continues with Needham's "ordeal by guzzle, gabble and gorge"?

Ideas:

1. Is Needham's only aim to amuse us, or is he at least partly serious in portraying a cocktail party as "a form of shock treatment"?

2. Are there topics so serious that they cannot be developed through SATIRE?

3. Why do people go to parties? Give some good reasons. Give some bad reasons.

4. What STEREOTYPES do you recognize in Needham's thumbnail portraits of the guests?

5. Does the narrator hate only cocktail parties, or does he seem cynical about humanity in general? Give reasons for your answer.

6. Write an essay describing the best or worst party you have ever attended. Supply frequent and colourful *examples,* as Needham has.

(NOTE: See also the Topics for Writing at the end of this chapter.)

Topics for Writing

Chapter 2: Example

(Note also the topics for writing that appear after each selection in this chapter.)

Write an essay that develops one of the following ideas either through a number of short examples or through one fully developed example.

1. Dreams express our lives.
2. Superstition is widespread even today.
3. Games imitate life.
4. Professional sports teach violence.
5. We learn best from our mistakes.
6. Children learn best from their parents' example.
7. Travel is the best education.
8. Hitchhiking is dangerous.
9. First impressions can mislead.
10. Opposites attract.
11. Short
12. Intelligent
13. Ugly
14. Illegitimate ⎫ people are discriminated against in
15. Adopted ⎬ our society.
16. Lefthanded
17. Disabled ⎭
18. Men have the power in our society.
19. Information is power.
20. Computers can make mistakes.
21. Books are friends.
22. Automation causes unemployment.
23. Some products are built to fall apart.
24. Prison is a school for criminals.
25. You have to give in order to receive.

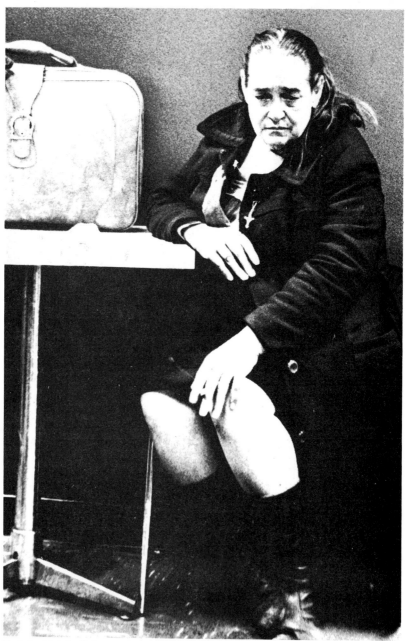

Photo by Christie McLaren.

" 'I bum on the street. I don't like it, but I have to. I have to survive. The only pleasure I got is my cigaret . . . . It's not a life.' "
Christie McLaren, "Suitcase Lady"

It's large and yellow and ....

3

DESCRIPTION

Consider the writer's tools: words in rows on the page. The writer cannot use gestures, facial expression or voice as the public speaker does. The writer cannot use colour, shape, motion or sound, as the filmmaker does. Yet words on the page can be powerful. We have all seen readers so involved in a book that they forget where they are; they will fail to hear their own name called or they will pass their own stop on the bus or subway. These readers have passed into another world, living at second-hand what the writer has lived or at least imagined at first-hand. How does writing convey experience so vividly? One way is through description.

In simulating direct experience, description makes frequent appeals to our senses:

sight
sound
touch
smell
taste

How many senses does Ian Adams appeal to in the opening of our first selection, "Living with Automation in Winnipeg"?

Hear it! The crunching smash of twenty-four bottles of beer, all splintering against each other as I misdeal on the packing machine. Smell the stink of the warm beer pouring over my clothes, washing over the sour sweat of my body. I can feel the unheard curse as I toss the wet, mangled carton down the rollers for some poor bastard to sort out.

Not all words are equal. Adams prefers the short and strong ones to the long and flabby ones. He does not write "perspiration" but "sweat," and he does not write "imprecation" but "curse." He seeks words that convey exact feelings as well as exact meanings. In a negative passage like this, could he have written "damaged" for "mangled," or "aroma" for "stink"? Choosing words carefully takes time, more time than was spent by one student who ended a pretty description of the ocean by saying that the water was "as still as a pan full of oil." The image of water as oil may imply stillness, but this water is not exactly something we would want to swim in or even watch at sunset — we'd be too busy thinking of pollution! Spend the time, then, to sense the emotional as well as logical meanings of your words. Search your first draft for weak or inexact or inappropriate words, and replace them. If the right word doesn't come, find it in a thesaurus or dictionary of synonyms.

Figures of speech — such as the similes and metaphors discussed in Chapter 6 — are powerful tools of description. When Thierry Mallet writes in "The Firewood Gatherers" that a woman's throat, "thin and bare as a vulture's neck, showed the muscles like cords," the idea of old age is swiftly and powerfully conveyed. Onomatopoetic language — words that sound like what they mean — can be another powerful tool of description. When Ian Adams writes of a "crunching smash" or a "teeth-jarring rattle," or when John Kenneth Galbraith writes of "joyful shrieks and loud crashes," we do more than just read words on paper; we share more fully and directly in the original experience of the writer.

The basic strategy behind all descriptive techniques is a preference for concrete language. In a description, avoid generalizations except where they are needed to make the point clear. In helping us to experience the great Halifax explosion, Hugh MacLennan *tells* us very little of theory; instead, he *shows* us houses swept off their foundations, trees and lamp posts snapped off and red-hot steel raining down from the skies. In fact, a good summation of how to describe is *show, don't tell.*

Ian Adams

Living with Automation in Winnipeg

Ian Adams was born in 1937 to missionary parents in Tanzania and came to Canada at age 16. In the mid-sixties, after several years of work and travel in other countries, Adams joined Maclean's *as a staff writer. For four years he covered Canadian events, Latin American revolutions and the Vietnam War. Two books of pointed social criticism followed:* The Poverty Wall *(1970) and* The Real Poverty Report *(co-authored in 1971). But since then Adams has said, "I used to have this idea that people could change their ideas . . . if you gave them information . . . but it really doesn't work that way." Now Adams clothes his social criticism in fiction, which "can have a much more powerful effect" (*Maclean's, *January 28, 1980). His first novel,* The Trudeau Papers, *appeared in 1971;* S, Portrait of a Spy *in 1977; and* Endgame in Paris *in 1979. Adams' new strategy may be effective, but when* The Toronto Sun *claimed that the main character of* S, Portrait of a Spy *(a double agent for the KGB and RCMP) was a thinly disguised version of an actual RCMP officer now retired in Australia, a sensational libel suit followed. Although the case was settled out of court, it cast some doubt upon the freedom of novelists to base fictional characters on actual persons. In its style our selection resembles fiction, but "Living with Automation in Winnipeg" is from* The Poverty Wall, *one of Adams' nonfiction books.*

H
ear it! The crunching smash of twenty-four bottles of beer, all splintering against each other as I misdeal on the packing machine. Smell the stink of the warm beer pouring over my clothes, washing over the sour sweat of my body. I can feel the unheard curse as I toss the wet, mangled carton down the rollers for some poor bastard to sort out. And back to the mother-eating machine where the bottles are already starting to pile up on the conveyor belt. The ten-second delay bell starts ringing. The jangling vibrations echo in my skull, and the foreman comes running over, screaming incoherently. How the hell can I hear him over the roar of four acres of machinery and the teeth-jarring rattle of 25,000 bottles, all clinking against each other as they ride down the hundred yards of clanking metal conveyor belts.

But don't try to figure out what the foreman's yelling, you'll only lose more time. The bottles will back up all the way to the pasteurizer, the thirty-second delay hooter will start whooping like an air-raid siren, then they'll pull you off this job for sure and send

1

2

you down to the washers, so forget him and just keep moving. With your left hand crush the right-hand corner of the next empty carton and ram it on the hydraulic lift. Kick your heel down on the pedal to send the drawer up. The bottles drop through the metal leaves this time with a nice *thonk*, thank God! And even as they are hitting the bottom of the box, stab the pedal with your toe to bring the drawer back down. Before it stops, spin off the loaded carton with your right hand to send it in the direction of the sealing machine. Don't wait for it to clear the drawer, reach for the next empty carton with your left hand. But you have to waste time, reaching in to push the "filler" down flat. And without even looking at him, you scream at the filler-man, "Look what you're doing, you son-of-a-bitch! Can't you even put these lousy pieces of cardboard in straight?" He, seeing only your lips curling, snarls obscenely back. Never mind him either. He's been here fourteen years, paying his union dues, kissing the foreman's ass. Look at the zombie, pot-bellied on all the free beer, draggy-eyed from a lifetime of night shifts, skin like a corpse, embrace your fellow industrial worker!

3   A group of tourists are coming through the brewery. Cowed by the noise, they shy away from the machines, cringing behind the protective eyeglasses issued at the front office. They stop to wonder at the frantic activity around the packing machine. And we, the sweat running down our faces, our shirts soaked, our hands and feet doing five different things at once, turn smiling and scream the crudest of obscenities at the women. And they, unhearing, smile and mouth thank you, then walk on with another uncertain smile for the monkeys in the freak show.

4   All this ten hours a day. Surrounded by four or five other workers who endlessly fold cardboard cartons in a bored blur of hand movements. Their hands turn flat shapes into square boxes, insert handles and fillers that will keep the bottles separated from each other. Behind them on scores of wooden platforms await thousands of unfolded cardboard cartons. They are literally unfolding a forest of trees between their hands. Other men tend the monotonous machines. One feeds thousands of bright little labels into slots; each label costs one cent, but that's more than the beer inside the bottle is worth. "Everything else is taxes and profit," that's what the brewmaster said. Another man sits dreamily beside a lighted yellow panel. In hypnotic progression, each bottle passes briefly in front of this panel before being filled with beer. The man tries to catch the ones that are still jammed with trapped mice, cigarette butts, and old safes, even after going through the washers.

5   All the men are wearing the same dingy uniforms, green workpants and shirts. They are my brotherhood, and we are men of

our time, working in feverish, mute activity, unable to communicate, drowned out by the roar of our age, the ass-end of this industrial epoch. Run this packing machine, you slob. Pack twenty-four bottles of beer every six seconds. Ten cases every minute, six hundred in an hour, six thousand in a ten-hour shift. Fill all those empty bottles full of beer so all the leisure-programmed people in this country can drink their beer in creepy bars and dirty, men-only beer parlours. Pack so the whores on Main Street can tease their fancy men over a couple, so the businessmen can pull on a three-o'clock beer and ease a contented fart. And you, you sad bastard, work! Work to fill up those empty boxes with bottles of beer so that all those beautiful people out there can piss it away.

Don't waste time thinking about the absurdity of this effort. Just pack and think about the $125 a week you're clearing. Pack and forget about the bills you can't pay. Pack and don't look at the man going around giving out pink slips. Just keep packing, you dummy. Because while you're sitting there running that machine, with the sweat running down into your eyes, with your hands and feet going like an epileptic's, they're already building a machine to do your job. And brother, nobody can hear a word you're screaming.

6

Structure:

1. To begin his description, Ian Adams boldly demands our attention with the words "Hear it!" What does he do in the rest of the opening paragraph?
2. What is the basic message of this selection and where is it most openly stated?
3. Later in this book we will examine process analysis — telling how a process is performed. Which paragraphs has Adams devoted to process analysis?

Style:

1. Why has Adams used racy language? Do the COLLOQUIAL and even vulgar expressions have a purpose? If so, what?
2. "Clinking" and "clanking" (par. 1) are examples of ONOMATOPOEIA — words that sound like what they mean. Point out other sound-effect words in this selection and discuss their contribution to the total effect.
3. Look up "thonk" (par. 2) in your dictionary. Is it a word? Can you imagine "thonk" appearing in a business letter? In the Bible? In a scientific report? In the comics? Why does Adams use it?

4. Adams says "Run this packing machine, you slob" (par. 5) and "Just keep packing, you dummy" (par. 6). What is the effect of these and other passages that seem addressed to the reader? Is use of the word "you" a good technique in essays?
5. Why is paragraph 2 so long? How long can a paragraph be?

Ideas:

1. Did this description make you feel as though you were in the brewery yourself? Why or why not?
2. What purposes can be served by reproducing for your reader an experience that you yourself had?
3. Is industrial work as sordid as Adams makes it seem? Have you had experiences that confirm or contradict Adams' view? If so, describe them.
4. In paragraph 5, Adams writes of his co-workers: "They are my brotherhood, and we are men of our time, working in feverish, mute activity, unable to communicate, drowned out by the roar of our age, the ass-end of this industrial epoch." Where else in Adams' description do you find evidence of isolation among the workers? Do you agree with Adams that workers are "drowned out by the roar of our age"?
5. Do you think automation helps or harms society? Should we allow further automation to eliminate jobs like the already automated ones Adams describes, or is unemployment a worse evil? Does automation necessarily mean unemployment?
6. If you have read "Grinning and Happy," compare work as described by both Joy Kogawa and Adams. If you had to perform one of these jobs, which would you choose and why?
7. If you have read "Supermarket Technology," compare the effects of automation upon workers as seen by Bill Reno and by Ian Adams.
8. Using vivid appeals to the senses, as Adams does, write a *description* of the best or worst job you have ever held. Choose your details carefully to support the dominant impression.

(NOTE: See also the Topics for Writing at the end of this chapter.)

Thierry Mallet

The Firewood Gatherers *

Thierry Mallet joined the French fur company Revillon Frères as an apprentice trader and went on to establish and oversee a large group of trading posts in the Barrens of the Canadian Arctic. Through each of the twenty years before our selection was published, Mallet had travelled through the region, sometimes at great risk, inspecting those posts. His intimate knowledge of the land and of the people who lived on it led him to write a small book, Plain Tales of the North. *Then in 1930 appeared his second small volume,* Glimpses of the Barren Lands. *From it comes our selection, "The Firewood Gatherers." Both books were published in New York by Revillon Frères. As if to reflect the arctic itself, Mallet's style is spare but powerful.*

O ur camp had been pitched at the foot of a great, bleak, ragged   1
hill, a few feet from the swirling waters of the Kazan River.
The two small green tents, pegged down tight with heavy
rocks, shivered and rippled under the faint touch of the northern
breeze. A thin wisp of smoke rose from the embers of the fire.

Eleven o'clock, and the sun had just set under a threatening bank   2
of clouds far away to the northwest. It was the last day of June and
daylight still. But the whole country seemed bathed in gray,
boulders, moss, sand, even the few willow shrubs scattered far apart
in the hollows of the hills. Half a mile away, upstream, the
caribou-skin topeks of an Eskimo settlement, fading away amid the
background, were hardly visible to the eye.

Three small gray specks could be seen moving slowly above our   3
camp. Human shapes, but so puny, so insignificant-looking against
the wild rocky side of that immense hill! Bending down, then
straightening up, they seemed to totter aimlessly through the chaos
of stone, searching for some hidden treasure.

Curiosity, or perhaps a touch of loneliness, suddenly moved me to   4
leave camp and join those three forlorn figures so far away above me
near the sky line.

Slowly I made my way along the steep incline, following at first   5
the bed of a dried-up stream. Little by little the river sank beneath
me, while the breeze, increasing in strength, whistled past, lashing
and stinging my face and hands. I had lost sight momentarily of the

---

*Editor's title

three diminutive figures which had lured me on to these heights. After a while a reindeer trail enabled me to leave the coulee and led me again in the right direction, through a gigantic mass of granite which the frost of thousands of years had plucked from the summit of the hill and hurled hundreds of feet below.

6 At last I was able to reach the other side of the avalanche of rocks and suddenly emerged comparatively in the open, on the brim of a slight depression at the bottom of which a few dead willow bushes showed their bleached branches above the stones and the gray moss. There I found the three silent figures huddled close together, gathering, one by one, the twigs of the precious wood. Two little girls, nine or ten years old, so small, so helpless, and an aged woman, so old, so frail, that my first thought was to marvel at the idea of their being able to climb so far from their camp to that lonely spot.

7 An Eskimo great-grandmother and her two great-grand-daughters, all three contributing their share to the support of the tribe. Intent on their work, or most probably too shy to look up at the strange white man whom, until then, they had only seen at a distance, they gave me full opportunity to watch them.

8 All were dressed alike, in boots, trousers, and coats of caribou skin. The children wore little round leather caps reaching far over their ears, the crown decorated with beadwork designs. One of them carried on the wrist, as a bracelet, a narrow strip of bright red flannel. Their faces were round and healthy, the skin sunburned to a dark copper color, but their cheeks showed a tinge of blood which gave them, under the tan, a peculiar complexion like the color of a ripe plum. Their little hands were bare and black, the scratches caused by the dead twigs showing plainly in white, while their fingers seemed cramped with the cold.

9 The old woman was bareheaded, quite bald at the top of the head, with long wisps of gray hair waving in the wind. The skin of her neck and face had turned black, dried up like an old piece of parchment. Her cheeks were sunken and her cheek bones protruded horribly. Her open mouth showed bare gums, for her teeth were all gone, and her throat, thin and bare as a vulture's neck, showed the muscles like cords. Her hands were as thin as the hands of a skeleton, the tip of each finger curved in like a claw. Her eyes, once black, now light gray, remained half closed, deep down in their sockets.

10 She was stone blind.

11 Squatting on her heels, she held, spread in front of her, a small reindeer skin. As soon as the children dropped a branch beside her,

she felt for it gropingly; then, her hands closing on it greedily, like talons, she would break it into small pieces, a few inches long, which she carefully placed on the mat at her feet.

Both little girls, while searching diligently through the clumps of   12
dead willows for what they could break off and carry away, kept absolutely silent. Not only did they never call to one another when one of them needed help, but they seemed to watch each other intently whenever they could. Now and then, one of them would hit the ground two or three times with the flat of her hand. If the other had her head turned away at the time, she appeared to be startled and always wheeled round to look. Then both children would make funny little motions with their hands at one another.

The little girls were deaf and dumb.   13

After a while they had gathered all the wood the reindeer skin   14
could contain. Then the children went up to the old woman and conveyed to her the idea that it was time to go home. One of them took her hands in hers and guided them to two corners of the mat, while the other tapped her gently on the shoulder.

The old, old woman understood. Slowly and carefully she tied up   15
the four corners of the caribou skin over the twigs, silently watched by the little girls. Groaning, she rose to her feet, tottering with weakness and old age, and with a great effort swung the small bundle over her back. Then one little girl took her by the hand, while the other, standing behind, grasped the tail of her caribou coat. Slowly, very slowly, step by step they went their way, following a reindeer trail around rocks, over stones, down, down the hill, straight toward their camp, the old woman carrying painfully for the young, the deaf and dumb leading and steering safely the blind.

Structure:

1. "The Firewood Gatherers" is narrated in chronological order. Point out at least fifteen words or phrases that signal the flow of time.
2. Which paragraphs are devoted so fully to description that they interrupt completely or almost completely the flow of time?
3. To what extent is the effect of "The Firewood Gatherers" based upon comparisons and contrasts?
4. In what way does the last sentence summarize the entire selection?

Style:

1. How CONCRETE or ABSTRACT is the language of this selection? Point out three or four passages that illustrate your answer.
2. How economical or wasteful is Mallet's use of words? Does the large amount of description cause this passage to be wordy? Why or why not?
3. Mallet's description of the old woman, in paragraph 9, makes extensive use of SIMILE. For example, her throat is "thin and bare as a vulture's neck. . . ." Point out all the other similes in this paragraph.
4. In paragraph 5, Mallet writes of "a gigantic mass of granite which the frost of thousands of years had plucked from the summit of the hill and hurled hundreds of feet below." Where else in this selection does he use the device of PERSONIFICATION, in which inanimate things are described in human terms?

Ideas:

1. How often do we take the time to fully observe our surroundings, as Mallet has observed his? What prevents us from doing so? What are the rewards of such observation?
2. Judging by the evidence in "The Firewood Gatherers," how do this traditional society and our modern society differ in their views of the old and the handicapped? What do you imagine the old blind woman and her deaf and dumb great-granddaughters would be doing if they lived today in your town or city?
3. Does compulsory retirement at age 65 help or harm our society? Does it help or harm the people who have reached that age? What are the alternatives? When would you retire if you had the choice? And what will you do in retirement to retain a sense of your own worth?
4. What are some advantages and disadvantages of the extended family? If you live in the same house as your grandparents, describe what they do for you that your parents cannot do. Describe also the problems, if any, that their presence creates. When you grow old will you prefer to live with your descendants or in a home for the aged? Why?
5. If you have read "Suitcase Lady," by Christie McLaren, compare the two women: If you had to be one or the other, would you choose to be the Eskimo great-grandmother of the Barrens or the homeless "suitcase lady" of Toronto? Why?

6. *Describe* the oldest person you know or the youngest person you know. Use concrete details, as Mallet has done, and if possible write from life rather than from memory.

***

(NOTE: See also the Topics for Writing at the end of this chapter.)

Christie McLaren

Suitcase Lady*

Christie McLaren, now on the editorial staff of the Toronto Globe and Mail, wrote "Suitcase Lady" while she was a student at the University of Waterloo, reporting for the Globe as a part of her English co-op work experience. McLaren was born in 1958 in Kitchener, Ontario. She has hitchhiked over much of western Canada, has been a helicopter hiking guide in the Cariboo Mountains of British Columbia, has reported on the mentally ill and mental health care in Ontario, and hopes to report on native issues and resources in the Yukon or Northwest Territories. Among her other interests are photography (she took the portrait accompanying her article), skiing and canoeing. Although a professional journalist, she says that "writing . . . is nothing but pain while you're doing it and nothing but relief when it's done. Any joy or satisfaction, I think, is a bit of fleeting luck." McLaren spent several nights with "the Vicomtesse" before hearing the story she reports in "Suitcase Lady." The article and photograph (see p. 78) appeared in 1981 in the Toronto Globe and Mail.

1   Night after night, the woman with the red hair and the purple dress sits in the harsh light of a 24-hour doughnut shop on Queen Street West.

2   Somewhere in her bleary eyes and in the deep lines of her face is a story that probably no one will ever really know. She is taking pains to write something on a notepad and crying steadily.

3   She calls herself Vicomtesse Antonia The Linds'ays. She's the suitcase lady of Queen Street.

4   No one knows how many women there are like her in Toronto. They carry their belongings in shopping bags and spend their days and nights scrounging for food. They have no one and nowhere to go.

5   This night, in a warm corner with a pot of tea and a pack of Player's, the Vicomtesse is in a mood to talk.

6   Out of her past come a few scraps: a mother named Savaria; the child of a poor family in Montreal; a brief marriage when she was 20; a son in Toronto who is now 40. "We never got along well because I didn't bring him up. I was too poor. He never call me mama."

7   She looks out the window. She's 60 years old.

8   With her words she spins herself a cocoon. She talks about drapes and carpets, castles and kings. She often lapses into French. She lets her tea get cold. Her hands are big, rough, farmer's hands. How she

---
*Editor's title

90

ended up in the doughnut shop remains a mystery, maybe even to her.

"Before, I had a kitchen and a room and my own furniture. I had to leave everything and go."   9

It's two years that she's been on the go, since the rooming houses stopped taking her. "I don't have no place to stay."   10

So she walks. A sturdy coat covers her dress and worn leather boots are on her feet. But her big legs are bare and chapped and she has a ragged cough.   11

Yes, she says, her legs get tired. She has swollen ankles and, with no socks in her boots, she has blisters. She says she has socks — in the suitcase — but they make her feet itch.   12

As for money, "I bum on the street. I don't like it, but I have to. I have to survive. The only pleasure I got is my cigaret." She lights another one. "It's not a life."   13

She recalls the Saturday, a long time ago, when she made $27, and laughs when she tells about how she had to make the money last through Sunday, too. Now she gets "maybe $7 or $8," and eats "very poor."   14

When she is asked how people treat her, the answer is very matter-of-fact: "Some give money. Some are very polite and some are rude."   15

In warm weather, she passes her time at the big square in front of City Hall. When it's cold she takes her suitcase west to the doughnut shop.   16

The waitresses who bring food to the woman look upon her with compassion. They persuaded their boss that her sitting does no harm.   17

Where does she sleep? "Any place I can find a place to sleep. In the park, in stores — like here I stay and sit, on Yonge Street." She shrugs. Sometimes she goes into an underground parking garage.   18

She doesn't look like she knows what sleep is. "This week I sleep three hours in four days. I feel tired but I wash my face with cold water and I feel okay." Some questions make her eyes turn from the window and stare hard. Then they well over with tears. Like the one about loneliness. "I don't talk much to people," she answers. "Just the elderly, sometimes, in the park."   19

Her suitcase is full of dreams.   20

Carefully, she unzips it and pulls out a sheaf of papers — "my concertos."   21

Each page is crammed with neatly written musical notes — the careful writing she does on the doughnut shop table — but the bar lines are missing. Questions about missing bar lines she tosses aside. Each "concerto" has a French name — Tresor, La Tempete, Le   22

Retour — and each one bears the signature of the Vicomtesse. She smiles and points to one. "A very lovely piece of music. I like it."

23 She digs in her suitcase again, almost shyly, and produces a round plastic box. Out of it emerges a tiara. Like a little girl, she smooths back her dirty hair and proudly puts it on. No one in the doughnut shop seems to notice.

24 She cares passionately about the young, the old and the ones who suffer. So who takes care of the suitcase lady?

25 "God takes care of me, that's for sure," she says, nodding thoughtfully. "But I'm not what you call crazy about religion. I believe always try to do the best to help people — the elderly, and kids, and my country, and my city of Toronto, Ontario."

Structure:

1. "Suitcase Lady" appeared as a feature article in the Toronto *Globe and Mail*. Name all the ways that you can think of in which, as a piece of newspaper journalism, it differs from the typical ESSAY in this book.
2. What does McLaren achieve in the opening description?
3. How do the frequent quotations help McLaren to build her description?
4. McLaren's photograph of "the Vicomtesse" originally accompanied McLaren's article in the *Globe and Mail*. Does a descriptive piece of writing like "Suitcase Lady" need an illustration? What does the photograph do that the article cannot do? And what does the article do that the photograph cannot do?
5. What effect does McLaren achieve in the closing?

Style:

1. How difficult or easy is the vocabulary used in "Suitcase Lady" compared to that of most essays you have read in this book? Why?
2. "With her words she spins herself a cocoon," states McLaren in paragraph 8. Point out another vivid METAPHORE, a statement that is literally false but poetically true.
3. Of the many concrete details, point out the ones that you think most strongly convey the flavour of this suitcase lady's life and discuss why these particular details are effective.

Ideas:

1. If you have read "The Firewood Gatherers," by Thierry Mallet, compare the hardships faced by the Eskimo great-grandmother

in the Arctic with those faced by the suitcase lady in Toronto. In what ways is each of these two persons better off? In what ways is each worse off? If you had to be one of these two women, which would you choose to be and why?

2. "It's not a life," says "the Vicomtesse" in paragraph 13. What is our society doing, either through acts of individuals or acts of institutions such as church and government, to try to make it "a life" for people like the suitcase lady? What more could society do? What prevents society from doing more?

3. How do you react to people who, like the suitcase lady, "bum on the street"? Do you divide them into categories? When do you give and when do you not give? How does the giving or not giving make you feel, and why? Have you ever "bummed on the street" yourself? How much did you make? How did it make you feel, and why?

4. If you have read Ian Adams' "Living with Automation in Winnipeg," compare the ways in which our urban and industrialized society affects the narrator of that description with the ways in which society affects McLaren's suitcase lady.

5. In paragraph 6, the suitcase lady talks of her son in Toronto: "We never got along well because I didn't bring him up. I was too poor. He never call me mama." Discuss the effects of poverty on family life: In the area where you live, how much money does a family need to stay together? To avoid quarrels over money? To feel hopeful about the future?

6. Interview a person who in economic status, age, culture, values or in some other way is radically different from yourself. Then write a vividly *descriptive* profile of that person, as Christie McLaren has of the suitcase lady.

(NOTE: See also the Topics for Writing at the end of this chapter.)

John Kenneth Galbraith

The McIntyre House

John Kenneth Galbraith is one of the world's foremost economists and perhaps the most notable American Canada has ever produced. Born in 1908 near the village of Iona Station in Elgin County, Ontario, he earned his B.S. in 1931 at the Ontario Agricultural College in Guelph and his Ph.D. in 1934 at the University of California at Berkeley. Although most of his working life has been spent as professor of economics at Harvard, Galbraith has also been deeply involved in American liberal politics. He has been a trusted advisor to John Kennedy and other Democratic presidents, has campaigned tirelessly for Democrats in election campaigns, has served in numerous governmental agencies and from 1961 to 1963 was American ambassador to India. From his height of six feet eight and a half inches Galbraith looms over the audiences of his many public lectures; he also appears on television, most notably in his series on economics, The Age of Uncertainty. *But most important of all are his books. Galbraith was deeply affected by the human suffering he saw during the Great Depression. Since that time he has waged a ceaseless battle of words on behalf of the "little man" and against the great corporations: in 1952 appeared* American Capitalism *and* A Theory of Price Control; *in 1958 his influential best-seller,* The Affluent Society; *in 1967 his masterpiece,* The New Industrial State; *in 1973* Economics and the Public Purpose; *in 1979* The Nature of Mass Poverty; *and in 1983* The Anatomy of Power. *Galbraith once told a group of students, "You'll find that most of your opponents can't strike back because they can't write . . . . If you are going into politics or government I suggest that you postpone studying economics until you have mastered the English language." Galbraith's own way with words is nowhere better demonstrated than in* The Scotch *(1964), his own favourite of all his books, the memoir of his childhood among the Scots of Ontario. From it comes our selection, his description of a local landmark.*

1   The McIntyre House stood nearly in the center of the east side of the single block that comprised Main Street. Unlike the square brick-fronted buildings across and on either side, it was longer, lower and of frame construction. Once it had been white with green trim, and traces of the original paint remained. At the north end was an arch cut through the building which gave access to the livery stables behind and to another blacksmith shop run by Jim Bruce who, on all festival occasions and for a moderate fee, closed his shop, donned the ancient tartan of the Bruce and took up his pipes to provide the only music the Scotch understood and loved. Also in the hotel yard were the privies, a massive bank of cells,

undifferentiated as to sex or precision of user, each cell giving on to a single trench which was cleaned out only at infrequent intervals. They gave off an astonishing smell. Immediately adjacent was the kitchen.

However, it was not for its food that the McIntyre House was renowned but its drink. A door within the arch led into the bar; there was another in from the street. In the 1920's this valiant room was already in decline; pool tables had been moved in to retrieve, however ingloriously, some of the revenues that had once accrued exclusively to whisky. But the scars of the greater days could still be seen on the wainscotting, the doors and deep in the bar itself. Before prohibition came to Ontario in 1916, it had been the resort of the drinking Scotch. As the result, it had been the scene of some of the most uproarious violence that alcohol has ever produced. 2

The effect of alcohol on different races is as remarkable as it is invariable. An Englishman becomes haughty; a Swede sad; an Irishman sentimental; a Russian fraternal; a German melodious. A Scotchman always becomes militant. It was on Saturday night that the Scotch gathered at the McIntyre House to make merry and seek one another's destruction. Whisky bottles were emptied and used as weapons; sometimes the bottom was knocked off to make a better impression on the thick epidermis that so admirably protected the average clansman. Boots and even furniture were also used, although on gala occasions the furniture was removed. On a Sunday after one of these festivals, men would be in poor condition from Port Talbot to Campbellton and from Iona Station nearly to West Lorne. 3

Even among the nondrinking Scotch, the tales of the McIntyre House were part of the legend. Once a commercial traveler from Toronto had called for a cocktail and gave instructions on how to make it. The patrons were outraged but Johnnie McIntyre quieted them down and went out for ice. This he got from a little iceberg by a tree in the yard. It owed its origins to the dogs who frequented the tree and to the Canadian winter which quickly converted all moisture to ice. Johnnie thought this would return the man to whisky and so did those to whom he quietly confided the stratagem. The man from Toronto praised the flavor and called for another. 4

There was also the night that my great-uncle Duncan, then the family ambassador to the drinking Scotch, sat next to one of the McPherson boys who had begun to worry lest whisky was getting the better of him. After once again confiding sadly of his fears, he drank a large bottle of carbolic acid. To the surprise of all who had known his capacity, he died a horrible death. 5

Finally, there was the gala evening — it must have been about 1910 — when one of the Campbells who inhabited the country north 6 and west of town mounted the bar and announced his intention of avenging, once and for all, the insults that had been heaped on the Clan Campbell ever since it had fought on the wrong side at Culloden* a hundred and sixty-five years before. He specifically promised to lick any man who lived between Lake Erie and the Michigan Central Railway. A score leaped to the challenge; the Campbells rallied round. It was a glorious struggle. The outcome was indeterminate although it was said that the Campbells acquitted themselves well. Next morning a half-dozen clansmen were still stacked like cordwood in the livery stable back of the hotel. None was seriously hurt.

2

7   Prohibition was advocated in Ontario partly as a product of the natural desire of better men to impose their virtue on the worse. But partly it was considered an important pacifying influence which would raise markedly the productivity of the farm labor force. The slogan of the prohibitionists, "Abolish the bar," showed the way in which their concern had become associated not with whisky but with the theater of combat. Prohibition came and when it was later repealed in Ontario, the principal concern was not to control the intake of alcohol but to insure that it occurred in surroundings which were inconsistent with physical violence. This the institution of the cocktail lounge accomplished.

8   Once the bar of the McIntyre House was closed, the Scotch deserted it in droves. The poolroom was taken over by the idlers of the town and no good was thought to come of anyone who frequented the place. In point of fact, none did.

9   Commercial travelers must have stopped at the McIntyre House. Certainly a horse-drawn bus went down to meet each train at the MCR station. Occasionally one of the girls of the town who worked there as chambermaid would be seen leaning out an upstairs window exchanging insults with a boy friend in the street. In the main lobby adjoining the bar was a desk and a yellowed and dog-eared guest register. Out back was the dining room. But in its days of glory, the McIntyre House meant the bar. The rest must have been operated as an afterthought.

3

10   I have memory of only one moment when the McIntyre House was in its glory. It must have been on the first of July of 1914 or 1915

*Culloden: a village near Inverness, Scotland, where in 1746 English forces won a decisive victory over Scottish nationalists who had risen in arms to restore the Stuart dynasty to the throne when I was approaching the age of either six or seven. We had gone to Dutton to celebrate Dominion Day, the Canadian Fourth of July, and to attend the Caledonian games. There had been running and broad-jumping, and throwing of weights for distance and height, and a great deal of sword dancing and piping. Some of the dancing we found tedious but the rest was wholly fascinating. My father, one of the officials of the West Elgin Caledonian Society, had looked very grand in a modified kilt of the McDonald tartan — not many of the clansmen owned a complete kilt so they made do with what they had. Then at four o'clock my sister and I were bundled into the family democrat, a large four-wheeled affair with a fringed top, and we started for home because word had come that the fighting had begun. As we passed the McIntyre House, we saw it. Some forty or fifty clansmen, the drinking Scotch at nearly their maximum effective strength, had been reinforced by elements of a Scottish regiment which had come to grace the celebration and provide music. Some of the celebrants were in the bar; others were struggling to approach it or shouting to those inside to pass out the bottles. A number of fights were already in progress in the crowd outside; from within came joyful shrieks and loud crashes indicating that hostilities were much more advanced inside. Pipers around the edge of the struggling mass were offering a competitive combination of pibrochs, marches and laments to inspire the combatants to greater feats of violence. We got by as quickly as the traffic and our alarmed mare would allow.

We drove down Shackleton Street and across Willey's Sideroad, 11 and the memory of that journey on a summer evening by the bare hayfields and through the fields of ripening wheat has never forsaken me. The sound of the pipes did not recede and fade; on the contrary, it grew in volume as the whisky was passed out and the pipers warmed to their work. And at intervals, over the spiel of the pipes came the high demoniac shrieks which for a thousand years on ten thousand battlefields have struck terror to the hearts of the brave. It is the cry of uncontrollable joy of a drunken Highlander as he rushes toward personal immolation.

A year or two later, the McIntyre House was selling nothing more 12 dangerous than Orange Crush.

Structure:

1. Which is described more fully in this selection, the McIntyre House or the activities that took place there? Why does Galbraith describe both? Why does he place them in their present order?

2. Just after stating that the privy "gave off an astonishing smell" (par. 1), Galbraith notes that "Immediately adjacent was the kitchen." Why does he place these two facts together? Do you see other significant examples of JUXTAPOSITION in this selection? How does this device work?

3. In what major way is this selection based on cause and effect? In what part or parts is this device most obvious?

Style:

1. How would you describe the vocabulary of this selection? How would you describe the sentence structure? For what sort of reader do you think Galbraith is writing? Give examples to support your answers.

2. In paragraph 4 Galbraith tells of the Torontonian who called for a second cocktail. What are the sources of humour in this example?

3. About what proportion of this selection would you say consists of examples? Which component has the greater effect, the examples or the rest? Explain why.

Ideas:

1. Why do you think John Kenneth Galbraith, the celebrated American economist, wrote about his village and his childhood in Ontario and even considers *The Scotch* his favourite of all his books?

2. "The McIntyre House" is in large part an account of violence. If you have read "Coming of Age in Putnok," "In the Trenches," "The Scar" or "Profile of the Rapist as an Ordinary Man," compare Galbraith's treatment of violence with that of George Gabori, Charles Yale Harrison, Kildare Dobbs or Myrna Kostash. Do you view as peculiar the image of clansmen "stacked like cordwood" though "none was seriously hurt" (par. 6)? Discuss your own perception of this alcoholic violence and compare it to that of Galbraith.

3. Where in this selection does Galbraith take an economist's view of his subject?

4. In describing the exploits of the "drinking Scotch," has Galbraith unjustly maligned an ethnic group? Or does his own Scottish background free him to write this selection with no danger of blame? Compare Mordecai Richler's rendition of his own culture in "My Father's Life."

5. How do you react to Galbraith's description of Dominion Day in paragraphs 10 and 11? Does he basically criticize the Ontario Scots for their "hostilities," does he basically praise the vitality of their culture, or is he merely having fun telling a good story?
6. When members of your own cultural group get together, how do they celebrate? Describe such an occasion in essay form, giving many details and examples, as Galbraith does.
7. Write an essay *describing* an important establishment in your own neighbourhood (a restaurant, a bar, a hotel, a church, a store, etc.). Give many CONCRETE details, both of the structure and of the activities that take place inside it.

(NOTE: See also the Topics for Writing at the end of this chapter.)

Claude Jasmin

The Mysterious and Bizarre World of Adults*

Translated from the French by Ronald Conrad

Claude Jasmin, born in 1930 in Montreal, is one of Quebec's most prolific novelists. He has also been a ceramic artist and teacher of art, an actor, a designer and script writer for television, and director of the literary and art sections of the Journal de Montréal. *Jasmin's best-known novel is based on an FLQ incident:* Ethel et le terroriste *(1964), translated in 1965 as* Ethel and the Terrorist. *Another major success was* La Sablière *(1979), translated in 1985 as* Mario *and produced as a feature film under the same title. From his first novel to his recent crime fiction, most of Jasmin's books have been set in the working-class area of Montreal where he grew up. This neighbourhood was immortalized in his 1972 memoir* La Petite Patrie, *a loving description of his "little fatherland." The book was enormously popular in Quebec, going through seven printings in seven years, being adapted as a 75-part television series and entering its title phrase, "la petite patrie," into the jargon of sociologists, broadcasters and politicians. From this work comes our selection.*

1   On certain Sundays my aunts would come to spend the afternoon at our house. These visits were ideal times to observe the world of big people, the mysterious and bizarre world of adults. Aunt Alice and Aunt Lucienne would arrive first, then Aunt Maria, and then Aunt Gertrude who came from far away — from Verdun, just think of it, three streetcar lines away! — just to see us. And sometimes even Aunt Pauline would come to these little family reunions where my mother — would you believe it? — rediscovered her youth and even her rare good humour. To us Aunt Pauline might as well have come from the arctic, because she lived at Saint-Donat so far north. She would tell us about those famous "snowmobiles" where she lived in the Laurentians, and her photos of these machines that we had never seen would amaze us.

2   Filled with Mother's sisters, the living room grew louder and louder from the chattering and prattling and cackling. We hid in the hallway or the dining room to hear this cacophony of the little sisters who still got together, all the Sunday afternoon long.

*Editor's title

100

They talked about their clothes: "Look, dear, it's only my old dress   3
I fixed up." Laughter burst out: "Look, it's the same apple-green
outfit, I wore it when your little Nicole was baptised!" They passed
the plates of hard candies and the dish of sugar cream fudge. Aunt
Alice laughed so loudly that we shut ourselves in the bathroom to
imitate her, and when Aunt Maria raised her authoritative
big-sister voice to blame Aunt Lucienne for her behaviour or to scold
Aunt Pauline for her latest decision, it was all we could do not to
break out laughing.

We were astonished when Aunt Pauline and Aunt Alice lit   4
cigarettes: we watched while the grey and blue spirals of smoke
rivalled the lace of the living-room curtains. Sometimes the talk
grew livelier and louder, till suddenly an insult broke out: "You
always were an ignoramus!" We grew silent as death. It was a
comical fight: would Mother win against one of her sisters? She
couldn't lose. . . . To lighten the atmosphere Aunt Maria and Aunt
Alice changed the subject, comparing the one's necklace with the
other's bracelet. Calm again, Mother called my big sister Lucille,
and it was a rush to the kitchen for the soft drinks — the moment
we'd been waiting for.

Mother said, "Marielle, come greet your aunts. You too, Claude,   5
come on kids!" We had to go. Oh, what torture! The Lefebvre sisters
examined us, scrutinized us, made us show our arms or our thighs,
our scars, our bruises. And the remarks began:

"My gosh, look how she's grown!"   6

"I can't believe how fat your Raynald has got, he was always so   7
thin."

"Look how Marielle's scar has disappeared, you hardly notice it."   8

"Funny how her hair isn't growing."   9

"Eat, you're a real bean-pole, Marielle, eat!"   10

And then one of the aunts would say, with a contented smile, "You   11
know my Yvette has been a *big girl* for almost a year now!" My
mother would shoot an accusing glance at my older sister and sigh,
"Well, mine isn't a *big girl* yet but she should be, she's over
fourteen." Mortified, my sister emptied her glass of cream soda and
went to hide her shame at the back of the kitchen. This term "*big
girl*" seemed a rare honour, but I sensed it was a feminine secret, one
of many secrets belonging to the world of women. Once my aunts
had inspected us, their attention returned to more ordinary
concerns. The comparisons — "My girl is stronger"; "My boy seems
less fragile" — stopped. And one by one we drew back from this
arena, still fascinated, to watch from more distant and neutral
territory. The cackling resumed, louder than ever. We were happy to
hear our mother's sudden peals of laughter and her cries of "Gee

whiz" or "By God, is it possible!" Aunt Alice, roaring in laughter too, wiped her eyes with a little silk handkerchief embroidered in delicate designs, flashing the diamonds of her big engagement ring. They seemed happy recalling their days at the convent school and sharing their latest news. Sometimes their voices dropped lower and lower till we couldn't understand a thing. Now it was a question of the neighbour and his maid, or a cousin and her no-good boyfriend: "Really, just a little gigolo!" . . . and by now they were whispering. New words, forbidden words, came out. We looked at each other, nervous at spying, at being hidden witnesses. Oh, this world of big people was full of luxurious mysteries! How exciting to be fully adult, to know all, to understand all!

12 And emptying the plate of nuts, eating the remains of the sugar cream fudge and the toffee, sucking the bottoms of the soft drink glasses, we dreamed of growing older, of growing up — and the sooner the better.

Structure:

1. To what extent is this selection a narrative? Point out at least ten words or phrases that signal time passing.
2. This selection is to a great extent based on contrast. Who or what is being contrasted, and in what major ways?
3. Which group does this selection *describe* more vividly, the children or the adults? And is the description mostly of appearance? Of behaviour? Or of anything else? Give examples to support your answers.
4. Which does Jasmin describe more clearly, what he *saw* or what he *heard*? Give examples to support your answer.

Style:

1. How realistically has Jasmin described a young boy's perceptions of adults? Is the vocabulary appropriate? Do the perceptions and attitudes seem those of a child? Give examples to support your answers.
2. Read paragraph 2 aloud. Which words *sound* like what they mean? Do you often find ONOMATOPOEIA when you read? Do you ever consciously use it when you write?

Ideas:

1. Which phase of life do you view as happier, childhood or adulthood? Why? Which group seems happier in this selection, the children or the adults? Why?
2. Longing for a return to childhood is a prominent theme in many of Claude Jasmin's books. Why, then, does young Claude in "The Mysterious and Bizarre World of Adults" dream ". . . of growing older, of growing up — and the sooner the better"?
3. Do you think the women in the living room are insensitive, even rude, toward the children? Or as adults are they simply honest, frank and outspoken?
4. Do you agree with our young narrator that the world of adults is "mysterious and bizarre"? Is this a truth known by children but forgotten by adults? Or is the world of adults ordinary and hum-drum — exotic only to those who have not yet experienced it?
5. Write a *description,* based on your own observation, entitled "The Mysterious and Bizarre World of

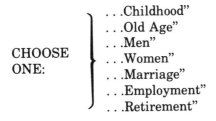

CHOOSE ONE:
. . .Childhood"
. . .Old Age"
. . .Men"
. . .Women"
. . .Marriage"
. . .Employment"
. . .Retirement"

(NOTE: See also the Topics for Writing at the end of this chapter.)

Hugh MacLennan

*A Sound Beyond Hearing**

Hugh MacLennan is one of Canada's best-known novelists and essayists, the author of over a dozen books and winner of five Governor-General's Awards. He was born in 1907 in Glace Bay, Cape Breton, Nova Scotia, and studied at Dalhousie, Oxford and at Princeton, where he earned a Ph.D. in classics. From 1951 until his retirement in 1982, he taught in the English Department of McGill University. MacLennan has published several books of essays: Cross-Country (1949), Thirty and Three (1954), Scotchman's Return and Other Essays (1960) and The Other Side of Hugh MacLennan (1978). Among his novels are Each Man's Son (1951), The Watch that Ends the Night (1959) and Voices in Time (1980). Two Solitudes (1945), which contrasts the French- and English-Canadian cultures, is his most widely read novel; but Barometer Rising (1941), from which our selection comes, is thought by many to be his best. "A Sound Beyond Hearing," MacLennan's account of an event he witnessed at age 10, is one of the best-known passages in Canadian literature: it describes the explosion that, on December 6, 1917, levelled much of Halifax and killed over 1600 people.

1   The *Mont Blanc* was now in the Narrows and a detail of men went into her chains to unship the anchor. It would be dropped as soon as she reached her appointed station in the Basin. A hundred yards to port were the Shipyards and another hundred yards off the port bow was the blunt contour of Richmond Bluff; to starboard the shore sloped gently into a barren of spruce scrub. During the two minutes it took the *Mont Blanc* to glide through this strait, most of Bedford Basin and nearly all its flotilla of anchored freighters were hidden from her behind the rise of Richmond Bluff.

2   Around the projection of this hill, less than fifty fathoms off the port bow of the incoming *Mont Blanc,* another vessel suddenly appeared heading for the open sea. She flew the Norwegian flag, and to the startled pilot of the munitioner the name *Imo* was plainly visible beside the hawse. She was moving at half-speed and listing gently to port as she made the sharp turn out of the Basin to strike the channel of the Narrows. And so listing, with white water surging away from her fore-foot, she swept across the path of the *Mont Blanc,* exposing a gaunt flank labeled in giant letters BELGIAN RELIEF. Then she straightened, and pointed her bow directly at the

*Editor's title

fore-quarter of the munitioner. Only at that moment did the men on the *Imo's* bridge appear to realize that another vessel stood directly in their path.

Staccato orders broke from the bridge of the *Mont Blanc* as the two ships moved toward a single point. Bells jangled, and megaphoned shouts came from both bridges. The ships sheered in the same direction, then sheered back again. With a violent shock, the bow of the *Imo* struck the plates of the *Mont Blanc* and went grinding a third of the way through the deck and the forward hold. A shower of sparks splashed out from the screaming metal. The canisters on the deck of the *Mont Blanc* broke loose from their bindings and some of them tumbled and burst open. Then the vessels heeled away with engines reversed and the water boiling out from their screws as the propellers braked them to a standstill. They sprawled sideways across the Narrows, the *Mont Blanc* veering in toward the Halifax shore, the *Imo* spinning about with steerageway lost entirely. Finally she drifted toward the opposite shore.

For a fraction of a second there was intense silence. Then smoke appeared out of the shattered deck of the *Mont Blanc,* followed by a racing film of flame. The men on the bridge looked at each other. Scattered shouts broke from the stern, and the engine-room bells jangled again. Orders were half-drowned by a scream of rusty metal as some sailors amidships followed their own inclination and twisted the davits around to lower a boat. The scurry of feet grew louder as more sailors began to pour out through the hatches onto the deck. An officer ran forward with a hose, but before he could connect it his men were ready to abandon ship.

The film of flame raced and whitened, then it became deeper like an opaque and fulminant liquid, then swept over the canisters of benzol and increased to a roaring tide of heat. Black smoke billowed and rolled and engulfed the ship, which began to drift with the outgoing tide and swing in toward the graving-dock of the Shipyards. The fire trembled and leaped in a body at the bridge, driving the captain and pilot aft, and there they stood helplessly while the tarry smoke surrounded them in greasy folds and the metal of the deck began to glow under their feet. Both men glanced downward. Underneath that metal lay leashed an incalculable energy, and the bonds which checked it were melting with every second the thermometers mounted in the hold. A half-million pounds of trinitrotoluol and twenty-three hundred tons of picric acid lay there in the darkness under the plates, while the fire above and below the deck converted the hollow shell of the vessel into a bake-oven.

6   If the captain had wished to scuttle the ship at that moment it would have been impossible to do so, for the heat between decks would have roasted alive any man who tried to reach the sea-cocks. By this time the entire crew was in the lifeboat. The officers followed, and the boat was rowed frantically toward the wooded slope opposite Halifax. There, by lying flat among the trees, the sailors hoped they would have a chance when their ship blew up. By the time they had beached the boat, the foredeck of the *Mont Blanc* was a shaking rampart of fire, and black smoke pouring from it screened the Halifax waterfront from their eyes. The sailors broke and ran for the shelter of the woods.

7   By this time men were running out of dock sheds and warehouses and offices along the entire waterfront to watch the burning ship. None of them knew she was a gigantic bomb. She had now come so close to the Shipyards that she menaced the graving-dock. Fire launches cut out from a pier farther south and headed for the Narrows. Signal flags fluttered from the Dockyard and the yardarms of ships lying in the Stream, some of which were already weighing anchor. The captain of the British cruiser piped all hands and called for volunteers to scuttle the *Mont Blanc;* a few minutes later the cruiser's launch was on its way to the Narrows with two officers and a number of ratings. By the time they reached the burning ship her plates were so hot that the seawater lapping the plimsoll line was simmering.

8   The *Mont Blanc* had become the center of a static tableau. Her plates began to glow red and the swollen air inside her hold heated the cargo rapidly towards the detonation point. Launches from the harbour fire department surrounded her like midges and the water from their hoses arched up with infinite delicacy as they curved into the rolling smoke. The *Imo,* futile and forgotten, was still trying to claw her way off the farther shore.

9   Twenty minutes after the collision there was no one along the entire waterfront who was unaware that a ship was on fire in the harbor. The jetties and docks near the Narrows were crowded with people watching the show, and yet no warning of danger was given. At that particular moment there was no adequate centralized authority in Halifax to give a warning, and the few people who knew the nature of the *Mont Blanc's* cargo had no means of notifying the town or spreading the alarm, and no comfort beyond the thought that trinitrotoluol can stand an almost unlimited heat provided there is no fulminate or explosive gas to detonate it.

10   Bells in the town struck the hour of nine, and by this time nearly all normal activity along the waterfront had been suspended. A tug

had managed to grapple the *Mont Blanc* and was towing her with imperceptible movement away from the Shipyards back into the channel of the Narrows. Bluejackets from the cruiser had found the bosun's ladder left by the fleeing crew, and with flesh shrinking from the heat, were going over the side. Fire launches surrounded her. There was a static concentration, an intense expectancy in the faces of the firemen playing the hoses, a rhythmic reverberation in the beat of the flames, a gush from the hose-nozzles and a steady hiss of scalding water. Everything else for miles around seemed motionless and silent.

Then a needle of flaming gas, thin as the mast and of a brilliance   11
unbelievably intense, shot through the deck of the *Mont Blanc* near the funnel and flashed more than two hundred feet toward the sky. The firemen were thrown back and their hoses jumped suddenly out of control and slashed the air with S-shaped designs. There were a few helpless shouts. Then all movement and life about the ship were encompassed in a sound beyond hearing as the *Mont Blanc* opened up. . . .

Three forces were simultaneously created by the energy of the   12
exploding ship, an earthquake, an air-concussion, and a tidal wave. These forces rushed away from the Narrows with a velocity varying in accordance with the nature of the medium in which they worked. It took only a few seconds for the earthquake to spend itself and three minutes for the air-expansion to slow down to a gale. The tidal wave traveled for hours before the last traces of it were swallowed in the open Atlantic.

When the shock struck the earth, the rigid ironstone and granite   13
base of Halifax peninsula rocked and reverberated, pavements split and houses swayed as the earth trembled. Sixty miles away in the town of Truro windows broke and glass fell to the ground, tinkling in the stillness of the streets. But the ironstone was solid and when the shock had passed, it resumed its immobility.

The pressure of the exploding chemicals smashed against the   14
town with the rigidity and force of driving steel. Solid and unbreathable, the forced wall of air struck against Fort Needham and Richmond Bluff and shaved them clean, smashed with one gigantic blow the North End of Halifax and destroyed it, telescoping houses or lifting them from their foundations, snapping trees and lamp posts, and twisting iron rails into writhing, metal snakes; breaking buildings and sweeping the fragments of their wreckage for hundreds of yards in its course. It advanced two miles southward, shattering every flimsy house in its path, and within thirty seconds

encountered the long, shield-like slope of the Citadel which rose before it.

15   Then, for the first time since it was fortified, the Citadel was able to defend at least a part of the town. The airwall smote it, and was deflected in three directions. Thus some of its violence shot skyward at a twenty-degree angle and spent itself in space. The rest had to pour around the roots of the hill before closing in on the town for another rush forward. A minute after the detonation, the pressure was advancing through the South End. But now its power was diminished, and its velocity was barely twice that of a tornado. Trees tossed and doors broke inward, windows split into driving arrows of glass which buried themselves deep in interior walls. Here the houses, after swaying and cracking, were still on their foundations when the pressure had passed.

16   Underneath the keel of the *Mont Blanc* the water opened and the harbor bottom was deepened twenty feet along the channel of the Narrows. And then the displaced waters began to drive outward, rising against the town and lifting ships and wreckage over the sides of the docks. It boiled over the shores and climbed the hill as far as the third cross-street, carrying with it the wreckage of small boats, fragments of fish, and somewhere, lost in thousands of tons of hissing brine, the bodies of men. The wave moved in a gigantic bore down the Stream to the sea, rolling some ships under and lifting others high on its crest, while anchor-chains cracked like guns as the violent thrust snapped them. Less than ten minutes after the detonation, it boiled over the breakwater off the park and advanced on McNab's Island, where it burst with a roar greater than a winter storm. And then the central volume of the wave rolled on to sea, high and arching and white at the top, its back glossy like the plumage of a bird. Hours later it lifted under the keel of a steamer far out in the Atlantic and the captain, feeling his vessel heave, thought he had struck a floating mine.

17   But long before this, the explosion had become manifest in new forms over Halifax. More than two thousand tons of red hot steel, splintered fragments of the *Mont Blanc,* fell like meteors from the sky into which they had been hurled a few seconds before. The ship's anchor soared over the peninsula and descended through a roof on the other side of the Northwest Arm three miles away. For a few seconds the harbor was dotted white with a maze of splashes, and the decks of raddled ships rang with reverberations and clangs as fragments struck them.

18   Over the North End of Halifax, immediately after the passage of the first pressure, the tormented air was laced with tongues of flame

which roared and exploded out of the atmosphere, lashing down-wards like a myriad blowtorches as millions of cubic feet of gas took fire and exploded. The atmosphere went white-hot. It grew mottled, then fell to the streets like a crimson curtain. Almost before the last fragments of steel had ceased to fall, the wreckage of the wooden houses in the North End had begun to burn. And if there were any ruins which failed to ignite from falling flames, they began to burn from the fires in their own stoves, onto which they had collapsed.

Over this part of the town, rising in the shape of a typhoon from the Narrows and extending five miles into the sky, was poised a cloud formed by the exhausted gases. It hung still for many minutes, white, glossy as an ermine's back, serenely aloof. It cast its shadow over twenty miles of forest land behind Bedford Basin. 19

Structure:

1. To what extent is "A Sound Beyond Hearing" based on chronological order? Could it have been placed in our first chapter, "Narration"? What qualifies it to appear in this chapter instead?
2. To what extent does this selection trace the causes and effects of the great Halifax explosion? Could it have appeared in our later chapter, "Cause and Effect"?
3. Why does MacLennan classify the effects of the explosion into three parts, one each for land, air and sea? Could "A Sound Beyond Hearing" have appeared in our later chapter, "Classification"? Why do you think it appears in this chapter instead?
4. Roughly what percentage of this selection is devoted to description? How close did MacLennan come to making you feel as though you were there? Which passage most strongly gave you the feeling of being a spectator?
5. Does MacLennan's use of narration, cause and effect, classification and description, all in the same selection, give an effect of confusion? Or do these methods of development work smoothly together? Do you think MacLennan consciously planned all these interlocking methods? Would you attempt to combine methods as you plan a piece of writing?

Style:

1. This explosion scene, from MacLennan's novel *Barometer Rising,* is recognized as one of the most vivid passages in all of Canadian

literature. One reason is the profusion of SENSE IMAGES. Point out one striking example each of appeals to sight, hearing, touch and smell.

2. In paragraph 3, MacLennan uses the image of "screaming metal" and in paragraph 18, the image of "tongues of flame." Point out three other examples of PERSONIFICATION, in which an inanimate object is described in human terms.

3. In paragraph 17, MacLennan writes that fragments of red hot steel "fell like meteors." Point out at least five other SIMILES, figures of speech in which one thing is said to be like another.

4. In paragraph 15, MacLennan writes that "windows split into driving arrows of glass." Point out at least five other METAPHORS, figures of speech in which one thing is said to *be* another.

5. What do "port," "starboard," "hawse," "scuttle" and all the other nautical terms do for this selection? Would a reader's unfamiliarity with some of these specialized words detract from the effect? Why or why not?

Ideas:

1. Name all the novels and films you can think of that are about disasters. Why is such entertainment popular? Do people like to be scared? If so, why?

2. The blast that killed over 1600 people in Halifax, on December 6, 1917, is said to be the world's most disastrous man-made explosion before the atomic bomb. If you have read about the atomic blast that destroyed Hiroshima, in Kildare Dobbs' essay "The Scar," compare the two events in their magnitude and their effect upon the inhabitants.

3. Do you sense moments of beauty in MacLennan's description of the disaster? If so, where? Is it appropriate or even moral to see beauty in destruction?

4. Write a *description* of a disaster that you have seen or of whatever you have seen that comes closest to being a disaster. Your subject could be a fire, an explosion, an automobile accident, a drowning, etc. Use a great many SENSE IMAGES to recreate for the reader what you experienced in person.

(NOTE: See also the Topics for Writing at the end of this chapter.)

Topics for Writing

Chapter 3: Description

(Note also the topics for writing that appear after each selection in this chapter.)

Describe one of the following as vividly as you can:

1. The nursery of a maternity ward
2. The locker room before or after a game
3. A retirement home or nursing home
4. A funeral parlour during visiting hours
5. Your attic or basement
6. A swamp, a meadow, the deep woods or the seashore
7. Your favourite park
8. A garbage dump or junkyard
9. A thunderstorm, blizzard, tornado, hurricane, flood or earthquake
10. The most architecturally interesting building in your town or city
11. A building that seems out of place in your neighbourhood
12. The interior of your church, synagogue, mosque or temple during a service
13. The waiting room of a doctor's office or of the emergency ward of a hospital
14. A crowded beach
15. A cafeteria at lunch or dinner
16. A police station, courtroom or jail
17. A garage or body shop in operation
18. The appearance of your best friend
19. The appearance of your best-remembered public- or high-school teacher
20. Rush hour on the expressway, subway, streetcar, bus or sidewalk
21. A pool hall, bowling alley or amusement arcade
22. A strike or demonstration
23. A carnival, a circus or the midway of an amusement park
24. The entertainment district of your town or city on a Saturday night
25. The sky on a clear night

"As far, far back as I could remember, I had a dread of cats. Dread, I think, is the word. Not fear. Not hatred. Not revulsion. Just dread."

Gregory Clark, "The Cat"

Here's why . . . .

CAUSE AND EFFECT

One of our most human traits is a desire to make sense of things by asking *"why?"*. If something good happens, we naturally want to know *why* so we can repeat it. If something bad happens, we want to know *why* so we can avoid it in the future. And other times we want to know *why* out of plain curiosity. These motives are so strong that cause and effect reasoning is one of our chief ways of thinking and one of our most effective ways of organizing essays.

When you investigate causes and effects, try to get them right. A few years ago, a church in Florida began a campaign to burn records by Elton John and other rock stars. A survey had reported that 984 out of 1000 girls who had become pregnant out of wedlock had "committed fornication while rock music was played." The assumption was automatic: rock music causes pregnancy. Before it lit the first match, though, the church might have asked what *other* causes contributed to the effect. How many of the music lovers had also taken alcohol or drugs? How many had failed to use means of birth control? Was the music played because "fornication" generally takes place inside a building, where sound systems also happen to be? The church might also have investigated causes further in the past: What kinds of family backgrounds and what influences of society prepared the fornicators to enter the situation in the first place? And, finally, the church might have asked how often people in this age group listened to Elton John and his friends while *not* fornicating. Rock music may still be to blame — but who knows without a more objective and thorough search of causes? When you trace causes and effects, consider these principles:

Just because one event follows another, don't assume the first causes the second. If a black cat crosses the road just before your car blows up, put the blame where it belongs: not on the cat but on the mechanic who forgot to replace your crankcase oil.

Control your prejudices. If the bank manager refuses to give you a loan, is it because bankers are capitalist exploiters who like to keep the rest of us down? Or is it because this one had to call the collection agency to get his last loan back from you?

Explore causes behind causes. Your employer promoted you because you work hard. But why do you work hard: because you are afraid of being fired? Because you need the money to pay off your car? Because your parents set a workaholic example for you? Or because in fact you like the job?

Many events have multiple causes and multiple effects:

In addition, each of these causes may have one or more causes behind it, and each of these effects may produce further effects, leading to an infinite chain of causality receding into the past and reaching into the future. Where, then, do you draw the boundaries as you plan an essay of cause and effect? The answer lies in your own common sense: Include enough to make your point clearly and fairly, then stop. If your parents are workaholics, a description of their behaviour may help a reader to understand your own. But do we need to hear about your grandparents as well? If we do, would a quick summary be enough, since we've already heard the details in your parents' case?

Some events or situations have very clear-cut causes, as in Gregory Clark's essay, which uncovers the origin in childhood of a "dread" held by Clark in adulthood. Others have numerous or complicated causes, as in Margaret Atwood's analysis of Canadians' attitudes toward Americans. Like Clark, Atwood and other effective essayists, tailor your argument to the requirements of your subject.

Allan Fotheringham

When the Natives Surrender

Allan Fotheringham has been called the "most admired and detested political columnist in the country." He heaps humorous scorn on his targets: the corrupt, the inept, the arrogant, the powerful and almost every aspect of our national capital, Ottawa. This high-living and influential journalist was born in 1932 in Hearne, Saskatchewan, a village of 30 persons. Working in summers as a logger and a steelworker, Fotheringham put himself through school at the University of British Columbia, then joined the staff of the Vancouver Sun. *When several years later he was given his own column to write, he quickly made a name for himself as a brash and fearless journalist: he demolished local politicians with his attacks and gave his readers a larger view of the world outside Vancouver. In 1980 he became an Ottawa columnist for the Southam newspaper chain. But it is his weekly column on the last page of* Maclean's *that since 1975 has made "The Foth," as he calls himself, the best-known personality in Canadian journalism. Our selection was one of these columns in 1983. While it is not overtly political, its vivid style and what has been called the "outrageous" personality of its author make it vintage Fotheringham.*

1   I have been going, you see, to the island for some 25 years. It supplies the annual brain transplant (badly needed, as faithful readers will testify). The sand is smoother than Brian Mulroney's voice. The sun sears and heals. The sun goes down at 6:21, transforming the sky into a mauve and pink canvas that hypnotizes and reduces one to helpless little murmurs of ineptitude. The body goes down to the pillow at 8:00 p.m., rising sharply at 11:00 p.m. It is children's hours for the soul, a surefire cure, washing away thoughts of Bill Bennett's* humanity, Pierre Trudeau's humility, Mark MacGuigan's* charisma, Eugene Whelan's* eloquence, Robert Bourassa's* resurrection. The first act, on arrival on the island, is the removal of one's watch and one's shoes. They are stored away, unseen, until it is time reluctantly to seek out the great silver bird and return to distasteful reality.

---

*Bill Bennett: former premier of British Columbia
*Mark MacGuigan, Eugene Whelan: cabinet ministers under the Trudeau government
*Robert Bourassa: premier of Quebec who was returned to office in the election of 1985

The yearly visitor to the island becomes, of course, an expert, his brief glimpses at intervals revealing trends and developments in the evolving of the island not so easily apparent to the resident. Some years back, your diligent pursuer of the rough life, ahead of his time as usual, issued a warning. Trouble could be spied ahead in paradise. There is a certain inexorable effect when the privileged portion of the world finds a pleasant spot to acquire the most desirable attribute in North America: a tan. The residents of the spot, grateful for the money at first, have to service the visitors. Each year, the diligent pursuer found more waitresses, more taxi drivers, more bartenders, more beach boys. You can't turn the entire population of an island into cocktail waitresses and tour guides, I argued, without breeding resentment and bitterness and eventual backlash.

This was considered troublemaking heresy at the time, harmful mischief that would hurt the tourist trade and be offensive to the travel industry. I thought, myself, that it was quite prescient, noble in concept and, as usual, far ahead of its time. No one paid any attention to the columns, except those who accused your agent of being a dolorous doomsayer, my usual title.

In time, the shrewd prediction began to take shape and form. At each visit, the creeping disease of condominiums marched resolutely onward so as to blot out the sunset. Ever upward the mountain slope the pineapple and sugar cane fields were ripped out, the rich red soil instead growing condos and golf courses. The curse of the electric golf cart was upon the land.

As so wisely predicted, the resentments festered and grew on the island. There was the bittersweet saying that when the white man first came to the island the natives were lying on the beach, eating, drinking and making love — shocking the missionaries with their indolence. As a result, after years of colonization, the natives are all working. And the white men? Lying on the beach, eating, drinking and making love.

There was the bitter realization that fewer and fewer stretches of the precious, achingly lovely beaches were left for public access — the hotels reserving them for "guests only." The real residents, the natives of the island, had trouble finding access to their own beaches (on those weekend hours when they weren't bartending, doing the hotel laundry or waiting on tables). There were, first isolated then more frequent, cases of violence on the island. Strange, illogical violence. Youths, beered-up, would pounce on tourists who were camped alone, sleeping in paradise. There seemed no motive, but there was — the pent-up resentment of the natives against the white visitors who, if only penny-pinching campers, represented affluence that would be forever foreign (and grating).

7   As the condos marched through the pineapple fields, the Teamsters and the other big unions moved in on the island, finding eager supplicants. As the native workers escalated their pay demands and the strike syndrome hit paradise, the big multinationals did what they always do: seek cheaper labor. The pineapple and sugar companies suddenly found that they were developing new fields on other, less evolved, islands further across other oceans. The condos marched on, ever higher on the mountain, ever thicker on the beaches, more and more pineapple workers and sugar cane toilers being turned into cocktail waitresses and taxi drivers. The publicity about the violence in paradise — greatly headlined because of its shock value — caused the tourism dollars to fall off.

8   On this visit, the cranium being soothed by the sun and bathed by the limpid sea, one notices the change. The surliness is gone. The mindless violence against isolated campers has disappeared. The newspaper is upbeat, singing a siren song to visitors, betraying an underlying nervousness about the dicey times of the last few summers. The waitresses are cheerful. As the sun goes down at 6:21, sending soft shafts of purple and scarlet into the backlit clouds, a restaurant bar looks over a vast swimming pool which looks over the palm-girt sea. Behind the bar is Lyle, a young man in his 20s, neat, polite, impassive, with the mandatory moustache that goes with his age. He does not resent anyone is the message. Your diligent pursuer of the truth suddenly sees it all. Lyle is the son of the resentful unemployed pineapple worker. He represents a different generation. He likes his job as a bartender, union rates, union hours, medical benefits no doubt, guaranteed retirement plan. Lyle represents the surrender. The subversion is complete.

9   The missionaries, in the end, have won.

Structure:

1. Why does Allan Fotheringham specify, in his very first sentence, how many years he has gone to "the island"?
2. In Fotheringham's analysis, many of the *effects* of tourism on "the island" become the *causes* of further *effects*. Point out a chain of at least five causes and effects, and explain the relationship of each item to the next.
3. Why are some of the paragraphs so long? Why is the last one so short?

4. What principle does Fotheringham follow in choosing "won" as his final word?

Style:

1. Allan Fotheringham has perhaps the most individualistic STYLE of any major Canadian journalist. What aspects of this style strike you the most strongly? Cite examples to illustrate your answers.
2. How do we acquire our own writing STYLE? Do we choose the one we want, perhaps after reading an author we admire? Do we practise a certain style to make it our own? Or does a style just happen? Explain which you believe to be the best approach, and why.
3. If you have already read a number of other selections in this book, roughly what percentage are written in the first person, as a large part of this selection is? What are some advantages of first-person narration in an essay? What are some disadvantages?
4. In paragraph 5, Fotheringham describes how "the natives were lying on the beach, eating, drinking and making love" when the first white men arrived; now it is the white men who lie on the beach "eating, drinking and making love" while the natives work. This is a good example of Fotheringham's central device, IRONY. Point out at least five other good examples of irony in this selection, and explain how each works.

Ideas:

1. Are the islanders better off or worse off now than when the first missionaries arrived? Better or worse off than when the plantations were thriving? Give reasons.
2. Is Lyle right to "surrender" — to like his "job as a bartender, union rates, union hours, medical benefits no doubt, guaranteed retirement plan"? Is his acceptance of the new situation a weakness or a strength?
3. Is Fotheringham criticizing, praising or merely noting cause and effect when he states in his final sentence that "the missionaries, in the end, have won"? Explain.
4. If you have read "Old Year's Night," compare the effects of tourism upon a southern island as seen by an islander (Austin Clarke) and a tourist (Allan Fotheringham).
5. Does Allan Fotheringham's role as a political columnist justify his poking fun at Brian Mulroney and other politicians in

paragraph 1 of an essay about a tropical island? If so, explain how.

6. Great numbers of Canadians go south in winter to a "paradise" like Fotheringham's. A great many others go skating or skiing or snowmobiling, in an attempt not to escape winter but to enjoy it. Which side do you take? Why? Describe your most successful techniques, if any, for coping with winter in a northern country.

7. Write an essay analyzing the *cause(s) and/or effect(s)* of your most recent holiday, whether at home or elsewhere. Focus the argument, and give specific details to illustrate your points.

(NOTE: See also the Topics for Writing at the end of this chapter.)

Margaret Atwood

Canadians: What Do They Want?

If an American or German or Briton knows only one Canadian writer, that writer is likely to be Margaret Atwood. Both poet and novelist, Atwood is a rare example of the serious writer who has met with popular success. Ironically, it is her poetry that many critics consider her best work, while it is her novels that have brought wide recognition from the public. Atwood was born in Ottawa in 1939, earned a B.A. at the University of Toronto in 1961 and a master's at Radcliffe in 1962. Since then she has published over 20 books. The best-known is her novel Surfacing *(1972), also produced as a film. Her other works include* The Circle Game *(poetry, 1966);* The Journals of Susanna Moody *(poetry, 1970);* Power Politics *(poetry, 1971);* You Are Happy *(poetry, 1974);* Selected Poems *(1976);* The Edible Woman *(novel, 1969);* Lady Oracle *(novel, 1976);* Life Before Man *(novel, 1979);* Bodily Harm *(novel, 1981);* Bluebeard's Egg *(short stories, 1983);* The Handmaid's Tale *(novel, 1985);* Survival: a Thematic Guide to Canadian Literature *(1972); and* The New Oxford Book of Canadian Verse in English *(editor, 1982). Atwood's feminism and Canadian nationalism are evident in her books and also in our selection, "Canadians: What Do They Want?" This essay, written for Americans, appeared in 1982 in* Mother Jones, *an American political magazine. Editor Mark Dowie wrote, "... we asked Canadian novelist and poet Margaret Atwood to explain why her fellow Canadians feel so strongly about their neighbors to the south."*

L ast month, during a poetry reading, I tried out a short prose poem called "How to Like Men." It began by suggesting that one start with the feet. Unfortunately, the question of jackboots soon arose, and things went on from there. After the reading I had a conversation with a young man who thought I had been unfair to men. He wanted men to be liked totally, not just from the heels to the knees, and not just as individuals but as a group; and he thought it negative and inegalitarian of me to have alluded to war and rape. I pointed out that as far as any of us knew these were two activities not widely engaged in by women, but he was still upset. "We're both in this together," he protested. I admitted that this was so; but could he, maybe, see that our relative positions might be a little different.

This is the conversation one has with Americans, even, uh, *good* Americans, when the dinner-table conversation veers round to

1

2

121

Canadian-American relations. "We're in this together," they like to say, especially when it comes to continental energy reserves. How do you *explain* to them, as delicately as possible, why they are not categorically beloved? It gets like the old Lifebuoy ads: even their best friends won't tell them. And Canadians are supposed to be their best friends, right? Members of the family?

3   Well, sort of. Across the river from Michigan, so near and yet so far, there I was at the age of eight, reading *their* Donald Duck comic books (originated, however, by one of *ours;* yes, Walt Disney's parents were Canadian) and coming at the end to Popsicle Pete, who promised me the earth if only I would save wrappers, but took it all away from me again with a single asterisk: Offer Good Only in the United States. Some cynical members of the world community may be forgiven for thinking that the same asterisk is there, in invisible ink, on the Constitution and the Bill of Rights.

4   But quibbles like that aside, and good will assumed, how does one go about liking Americans? Where does one begin? Or, to put it another way, why did the Canadian women lock themselves in the john during a '70s "international" feminist conference being held in Toronto? Because the American sisters were being "imperialist," that's why.

5   But then, it's always a little naive of Canadians to expect that Americans, of whatever political stamp, should stop being imperious. How can they? The fact is that the United States is an empire and Canada is to it as Gaul was to Rome.

6   It's hard to explain to Americans what it feels like to be a Canadian. Pessimists among us would say that one has to translate the experience into their own terms and that this is necessary because Americans are incapable of thinking in any other terms — and this in itself is part of the problem. (Witness all those draft dodgers who went into culture shock when they discovered to their horror that Toronto was not Syracuse.)

7   Here is a translation: Picture a Mexico with a population ten times larger than that of the United States. That would put it at about two billion. Now suppose that the official American language is Spanish, that 75 percent of the books Americans buy and 90 percent of the movies they see are Mexican, and that the profits flow across the border to Mexico. If an American does scrape it together to make a movie, the Mexicans won't let him show it in the States, because they own the distribution outlets. If anyone tries to change this ratio, not only the Mexicans but many fellow Americans cry "National chauvinism," or, even more effectively, "National socialism." After all, the American public prefers the Mexican product. It's what they're used to.

Retranslate and you have the current American-Canadian 8
picture. It's changed a little recently, not only on the cultural front.
For instance, Canada, some think a trifle late, is attempting to
regain control of its own petroleum industry. Americans are
predictably angry. They think of Canadian oil as *theirs*.

"What's mine is yours," they have said for years, meaning exports; 9
"What's yours is mine" means ownership and profits. Canadians are
supposed to do retail buying, not controlling, or what's an empire
for? One could always refer Americans to history, particularly that
of their own revolution. They objected to the colonial situation when
they themselves were a colony; but then, revolution is considered
one of a very few home-grown American products that definitely are
not for export.

Objectively, one cannot become too self-righteous about this state 10
of affairs. Canadians owned lots of things, including their souls,
before World War II. After that they sold, some say because they had
put too much into financing the war, which created a capital
vacuum (a position they would not have been forced into if the
Americans hadn't kept out of the fighting for so long, say the sore
losers). But for whatever reason, capital flowed across the border in
the '50s, and Canadians, traditionally sock-under-the-mattress
hoarders, were reluctant to invest in their own country. Americans
did it for them and ended up with a large part of it, which they
retain to this day. In every sellout there's a seller as well as a buyer,
and the Canadians did a thorough job of trading their birthright for
a mess.

That's on the capitalist end, but when you turn to the trade union 11
side of things you find much the same story, except that the sellout
happened in the '30s under the banner of the United Front. Now
Canadian workers are finding that in any empire the colonial
branch plants are the first to close, and what could be a truly
progressive labor movement has been weakened by compromised
bargains made in international union headquarters south of the
border.

Canadians are sometimes snippy to Americans at cocktail parties. 12
They don't like to feel owned and they don't like having been sold.
But what really bothers them — and it's at this point that the
United States and Rome part company — is the wide-eyed innocence
with which their snippiness is greeted.

Innocence becomes ignorance when seen in the light of interna- 13
tional affairs, and though ignorance is one of the spoils of conquest
— the Gauls always knew more about the Romans than the Romans
knew about them — the world can no longer afford America's
ignorance. Its ignorance of Canada, though it makes Canadians

bristle, is a minor and relatively harmless example. More dangerous is the fact that individual Americans seem not to know that the United States is an imperial power and is behaving like one. They don't want to admit that empires dominate, invade and subjugate — and live on the proceeds — or, if they do admit it, they believe in their divine right to do so. The export of divine right is much more harmful than the export of Coca-Cola, though they may turn out to be much the same thing in the end.

14   Other empires have behaved similarly (the British somewhat better, Genghis Khan decidedly worse); but they have not expected to be *liked* for it. It's the final Americanism, this passion for being liked. Alas, many Americans are indeed likable; they are often more generous, more welcoming, more enthusiastic, less picky and sardonic than Canadians, and it's not enough to say it's only because they can afford it. Some of that revolutionary spirit still remains: the optimism, the 18th-century belief in the fixability of almost anything, the conviction of the possibility of change. However, at cocktail parties and elsewhere one must be able to tell the difference between an individual and a foreign policy. Canadians can no longer afford to think of Americans as only a spectator sport. If Reagan blows up the world, we will unfortunately be doing more than watching it on television. "No annihilation without representation" sounds good as a slogan, but if we run it up the flagpole, who's going to salute?

15   We *are* all in this together. For Canadians, the question is how to survive it. For Americans there is no question, because there does not have to be. Canada is just that vague, cold place where their uncle used to go fishing, before the lakes went dead from acid rain.

16   How do you like Americans? Individually, it's easier. Your average American is no more responsible for the state of affairs than your average man is for war and rape. Any Canadian who is so narrow-minded as to dislike Americans merely on principle is missing out on one of the good things in life. The same might be said, to women, of men. As a group, as a foreign policy, it's harder. But if you like men, you can like Americans. Cautiously. Selectively. Beginning with the feet. One at a time.

Structure:

1. How does the opening ANECDOTE lead to Margaret Atwood's main topic? Upon what organizational device is it based?
2. What technique underlies the closing of Atwood's essay? How effective is it?

3. Identify Atwood's THESIS STATEMENT, the passage that most clearly tells what the essay will be about.
4. As editor Mark Dowie states in his introduction, ". . . we asked Canadian novelist and poet Margaret Atwood to explain why her fellow Canadians feel so strongly about their neighbors to the south." Point out at least ten *causes* given by Atwood for anti-Americanism in Canada.
5. Atwood's economic "translation" in paragraph 7 is a comparison of American control over Canada with a hypothetical Mexican control over the United States. What purpose does this passage serve for the readers it was meant to instruct?

Style:

1. How FORMAL or INFORMAL is Atwood's TONE in this essay? Give examples to illustrate your answer.
2. Like most of Atwood's writing, this selection is charged with IRONY. Point out the strongest examples of it. What effect do they achieve?

Ideas:

1. How well do you think this essay, written for Americans, communicates to Canadians?
2. In paragraph 13, Atwood writes that "empires dominate, invade and subjugate — and live on the proceeds . . . ." Do you agree with her that the United States is an "empire"? And if so, to what extent has it dominated, invaded and subjugated Canada? Give specific examples to support your point of view.
3. What degree of American influence do you detect in these aspects of Canadian life?

transportation	hockey
clothing	music
food	books
housing	language
television	law
films	foreign policy
inflation	interest rates

4. One concern of the Canadian military is a possible invasion by the Soviets. But in his novel *Exxoneration* (1974), Richard Rohmer describes a future military invasion of Canada by the United States. Tell why you think such an event might or might not happen. If it did, what would you do?

5. Discuss the benefits and dangers of nationalism. How nationalistic do you think most Canadians are? Should they become more or less nationalistic? What might be the results?
6. Point out the similarities and/or differences that you have noticed between Americans and Canadians as individuals. Give specific details.
7. If you have read "When the Natives Surrender," by Allan Fotheringham, compare the *effects* of northern influence on "the island" with the *effects* of American influence on Canada.
8. If you oppose Atwood's point of view, write a *cause and effect* essay entitled "What America Has Done for Me." If you agree with Atwood's point of view, write a *cause and effect* essay entitled "What America Has Done to Me." In either case, give specific examples.

(NOTE: See also the Topics for Writing at the end of this chapter.)

Gregory Clark

The Cat

Greg Clark (1892-1977) was a story teller. For many years on the inside back page of Weekend Magazine *he told a story each week about the war, or his hunting and fishing pals, or characters he knew or the odd events that came his way in Toronto. And in his last years, living in Toronto's old King Edward Hotel, he would delight staff and friends in the dining room by spinning tales from a long and colourful life. Hardly believing that so many things could happen to one person, his readers or listeners often wondered if the stories were true. "What a question to ask!" Clark would reply. He was born in Toronto and was a newspaperman — reporter, feature writer and columnist — for over sixty years. He began with the paper his father edited,* The Toronto Star. *When World War I came, he tried several times to enlist but was turned down for being too small. When Clark finally got into the army, though, he rose quickly from private to major and won the Military Cross for courage under fire at Vimy Ridge. Afterwards he returned to the* Star, *where he worked with Ernest Hemingway, Morley Callaghan and Gordon Sinclair. During the next war, he served as a war correspondent until his own son was killed in action. Clark's greatest popularity came with the column he wrote for* Weekend Magazine *from 1952 almost to the end of his life. Many of these pieces — short, funny, warm-hearted and full of homely wisdom — were gathered in books, among them* Hi There! *(1963), from which our selection comes.*

A s far, far back as I could remember, I had a dread of cats. 1
Dread, I think, is the word. Not fear. Not hatred. Not revulsion. Just dread.

One time, my fishing companion, W.C. Milne, asked me to pick up 2
his fishing tackle at his house, and gave me the key. His wife was out of town.

I didn't know the Milnes had acquired a cat. I opened the front 3
door and started through the vestibule for the living room, where the tackle was heaped on a chair. I froze in my tracks.

Somebody was in the house! 4

"Margaret?" I called. 5

No answer. 6

From a golf bag in the vestibule I took an iron. 7

Everything in my nature told me SOMEBODY was in the house. As 8
an old soldier, though only 30, I had an instinct for danger. I could FEEL it.

9   From wall to wall, I slid to the back door, finding it locked. With the niblick ready to throw or to swing, I sidled up the stairs, knowing any instant I would have to strike. In those days, I was not afraid of men.

10   Along the hall, into one room, then another, I moved, all tight as a stretched elastic band. In the front bedroom, on the bed was a black-and-yellow cat, arching aristocratically on being disturbed. I yelled, and chased it from the room and down the stairs and out the back door, which I opened, banging the golf stick.

11   "Ah, yes," said Billy Milne, when I told him. "That's our new cat."

12   But as I remember it, it never came home.

13   As a child, I used to cross the street, on my way to school, if I saw a cat in my path. In my teens, at the age when we look for chosen friends, I lost sundry friends because they had a cat in the house. In World War I, as a young fellow with the lives of thirty-eight men on my mind and soul, I led a night patrol into a ruined farmhouse and made an utter ass of myself because I let fly with a Very light pistol into a black cellar empty save for a poor mangy cat.

14   But I was certain it had been the enemy.

15   It took me weeks to restore the faith of my thirty-eight men.

16   Ah, cats!

17   "It," said my doctor friends, consolingly, "is one of those mysterious, unexplainable phobias . . . ."

18   I was in the back half of my fifties when I visited my Aunt Minnie Greig, in Seaforth, Ont. She was my stylish aunt, a beautiful woman.

19   We sat on her veranda, rocking; and she, being my elder by twenty or more years, was regaling me with stories of times past.

20   "You were an awful little shrimp," she said.

21   "Was I?" I regretted.

22   "So timid," said Aunt Min.

23   "Was I?" I muttered.

24   "Do you remember your white cat?" she asked.

25   "MY white cat?" I barely whispered.

26   "Joe, your dad," said Aunt Minnie, rocking idly, "bought you a white cat, since your mother wouldn't have a dog in the house. It was a beauty, that cat. Snow white."

27   I had a strange feeling, as I sat watching Aunt Minnie rocking, that I was in the act of taking off a heavy coat, a coat with pockets full of things.

28   "How old was I?" I said.

29   "Two," said Aunt Minnie. "You still had diapers. Do you remember what the back yard was like?"

30   "Yes," I said. "I was eight when we left there. There was a grape vine on the fence at the far end."

"Right," said Aunt Minnie. "A grape arbor." 31

"And over that fence," I said, "was Lilley's greenhouses." 32

"Good for you!" cried Aunt Minnie. "The Lilleys were the florists, 33
and they had those greenhouses. . . ."

"What," I interrupted cautiously, "about the cat?" 34

"I'm coming to that," said Aunt Minnie. "Well, the Lilleys had 35
trouble with mice and rats in the greenhouses. So they used to put
out poison."

"Did I," I asked, "like the cat? The white cat?" 36

"LIKE it!" cried Aunt Minnie. "There you'd go, staggering around 37
with that cat draped over your skinny little arm."

"I. . ." I said, and stopped. 38

"You took the cat to BED with you," said Aunt Min. "I told your 39
mother, Sarah Louisa, never, never to let a cat in bed with an infant.
But there you were with that blamed cat on the pillow beside your
head."

"Well, I . . ." I tried again, my body prickling, my back hair 40
creeping as it did in that ruined farmhouse in Flanders.

"The cat," said Aunt Min, "seemed as attached to you as you were 41
to it. It followed you everywhere, around the house, out the door, in
the back yard."

I pressed my back against the back of my chair. 42

"It was white?" I asked. 43

"Snow white, I told you," said Aunt Min. "Well, here's what 44
happened. Your lovely white cat disappeared!"

"Disappeared?" 45

"I was staying with your mother at the time," said Aunt Min. "The 46
cat vanished. It was gone all night. It didn't come home the next day.
You kept toddling around, hunting for it, upstairs, downstairs, out
the door, all around the yard, back in the door, upstairs, downstairs,
until we were sick of the sight of you."

"Did I cry?" 47

"No, you just went wandering around, looking under everything. 48
It was kind of pitiable, really."

"So?" I said, my back no longer twitching. 49

"We were sitting in the kitchen, having a cup of tea," said Aunt 50
Minnie. "Your mother, Mamie Armour, Mrs. Taylor from next door,
and your Aunt Mart.

"Then," said Aunt Min, "up the back steps from the yard you 51
came, CARRYING your white cat!"

I tightened. 52

"It was DEAD!" cried Aunt Min. "STIFF dead! It had been dead two 53
days. Poisoned from Lilley's greenhouses. Its tail was sticking out
stiff. Its white fur was all matted, damp. And you were HUGGING it to
your little chest, your chin over it."

54   "What happened?" I got the question out.

55   "Why, we all screamed!" said Aunt Min. "Your mother was first to reach you, and she snatched the cat from you so violently, you fell back on the steps; and she THREW it half way down the yard, and we were all screaming and yelling, and Aunt Mart had a fainting spell, and you were howling, and your mother was grabbing at you . . ."

● ● ● ● ● ● ●

56   Do you know what I wish you for a Happy New Year?

57   I wish you the luck to find YOUR Aunt Min, and have her tell you anecdotes about your childhood.

58   For in them, you may find, as I found, absolution from ancient fears, and mysterious dreads, and the strange darknesses that lie beyond the horizon of consciousness.

59   To know is to understand, even yourself.

Structure:

1. Point out several effects achieved by the introduction (par. 1-17).
2. Is Clark's "dread" of cats caused by only one event? Or is there a chain of cause and effect? If so, point out all the links in the chain.
3. Most of this selection takes the form of narration. Why are there two narrators?
4. Gregory Clark's usual way of exploring a subject was to tell a story. Do you think the cause and effect analysis of this selection is helped or harmed by the narrative form in which it appears?

Style:

1. Although this selection is short, it contains 59 paragraphs. Give as many reasons as you can for their short length.
2. How FORMAL or INFORMAL is the STYLE of this selection? Refer to passages that illustrate your answer.
3. Explain the effect of paragraph 27: "I had a strange feeling, as I sat watching Aunt Minnie rocking, that I was in the act of taking off a heavy coat, a coat with pockets full of things."

Ideas:

1. For many years the inside back page of *Weekend Magazine* featured Clark's "shorties," as he called them. When he was first

offered that page to fill, he wondered if he could write anything in so few words. "It's quite simple," his editor said. "Write about small things." Is Clark's story of the cat a "small thing"? In what ways may it be larger than it seems at first?

2. Discuss the emotions that the women exhibit to young Clark in paragraph 55. How would you have reacted if you had been one of those women, and why?

3. The process that Clark describes is similar to that of psychoanalysis: learning about oneself in order to find "absolution from ancient fears, and mysterious dreads, and the strange darknesses that lie beyond the horizon of consciousness" (par. 58). Clark found his "absolution." Do you believe that self-knowledge always has a good result? How does self-knowledge help us in life? Can you think of any way in which it could harm us?

4. Do you have any unexplained "dreads," like Clark's dread of cats? Name one or two and invent possible causes for them. Join class members in inventing possible causes of each other's dreads.

5. Write a true narrative or invent a fictitious but plausible one to explain the *cause or causes* of one of your strongest attitudes (the attitude could be a fear, a hatred, a love, a prejudice, etc.).

(NOTE: See also the Topics for Writing at the end of this chapter.)

Bill Reno

Supermarket Technology

Born in 1948, Bill Reno studied economics at the University of Chicago, then cinematography at Ryerson Polytechnical Institute in Toronto. For a time he worked in the film industry, then found his true interest in the labour movement. At present he is Research and Education Director for the Ontario Retail Council of the United Food and Commercial Workers. He serves on the board of directors of IDEA. Corporation, an Ontario crown corporation that promotes high tech industry; the board of governors of George Brown College, Toronto; the Ontario Council of Regents for the Colleges of Applied Arts and Technology; and the Ontario Advisory Council on Equal Opportunity for Women. Reno has also served on several governmental task forces on the Canadian food and beverage industries and does frequent public speaking on technology. He views his main accomplishment as the increased recognition which the Workers' Compensation Board in Ontario now gives to cashiers' disabilities caused by the new supermarket technology. His essay "Supermarket Technology" appeared in 1982 in The Canadian Forum.

1   Perhaps because it satisfies some basic human needs the supermarket is a remarkably successful cultural institution. The availability of a wide range of foods, most of which can be saved for later use, is certainly comforting to any animal addicted to eating daily. But for humans, the exercise of the personal executive skills shoppers must exercise in deciding which resources to trade for which products and how to devote less time to the process has helped to make the modern supermarket a hit almost everywhere.

2   In Canada large self-service retail food stores took root in the 1920s and throughout most of their history supermarkets were simply purveyors of goods which management hoped customers would buy. Early marketing strategies were essentially the same as those of today: lure shoppers into the store with promises of low prices, and keep them coming back with cleanliness, selection and good service. It worked. The chains prospered with few casualties throughout the depression and war years, expanding even more aggressively in the 1950s and 60s.

3   In the early 1970s, however, food prices began a sustained rise that outpaced the overall inflation rate. An alarming number of formerly loyal customers began to grumble and shop around for better prices. For assiduously price conscious consumers who viewed "shopping around" as simply visiting other large chain stores, it was

a frustrating endeavour. The fostering of the illusion of price competition had already become a sophisticated craft practiced by marketing specialists, particularly in the retail "war zone" of the major metropolitan areas of Ontario and Quebec. Except for loss leaders and coupon blitzes, price competition developed into an industry-wide holding action, with no chain having more than a marginal advantage at any one time against its rivals. To increase profits, the major retailers moved to larger, higher-volume premises and launched a crusade against labour costs.

Although wages account for less than ten per cent of the input 4 costs of even unionized supermarkets, they are the factor most easily manipulated. Skimping on lighting, heat and product selection drives customers away. Cutting back on advertizing depresses volume sales. Making do with fewer employees, however, was a tactic that shoppers might not notice or object to, provided they weren't inconvenienced and prices remained competitive.

How could this be done? Increased personal effort by workers can 5 raise productivity somewhat, but not consistently and permanently because of the high turnover of store personnel. Careful scheduling may help reduce the number of employees working during slack hours; hiring more part-time than full-time help assists efficient time management. But the needs of supermarket workers for higher wages and better work conditions were similar to those of their neighbours, and retail unions were just as effective as others in winning inflation-matching pay settlements for their members. Yet labour cost containment, though successful to a degree, failed to meet the expectations of those in management seeking to build their careers by dramatically cutting the cost of doing business in an already lean industry.

Onto this scene descended a remarkable corporate *deus ex* 6 *machina:* high technology hit the retail food industry with a muffled thump, but rapidly upstaged all other cost-cutting strategies.

After the invention of the cash register in 1878 by U.S. 7 restauranteur James J. Ritty, retail technology evolved quite slowly for nearly ninety years. Productivity gains were largely the result of changed work methods and increased store size. But the recent marriage of lasers, computers and microtechnology has fuelled an explosion of change in the industry. The new technology could turn the tide of consumerism which has plagued retail marketing specialists during the last decade. There is also a restrained hope among corporate planners that technology may prove to be the final solution in their normally polite but still deadly battles with the unions.

8   High technology in food stores begins with the now innocuous Universal Product Code (UPC), the series of bars and numbers found on over 90 per cent of all packaged items carried by supermarkets. To the untrained eye, all UPC symbols look more or less alike. To the scanning laser beam, embedded in the checkout counter, however, those bars of varying thickness reveal the product's manufacturer, the brand name and package size. When matched with the corresponding code in the store's computer, today's price for that product is electronically relayed to the cash register, which is wired to the scanner. Should the scanner be unable to read the bars for any reason, the numbers underneath them can be manually punched in by the cashier.

9   Some of the business advantages of the UPC system are obvious. As the can of tomato juice is run over the scanner, it is subtracted from the store's inventory; inventory control and re-ordering become automatic. Sales volume and gross margins for a single store or an entire chain can be obtained at the push of a button on the master computer. The potential for productivity gains, loss control and useful marketing data is substantial; but this is only the tip of the iceberg.

10   Any manager can name the ways in which scanning can eliminate jobs in his store. Individual item prices can be eliminated and replaced with a single shelf tag. After all, the cashier doesn't need to know the prices; the computer she's wired to can recall those speedily and accurately. Naturally clerks involved in pricing, controlling and maintaining inventory are redundant, as are the many cashiers who cannot ring in prices as fast as the scanner can read them. Additional cashier jobs are lost through the computer's ability to chart weekly sales volume in half-hour increments. This allows management to schedule workers for the minimum number of checkout lanes that need to be open to handle the normal customer flow at any point during the sales week. This last "benefit" for cost-cutters has become a source of physical and psychological stress for many cashiers. As the number of impatient customers in their line increases, the pressure to work at top speed throughout the shift builds correspondingly, eventually causing muscular and cervical strain as well as eliminating much of the personal interaction with shoppers which was once the most enjoyable aspect of the cashier's job.

11   Fewer jobs and more stress may be the cost workers must pay for store modernization, but how will shoppers be affected? How can UPC-based systems neutralize consumer awareness and transfer more dollars from shoppers' purses into the till? Put simply, the various schemes for gaining maximum corporate benefits from

scanning can be summed up by those watchwords of the microtechnological revolution: "Information is power." Collecting and analyzing data on the transactions which go through scanner-equipped registers is the fastest growing area of the retail food industry, with substantial spin-off benefits available to food manufacturers who want to pay for information which may assist their marketing programmes.

A typical example of this new approach to market research is A.C. Neilsen's Electronic Diary Service, which provides weekly reports to subscribers on the buying behaviour of 600 selected households in Toronto which purchase groceries in stores using scanners. The reports include an assessment of household penetration of products by individual brand size and price, buying frequency and size/flavour duplication within households, as well as consumer profiles and shopping characteristics of different types of households, income groups, working housewives, coupon users and convenience food lovers, to cite only a few of the categories studied by researchers. 12

Because their most profitable products are hit badly by generics, major manufacturers gladly pay for information on name brands; trial and repeat sales, brand loyalty and switchovers and cross-category relationships are all examined by the high priests of marketing to determine what makes a shopper select one product over another. Cross-category relationships are also very useful to retailers. A simple example can be noticed during the brief strawberry season in early summer. When strawberries move, so do shortcakes, ice cream and whipped cream. A loss leader on one of these items may stimulate sales of all the others. Likewise, a slight drop in the price of hot dogs during the barbecue season may trigger additional sales in condiments, buns, ground beef and charcoal. All of these associated products can be marked up slightly, if necessary, to more than compensate for lower profits on the hot dogs. 13

How much to charge for a product is resolved much more easily — and profitably — with scanners on the job. Marketing programmes to evaluate how high you can push the price of an item without losing sales movement was a strategy for using scanning data proposed at a 1977 seminar for food retailers in Chicago. Executives for *Ralph's*, a large U.S. chain, may have attended that session and listened closely. Last year the chain tested a substantial price increase for its private-label orange juice at two of its scanner stores, monitoring the results by calling up daily sales data from in-store computers. When no loss of sales volume was detected, the price increase was made chain-wide. This new ability to quickly judge price elasticity on its own brand products could by itself bring *Ralph's* an additional $1.5 million in profits annually. Canadian 14 retailers are close-mouthed about any of their own experiments in this area.

15   None of these schemes for milking consumers, however, has nearly the short-run profit potential of the simplest and most noticeable effect of scanning technology: the loss of item pricing. Eliminating individual price stickers on packaged products represents a major turnaround in the war on consumer price consciousness, and demonstrates the obverse of the maxim that knowledge is power — a lack of knowledge is powerlessness. Price conscious consumers don't respond as well to slick advertizing and they exhibit a low degree of brand loyalty. They mess up shelves by searching for cans with last week's prices still on them and buy fewer impulse, high-profit items. Price consciousness is the only marketing tool consumers have at their disposal to keep their necessary expenditures down. Any tactic which reduces such awareness will help enrich the industry.

16   The only argument advanced by retail industry apologists for eliminating item pricing emphasizes the corresponding elimination of all the labour now needed to affix all those price stickers in the store. But figures to verify this implied benefit to consumers are never supplied, because the per-item cost of individual price marking when passed on to the shopper is negligible. On an $80 grocery bill, item pricing accounts for less than 25 cents, and is a real bargain when placed against the power the shopper retains by having access to that most useful bit of pricing information.

17   No estimates are available on how much the retail food industry will profit from price removal, though the corporate chains in the U.S. have spared no expense in fighting lobbying efforts for legislated item pricing. In Ontario, the major chains have contentedly watched the provincial government defuse similar lobbying attempts. An extensive survey conducted by the Ministry of Consumer and Commercial Relations (known to consumer activists in Ontario as the Ministry of Foxes and Chickens) showed that 87 per cent of shoppers favoured legislated item pricing. It was ignored by the Minister, Frank Drea, though he had earlier promised that "the consumers will have the last word on this issue." Presently only Quebec enforces item pricing, though this is done in that province through the threat of a strict pricing law which has already been passed by the National Assembly, but not yet proclaimed.

18   What effects will the new technology have on the future of food retailing? Predictions agree on one vital point: with their advantages in technology and productivity, large supermarkets will grow in size and almost completely cannibalize small and medium-sized

stores in the next fifteen years. This will further concentrate retail food sales in an industry where five major chains already control about 60 per cent of all sales. Reduced competition and higher profits are the natural outcome of such an oligopoly — an economic truism already well known to Canadians in the West, where U.S. retailing giant Safeway controls over 50 per cent of the food sales, with nearly double the profit ratio of its eastern cousins.

Small stores won't be entirely eliminated, but they will have to adapt. As "superstores," which sell everything from tuna fish to televisions, continue to sprout in the quest for higher volumes, narrow specialty stores — food boutiques — will attract more middle- to upper-income shoppers. The big chains will fight this trend with their own high-priced specialty areas located on the periphery of their stores. 19

Longer-range prospects for the retail food industry may render even UPC-based technology obsolete. Shopping for food in the year 2000 may be a solitary experience. Energy costs and the emergence of television shopping systems along the Telidon* model will encourage the phasing out of neighbourhood stores and their substitution by large, automated warehouses where orders are made up and delivered in response to selections made in the home from electronic catalogues. Even before this shopping style takes hold, however, the local supermarket may be transformed into a businessman's dream, a store barren of paid help. This is possible with the technology available today. Automated Funds Transfer systems, now in use in pilot projects in the U.S. coupled with antitheft devices similar to those used by libraries to stop unauthorized removal of books, could make all cashiers redundant. Shoppers can easily be trained to scan and package their own groceries, paying for them with their plastic AFT card. Complete self-service, all supposedly in the name of "lower prices." 20

By that point, the consumer's mind may well be an open book to retailers and manufacturers alike; preferences, vulnerabilities and presently unpredictable behaviour will have been reduced to a few factors which can be computed and manipulated easily by those in control of twenty years' worth of scanning data. Whether organized consumers and organized labour can safeguard their interests in the struggle for jobs and dollars is uncertain. We know that the price will always be right, but for whom? 21

*Telidon: a system of television linked with computers, which enables the user, at home, to receive and send information

Structure:

1. Bill Reno introduces his argument with an unusually large amount of background information. Why? Where does the introduction end and the main argument begin?
2. Point out the THESIS STATEMENT of Reno's argument.
3. Reno divides the effects of supermarket high tech into two parts: effects on store employees and effects on customers. Point out the transitional passage between these parts.
4. Point out five *effects* of supermarket technology on clerks and/or cashiers.
5. Point out three *effects* of supermarket technology on customers.
6. Point out three paragraphs that are devoted mainly to examples. How convincing are these examples?
7. In his last two paragraphs, what is Reno's basic strategy for concluding the argument? How well does it work on you?

Style:

1. It is unlikely that Bill Reno, as a union employee, has set out to produce an OBJECTIVE analysis of supermarket technology. Discuss the following terms from his argument. Which of them appeal more to our emotions than to our intellect? Do any go so far as to openly encourage bias?
   "crusade against labour costs" (par. 3)
   "turn the tide of consumerism" (par. 7)
   "the final solution" (par. 7)
   "the tip of the iceberg" (par. 9)
   "transfer more dollars from shoppers' purses into the till" (par. 11)
   "the high priests of marketing" (par. 13)
   "close-mouthed" (par. 14)
   "schemes for milking consumers" (par. 15)
   "war on consumer price consciousness" (par. 15)
   "the Ministry of Foxes and Chickens" (par. 17)
   "cannibalize" (par. 18)
   "oligopoly" (par. 18)
   "sprout" (par. 19)
   "a store barren of paid help" (20)
2. Suppose that Bill Reno were not the "Education Director" of a union organization but an executive for Loblaws, Safeway or Dominion. Rewrite his argument (a short version if you prefer), using the same basic information but from his new point of view.

3. Is an OBJECTIVE analysis better than a SUBJECTIVE one? How often does our choice depend on the situation? Name a topic that you might treat objectively. Name another that you might treat subjectively. Name a reader or group of readers for whom you would probably write objectively. Name another individual or group for whom you would probably write subjectively. Would you tend to write the same way on one topic to all groups, or the same way to one group on all topics? Why or why not?

Ideas:

1. Americans spend about 16.1 per cent of their disposable income on food — less than any other people in the world. In 1982 Canadians came next at 16.4 per cent. West Germans spent 23.7 per cent, Japanese 24.8 per cent, Italians 29.1 per cent and Russians over 35 per cent (figures from Statistics Canada, quoted in *The Canadian Encyclopedia*). What do these figures suggest? Should we stop worrying about the cost of food because others pay more? Or should we resist any "war on consumer price consciousness" to guard our present status? Should we eat better because the price is right? Should we send more food to victims of drought overseas?

2. In paragraph 20 Reno envisions ". . . the phasing out of neighbourhood stores and their substitution by large, automated warehouses where orders are made up and delivered in response to selections made in the home from electronic catalogues." What do you imagine the effects of this would be on employees? On consumers? Write a narrative describing the future equivalent of a grocery shopping trip.

3. Do you do your banking by machine? Or do you prefer a teller even if it means waiting longer? What are the main effects of electronic banking on the employees? On management? On customers?

4. Do you know anyone who has lost a job because of automation? Tell the details. Do you believe that, in general, automation causes unemployment? If so, is automation justified? How much unemployment might result if Canada resisted automation while other countries did not?

5. In paragraph 10 Reno suggests that tighter scheduling of work hours rushes cashiers and thus eliminates ". . . much of the personal interaction with shoppers which was once the most enjoyable aspect of the cashier's job." How important is personal interaction in shopping? Are you willing to pay more for a less

efficient system that allows time for human contact? Or is price the only factor?

6. If you have read "Living with Automation in Winnipeg," compare the effects of technology on employees as seen by Ian Adams and Bill Reno.

7. What are your techniques for buying the food you want at the price you are willing to pay? Write an essay explaining the *effects* of your strategy as a grocery shopper.

(NOTE: See also the Topics for Writing at the end of this chapter.)

Wendy Dennis

A Tongue-Lashing for Deaf Ears

Wendy Dennis is an editor, teacher and free-lance writer. Born in 1950, she has lived in Toronto all her life. After attending York University and the University of Toronto, she taught high-school English for seven years, then, "terminally bored with that line of work," discovered a deeper interest while attending Ryerson Polytechnical Institute's journalism program. Since that time she has published extensively in periodicals such as Maclean's, Toronto Life, City Woman, Homemaker's, Chatelaine, Ontario Living *and* New Woman. *She is also features editor of* Toronto Life *and an instructor in Ryerson's magazine journalism program. Dennis states that our selection ". . . is one of my favorites because I got to sound off about one of my pet peeves and get paid for it! I wrote the thing very quickly, because I had been steaming about it for a while. . . . If you have a strong view about something and it means a lot to you to share it with others, there's nothing like writing it down. . . ." "A Tongue-Lashing for Deaf Ears" appeared in 1981 in the "Podium" column of* Maclean's.

The last time I went to the movies and got stuck beside a motor-mouth whose IQ bore an uncanny resemblance to his shoe size, I vowed, like Peter Finch in *Network*, that I was mad as hell and I wasn't going to take it anymore. That night I dreamt that my own rage-twisted face was projected in cinemascopic grandeur on the screen, while my Charlton Heston voice boomed hideous warnings in Dolby sound at foolish would-be noisemakers. No longer would I smile sweetly and apologize for the unusual craving I had to follow the plot without a Howard Cosell play-by-play; no longer would I stand miserably by while some pimply-faced prefect with a flashlight solemnly asked the buffoon on my right to please stop belching through the love scenes. It was time to retaliate.

I considered my options carefully. I thought of Nancy Reagan, who reportedly sleeps with "a tiny little gun" beside her bed, and had to admit that her solution, like the First Lady herself, possessed a certain clean elegance. But I didn't require a lethal weapon. A canister of tear gas maybe? Or a branding iron? Perhaps one of those guns they use to stun cattle before transforming them into the neat little cellophane packages you find under the red lights at supermarkets. I liked the poetic justice of that. Stun the beast and call four of those scrubbed choirboys theatres inevitably hire as ushers to deposit him under the marquee, where he would symbolize the long-overdue revolt of the Silent Movie Majority.

3   Noisy invasion of public spaces by yahoos is hardly a new problem but, unless my experience has been atypical, it seems to be nearing epidemic proportions. And the brutes are branching out. No longer content merely to destroy the sweet holy silence of the movie houses, like nasty malignant cells, they're now everywhere — and they're out for blood. I see them on subway platforms, where their infernal amplified radios bring demented stares to other passengers' faces but never seem to rouse the offenders from their somnambulant stupor. I've pulled up beside roving packs of them at red lights, where they stare like zombies, blithely unaware that the decibel level of their tape decks is precipitating anxiety attacks in passers-by for miles. I've come face to face with them as close to home as a campsite in Algonquin Park and as far away as a surf-washed beach in Bali; recently I've even encountered them at live theatre. All of which convinces me there's something awry in the land.

4   But to blame it entirely on a lapse in good manners is, I think, to miss the whole point. It has to do with something much larger and scarier than rudeness. What brought it all home to me was an incident that occurred in a Grade 12 English class I was teaching a few years ago. While we discussed a movie everyone had seen, I saw a wonderful opportunity to interject a few comments about my pet obsession — the invasion of movies by morons. Before I could sermonize, one of the boys said, "I know just what you're going to say and it bugs me too." Delighted I'd be preaching to the converted, I tried to continue, but he interrupted me again: "It really burns me when I go to the movies with my friends and we're horsing around and some jerk turns around and asks us to be quiet." When my berserk ravings had melted into a whimpering whine, I was struck by an overwhelming sadness — the kind of sadness one feels when a familiar touchstone has been lost. Here was someone I knew to be quite normal, sometimes even thoughtful, explaining how people who requested quiet in movies constituted an invasion of *his* rights. There was no doubt about it — something was certainly rotten.

5   I blame television. Though TV is a convenient whipping boy, what else could have so warped that boy's perception of what a movie ought to be? Like the tube he switches on for company the moment he gets home, the movie screen is just supposed to be there — several dollars worth of objective background noise for *his* performance. Add to that insidious ethic a healthy dose of egocentricity, and you begin to understand the value system of the

radio-schleppers too. If they travel in hermetically sealed vacuum-packed capsules of indifference, so must everyone else. Sadly then, all the reliable approaches to solving such a problem, like asking the offenders to quieten down, no longer work. What's worse, it has been my experience that *any* approach tends to evoke obscene remarks or the verbal equivalent of two longs and a short. Perhaps soon the home video revolution will keep them safely locked up and they will venture into the public domain only spasmodically to cart away armloads of tapes from the corner video outlet. Until then, however, this travesty demands a little noisemaking from the rest of us.

6   Now I've never been one to shirk a struggle, but I'll admit this one is getting me down. I'm weary of paying to see a film and getting a rumble instead. I'm tired of cowardly theatre managers who won't throw the bums out. But most of all I'm sick of this rabid Canadian disease of deferential politeness — even to neanderthals who deserve nothing better than to have their eyes burned out with projector bulbs. I figure we've got one chance only. If, in a few short years, the nonsmokers could make us feel like social lepers for lighting up in public, maybe we can do the same to the noise polluters. Is anybody out there listening?

Structure:

1. What basic technique does Wendy Dennis use to introduce her essay?
2. In paragraph 2 Dennis names her "options" for controlling noisy people in public places: a gun, tear gas, a branding iron, etc. How do you react to this passage? What is its real purpose?
3. In what major way does paragraph 3 contribute to Dennis' argument?
4. Roughly what proportion of this essay consists of examples? How effective would the argument be without them? Choose the best example and explain what it achieves.
5. Paragraph 5 blames the epidemic on television and "egocentricity." Why do you think Dennis waits until almost three-quarters of the way through her argument to analyze these *causes*? What is the effect of this strategy?
6. Point out all the comparisons and contrasts that Dennis uses in paragraph 6 to heighten the force of her closing.
7. "Is anybody out there listening?" asks Dennis in the last line. What does this question attempt to achieve? Does it succeed?

Style:

1. Wendy Dennis tells us in her opening sentence that she is "mad as hell." What other COLLOQUIAL or SLANG expressions do you find in her essay? Could she have expressed her feelings as clearly using more FORMAL language?
2. What FIGURE OF SPEECH does Dennis use in paragraph 3 when she says that noise polluters are "like nasty malignant cells"? Point out five more SIMILES or METAPHORS in this selection.
3. The term "yahoos" (par. 3) is an ALLUSION to the semi-human monsters of Jonathan Swift's book *Gulliver's Travels*. To what does "the Silent Movie Majority" of paragraph 2 allude? What is the effect of this allusion? In what way can allusions help to create a CONCISE STYLE?

Ideas:

1. There is no doubt that Wendy Dennis is angry. Why, then, does she also give her essay a humorous TONE, as in paragraph 1? Is anger a good motivation for writing? In what ways may it help? In what ways may it harm? In your opinion, what is the overall effect of Dennis' anger on the quality of her essay?
2. Do you agree with Dennis that noise in public places is disagreeable? That it is a real problem? If so, give two or three examples from your own experience. Or are you on the side of the "noise polluters"? Is Dennis unjustly trying to stop your legitimate fun? If so, explain why you should be allowed to talk in "the sweet holy silence of the movie houses" or play your radio on the beach.
3. Is life louder today than in past times? Name at least five forms of "noise pollution" that you hear every day. How many of them would you have heard a century ago? Is most "noise pollution" caused simply by the advance of technology or is it caused mainly by a deterioration of our regard for others?
4. Explain the meaning of "touchstone" (par. 4), using a dictionary if necessary. Through her encounters with people who make noise, Wendy Dennis has lost one of her "familiar touchstones." Name a few of your "familiar touchstones." Have you "lost" any of them in your lifetime so far? If so which, and how? And how has the "loss" affected you?
5. Have you noticed the "rabid Canadian disease of deferential politeness" that Dennis laments in her final paragraph? Are we too tolerant toward those who violate social norms? Or even

toward other countries that violate our national norms? If so, give examples. If not, explain why not.

6. Do you think Dennis is right that television is a *cause* of noisemaking in theatres? Has television had other *effects* on society? If so, choose one of them and explore it in an essay of *cause and effect.*

7. Wendy Dennis' "pet obsession" is noise in public places. For many other people (par. 6) it is smokers who light up in public. What is your own "pet obsession"? Write an essay analyzing the *cause* or *causes* of the thing that bothers you. Like Dennis, give vivid and concrete examples to illustrate the problem.

(NOTE: See also the Topics for Writing at the end of this chapter.)

Franklin Russell

The Capelin

Once a professional hunter, Franklin Russell is now a naturalist and an internationally respected writer about nature. He was born in 1922 in New Zealand, but he has also lived in Australia, Great Britain, Canada (he is a Canadian citizen) and, since 1963, the United States. Having been a farmer, hunter, forester and erosion control specialist and having travelled to most parts of the globe, Russell has experienced nature first-hand in a multitude of environments. It is from these experiences that he has written a succession of vivid and wise books about nature — among them the much-beloved Watchers at the Pond *(1961). Margaret Laurence once stated, "Franklin Russell is one of the very few writers who can communicate the essential fact that the planet is totally alive." In a prose of rare power, Russell demonstrates this gift in "The Capelin," a chapter from his book* The Hunting Animal *(1983).*

1   Beyond the northern beach, a gray swell rolls in from Greenland and runs softly along the shore. The horizon is lost in a world of gray, and gulls glide, spectral in the livid air. Watching, I am enveloped in the sullen waiting time and feel the silence, drawn out long and thin. I wait for the sea to reveal a part of itself.

2   A capelin is perhaps the best-hunted creature on earth. It is not more than five inches long, about the size of a young herring, and undistinguished in appearance, except that when it is freshly caught, it is the color of mercury. As the capelin dies, its silvery scales tarnish and the glitter goes out like a light, ending a small allegory about nature, a spectacle of victims, victors, and an imperative of existence. Its death illuminates a dark process of biology in which there are shadows of other, more complex lives.

3   The capelin are born to be eaten. They transform oceanic plankton into flesh which is then hunted greedily by almost every sea creature that swims or flies. Their only protection is fecundity. One capelin survives to adulthood from every ten thousand eggs laid, and yet a single school may stir square miles of sea.

4   In mid-June, the capelin gather offshore. They can be seen everywhere and at all times in history, symbols of summer and fertility, of Providence and danger. I see them along the shores of Greenland, Iceland, Norway, and near Spitsbergen. I follow them across the northern coast of Russia. Chill air, gray seas, the

northern silences, are the capelin's world in Alaska, in the
Aleutians, around Hudson Bay, and along the northeastern shores
of North America. But the capelin of the Newfoundland coast are
the most visible. Here, they spawn on the beaches rather than in
deep water offshore, and I have to see their rush for eternity.

They gather a thousand feet offshore, coalescing into groups of a 5
hundred thousand to break the water's surface with bright
chuckling sounds. They gather, and grow. Soon they are in the
millions, and with other millions swimming up from the offshore
deeps. They gather, now in the billions, so densely packed together
in places that the sea shimmers silver for miles and flows,
serpentine, with the swelling body of a single, composite creature.

The fish do, in fact, possess a common sense of purpose. Nothing 6
can redirect their imperative to breed. I once swam among them and
saw them parting reluctantly ahead of me, felt their bodies flicking
against my hands. Looking back, I saw them closing in, filling up
the space created by my passage. The passive fish tolerated me, in
their anticipation of what they were about to do.

At this time of the year they are so engrossed that they barely 7
react when a host of creatures advances to kill them. Beneath and
beyond them, codfish pour up out of the deep. They overtake the
capelin, eat them, plunge their sleek dark bodies recklessly into
shallow water. Some have swum so rapidly from such depths that
their swim bladders are distended by the sudden drop in water
pressure. The cod are gigantic by comparison with the capelin.
Many weigh one hundred pounds or more, and will not be sated until
they have eaten scores of capelin each. The water writhes with
movement and foam where cod, headlong in pursuit, drive
themselves above the surface and fall back with staccato slaps.

The attack of the codfish is a brutal opening to a ritual, and a 8
contradiction in their character. Normally, they are sedentary
feeders on the sea floor. Now, however, they are possessed. Their
jaws rip and tear; the water darkens with capelin blood: the
shredded pieces of flesh hang suspended or rise to the surface.

Now a group of seabirds, the parrotlike puffins, clumsy in flight, 9
fly above the capelin, their grotesque, axlike beaks probing from
side to side as they watch the upper layers of the massacre. They are
joined by new formations of birds until several thousand puffins are
circling. They are silent, and there is no way of knowing how they
were summoned from their nesting burrows on an island that is out
of sight. They glide down to the water — stub-winged cargo planes
— land awkwardly, taxi with fluttering wings and stamping,
paddling feet, then dive.

At the same time, the sea view moves with new invasions of 10
seabirds. Each bird pumps forward with an urgency that suggests it

has received the same stimulus as the cod. The gulls that breed on cliffs along a southern bay come first, gracefully light of wing, with raucous voice as they cry out their anticipation. Beneath them, flying flat, direct, silent, come murres, black-bodied, short-tailed, close relatives of the puffins. The murres land and dive without ceremony. Well offshore, as though waiting confirmation of the feast, shearwaters from Tristan da Cunha turn long pointed wings across the troughs of waves and cackle like poultry.

11   The birds converge, and lose their identity in the mass thickening on the water. Small gulls — the kittiwakes, delicate in flight — screech and drop and rise and screech and drop like snowflakes on the sea. They fall among even smaller birds, lighter than they, which dangle their feet and hover at the water's surface, almost walking on water as they seek tiny pieces of shredded flesh. These are the ocean-flying petrels, the Mother Carey's chickens of mariners' legends, which rarely come within sight of land. All order is lost in the shrieking tumult of hundreds of thousands of birds.

12   Underwater, the hunters meet among their prey. The puffins and murres dive below the capelin and attack, driving for the surface. The cod attack at mid-depth. The gulls smother the surface and press the capelin back among the submarine hunters. The murres and puffins fly underwater, their beating wings turning them rapidly back and forth. They meet the cod, flail their wings in desperate haste, are caught, crushed, and swallowed. Now seabirds as well as capelin become the hunted. Puffin and murre tangle wings. Silver walls of capelin flicker, part, re-form. Some seabirds surface abruptly, broken wings dangling. Others, with a leg or legs torn off, fly frantically, crash, skitter in shock across the water.

13   I see the capelin hunters spread across the sea, but also remember them in time. Each year, the hunters are different, because many of them depend on a fortuitous meeting with their prey. A group of small whales collides with the capelin, and in a flurry of movement, they eat several tons of them. Salmon throw themselves among the capelin with the same abandon as the codfish, and in the melee become easy victims for a score of seals which kill dozens of them, then turn to the capelin and gorge themselves nearly stuporous. They rise, well beyond the tumult of the seabirds, their black heads jutting like rocks from the swell, to lie with distended bellies and doze away their feast. Capelin boil up around them for a moment but now the animals ignore them.

14   The capelin are hosts in a ceremony so ancient that a multitude of species have adapted to seeking a separate share of the host's bounty. The riotous collision of cod, seal, whale, and seabird obscures the smaller guests at the feast. Near the shore are small brown fish — the cunner, one of the most voracious species. Soon

they will be fighting among themselves for pieces of flesh as the capelin begin their run for the beach, or when the survivors of the spawning reel back into deep water, with the dead and dying falling to the bottom. If the water is calm and the sun bright, the cunner can be seen working in two fathoms, ripping capelin corpses to pieces and scattering translucent scales like silver leaves in a wind of the sea.

Closer inshore, at the wave line, the flounder wait. They know the   15
capelin are coming and their role is also predetermined. They cruise rapidly under the purling water in uncharacteristic excitement. They are not interested in capelin flesh. They want capelin eggs, and they will eat them as soon as spawning starts.

Now the most voracious of all the hunters appears. Fishing   16
vessels come up over the horizon. They brought the Portuguese of the fifteenth century, who anchored offshore, dropped their boats, and rowed ashore to take the capelin with hand nets, on beaches never before walked by white men. They brought Spaniards and Dutchmen, Englishmen and Irish, from the sixteenth to the twentieth centuries. Americans, Nova Scotians, Gloucestermen, schoonermen, bankermen, long-liner captains, have participated in the ritual. All of them knew that fresh capelin is the finest bait when it is skillfully used, and can attract a fortune in codfish flesh, hooked on the submarine banks to the south.

But presently, these hunters are Newfoundlanders. They bring   17
their schooners flying inshore like great brown-and-white birds, a hundred, two hundred, three hundred sail. They heel through the screaming seabirds, luff, anchor, and drop their dories with the same precision of movement of the other figures in the ritual. In an hour, three thousand men are at work from the boats. They work as the codfish work, with a frenzy that knots forearms and sends nets spilling over the sterns to encircle the capelin. They lift a thousand tons of capelin out of the sea, yet they do not measurably diminish the number of fish.

Meanwhile, landbound hunters wait for the fish to come within   18
range of their lead-weighted hand nets. Women, children, and old people crowd the beach with the ablebodied men. The old people have ancestral memories of capelin bounty. In the seventeenth and eighteenth centuries, when food was often short, only the big capelin harvest stood between the shore people and starvation during the winter.

Many of the shore people are farmers who use the capelin for   19
fertilizer as well as for food. Capelin corpses, spread to rot over thin northern soils, draw obedient crops of potatoes and cabbages out of the ground, and these, mixed with salted capelin flesh, become winter meals.

20   The children, who remember dried capelin as their candy, share the excitement of waiting. They chase one another up and down the beach and play with their own nets and fishing rods. Some are already asleep because they awoke before dawn to rouse the village, as they do every capelin morning, with the cry: "They've a-come, they've a-come!"

21   At the top of the beach, old women lie asleep or sit watching the seabirds squabbling and the dorymen rowing. They are Aunt Sadie and Little Nell and Bessie Blue and Mother Taunton, old ladies from several centuries. They know the capelin can save children in hard winters when the inshore cod fishery fails. They get up at two o'clock in the morning when the capelin are running, to walk miles to the nearest capelin beach. They net a barrel of fish, then roll the barrel, which weighs perhaps a hundred pounds, back home. They have finished spreading the fish on their gardens, or salting them, before the first of their grandchildren awakes.

22   They have clear memories of catching capelin in winter, when the sea freezes close inshore and the tide cracks the ice in places. Then millions of capelin, resting out the winter, rise in the cracks. An old woman with a good net can take tons of passive fish out of the water for as long as her strength lasts and the net can still reach them.

23   A cry rises from the beach: "Here they come!"

24   The ritual must be played out, according to habit. The dorymen and the seabirds, the rampaging cod and cunner, cannot touch or turn the purpose of the capelin. At a moment, its genesis unknown, they start for the shore. From the top of some nearby cliffs I watch and marvel at the precision of their behavior. The capelin cease to be a great, formless mass offshore. They split into groups that the Newfoundlanders call wads — rippling gray lines, five to fifty feet wide — and run for the shore like advancing infantry lines. One by one, they peel away from their surviving comrades and advance, thirty to forty wads at a time.

25   Each wad has its discipline. The fish prepare to mate. Each male capelin seeks a female, darting from one fish to another. When he finds one, he presses against her side. Another male, perhaps two males, press against her other side. The males urge the female on toward the beach. Some are struck down by diving seabirds but others take their places. Cod dash among them and smash their sexual formations; they re-form immediately. Cunner rise and rip at them; flounder dart beneath them toward the beach.

26   The first wad runs into beach wavelets, and a hundred nets hit the water together; a silver avalanche of fish spills out on the beach. In each breaking wavelet the capelin maintain their formations, two or three males pressed tightly against their female until they are all flung up on the beach. There, to the whispering sound of tiny fins

and tails vibrating, the female convulsively digs into the sand, which is still moving in the wake of the retreating waves. As she goes down, she extrudes up to fifty thousand eggs, and the males expel their milt.

The children shout; their bare feet fly over the spawning fish; sea   27
boots grind down; the fish spill out; gulls run in the shallows under the children's feet; the flounder gorge. A codfish, two feet long, leaps out of the shallows and hits the beach. An old man scoops it up. The wads keep coming. The air is filled with birds. The dorymen shout and laugh.

The flood of eggs becomes visible. The sand glistens, then is   28
greasy with eggs. They pile in drift lines that writhe back and forth in each wave. The female capelin wriggle into masses of eggs. The shallows are permeated with eggs. The capelin breathe eggs. Their mouths fill with eggs. Their stomachs are choked with eggs. The wads keep pouring onward, feeding the disaster on the beach.

Down come the boots and the nets, and the capelin die, mouths   29
open, and oozing eggs. The spawning is a fiasco. The tide has turned. Instead of spawning on the shore with the assurance of rising water behind them, each wad strikes ashore in retreating water. Millions are stranded, but the wads keep coming.

In the background, diminished by the quantity of fish, other   30
players gasp and pant at their nets. Barrels stack high on the beach. Horses whinny, driven hard up the bank at the back of the beach. Carts laden with barrels weave away. Carts bringing empty barrels bounce and roar down. The wads are still coming. Men use shovels to lift dead and dying fish from drift lines that are now two and three feet high. The easterly wind is freshening. The wavelets become waves. The capelin are flung up on the beach without a chance to spawn. They bounce and twist and the water flees beneath them.

It is twilight, then dark; torches now spot the beach, the offshore   31
dories, and the schooners. The waves grow solidly and pile the capelin higher. The men shovel the heaps into pyramids, then reluctantly leave the beach. Heavy rain blots out beach and sea.

I remain to watch the blow piling up the sea. At the lowest point of   32
the tide, it is driving waves high up on the beach, roiling the sand, digging up the partially buried eggs, and carrying them out to sea. By dawn most of the eggs are gone. The capelin have disappeared. The seabirds, the schooners, the cod, flounder, cunner, seals, whales, have gone. Nothing remains except the marks of human feet, the cart tracks on the high part of the beach, the odd pyramid of dead fish. The feast is done.

The empty arena of the beach suggests a riddle. If the capelin   33
were so perfectly adapted to spawn on a rising tide, to master the task of burying eggs in running sand between the waves, to know

when the tide was rising, why did they continue spawning after the tide turned? Was that, by the ancient rules of the ritual, intentional? If it was, then it indicated a lethal error of anticipation that did not jibe with the great numbers of the capelin.

34   I wonder, then, if the weak died and the strong survived, but dismiss the notion after recalling the indiscriminate nature of all capelin deaths. There was no Darwinian selection for death of the stupid or the inexperienced. Men slaughtered billions, this year and last year and for three hundred years before, but the capelin never felt this pinpricking of their colossal corporate bodies. Their spawning was a disaster for reasons well beyond the influence of man.

35   A nineteenth-century observer, after seeing a capelin spawning, recorded his amazement at "the astonishing prosperity of these creatures, cast so willfully away." It was in the end, and indeed throughout the entire ritual, the sheer numbers of capelin that scored the memory. The prosperity of the capelin preceded the disaster but then, it seemed, created it. Prosperity was not beneficial or an assurance of survival. The meaning of the ritual was slowly growing into sense. Prosperity unhinges the capelin. It is a madness of nature. Prosperity, abundance, success, drive them on. They become transformed and throw themselves forward blindly. . . .

36   I turn from the beach, warm and secure, and take a blind step forward.

Structure:

1. This "ritual" of the capelin's spawning and death is organized roughly by time sequence. Point out the major steps in Russell's chronology. Is every step in chronological order? Why or why not?
2. In paragraph 4 Russell states that the capelin ". . . can be seen everywhere and at all times in history. . . ." and in paragraph 13 he writes, "I see the capelin hunters spread across the sea, but also remember them in time." In describing fishing schooners and persons long dead as if he sees them in the present with his own eyes, is Russell violating our sense of realism? Or in distorting time does he seek a greater effect? If so, what? Does he succeed?
3. Although we are discussing "The Capelin" as an example of development by cause and effect, Russell supports his argument with *description* as vivid as any in this book. Select the two or

three paragraphs of description that most strongly affect you, and point out their most vivid words or phrases.

4. The climactic *effect* of Russell's account is the "disaster" — the seemingly needless death of countless spawning capelin as a falling tide leaves them stranded on the beach. What possible *causes* for this disaster does he reject in paragraphs 33 and 34? Which cause does he accept in paragraph 35? And in what way does he relate that cause to his own actions in the closing sentence? What are the overall implications for the human race?

5. Through this long examination of the capelin's mating and death, Russell waits until the very last two paragraphs to reveal the *cause* of the "disaster." Why? And are there smaller examples of cause and effect along the way? If so, point out the most vivid ones.

Style:

1. On a scale of one to ten, with OBJECTIVE as one and SUBJECTIVE as ten, where would you rank "The Capelin"? Do you approve of Russell's approach? Is it scientific? Is it interesting or even dramatic? Can writing be both scientifically valid and dramatic at the same time?

2. Why does Russell use the pronoun "I" in this essay? Have you ever been told not to? If so, have you always followed that rule? Or does choice of first-person or third-person narration depend on the situation? If so, what are some factors in our choice?

3. Read paragraph 27 aloud. Raise your hand to signal each SENSE IMAGE (each appeal to our senses of sight, hearing, touch, taste and smell).

4. Read paragraph 28 aloud. What word is deliberately repeated several times, and why?

5. In paragraph 9 puffins are called "stub-winged cargo planes." Find at least five more METAPHORS in this selection. In paragraph 14 cunner are described "ripping capelin corpses to pieces and scattering translucent scales like silver leaves in a wind of the sea." Find at least five more SIMILES in this selection. What is the overall effect of so many FIGURES OF SPEECH?

Ideas:

1. Russell's introduction states that the capelin's death "...illuminates a dark process of biology in which there are

shadows of other, more complex lives" (par. 2). Shadows of whose lives? Do you sense any connection between this statement and the fact that Russell seems so personally involved in the capelin's "rush for eternity"? Explain.

2. If we view "The Capelin" as an ALLEGORY of the human race, what forces may we see as propelling us on our own "rush for eternity"?

3. In paragraph 16 Russell calls humans "...the most voracious of all the hunters...." After his description of voracious fish and birds slaughtering capelin, is this judgment accurate? In what ways are we more or less "voracious" than other species?

4. Franklin Russell reacts emotionally to nature. Do you? If so, describe a specific reaction that you had. Tell its *cause* or *causes*. Tell its *effect* or *effects*.

5. Russell has discussed the *effects* of "prosperity" (his term for density of population) among the capelin. Write your own essay analyzing the *effects* of population density among humans (if the whole human race is too large a group, focus on a subgroup: a nation, city, town, neighbourhood or even a family).

(NOTE: See also the Topics for Writing at the end of this chapter.)

Topics for Writing

Chapter 4: Cause and Effect

(Note also the topics for writing that appear after each selection in this chapter.)

Analyze the cause(s) and/or effect(s) of one of the following:

1. The use of credit cards
2. Divorce
3. Sexual promiscuity
4. Alcoholism
5. Gambling
6. Smoking
7. AIDS
8. Terrorism
9. Religious conversion
10. Learning a second language
11. Chemical additives in food
12. Anorexia nervosa
13. Overeating
14. Heart disease
15. Unemployment
16. Lotteries
17. Playing video games
18. Using a VCR
19. Using a Walkman
20. Using a bicycle or motorcycle
21. Owning a car
22. Immigration
23. High-rise development
24. Arson
25. Acid rain

"Well, the things you can see just standing for ten minutes at a big-city intersection. Lynda can't get over it. But, of course, she comes from a town where the main recreation is drinking."

Philip Marchand, "Learning to Love the Big City"

It's just the opposite of . . . .

5

COMPARISON AND CONTRAST

One of the most dramatic ways to make an argument is to compare and contrast. The term "comparison" is often used to mean the showing of both similarities and differences, but in its narrower sense refers only to the showing of similarities. A "contrast" shows differences. Of the two, contrast is the more dramatic and the more frequently used in essays.

You have experienced contrast to the fullest if you have ever experienced culture shock. As you arrive in a new country, the look of the buildings and streets, the smells in the air, the sounds, the language and customs all seem strange — because you are contrasting them to what you just left. And if you stay a long time, the same thing happens in reverse when you come back: home seems strange because you are contrasting it to the place where you've just been. The cars may seem too big, the food too bland, the pace of life too fast. Travel is one of the great educational experiences: through contrast, one culture puts another in perspective.

In writing an essay you can show similarities only or show both similarities and differences or show differences only. Do whatever best fits your subject and your message. But whichever way you do it, *choose subjects of the same general type:* two countries, two sports, two poems or two solutions to unemployment. Like Philip Marchand in "Learning to Love the Big City," you might contrast two centres of population — a town and a city — and in doing so make a logical point. But if you write about a city and an ant hill, no matter how much fun you have or what insights you get across, you will prove nothing — because people are not insects. Your argument will be an *analogy,* a more imaginative but less logical kind of argument, which we will explore in the next chapter.

Once you have chosen your two subjects of the same general type, you face another choice: how to arrange them. There are two basic ways:

Divide the essay into halves, devoting the first half to the town and the second to the city. This system is natural in a very short essay, because your reader remembers everything from the first half while reading the second half. It is also natural when for some reason the items seem most clearly discussed as a whole rather than in parts.

Divide the subjects into separate points. First contrast employment in both town and city, then recreation in both town and city, then social life in both town and city, and so on. This system is most natural in long essays: putting related material together helps the reader to grasp comparisons or contrasts without the strain of recalling every detail from ten pages back.

Marchand organizes mainly by halves, even though his essay is long. The feeling for life in both town and city develops best in long sections that have time to build their effects; if the contrasting feelings appeared in short alternating sections, they would merely cancel each other out. Like Marchand, do whatever works — that is, whatever fits your subject and your message.

Doris Anderson

The 51-Per-Cent Minority

Doris Anderson is one of Canada's most effective advocates of women's rights. She was born in Calgary in 1925. After earning her B.A. at the University of Alberta in 1945, she wrote radio scripts, worked in advertising, then in 1951 joined the staff of Chatelaine. As editor-in-chief from 1958 to 1977, Anderson added to the magazine's family emphasis an advocacy of higher social and economic status for women. She served as president of the Canadian Advisory Council on the Status of Women. Her sudden resignation from the council in 1981, in protest against the government's interference and its reluctance to guarantee equality of men and women in the Constitution, sparked a campaign by women that did achieve a constitutional guarantee of their rights. From 1982 to 1984 she was president of the National Action Committee on the Status of Women, an umbrella group that represents over a million women in 190 organizations. Anderson has published novels, Two Women *in 1978 and* Rough Layout *in 1981, in addition to her many editorials and articles. Our selection, "The 51-Per-Cent Minority," appeared in 1980 in* Maclean's. *Anderson has revised it slightly for this book.*

In any Canadian election the public will probably be hammered   1
numb with talk of the economy, energy and other current issues.
But there will always be some far more startling topics that no
one will talk about at all.

No one is going to say to all new Canadians: "Look, we're going   2
through some tough times. Three out of four of you had better face
the fact that you're always going to be poor. At 65 more than likely
you'll be living below the poverty level."

And no one is going to tell Quebeckers: "You will have to get along   3
on less money than the rest of the country. For every $1 the rest of
us earn, you, because you live in Quebec, will earn 61 cents."

I doubt very much that any political party is going to level with   4
the Atlantic provinces and say: "We don't consider people living
there serious prime workers. Forget about any special measures to
make jobs for you. In fact in future federal-provincial talks we're not
even going to discuss your particular employment problems."

And no politician is going to tell all the left-handed people in the   5
country: "Look, we know it looks like discrimination, but we have to
save some money somewhere. So, although you will go on paying
unemployment insurance at the same rates as everyone else, if you
get laid off your job, you'll only collect 50 per cent of your salary,
whereas everyone else will collect 66 per cent."

6   And no one is going to say to Canadian doctors: "We know you perform one of the most important jobs any citizen can perform, but from now on you're going to have to get along without any support systems. All hospital equipment and help will be drastically reduced. We believe a good doctor should instinctively know what to do — or you're in the wrong job. If you're really dedicated you'll get along."

7   As for blacks: "Because of the color of your skin, you're going to be paid less than the white person next to you who is doing exactly the same job. It's tough but that's the way it is."

8   As for Catholics: "You're just going to have to understand that you will be beaten up by people with other religious beliefs quite regularly. Even if your assailant threatens to kill you, you can't do anything about it. After all, we all need some escape valves, don't we?"

9   Does all of the above sound like some nihilistic nightmare where Orwellian forces have taken over? Well, it's not. It's all happening right now, in Canada.

10   It's not happening to new Canadians, Quebeckers, residents of the Atlantic provinces, left-handed people, doctors, blacks or Indians. If it were, there would be riots in the streets. Civil libertarians would be howling for justice. But all of these discriminatory practices are being inflicted on women today in Canada as a matter of course.

11   Most women work at two jobs — one inside the home and one outside. Yet three out of four women who become widowed or divorced or have never married live out their old age in poverty. And the situation is going to get worse.

12   Women workers earn, on an average, only 61 cents for every $1 a man gets — even though on an average, women are better educated than men.

13   And when governments start talking about basing unemployment insurance on family income or introducing the two-tier system of family income, they mean women will pay the same rates as other Canadians but if they lose their jobs, they will collect less, or may not collect at all.

14   What politician could possibly tell doctors to train each other and get along without all their high technology and trained help? Yet a more important job than saving lives is surely creating lives. But mothers get no training, no help in the way of more than a token family allowance, inadequate day-care centres, and almost nonexistent after-school programs.

15   No politician would dream of telling blacks they must automatically earn less than other people. But women sales clerks, waitresses and hospital orderlies almost always earn less than

males doing the same jobs. It would be called discrimination if a member of a religious group was beaten up, and the assailant would be jailed. But hundreds of wives get beaten by their husbands week in and week out, year after year. Some die, yet society acts as though it isn't happening at all.

Women make up 51 per cent of the population of this country. 16 Think of the kind of clout they could have if they used it at the polls. But to listen to the political parties, the woman voter just doesn't exist. When politicians talk to fishing folk they talk about improved processing plants and new docks. When they talk to wheat farmers they talk of better transportation and higher price supports. When they talk to people in the Atlantic provinces they talk about new federal money for buildings and more incentives for secondary industry. When they talk to ethnic groups they talk about better language training courses. But when they think of women — if they do at all — they assume women will vote exactly as their husbands — so why waste time offering them anything? It's mind-boggling to contemplate, though, how all those discriminatory practices would be swept aside if, instead of women, we were Italian, or black, or lived in Quebec or the Atlantic provinces.

Structure:

1. Is this essay mainly a comparison or a contrast?
2. Is the essay organized point by point or by halves?
3. Point out the passage of transition between Anderson's description of minorities and her description of women.
4. In this essay about women, why does Anderson never mention women until halfway through, at paragraph 10?
5. If you have read *1984* or *Animal Farm,* by George Orwell, tell how the reference to Orwell in paragraph 9 helps to explain Anderson's point.
6. Why does the closing bring in a series of new examples? And why are these examples so short?

Style:

1. How important is the title of an essay? What should it do? How effective is this one, and why?
2. Anderson's essay appeared in *Maclean's,* a magazine for the general reader. Name all the ways you can think of in which her essay seems designed for that person.

Ideas:

1. Explain the IRONY of Anderson's claim: in what sense are women, 51 per cent of the population, a "minority" in Canada?
2. Anderson describes numerous groups as not being exploited in the ways that women are. Has she missed other groups that you know to be exploited in Canada? If so, name them.
3. Anderson states in paragraph 11, "Most women work at two jobs — one inside the home and one outside." Suppose that at some time you and your spouse both have full-time jobs. If you are a woman, how much of the housework will you expect your husband to do? If you are a man, how much of the housework will you expect your wife to do? Whatever your answer, give reasons to support it.
4. Anderson writes in paragraph 12, "Women workers earn, on an average, only 61 cents for every $1 a man gets — even though on an average, women are better educated than men." Whether you are male or female, have you personally experienced this difference in wage levels? If so, give an example. How did you feel about it? How do some employers manage to pay men more than women? If you believe the practice is wrong, how could it be fought?
5. In paragraph 16, Anderson writes, "Women make up 51 per cent of the population of this country. Think of the kind of clout they could have if they used it at the polls." Do you agree that women have not yet used their voting power to best advantage? If so, why haven't they? And how could they begin to?
6. In "Canadians: What Do They Want?" Margaret Atwood points out that war and rape are ". . . two activities not widely engaged in by women . . . ." (par. 1). Do you think our world would be different if it were run by women? If so, why and in what ways? If not, why not?
7. Write an essay in which you *contrast* the way society trains girls to be women with the way society trains boys to be men.
8. Write an essay that *compares* either women or men to one of these:

servants	prison guards
masters	children
slaves	employers
prison inmates	employees

(NOTE: See also the Topics for Writing at the end of this chapter.)

Austin Clarke

Old Year's Night *

Austin Chesterfield Clarke is Canada's best-known black writer. He was born in Barbados in 1932, went to school there, then in 1955 moved to Canada and studied at the University of Toronto. Not all of Clarke's professional life has been spent in Canada. He has served as advisor to the prime minister of Barbados, as cultural attaché of the embassy of Barbados in Washington, D.C., and as general manager of the Caribbean Broadcasting Corporation. He has also been a visiting professor at numerous universities in the United States as well as in Canada. Now he lives in Toronto. Since 1964 Clarke has written or edited some twenty books, among them a widely read trilogy of novels about West Indians living in Toronto: The Meeting Point *(1967),* Storm of Fortune *(1973) and* The Bigger Light *(1975). Although our selection comes from* Growing Up Stupid Under the Union Jack *(1980), Clarke's account of his own boyhood, it shares the vivid dialogue and rich style of his fiction.*

E veryone in the village — our mothers, big sisters, aunts, uncles and fathers — worked at some time at the Marine Hotel. It was a huge building washed in pink, with tall casuarina trees for miles and miles up in the blue sky; and at night it almost touched the stars which we counted beyond five hundred, although the sages of little boys among us said, "If you ever count past five hundred stars, yuh going *drop-down* dead, yuh!"   1

After midnight only ghosts and fowl-cock thieves walked the streets from the Marine, past the church which had a graveyard of dead Englishmen and English vicars and an English sailor which a tombstone called an "ensign."   2

And when we ventured too close to the walls of the Marine Hotel on Old Year's Night — the highest moment in our lives — the watchman, dressed in an old black jacket to suit the night, and khaki trousers rolled up above the ankles, and who knew the lay and geography of each rock and glass-bottle in the roads and lanes surrounding the grounds, this night watchman would challenge us. "Where the arse wunnuh think wunnuh going?"   3

If we stood our ground, which we never did, and stated our mission, which he never accepted, we would end up running from him, with the fear of his bull-pistle* in our back. We soon learned   4

---

*Editor's title
*bull-pistle: a whip made from the penis of a bull

163

that we could take liberties only when he had a woman in the flower bed of blooming begonias.

5 On Old Year's Night there would be balloons with faces painted on them, bigger and prettier than we had ever seen before. And music by the best dance bands in the country. Coe Alleyne's Orchestra, Percy Greene's Orchestra and others. The music would slip over the wall which was too high and treacherous for us to climb.

6 Outside the free wall hundreds of boys and unemployed men, and some girls who were old enough to have boyfriends and be out at night, would stand in the dew dressed in men's jackets, always black, to keep the dew from seeping into our bones, so the old people said, and to give us consumption, which was our term for tuberculosis. We would dance to the music in our native rhythmic steps, moving over the pebbles in the road, and watch the white people inside because the Marine was "blasted serrigated."*

7 The men inside wore formal black suits that turned them into undertakers. And the women were white in long dresses skating over the huge dance floor, slippery and dangerous to unpractised steps from the waxing which the watchman had given it the day before. "Woe betide the man who don't know a waltz from a trot when he step 'pon that floor!" he would boast to us.

8 We watched them from below the wall. And we dreamed of becoming powerful and rich, to join them, to be like them. The waiters, our "relatives," our family, were mingling among them now: our fathers, uncles and older brothers. And if we were looking at the right moment, we would see a wink cast in our direction, and in the wink the promise of a turkey leg, or a rum for the older boys. Perhaps a funny hat or a balloon that was not trampled at the stroke of midnight.

9 Once one of them, braver than the watchman, and smarter, sneaked a leg of turkey out to us before the ball was over. And we chomped on the cold strange-tasting meat all the way through "The Blue Danube," all the while making mincemeat with prettier steps than those trudging ladies and drunken gentlemen on the grand ballroom floor.

10 Five minutes before midnight it would become very quiet. Quiet like my old school down the gap fifty yards away, silent and asleep at this time of grave-digging darkness. The watchman would stand at attention. And when he knew that we had all seen him, he would walk through the midst of us like a general, like a plantation overseer; come right up to each one of us, twirling his stick right in

---

*serrigated: segregated

our faces, like the drum major in the Volunteer Force, and say, "Don't mek no noise in front of the white people, you hear me?"

Four minutes before midnight. And we can see the *musicianers*   11
with their instruments at the ready, and the ladies and gentlemen in the grand ballroom skipping here and there, looking for husbands or partners. And the lights would go off one by one, and suddenly the place would be like a fairy garden with only coloured bulbs, and the balloons like beads of sea water on the skin. And then the counting in a collection of voices, ours and theirs inside. "Twelve . . . eleven . . . ten . . . nine . . ."

All of us outside counting in a year that would bring us more war,   12
and nothing like what it would bring the ladies and gentlemen on the other side of the wall.

The counting growing louder now. ". . . five . . . four . . ." And we   13
continue to ignore the watchman, whom we had long ago nicknamed "Hitler." And suddenly he too joins in the counting.

And then, on the stroke of midnight, the eruption of motorcar   14
horns blowing, balloons popping; the waiting taxicabs honking, with a hint of deliberate impatience; and the ringing of bells, dinner bells and church bells; and the bursting of balloons, and the scuffling and fighting for the balloons thrown over the wall and floating in our direction; and the good fortune of a funny hat which has landed in our midst, barely destroyed, which we patched and for days afterwards wore as a statement: "Man, you went to the Marine Old Year's Ball? I went, man. I got this hat. Look!" Or a noise-maker sneaked out from behind the wall by a maid or a mother; and the boiled unsalted rice carried in paperbags; "them tourisses is people who suffer from sugar in the blood!"

We would walk back, happy, to our district, memorizing the night   15
of magic and revelry and choruses and words of the most popular tune played by the Percy Greene Orchestra. *Goodnight, Irene* . . .

"Percy blow that tenor sax like po'try, boy! You hear how he take   16
them riffs in the first chorus? Pure po'try, boy!"

Structure:

1. How fully does Clarke develop a *contrast* between the tourists and the islanders? What are the main differences that he describes?
2. To what extent does Clarke *compare* the tourists and the islanders? Point out the main similarities that he describes.

3. How does Clarke organize his comparison and contrast: by halves, or by switching from one side to the other with each new topic?
4. To what extent is "Old Year's Night" a narrative? Point out at least ten words or phrases that signal the flow of time.
5. To what extent is "Old Year's Night" supported by description? Point out the most vivid passages.

Style:

1. Point out all the passages of local dialect quoted in this selection and discuss what they contribute to Clarke's description of life in Barbados. Why didn't Clarke write the whole selection in dialect, since he is narrating in first person?
2. In what ways do the visual images of the opening paragraph appeal to our attention?
3. Point out all the appeals that paragraph 14 makes to our sense of sound.
4. When Clarke says the tourists are "skating over the huge dance floor" (par. 7), he uses a METAPHOR — a figure of speech that is literally false but poetically true. And when he says the watchman is "like a general" (par. 10), he uses a SIMILE — a figure of speech saying that one thing is like another. Which of the following are metaphors and which are similes? And what is the effect of these FIGURES OF SPEECH?
   A. "It was a huge building washed in pink. . ." (par. 1).
   B. "The men inside wore formal black suits that turned them into undertakers" (par. 7).
   C. ". . .all the while making mincemeat with prettier steps. . ." (par. 9).
   D. "Five minutes before midnight it would become very quiet. Quiet like my old school down the gap fifty yards away, silent and asleep at this time of grave-digging darkness" (par. 10).
   E. "And the lights would go off one by one, and suddenly the place would be like a fairy garden with only coloured bulbs, and the balloons like beads of sea water on the skin" (par. 11).
   F. ". . .the eruption of motorcar horns blowing. . ." (par. 14).
   G. " 'Percy blow that tenor sax like po'try, boy!' " (par. 16).
5. In what ways is the wall a SYMBOL?

Ideas:

1. The islanders described by Clarke envy the tourists (". . . we dreamed of becoming powerful and rich, to join them, to be like

them" — par. 8), yet the same islanders "would walk back happy" to their "district" (par. 15). How do you explain this apparent discrepancy?
2. In what ways do the islanders feel superior to the tourists?
3. What benefits does tourism bring to a small country like Barbados? What economic and cultural problems can extensive tourism bring?
4. Is it possible for a tourist from a relatively wealthy country like Canada to be responsible in visiting a poor country? If so, name some characteristics of the responsible tourist.
5. If you have read "When the Natives Surrender," compare the effects of tourism upon a southern island as seen by a tourist (Allan Fotheringham) and an islander (Austin Clarke).
6. Write an essay *contrasting* either of these two pairs:
   The good tourist and the bad tourist
   My best holiday and my worst holiday

(NOTE: See also the Topics for Writing at the end of this chapter.)

Pierre Berton

The Dirtiest Job in the World

Few people are better known to Canadians than Pierre Berton — journalist, humorist, social critic, popular historian and television personality. He was born in 1920 in Whitehorse, the Yukon, and studied at the University of British Columbia. In 1942 he began his career in journalism at the Vancouver News-Herald. *After wartime service in the Canadian Information Corps, Berton returned to journalism as a feature writer for the* Vancouver Sun, *moved in 1947 to an editorial position at* Maclean's, *then in 1958 became a daily columnist for* The Toronto Star. *For well over two decades Berton has appeared regularly on television series such as* Front Page Challenge, The Great Debate *and* My Country, *and since 1954 has written over twenty books, several of them best-sellers. His most widely read have been* The National Dream *(1970) and* The Last Spike *(1971), the massively researched and highly readable two-volume history of the CPR that in 1974 was serialized on CBC-TV with Berton as narrator.* The Invasion of Canada, 1812-13 *appeared in 1980,* Flames Across the Border *in 1981 and* The Promised Land *in 1984. Whatever Berton's subject, his writing is full of human interest and concern for social justice. Nowhere are these traits more evident than in our selection, "The Dirtiest Job in the World," which appeared in Berton's 1968 book,* The Smug Minority.

1   On my seventeenth birthday, which fell on July 12, 1937, one of the worst years of the Depression, I went to work for pay and there was jubilation among my friends and relatives. In an era when jobs were scarce I had a job; and having a job was the goal of everyone in those days. Having a job in the Thirties was a bit like having a swimming pool in the Sixties; it conferred status. It didn't really matter what the job was. It could be unrewarding, mindless, foolish, unproductive, even degrading — no matter: it set you apart as a paying member of a society whose creed was that everyone must work at something, and the harder the better, too.

2   My job was in a mining camp in the Yukon some 1,500 miles from my home in Victoria, B.C. I worked ten hours a day, seven days a week, and I was paid $4.50 a day plus my board. Almost everybody who learned about my job had the same thing to say about it: "It will make a man out of you!" And when the job came to an end at the start of my university term, almost every adult I knew examined my hands to note with satisfaction the heavy callouses. Back-breaking

work was considered to be a high form of human endeavour. A man who worked hard couldn't be all bad, whether he was a convict breaking rocks in a prison yard or an executive neglecting his family by toiling weekends at the office.

I worked for three summer seasons at that same job and it was 3 commonly held that I was "working my way through college," another laudable endeavour in a society which believed, and still believes, that every individual must pay his own way regardless of position, health, mental ability, or physical condition.

The first year I worked on a construction gang; the following years 4 I worked on the thawing crew, engaged in preparing the ground for the actual gold mining that was to follow. Thawing permafrost with cold water is a fascinating process to almost everyone except those actually employed in it. As far as I know, it is the world's muddiest job, involving as it does the pumping of millions of gallons of cold water into the bowels of the earth.

In earlier days steam had been used to thaw the permanently 5 frozen ground so that the dredges could reach the gold; but the lovely, verdant valleys had long since been denuded of their timber and no fuel was left to operate the old-time boilers. So now a new process had been devised to tear the valley apart and convert it into a heaving sea of mud.

On Dominion Creek in the Klondike watershed, where I toiled 6 those three Depression summers, the gold lay hidden in crevices of bedrock some twenty or thirty feet beneath the surface. The valley was perhaps a mile wide at this point and it was being ripped to pieces so that man might reach this gold. First, every shred of plant life was sheared off by a bush-cutting crew. Then all the black topsoil, most of it frozen hard as granite, was sluiced away by giant nozzles flinging water against the banks at a pressure so high it could cut a man in half. By the time the thawing crew arrived, the sinuous valley, misty green each spring, flaming orange each fall, had been reduced to a black, glistening scar.

It was our task to dam the creek anew to build up water pressure 7 and then introduce a spider web of pipes across the newly ravaged valley floor. From these pipes at sixteen-foot intervals there protruded an octopus-like tangle of hoses. On to each hose was fastened a ten-foot length of pipe, known as a "point," because of the chisel-bit at the end. This point was driven into the frozen soil by means of a slide hammer. When it was down the full ten feet, an extension pipe was screwed onto the end and this was driven down, too, inch by painful inch. If necessary, further extensions were added. And all the time, without cessation, ice cold water was being pumped through every pipe at high pressure. In this way an underground lake was created beneath the valley floor and, though its waters were only a few degrees above freezing, that small change in temperature was enough to thaw the permafrost.

8   And so we toiled away, up to our ankles, our knees, and sometimes even our hips in a pulsating gruel of mud and ice-water. The men who drove those points into the rock-like soil were soaking wet most of the time, for it was difficult to add extensions or withdraw a point without water spurting in all directions. All day long they laboured, with their fingers curled around the handles of their slide hammers, their torsos rising and falling as they drove each pipe inch by inch into the earth. When a point became plugged it had to be hauled up and unplugged while the ice-water squirted in their faces. Each man was logged on the amount of footage he had driven in a day, and if that footage was seen to be too low he could expect to draw his time slip that evening. There was a story current in my day that the general manager had come out from Dawson on a tour of inspection and seen a man standing immobile in the distance. "Fire that man!" he cried. "I've been watching him and he hasn't moved for half an hour." Later it was discovered that he *couldn't* move; he was up to his hips in mud.

9   As the water continued to flow into the ground, the floor of the valley began to go to pieces. Immense craters ten or twenty feet deep began to appear. Whole sections fell away, sometimes taking men with them. The mud grew thicker. The pipeline supports toppled as the soil crumbled, and the pipes themselves — mainlines and feeder lines — began to buckle and break and to shoot icy fountains in every direction. When this occurred it was the job of the pipeline crew, of which I was a member, to replace the pilings, drive new pipes and repair leaks. Sometimes the sun was out and we stripped to our shorts; sometimes a bone-chilling wind swept down the valley accompanied by a sleety rain. It did not matter. We worked our ten hours (later it was reduced to a merciful nine) day in and day out, without a holiday of any kind.

10   When you work for ten hours at hard labour, whether you are seventeen or fifty-seven, there is precious little time or energy left for anything else. We rose at six, performed our swift ablutions, wolfed an enormous breakfast, and headed off for the job which had to begin at seven. At noon we started back up the valley slopes through the mud to the messhall, wolfed another vast meal, and finished it just in time to head back once more. At six we were finished, in more ways than one. I have seen men so tired they could not eat the final meal of the day which was always consumed in silence and at top speed. (It was said that any man who stumbled on the messhall steps on the way in found himself trampled by the rush

coming out.) When this was over, large numbers of men of varying ages simply lay down on their bunks, utterly fagged out, and slept. There was nothing else to do anyway: no library, no recreation hall, no lounge, no radio or films — nothing but a roadhouse five miles distant where you could buy bootleg rum. Civilization was represented by Dawson, forty miles away; we never visited it. We were like men in a prison camp, except that we worked much harder.

Under such conditions any kind of creative act or thought is 11 difficult. I remember one man, a German immigrant, who was trying to learn to draw by correspondence. He had some talent but in the end he had to give it up. He was too tired to draw. I had brought along a pile of books required in my university course for summer reading, but most of the time I found I was too tired to read. Those who did not immediately go to sleep after supper spent their spare time washing their work clothes or lying in their bunks indulging in verbal sexual fantasies. I often wondered if this was what the adults meant when they said that mining camp life would make a man of me. Certainly I learned a great deal more from these sexual bull sessions than I had at my mother's knee. It was not until many years later that I discovered most of it was wrong.

It is difficult to describe the absolute dreariness and hopelessness 12 of this kind of job. The worst thing about it was that there was no respite, since — in a seven-day-a-week job — there were no breaks of any kind to look forward to until the coming of winter rendered further toil impossible. There was one wit among us who used to leap from his bunk once a week, when the bull cook banged the triangle at 6:00 A.M., crying jubilantly: "Thank God, it's Sunday!" This always provoked a bitter laugh. Without any change of pace, time moves sluggishly; without any break in the routine, a kind of lethargy steals over the mind. The blessed winter seemed eons away to all of us.

Yet for me, in my late teens, life in this mining camp was 13 immeasurably easier than it was for the others. There were men here in their sixties who had lived this way all their lives. There were men in their prime with wives and children to support — families they did not see for half of every year. There were all kinds of men here and few who were really stupid. I worked with immigrants from Austria, Germany, Switzerland, Italy, Sweden, Norway, and Denmark, as well as with Canadians. Most were intelligent and a great many were extremely sharp and able. All were industrious. Each had displayed enough courage and independence to somehow make his way several thousand miles to the one corner of North America where a job of sorts was comparatively easy to get. But all had one thing in common: according to my observation, none had been educated up to his ability.

14   There were many men in that mining camp easily capable of obtaining a university degree; and there were many more who might have completed high school and then gone on to technical school. I saw them each evening, lying on their bunks and trying to force their hands open — hands that had been curled into almost permanent positions around cold pipes; I saw them each morning, shambling down to that grotesque mud-pie of a valley; during the day I saw them — scores of ant-like figures, bent double over their slide hammers, struggling in the gumbo, striving and groaning; and the thought that came to my mind was ever the same: "What a waste of human resources!"

15   For this "job," which everybody had congratulated me upon getting, which was supposed to be so ennobling, which was to make a man of me, was actually degrading, destructive, and above all useless. It was degrading because it reduced men to the status of beasts. There was one wag who went around with his zipper purposely undone and his genitals exposed. "If I'm working like a horse, I might as well look like one," he'd say. It was destructive because it reduced a glorious setting to a black obscenity. And it was useless because the gold, which was mined at such expense and human cost, was melted into bars and shipped to Fort Knox in the United States where it was once again confined below ground. Every manjack of us knew this; it was the subject of much bitter banter and wisecracking; each of us, I think, was disturbed by the fact that we were engaged in an operation which was essentially unproductive. If we'd been growing wheat, we would at least have had the satisfaction of knowing our labours were useful. The whole, vast, complicated operation seemed to me to be pointless: even the stockholders failed to profit by it greatly; for years the company was forced to pass its dividends. Would we or the nation have been worse off if we had stayed drunk all summer?

16   For myself, as a teenager, there were certain minor advantages that did not apply to those older men who worked out of necessity and desperation. Certainly it was healthy enough. Certainly I got to know a bit more about my fellow men. It occurs to me now, however, that both these goals could have been achieved in a pleasanter and more productive fashion. As for the financial gain, much of that was illusory. After I paid for my equipment and my return fare home, there was precious little left. The first year I scarcely broke even. In succeeding seasons I was able to pay my university tuition but not much more. Like my fellow students, I could say that I was working my way through college, but like most of them I could not have

continued a university career had I not been able to board at home and take money for clothing and extras from my parents. During four years at university, I met only a handful of students who were able to support themselves wholly through summer employment.

The one valuable asset that I recovered from my mining camp 17 experience was status. It allows me to use a line in my official biography which I notice is seized upon joyfully by those who have to introduce me when I make after-dinner speeches: "During the Thirties, he worked in Yukon mining camps to help put himself through university." When that line is uttered the audience is prepared to forgive me almost anything: outlandishly radical opinions, dangerous views on matters sexual, alarming attitudes toward religion. I am pronounced worthy because, in that one sentence, is summed up the great Canadian myth: that work — *any* work — is the most important thing in life, and that anybody who is willing to work hard enough can by his own initiative get as far as he wants.

Structure:

1. In this contrast between society's high opinion of work and Pierre Berton's low opinion of his job, why is so much more of the argument devoted to the job than to society's opinions?
2. How is the essay organized? Does Berton finish with one view before presenting the other?
3. Berton's argument against the idea of hard labour as "a high form of human endeavour" basically takes the form of one extended example. Has this example enabled Berton to *disprove* society's view of work?
4. Paragraph 15 is filled with short comparisons and contrasts. Point out each one.

Style:

1. Is the TONE of Berton's essay OBJECTIVE or SUBJECTIVE? Point out passages that illustrate your answer.
2. In paragraph 5, Berton describes the valley as "a heaving sea of mud." Find other METAPHORS or SIMILES which poetically describe one thing as another.
3. In paragraph 10, the crew "wolfed an enormous breakfast" and later "wolfed another vast meal." Have you heard this figure of speech before? How effective is it?

Ideas:

1. Do we still believe, or did we ever believe, in what Berton calls "the great Canadian myth: that work — *any* work — is the most important thing in life, and that anybody who is willing to work hard enough can by his own initiative get as far as he wants"?
2. Is work necessary for human happiness? How are prisoners, pensioners, the unemployed and the rich affected by large amounts of leisure time? Give examples from the experience of people you know.
3. To what extent does our society still believe that "every individual must pay his own way regardless of position, health, mental ability, or physical condition" (par. 3)?
4. Berton seems to view education as the means of escape from "back-breaking work" (see par. 14). Was that view correct during the Depression, in which the essay is set? Was it correct in 1968, when the essay was first published? Is it correct now?
5. How much did Berton learn from his experience in the gold fields? How large a part of your own education has come from summer or part-time work?
6. If you have read "Living with Automation in Winnipeg," compare and contrast work as Ian Adams describes it with work as Berton describes it.
7. Write an essay *contrasting* the most socially useless job and the most socially useful job that you can think of.

(NOTE: See also the Topics for Writing at the end of this chapter.)

Philip Marchand

Learning to Love the Big City

Born in Massachusetts in 1946, Philip Marchand studied English language and literature at the University of Toronto. After earning his M.A. in 1970, he worked as a manuscript editor and freight car loader, then became a free-lance writer. Since 1971, his articles about social trends have appeared regularly in Saturday Night, Chatelaine *and other Canadian magazines. He says, "I like to write about individual personalities reacting to a larger social scene, reacting to expectations they feel this scene imposes on them." Until recently Marchand was heavily influenced by the "New Journalism" of the American writer Tom Wolfe. In this approach to writing, the subject is thoroughly researched but is presented in a subjective, personal style meant to heighten its appeal to the reader. One of these "non-fiction short stories," as they have been called, is our selection, "Learning to Love the Big City." It appeared first in* The Canadian, *then in Marchand's book* Just Looking, Thank You *(1976).*

Man does not live by bread alone, but by fantasy and daydream as well. Young men and women are sitting behind desks in downtown Toronto, Montreal, and Vancouver and thinking, when I get my grubstake I'm going to leave this scene for good. I'm heading for the country. Get a place ten miles from the nearest town and only come in on weekends for supplies, like lentils and Crunchy Granola. Yes. A little homestead far from the Great Urban Maw . . . and at the same time as these visions are being entertained, other young men and women are flocking to Toronto and Montreal and Vancouver, from places like Marathon, Ont., and Gypsumville, Man., and Vanderhoof, B.C., for jobs in life-insurance offices and a comfortable nook in some monstrous high-rise. It's not the popular dream, to settle down in the big city, but there you have it — real alternatives are simply too scarce. Small-town life practically doesn't *exist* in Canada anymore. Or rather it exists, but it's fading all the time. We're in a stage roughly analogous to the Late Roman Republic, when poets and politicians were praising the virtues of the simple old Roman country life, sturdy farmers worshipping the household gods and taking cold-water baths, while everybody who had the chance was heading for the city for some fast money and funky entertainment. 1

175

2   For people like Lynda, eighteen years old and fresh into Toronto
from a town of 5,000 in the wilds of northern Ontario, all this talk
about getting out of the city is definitely puzzling. For a weekend,
sure — who doesn't like the peace and quiet? But the city is
fascinating. The first few weeks she was here she would spend ten
minutes at a time standing on a street corner like the Bloor-Yonge
intersection, just watching. She would see, for instance, this young
man with a shaved head and a saffron robe dogging passersby on the
sidewalk, talking it up for the Lord Krishna. Disgusting! Nobody
she had ever known in her whole life would act like such an idiot,
but she had to watch. This guy would attack some poor timorous girl
going back to work at a reception desk and stick to her like a
horsefly, threatening her with his humbleness, his shamelessness,
asking for money, asking for her name, her address, silently hinting
that if she yielded a little bit he would never let up until she was
there in the temple babbling insane praise to Lord Krishna for the
rest of her natural life. He did this until he tried it on one guy in a
business suit, who just grabbed him by his saffron robes and threw
him off the sidewalk, into the traffic.

3   Well, the things you can see just standing for ten minutes at a
big-city intersection. Lynda can't get over it. But, of course, she
comes from a town where the main recreation is drinking. It
overshadows such country sports as ice-fishing, snowmobiling,
backpacking, even hockey. At school dances the Ontario Provincial
Police officer is standing by the door watching fourteen- and
fifteen-year-old kids reel in, and the only time he interferes is if they
start attacking each other. Of course, the booze is cheap up there in
the north country — you go to one of the three hotels in the town and
get a bottle of beer for 50 cents, or a shot of vodka for 70 cents. It
always surprised Lynda when people in Toronto would say they
were going out drinking, and then they'd end up having only three
shots of rye the whole evening. That was not Lynda's idea of serious
drinking. She would be having her sixth or seventh vodka, and
calmly watching her boyfriend knocking over chairs as he stumbled
back to their table from the men's room — she would be just getting
warmed up, you see, and here he was losing control of his basic
motor functions after consuming the same quantity of booze.

4   But after a while Lynda began to grasp the point, which is that
you don't really have to get drunk in the big city. Lynda gets drunk
in Toronto, and all she wants to do is go home and sleep. That
means, really, that she misses all the weird and wonderful action
around her, the satin freaks in star-spangled boots, the criminal
types with tattoos on their arms, premed students wearing
sleeveless sweaters and Bulova watches, the whole urban monkey

house drinking draught beer out of jugs and having their ear membranes warped from the rock music.

Back home there was a point to getting drunk. You could not   5
conceive, in fact, of having a party or a dance without getting ripped before 10 p.m. You'd end up rolling around on the floor, and the guys would be shouting at each other — "George, get your arms off me, you queer!" — like a class of ten-year-olds who had just been forced to sit a whole half-hour with their feet still and their hands on top of their desks, and the girls would be giggling at the sight of their boyfriends making such utter fools of themselves. And, of course, a few party games. In this one game a person would doodle a few lines on a piece of paper and then another person who didn't know what the game was about would take a strand of hair and try to bend and twist the hair so it covered the lines on the paper, and meanwhile some girl who knew Pitman shorthand would be recording his remarks on the sly. These remarks would then — surprise! — be read back to the guy later as the things he would say on his "wedding night." With half a pint of rye, rum, vodka, gin, or Zing under their belts, the kids would kill themselves laughing at remarks like "Geez, I can't keep hold of this thing." Party night for the young folks in ——, Ont.

But at least it was something to talk about in school on Monday,   6
the number of bottles consumed, and what happened to so and so who was found with his head resting on the toilet, and this other couple who disappeared a little after midnight, under a bed, or some place. A few of the guys, and the girls even, would have arguments about just how much each person drank, it being a point of honour, of course, to hold your liquor and not act too foolish unless the kidneys and the lobes of the brain were actually getting soggy from alcohol. These are all, indeed, lively topics of conversation . . . but after a while it does get tiresome, Monday after Monday, the endless gossip about drinking, and sometimes about sex. Kids couldn't possibly have a little sexual adventure without everybody they met on the street knowing about it within a few days. Sometimes the people on the street even knew about things that never happened. A girl might enter the hospital to have her appendix removed and come out to discover her friends and neighbours all firmly believed she'd had an abortion.

But what else is there to talk about? Lynda is not an intellectual,   7
but sometimes during conversations she tried to discuss topics of wider interest than, say, last night's alcoholic blowout — like what is the future of life in this town, for instance — and her friends started examining their fingernails and clearing their throats and after 30 seconds the conversation slid back into the old, hairy trough

of local gossip. Or she used words like "progressive" or "confrontation" in conversation, and they asked, "What's with the vocabulary?" These people are all carrying on like Leo Gorcey and his
Bowery Boys. Great for nostalgia, watching Gorcey movies from the
forties, but it's not so funny in real life.

8   The guys, for instance, have two alternatives facing them when
they leave high school. They can work in the mines or they can work
in a garage somewhere. Either way, they will get married and have
a family and try to get on the graveyard shift, so they can goof off
and sleep for a few hours and brag about it afterwards to their
buddies in the beverage room of the hotel. They will actually do
things like trade war comics with their co-workers, the kind that
feature granite-jawed Marines with five-o'clock shadows, blasting
away at Japs on Gizo Island. They will get their greatest excitement
from picking fights with guys who come in for the hockey
tournament with their team, from some town a hundred miles away,
and they will continue to do this until their bellies turn soft from
drinking and they can't take the punishment anymore. That will be
a sad day for them, incidentally, because they do like picking fights
with strangers. The adrenalin wash helps clear up the brainstem
and, besides, it's one of the few things they can do that girls can't,
with their blue jeans and T-shirts and ability, some of them, to
out-gross and out-drink even the hairiest males.

9   But this is their future, ladies and gentlemen. And their
girlfriends do not exactly have it better. They will work in the bank
or an insurance office after they leave school, and then they will get
married and tend to the kids. Some of them will skip the high school
graduation and employment part of it and get married out of Grade
11 or 12. Indeed, it is not uncommon for fourteen-year-old girls to
get married in this town. These blossoming children who would
prefer scar tissue to wearing something other than their blue-jean-
and-T-shirt ensemble — except maybe a short skirt with lime- or
raspberry-coloured nylons, for the glamorous occasions.

10   Lynda recalls that the girl she admired most in this town was a
secretary who had her own apartment, her own money, her own
definite views on life — she knew definitely where she was going in
this world. This was a girl Lynda actually thought stood out from
the crowd. This was a girl Lynda thought really had an interesting
point of view, some unique statements on life to make, as opposed to
the general numbness of intellect around town. If you want to know
what a boy you're thinking of marrying is going to be like 20 or 30
years from now, she would say to Lynda, take a look at his father.
That's what he's going to be like. Truly a sobering thought . . . and
she had more, much more, to say in this vein. Well, when Lynda

came back from Toronto for her first homecoming, her first Christmas visit, and met this girl again, somehow she appeared in an entirely different light. Instead of being a person of strongly held views and unique personal vision, she just seemed ... well, opinionated, and as set in her ways as any middle-aged lady with tortoise-shell glasses and menthol cigarettes whose greatest challenge in life is deciding on what cheese dip to serve for the weekly meeting of her canasta club. Now her discussion of young men centred on whether or not they were "self-starters". That, apparently, is more important than what their fathers are like, because she has just gotten herself engaged to a young engineer at the mines, whose father spends most of his time down in his basement with some ice water and Saltines, going over his stamp collection.

Had this girl changed — or had Lynda changed, in the four 11
months she had spent away from home for the first time in her life, back there in the big city? Lynda suspects that she herself has changed. She suspects that if she had lived in Toronto before, she would never have been taken in by this secretary. One thing she has learned in Toronto is not to take people for granted. They just aren't moulded in those cast-iron, unbreakable reputations that are given to people past the age of five in small towns. In Toronto you have to find out for yourself what they're like; you have to pick up all the subtle little indicators — practically in the first few minutes you meet them.

With guys, for instance, Lynda now can tell how promising they 12
look after two or three minutes. It's all based on the degree of shyness they present to you when they talk to you in your favourite bar, the Nickelodeon, say, or the Generator, or Zodiac I. At one end of this spectrum you find guys who are not shy at all. A guy like this sits down at your table and turns around and leans forward so his face is squarely in front of yours and there's an upbeat, lively tone in his voice as he starts talking about how boring this whole scene is, and what a drag so many of these girls are, they look like they're out on horse tranquillizers, and you know that before the evening's over he'll be suggesting that someone like you is obviously cut out for finer things, like going over to his apartment above an Army-Navy store on Yonge Street and shooting up. Most aren't this extreme, but if there's no *hint* of shyness in the character it often means there is a definite tilt to psychopathic lunacy here.

And at the other end of the spectrum is the guy who is tormented 13
by shyness, but obviously driven, forced, impelled to seek out contact, so he talks to you with his eyes fluttering back and forth between your own two eyes and the little pools of beer on the tabletop, talking with such effort that it is obvious he must have

worked himself up to come here tonight by performing unspeakable acts in front of some *Penthouse* nudes.

14 But Lynda has discovered that it isn't all that difficult to meet reasonable people somewhere in the middle of the shyness spectrum, even in bars. Curiously enough, the fact she was from a small town made it much easier, in a way, because she thought nothing of starting up a conversation with the people sitting next to her in the Nickelodeon or the Generator. Hard-bitten Torontonians do not as a rule do things like this, because they're already sure the person sitting next to them is somebody who will respond to their friendliness by putting a hand on their thigh, or quoting whole passages from the Book of Revelations at them, or shutting them up with their Penetrating Death Stare.

15 But Lynda, as I say, came from a small town where you speak to people who sit next to you in public places, as a matter of course. And not only does she meet a lot of *nice* guys this way, but she can tell how much other girls sitting around get absolutely burned up at her for it. I mean, she knows they're carrying on as if she were Little Orphan Annie befriending the poor and the outcast, and they're just sitting by doing a pictorial spread for *Vogue*, but — well, that's not her problem. Let them wobble by on their platform shoes, with their slithery satin gowns coming down low under the shoulder blades, let them entice these young men with such obvious displays of themselves; Lynda knows that guys also appreciate a girl who can talk to them, a girl they can approach without feeling they've strayed into a walk-in refrigerator. Good conversations can be sexy, too, as Lynda knows, who comes from a place where they are nonexistent. It kills her, for instance, that Lennox there, who she met at the Nickelodeon two or three months ago and with whom she has been more or less going steadily ever since, was actually interested, in one conversation they had, in the details of how people go about ice-fishing back home in ——. Lennox, who was born in Morocco and has lived in about three different countries in Europe, interested in how Lynda's friends and neighbours ice fish! I mean! Well, Lennox, how you do it is you start cutting a hole in the ice with a pick, and . . . and this is what Lynda came to Toronto for, to meet people and *talk*, to share experiences, to learn, to — oh, Lynda doesn't know, but to — to widen her horizons a bit beyond the world of the mines and incipient alcoholism.

16 This is what makes it worthwhile for Lynda — her boyfriend Lennox, who is interested in how you go about ice-fishing, and things like the whole variety of clothing stores in the city where you can buy practically anything outrageous or elegant, and you can dress like a lady and put on the nail polish and the green eyeliner

without people staring at you in the pub and your friends calling you "green eyes", and you can get your hair cut'n'curled any way you want, and you can get a decent Chinese meal and you can take long walks in the city and admire everything from the skyscrapers to odd little filigreed Victorian houses, and you can even stand at the corner of Yonge and Bloor and watch altercations between secretaries and Hare Krishna mendicants.

Yes, this is what makes it all worthwhile, and at times Lynda 17 actually has to remind herself that for the first two or three months she was here she was often on the verge of packing it in and going home. For those first few months, the fascination of life in Toronto was balanced by certain of its more frightening aspects. It was just all so *unknown*. Before she met Lennox, for instance, she really was dependent on some of the bars in town, the ones with the ear-warping rock music, for meeting people. But it was more than that. It was going into the subway at rush hour, and having people rush by you on the steps in panic, like a scene out of the fall of Berlin. It was the feeling of being a stranger, a foreigner almost, in your own country, riding the elevator in your apartment building every morning and hearing all these different languages, seeing black people for the first time, Sikhs, Chinese . . . I mean, Lynda is no bigot, but she was not quite ready for a lot of the cosmopolitan mix here in the city, the Detroit dudes in the peach-coloured suits, say, with matching fedoras, introducing some of that U.S.-patented pimp-flash to Toronto, looking as if any minute they would approach you on the sidewalk and say something like "Hey, honey, you so *fine*."

It was the feeling of having to be on your guard all the time, of 18 riding the subway and finding yourself sitting next to some drunk talking to you at the top of his voice, asking you all these questions, like did you know about this here Bermuda Triangle, and everybody else in the car looking at you to see how you're going to handle the situation. It was the feeling of wanting to go for a walk by yourself, late in the evening perhaps, and being afraid to, because guys on the street would be eyeing you, staring hard as if you were swinging a purse and wearing a leopard skin coat and white vinyl boots. One night Lynda was eating by herself in a restaurant and a table full of men in business suits kept *looking* at her the whole time. When Lynda walked by their table on her way out she couldn't take it anymore, she was so annoyed — she said something sarcastic to them like, "Have you fellas had a good look?" and one of them stood up and started yelling at her, calling her names, telling her to get out — it was a thoroughly bad scene. But why can't she eat by herself in a restaurant without being gawked at? And why can't she go out by herself late at night, if that is her wish? It's her right, isn't it? It was certainly her right back home. But then, of course, this is the big city, and we have different rules here, lady.

19   Most disturbing of all, perhaps, was something more subtle, something Lynda found hard to put her finger on. In its more extreme forms, it was, she guessed, simple big-city rudeness. All those waitresses who never seemed to crack a smile, for instance, and rolled their eyes in exasperation when you pointed out that you ordered your fried eggs done on both sides, not sunny-side up. But even when people in the city were not rude, when they had no intention of being anything other than decent and friendly and sociable, they still seemed curiously indifferent to other people's feelings. At work, for instance, Lynda will be doing these letters, not a rush job but she can't take forever on them. Her boss will ask another typist to do something, and that typist will say, right in front of Lynda, "Oh why can't you give it to Lynda? She never has that much to do." Or at lunch one of the girls will say to another, who is eating a full slice of rich, creamy cheesecake in spite of some obvious weight problems, "Are you sure you should be eating all that?" They don't seem to *care* about what other people think or feel, and they say these things that just cut you, things that people back home would never say.

20   But at Christmas, when Lynda went back home for the first time, she acquired a little perspective on the whole thing. She found that, yes, people in her town were friendly. Folks had a big smile for her when they met her on the street, and asked her questions — "Have you met anybody in Toronto?" — and seemed just full of concern. But after a while Lynda noticed how they kept giving her these surreptitious stares in the hotel bar when she walked in wearing a pantsuit and all this makeup. She noticed that when she talked about Toronto, especially in an enthusiastic tone of voice, the look on their faces began to get more and more quizzical, as if they couldn't figure her out, as if they were thinking — is this girl turning *strange* on us? And then she remembered all the times she felt she *had* to smile at people on the streets, greet them nicely, be careful of what she said, because, after all, this was a small town and you were going to have to live with these people whether you liked it or not. It was certainly true that she did have a definite place in this town, that her absence from it had been noted, that the merchants here never hesitated to cash one of her cheques. All this was a comfort when you thought about that big-city anonymity . . . but it hardly seemed worth it when you considered how hollow much of this recognition, this position in the community, actually was. I mean, Lynda's family happened to live in —— Heights, the most

prosperous area of town and her address alone guaranteed that a cheque of hers would be cashed anywhere in town, even if the merchant or clerk didn't know her personally. But there are, of course, other areas in town that aren't so nice, areas closer to the mines where families with eight or ten kids live and the old man works as a gas station attendant. Lynda recalls that a lot of this small-town friendliness begins to evaporate when it comes to dealing with people like this, and you will never find them hanging out with the —— Heights United Church Women, for instance.

So all in all, Lynda finds herself voting for the big city. People who 21 have lived in the city for a long time will no doubt continue to complain about it, and dream of the day they can settle down in the country on a farm perhaps, but for the vast majority of these people it will always be a dream. Economic pressure alone will continue to coerce people into living in the great cities. But there is something else involved. In 1806 John Loudon, in *A Treatise on Forming, Improving and Managing Country Residences,* wrote, "Such is the superiority of rural occupations and pleasures, that commerce, large societies, or crowded cities, may be justly reckoned unnatural. Indeed, the very purpose for which we engage in commerce is, that we may one day be enabled to retire to the country, where alone we picture to ourselves days of solid satisfaction and undisturbed happiness. It is evident that such sentiments are natural to the human mind." Such sentiments may indeed be natural to the human mind, but as long as there are cities there will always be a counter-appeal, expressed in the medieval proverb that city air breeds freedom. For the foreseeable future, the city will continue to draw people like Lynda with this lure — the freedom of lifestyle, the freedom of movement, the freedom of anonymity itself.

Structure:

1. What basic organizational technique underlies both the introduction, in paragraph 1, and the closing, in paragraph 21?
2. Most of the essay is divided into two sections, one describing the small town and the other describing the big city. Point out where each begins and ends.
3. What is the function of paragraph 11?
4. To what extent is "Learning to Love the Big City" based on narration? Where does the narrative begin?
5. To what extent is this essay based on examples? Point out a few of the more vivid ones.

Style:

1. On a scale of 1 to 10, with INFORMAL style as 1 and FORMAL style as 10, where would you place this essay?
2. Read paragraph 15 aloud, then describe its style, especially toward the end. How appropriate to the essay form is this style? When would you avoid it? Name other essays that you have read in this book whose style is in sharp contrast to that of "Learning to Love the Big City."
3. In paragraph 3, Marchand uses the word "booze" and in paragraph 5, the word "ripped." Point out other COLLOQUIAL and SLANG terms in the essay. Can any of these words be used in a more FORMAL sense?
4. A. What device does Marchand use in the phrase "stick to her like a horsefly" (par. 2)?
   B. What device does he use in "the whole urban monkey house" (par. 4)?
5. Read paragraph 16 aloud. How many sentences does it contain? Is this passage a grammatical error? Is it effective?

Ideas:

1. In closing, Marchand quotes the medieval proverb "City air breeds freedom." Name as many ways as you can in which this proverb holds true for modern city life. Name as many ways as you can in which it does not hold true.
2. If you, like Lynda, have come from the small town to the big city, describe as vividly as you can several of your first impressions. If you have been in the city for some time now, tell which of these first impressions were true and which were false.
3. If you live on a farm or in a small town, describe several ways in which your friends and neighbours amuse themselves.
4. If you live in the big city, describe rush hour as you experience it.
5. Do city dwellers really think that a stranger, when spoken to, "will respond to their friendliness by putting a hand on their thigh, or quoting whole passages from the Book of Revelation at them, or shutting them up with their Penetrating Death Stare" (par. 14)? Tell your techniques for meeting people in the city, or tell your techniques for avoiding people in the city.
6. If you have read "Suitcase Lady," by Christie McLaren, compare and contrast the experiences of "the Vicomtesse" with those of Lynda.
7. In essay form, *contrast* Saturday night in two different neighbourhoods, towns or cities.

(NOTE: See also the Topics for Writing at the end of this chapter.)

Terry Hackenberger

Michelle

Terry Hackenberger, born in 1965, lives in Oshawa, Ontario. When she wrote "Michelle" in 1985, she was a first-year social-work student at Ryerson Polytechnical Institute in Toronto. She hopes to go on for a M.A. and work with either juveniles or the emotionally or mentally handicapped. In her spare time Hackenberger draws and paints and — as a member of four book clubs — especially loves to read. Although the course for which she wrote "Michelle" was a writing laboratory in which students polished several drafts of most papers, applying suggestions from the teacher, Hackenberger produced "Michelle" in one draft. Her unusual ability to express ideas on the first try may be a result of her extensive reading. It may also be a result of her subject matter: whenever possible she chooses a topic so important to her that her reaction is strong and direct. Such was the case with "Michelle."

I began to worry two weeks ago when my half-sister was born. I worried about the present. I worried about the future. Oshawa isn't such a small place that it can't hold one more citizen. But the world is.

At first I feared the baby's closeness to my father. Will he love her more than me? Is he prouder of her than of me? Even the twenty-year advantage I have may not be any help.

She has so much pure untapped innocence. Watching her I see her resemblance to myself as a child. Her round-tipped nose is a family trait. Her soft and supple skin is unblemished by the world. The tiny spongy fingers open and close simply, grasping at thin air. Her moves seem to be in slow motion as the miniature arms and chubby legs flail. She uses them as a child uses a new toy: anxiously yet soon bored.

Crying alone among others, she gives me a familiar feeling of loneliness. She knows not of the dangers that exist. She knows not of our uncertainty of life.

Beaming faces surround her and I shudder with awe. They love her not knowing who she is or what she will become. They, too, are innocent.

Tears pressure my eyes to weep as I view a fresh new life. She is so much younger than I, yet I know inside I will cherish her all that I can. My jealousy can be overcome and little Michelle will be loved.

She lets out a howl and I am reassured that the world will listen to what she has to say. I hope that in twenty years she will be around to think what I am thinking about new life. Yet I hope she will be unafraid of the future.

Structure:

1. Is "Michelle" really long enough to be an ESSAY? Why or why not? How long are your shortest essays compared to this? How long are your longest essays compared to this? Name all the factors you can think of that determine the length of an essay.
2. In what ways is this composition a narrative? In what ways is it more than a pure narrative?
3. Is "Michelle" mainly a comparison? A contrast? Or is it both? Point out at least five passages to support your answer.

Style:

1. How wordy or CONCISE is this selection? Point out passages to support your answer.
2. Apart from paragraphs 1 and 2, Hackenberger has written almost entirely in the present tense. Is this a good choice? What are its effects?
3. Which passage is supported most strongly by description? Point out the details of this passage that you find most vivid.
4. Why are Hackenberger's paragraphs short? Could or should any of them be combined? If so, which?

Ideas:

1. In paragraph 1 Hackenberger writes, "Oshawa isn't such a small place that it can't hold one more citizen. But the world is." Explain her PARADOX: in what sense may the world be "smaller" than the town of Oshawa, Ontario? And for what reasons might adults hesitate to bring "one more citizen" into the world?
2. At age 20, Hackenberger looks at the newborn Michelle with adult eyes. Twenty years from now, will she at age 40 still know a great deal more than Michelle will at age 20? At what age does learning taper off or even end?
3. Is it natural to feel jealousy toward a new sister or brother? Did you? Did this feeling persist? Or was it resolved? If so, how?
4. Why is a person almost always the centre of attention as a newborn, yet often ignored as a teenager or adult?
5. In essay form, *compare and/or contrast* yourself with any one of these:

a child you know personally
a middle-aged adult you know personally
a pensioner you know personally

(NOTE: See also the Topics for Writing at the end of this chapter.)

Mordecai Richler

My Father's Life

Mordecai Richler is one of our most widely read novelists and is perhaps the best Canadian essayist of his generation. His carefully crafted, funny, ruthlessly satirical prose devastates its targets: hypocrisy, pretension, self-righteousness, prejudice, provincialism and nationalism. Sometimes, as in "My Father's Life," the devastation goes hand in hand with appreciation. It was in 1931 that Richler was born to the family he describes here. In 1951 he left the Jewish quarter of Montreal to spend two years in Paris, where he wrote his first novel. He returned to work at the CBC, then from 1959 to 1972 lived and worked in England. Since 1972 he has made his home in Montreal. Richler has maintained a steady output of novels: The Acrobats *(1954),* Son of a Smaller Hero *(1955),* A Choice of Enemies *(1957),* The Apprenticeship of Duddy Kravitz *(1959),* The Incomparable Atuk *(1963),* Cocksure *(1968),* St. Urbain's Horseman *(1971) and* Joshua Then and Now *(1980). Both* Duddy Kravitz *and* Joshua *have been made into films, as well as his children's book,* Jacob Two-Two Meets the Hooded Fang *(1975). Richler's essays, published widely in journals both here and abroad, have been collected in several volumes:* Hunting Tigers Under Glass *(1968),* Shovelling Trouble *(1972),* Notes on an Endangered Species *(1974),* The Great Comic Book Heroes *(1978) and* Home Sweet Home: My Canadian Album *(1984). It is from this last that our selection comes.*

1   After the funeral, I was given my father's *talis,** his prayer shawl, and (oh my God) a file containing all the letters I had written to him while I was living abroad, as well as carbon copies he had kept of the letters he had sent to me.

December 28, 1959: "Dear Son, Last week I won a big Kosher Turkey, by bowling, when I made the high triple for the week. How I did it I do not know, I guess I was lucky for once, or was it that the others were too sure of themselves, being much better at the game than I am."

February 28, 1963: "This month has been a cold one, making it difficult, almost impossible to work outside. Yes! it's been tough. Have you found a title for your last novel? What can you do with a title like this? 'UNTIL *DEBT* DO US PART'?"

---

*talis: a prayer shawl

His letter of February 28, 1963, like so many others written that   2
year, begins, "Thanks for the cheque." For by that time we had come
full circle. In the beginning it was my father who had sent checks to
me. Included in the file I inherited were canceled checks, circa 1945,
for $28 monthly child support, following the annulment of my
parents' marriage. A bill dated January 15, 1948, for a Royal
portable, my first typewriter; a birthday gift. Another bill, from
Bond Clothes, dated August 21, 1950, on the eve of my departure for
Europe, for "1 Sta. Wag. Coat, $46.49."

My own early letters to my father, horrendously embarrassing for   3
me to read now, usually begin with appeals for money. No, *demands*.
There is also a telegram I'd rather forget. March 11, 1951.
IMPERATIVE CHECK SENT PRONTO MADRID C O COOKS WAGON LITS
ALCALA NR 23 MADRID. BROKE. MORDECAI.

Imperative, indeed.   4

I was also left a foot-long chisel, his chisel, which I now keep on a   5
shelf of honor in my workroom. Written with a certain flourish in
orange chalk on the oak shaft is my father's inscription:

Used by M.I. Richler
Richler Artificial Stone Works
1922
De La Roche Street
NO SUCCESS.

My father was twenty years old then, younger than my eldest son   6
is now. He was the firstborn of fourteen children. Surely that year,
as every year of his life, on Passover, he sat in his finery at a
dining-room table and recited, "We were once the slaves of Pharaoh
in Egypt, but the Lord our God brought us forth from there with a
mighty hand and an outstretched arm." But, come 1922, out there in
the muck of his father's freezing backyard on De La Roche Street in
Montreal — yet to absorb the news of his liberation — my father was
still trying to make bricks with insufficient straw.*

Moses Isaac Richler.   7

Insufficient straw, *NO* SUCCESS, was the story of his life. Neither of   8
his marriages really worked. There were searing quarrels with my
older brother. As a boy, I made life difficult for him. I had no respect.
Later, officious strangers would rebuke him in the synagogue for the
novels I had written. Heaping calumny on the Jews, they said. If
there was such a thing as a reverse Midas touch, he had it. Not one

---

*". . . make bricks with insufficient straw": As slaves in Egypt, the Israelites
were forced to make bricks of mud, without being given the straw needed to
hold the bricks together.

of my father's penny mining stocks ever went into orbit. He lost regularly at gin rummy. As younger, more intrepid brothers and cousins began to prosper, he assured my mother, "The bigger they come, the harder they fall."

9   My mother, her eyes charged with scorn, laughed in his face. "You're the eldest and what are you?"

10   Nothing.

11   After his marriage to my mother blew apart, he moved into a rented room. Stunned, humiliated. St. Urbain's cuckold. He bought a natty straw hat. A sports jacket. He began to use aftershave lotion. It was then I discovered that he had a bottle of rye whiskey stashed in the glove compartment of his Chevy. My father. Rye whiskey. "What's that for?" I asked, astonished.

12   "For the femmes," he replied, wiggling his eyebrows at me. "It makes them want it."

13   I remember him as a short man, squat, with a shiny bald head and big floppy ears. Richler ears. My ears. Seated at the kitchen table at night in his Penman's long winter underwear, wetting his finger before turning a page of the *New York Daily Mirror*, reading Walter Winchell first. Winchell, who knew what's what. He also devoured *Popular Mechanics*, *Doc Savage*, and *Black Mask*. And, for educational purposes, *Reader's Digest*. My mother, on the other hand, read Keats and Shelley. *King's Row*. *The Good Earth*. My father's pranks did not enchant her. A metal ink spot on her new chenille bedspread. A felt mouse to surprise her in the larder. A knish* secretly filled with absorbent cotton. Neither did his jokes appeal to her. "Hey, do you know why we eat hard-boiled eggs dipped in salt water just before the Passover meal?"

14   "No, Daddy. Why?"

15   "To remind us that when the Jews crossed the Red Sea they certainly got their balls soaked."

16   Saturday mornings my brother and I accompanied him to the Young Israel synagogue on Park Avenue near St. Viateur. As I was the youngest, under bar-mitzvah age, and therefore still allowed to carry on the Sabbath, I was the one who held the prayer shawls in a little purple velvet bag. My father, who couldn't stomach the rabbi's windy speeches, would slip into the back room to gossip with the other men before the rabbi set sail. "In Japan," my father once said, "there is a custom, time-honored, that before he begins, a speaker's hands are filled with ice cubes. He can shoot his mouth off for as long as he can hold the ice cubes in his hands. I wouldn't mind it if the rabbi had to do that."

---

knish: a dumpling with filling, usually of meat

He was stout, he was fleshy. But in the wedding photographs that   17
I never saw until after his death the young man who was to become
my father is as skinny as I once was, his startled brown eyes
unsmiling behind horn-rimmed glasses. Harold Lloyd. Allowed a
quick no-promises peek at the world and what it had to offer, but
clearly not entitled to a place at the table.

My father never saw Paris. Never read Yeats. Never stayed out   18
with the boys drinking too much. Never flew to New York on a
whim. Nor turned over in bed and slept in, rather than report to
work. Never knew a reckless love. What did he hope for? What did
he want? Beyond peace and quiet, which he seldom achieved, I have
no idea. So far as I know he never took a risk or was disobedient. At
his angriest, I once heard him silence one of his cousins, a cousin
bragging about his burgeoning real estate investments, saying,
"You know how much land a man needs? Six feet. And one day that's
all you'll have. Ha, ha!"

Anticipating Bunker Hunt, my father began to hoard American   19
silver in his rented room. A blue steamer trunk filling with neatly
stacked piles of silver dollars, quarters, dimes. But decades before
their worth began to soar, he had to redeem them at face value. "I'm
getting hitched again," he told me, blushing. He began to speculate
in postage stamps. When he died at the age of sixty-five I also found
out that he had bought a city backlot somewhere for $1,200 during
the Forties. In 1967, however — riding a bloated market, every fool
raking it in — the estimated value of my father's property had
shrunk to $900. All things considered, that called for a real touch of
class.

I was charged with appetite, my father had none. I dreamed of   20
winning prizes, he never competed. But, like me, my father was a
writer. A keeper of records. His diary, wherein he catalogued
injuries and insults, betrayals, family quarrels, bad debts, was
written in a code of his own invention. His brothers and sisters used
to tease him about it. "Boy, are we ever afraid! Look, I'm shaking!"
But as cancer began to consume him, they took notice, fluttering
about, concerned. "What about Moishe's diary?"

I wanted it. Oh, how I wanted it. I felt the diary was my proper   21
inheritance. I hoped it would tell me things about him that he had
always been too reticent to reveal. But his widow, an obdurate lady,
refused to let me into the locked room in their apartment where he
kept his personal papers. All she would allow was, "I'm returning
your mother's love letters to her. The ones he found that time. You
know, from the refugee."

That would have been during the early Forties, when my mother   22
began to rent to refugees, putting them up in our spare bedroom.

The refugees, German and Austrian Jews, had been interned as enemy aliens in England shortly after war was declared in 1939. A year later they were transported to Canada on a ship along with the first German and Italian prisoners of war. On arrival at the dock in Quebec City, the army major who turned them over to their Canadian guards said, "You have some German officers here, very good fellows, and some Italians, they'll be no trouble. And over there," he added, indicating the refugees, "the scum of Europe."

23   The refugees were interned in camps, but in 1941 they began to be released one by one. My father, who had never had anybody to condescend to in his life, was expecting real *greeners* with sidecurls. Timorous innocents out of the *shtetl*,* who would look to him as a master of magic. Canadian magic. Instead, they patronized him. A mere junk dealer, a dolt. The refugees turned out to speak better English than any of us did, as well as German and French. After all they had been through over there, they were still fond of quoting a German son of a bitch called Goethe. "Imagine that," my father said. They also sang opera arias in the bathtub. They didn't guffaw over the antics of Fibber McGee 'n' Molly on the radio; neither were they interested in the strippers who shook their nookies right at you from the stage of the Gayety Theatre, nor in learning how to play gin rummy for a quarter of a cent a point. My mother was enthralled.

24   My father was afraid of his father. He was afraid of my unhappy mother, who arranged to have their marriage annulled when I was thirteen and my brother eighteen. He was also afraid of his second wife. Alas, he was even afraid of me when I was a boy. I rode streetcars on the Sabbath. I ate bacon. But nobody was ever afraid of Moses Isaac Richler. He was far too gentle.

25   The Richler family was, and remains, resolutely Orthodox, followers of the Lubavitcher rabbi. So when my mother threatened divorce, an all but unheard-of scandal in those days, a flock of grim rabbis in flapping black gabardine coats descended on our cold-water flat on St. Urbain Street to plead with her. But my mother, dissatisfied for years with her arranged marriage, in love at last, was adamant. She had had enough. The rabbis sighed when my father, snapping his suspenders, rocking on his heels — *speaking out* — stated his most deeply felt marital grievance. When he awakened from his Saturday afternoon nap there was no tea. "Me, I like a cup of hot tea with lemon when I wake up."

26   In the end, there was no divorce. Instead, there was an annulment. I should explain that in the Province of Quebec at that

---

*shtetl: a Jewish village, particularly in Eastern Europe

time each divorce called for parliamentary approval. A long, costly process. A lawyer, a family friend, found a loophole. He pleaded for an annulment. My mother, he told the court, had married without her father's consent when she had still been a minor. He won. Technically speaking, as I used to brag at college, I'm a bastard.

Weekdays my father awakened every morning at six, put on his   27
phylacteries, said his morning prayers, and drove his truck through the wintry dark to the family scrapyard near the waterfront. He worked there for my fierce, hot-tempered grandfather and a pompous younger brother. Uncle Solly, who had been to high school, had been made a partner in the yard, but not my father, the firstborn. He was a mere employee, working for a salary, which fed my mother's wrath. Younger brothers, determined to escape an overbearing father, had slipped free to form their own business, but my father was too timid to join them. "When times are bad they'll be back. I remember the Depression. Oh, boy!"

"Tell me about it," I pleaded.   28

But my father never talked to me about anything. Not his own   29
boyhood. His feelings. Or his dreams. He never even mentioned sex to me until I was nineteen years old, bound for Paris to try to become a writer. Clutching my Royal portable, wearing my Sta. Wag. coat. "You know what safes are. If you have to do it — *and I know you* — use 'em. Don't get married over there. They'd do anything for a pair of nylon stockings or a Canadian passport."

Hot damn, I hoped he was right. But my father thought I was   30
crazy to sail for Europe. A graveyard for the Jews. A continent where everything was broken or old. Even so, he lent me his blue steamer trunk and sent me $50 a month support. When I went broke two years later, he mailed me my boat fare without reproach. I told him that the novel I had written over there was called *The Acrobats* and he immediately suggested that I begin the title of my second novel with a B, the third with a C, and so on, which would make a nifty trademark for me. Writing, he felt, might not be such a nutty idea after all. He had read in *Life* that this guy Mickey Spillane, a mere *goy*, was making a fortune. Insulted, I explained hotly that I wasn't that kind of writer. I was a serious man.

"So?"   31

"I only write out of my obsessions."   32

"Ah, ha," he said, sighing, warming to me for once, recognizing   33
another generation of family failure.

34   Even when I was a boy his admonitions were few. "Don't embarrass me. Don't get into trouble."

35   I embarrassed him. I got into trouble.

36   In the early Forties, my father's father rented a house directly across the street from us on St. Urbain, ten of his fourteen children still single and rooted at home. The youngest, my Uncle Yankel, was only three years older than I was and at the time we were close friends. But no matter what after-school mischief we were up to, we were obliged to join my grandfather at sunset in the poky little Gallicianer *shul** around the corner for the evening prayers, a ritual I didn't care for. One evening, absorbed in a chemistry experiment in our "lab" in my grandfather's basement, we failed to appear. On his return from *shul*, my grandfather descended on us, seething, his face bleeding red. One by one he smashed our test tubes and our retorts and even our cherished water distiller against the stone wall. Yankel begged forgiveness, but not me. A few days later I contrived to get into a scrap with Yankel, leaping at him, blackening his eye. Oh boy, did that ever feel good. But Yankel squealed on me. My grandfather summoned me into his study, pulled his belt free of his trousers, and thrashed me.

37   Vengeance was mine.

38   I caught my grandfather giving short weight on his scrapyard scales to a drunken Irish peddler. My grandfather, Jehovah's enforcer. Scornful, triumphant, I ran to my father and told him his father was no better than a cheat and a hypocrite.

39   "What do you know?" my father demanded.

40   "Nothing."

41   "They're anti-Semites, every one of them."

42   My grandfather moved to Jeanne Mance Street, only a few blocks away, and on Sunday afternoons he welcomed all the family there. Children, grandchildren. Come Hanukkah, the most intimidating of my aunts was posted in the hall, seated behind a bridge table piled high with Parcheesi games one year, Snakes and Ladders another. As each grandchild filed past the table he was issued a game. "Happy Hanukkah."

43   My grandfather was best with the babies, rubbing his spade beard into their cheeks until they squealed. Bouncing them on his lap. But I was twelve years old now and I had taken to strutting down St. Urbain without a hat, and riding streetcars on the Sabbath. The next time my father and I started out for the house on Jeanne Mance on a Sunday afternoon, he pleaded with me not to disgrace him yet

---

**shul*: a synagogue

again, to behave myself for once, and then he thrust a *yarmulke** at me. "You can't go in there bareheaded. Put it on."

"It's against my principles. I'm an atheist." 44

"What are you talking about?" 45

"Charles Darwin," I said, having just read a feature article on him 46 in *Coronet*, "or haven't you ever heard of him?"

"You put on that *yarmulke*," he said, "or I cut your allowance right 47 now."

"O.K., O.K." 48

"And Jewish children are not descended from monkeys, in case 49 you think you know everything."

"When I have children of my own I'll be better to them." 50

I had said that, testing. Sneaking a sidelong glance at my father. 51 The thing is I had been born with an undescended testicle and my brother, catching me naked in the bathroom, had burst out laughing and assured me that I would never be able to have children or even screw. "With only one ball," he said, "you'll never be able to shoot jism."

My father didn't rise to the bait. He had worries of his own. My 52 mother. The refugee in the spare bedroom. His father. "When you step in the door," he said, "the *zeyda** will ask you which portion of the Torah they read in *shul* yesterday." He told me the name of the chapter. "Got it?"

"I'm not afraid of him." 53

My grandfather, his eyes hot, was lying in wait for me in the 54 living room. Before a court composed of just about the entire family, he denounced me as a violator of the Sabbath. A *shabus goy*. Yankel smirked. My grandfather grabbed me by the ear, beat me about the face, and literally threw me out of the house. I lingered across the street, waiting for my father to seek me out, but when he finally appeared, having endured a bruising lecture of his own, all he said was, "You deserved what you got."

"Some father you are." 55

Which was when I earned another belt on the cheek. 56

"I want you to go back in there like a man and apologize to the 57 *zeyda*."

"Like hell." 58

I never spoke to my grandfather again. 59

But when he died, less than a year after the annulment of my 60 parents' marriage, my mother insisted it was only proper that I attend his funeral. I arrived at the house on Jeanne Mance to find

yarmulke: a skullcap worn by Jewish males in the synagogue
zeyda: grandfather

the coffin set out in the living room, uncles and aunts gathered round. My Uncle Solly drove me into a corner. "So here you are," he said.

61   "So?"

62   "You hastened his death; you never even spoke to him even though he was sick all those months."

63   "I didn't bring on his death."

64   "Well, smart guy, you're the one who is mentioned first in his will."

65   "Oh."

66   "You are not a good Jew and you are not to touch his coffin. It says that in his will. Don't you dare touch his coffin."

67   I turned to my father. Help me, help me. But he retreated, wiggling his eyebrows.

68   So many things about my father's nature still exasperate or mystify me.

69   All those years he was being crushed by his own father, nagged by my mother, teased (albeit affectionately) by his increasingly affluent brothers and cousins, was he seething inside, plotting a vengeance in his diary? Or was he really so sweet-natured as not to give a damn? Finally, there is a possibility I'd rather not ponder. Was he not sweet-natured at all, but a coward? Like me. Who would travel miles to avoid a quarrel. Who tends to remember slights — recording them in my mind's eye — transmogrifying them — finally publishing them in a code more accessible than my father's. Making them the stuff of fiction.

70   Riddles within riddles.

71   My father came to Montreal as an infant, his father fleeing Galicia. Pogroms. Rampaging Cossacks. But, striptease shows aside, the only theatre my father relished, an annual outing for the two of us, was the appearance of the Don Cossack Choir at the St. Denis Theatre. My father would stamp his feet to their lusty marching and drinking songs; his eyes would light up to see those behemoths, his own father's tormentors, prance and tumble on stage. Moses Isaac Richler, who never marched, nor drank, nor pranced.

72   Obviously, he didn't enjoy his family. My mother, my brother, me. Sundays he would usually escape our cold-water flat early and alone and start out for the first-run downtown cinemas, beginning with the Princess, which opened earliest, continuing from there to the Capitol or the Palace, and maybe moving on to the Loew's, returning to us bleary-eyed, but satiated, after dark. Astonishingly, he kept a sharp eye out for little production errors. Discovering them filled

him with joy. Once, for instance, he told us, "Listen to this, Clark Gable is sitting there in this newspaper office and he tells Claudette Colbert he will be finished typing his story in an hour. But when she comes back and we are supposed to believe an hour has passed, *the hands on the clock on the wall haven't moved. Not an inch.*" Another time it was, "Franchot Tone is in this tank in the desert, you're not going to believe this, and he says 'O.K., men, let's go. Attack!' And they attack. But if you look closely inside the tank just before they push off, the fuel gauge is indicating EMPTY. No gas. Get it?"

The Best Years of Our Lives overwhelmed him.   73

"There's a scene in there where Fredric March burps. He's hung   74
over, he drinks an Alka-Seltzer or something, and he lets out a good one. Right there on screen. Imagine."

My mother was fond of reminding me that the night I was born,   75
my father had not waited at the hospital to find out how she was, or whether it was a boy or a girl, but had gone to the movies instead. What was playing, I wondered.

My father didn't dream of Italy, where the lemon trees bloomed.   76
He never went for a walk in the country or read a novel, unless he had to, because it was one of mine and he might be blamed for it. Bliss for him was the Gayety Theatre on a Saturday night. My father and a couple of younger brothers, still bachelors, seated front row centre. On stage, Peaches, Anne Curie, or the legendary Lili St. Cyr. My father rapt, his throat dry, watching the unattainable Lili simulating intercourse with a swan as the stage lights throbbed, then trudging home through the snow to sit alone at the kitchen table, drinking hot milk with matzohs before going to sleep.

We endured some rough passages together. Shortly after the   77
marriage annulment, I fought with my father. Fists flew. We didn't speak for two years. Then, when we came together again, meeting once a week, it wasn't to talk, but to play gin rummy for a quarter of a cent a point. My father, I began to suspect, wasn't reticent. He didn't understand life. He had nothing to say to anybody.

In 1954, some time after my return to Europe, where I was to remain 78
rooted for almost two decades, I married a *shiksa** in London. My father wrote me an indignant letter. Once more, we were estranged. But no sooner did the marriage end in divorce than he pounced: "You see, mixed marriages never work."

"But, Daddy, your first marriage didn't work either and Maw was   79
a rabbi's daughter."

"What do you know?"   80

---

*shiksa: gentile woman

81   "Nothing," I replied, hugging him.

82   When I married again, this time for good, but to another *shiksa,* he was not overcome with delight, yet neither did he complain. For after all the wasting years, we had finally become friends. My father became my son. Once, he had sent money to me in Paris. Now, as the scrapyard foundered, I mailed monthly checks to him in Montreal. On visits home, I took him to restaurants. I bought him treats. If he took me to a gathering of the Richler clan on a Sunday afternoon, he would bring along a corked bottle of 7-Up for me, filled with scotch whiskey. "There'll be nothing for you to drink there, and I know you."

83   "Hey, Daddy, that's really very thoughtful."

84   During the Sixties, on a flying trip to Montreal, my publishers put me up at the Ritz-Carlton Hotel, and I asked my father to meet me for a drink there.

85   "You know," he said, joining me at the table, "I'm sixty-two years old and I've never been here before. Inside, I mean. So this is the Ritz."

86   "It's just a bar," I said, embarrassed.

87   "What should I order?"

88   "Whatever you want, Daddy."

89   "A rye and ginger ale. Would that be all right here?"

90   "Certainly."

• • • • • • •

91   What I'm left with are unresolved mysteries. A sense of regret. Anecdotes for burnishing.

92   My wife, a proud lady, showing him our firstborn son, his week-old howling grandchild, saying, "Don't you think he looks like Mordecai?"

93   "Babies are babies," he responded, seemingly indifferent.

94   Some years later my father coming to our house, pressing chocolate bars on the kids. "Who do you like better," he asked them, "your father or your mother?"

95   In the mid-Sixties, I flew my father to London. He came with his wife. Instead of slipping away with him to the Windmill Theatre or Raymond's Revue Bar, another strip joint, like a fool I acquired theatre tickets. We took the two of them to *Beyond the Fringe.* "What did you think?" I asked as we left the theatre.

96   "There was no chorus line," he said.

97   Following his last operation for cancer, I flew to Montreal, promising to take him on a trip as soon as he was out of bed. The Catskills. Grossinger's. With a stopover in New York to take in

some shows. Back in London, each time I phoned, his doctor advised me to wait a bit longer. I waited. He died. The next time I flew to Montreal it was to bury him.

Structure:

1. "My Father's Life" is a huge topic for any writer to attempt in an essay. Has Richler succeeded? Has he done more than just scratch the surface of the topic? If so, how?
2. Why does Richler use spaces to divide his essay into sections? Have you tried this technique? Under what circumstances would it be useful?
3. Is "My Father's Life" mainly a *contrast* or mainly a *comparison*, or is it both? Point out the main contrasts between Moses Isaac Richler and his son Mordecai. Point out the main comparisons. And point out any major contrasts or comparisons between other persons or things as well.
4. Does the ambiguity of Richler's feelings about his father bother you? Would a clear feeling of hatred or of love have made for a better essay? Support your answer with reasons.

Style:

1. What device of humour does Richler's father use when he suggests, in paragraph 1, that his son's next novel be entitled *Until* Debt *Do Us Part?*
2. How do you react to Richler's use of Yiddish words such as *knish, shul, zeyda* and *shiksa?* Do they add authenticity, or atmosphere and flavour, or do they confuse? What guidelines would you suggest for use of foreign words in English?
3. What device of style underlies the first half of paragraph 18? Is it effective?
4. When in paragraph 17 Richler says that his father was "clearly not entitled to a place at the table," what FIGURE OF SPEECH does he use?
5. "Nothing" is the only word of paragraphs 10 and 40, and the key word of paragraph 81. Why is it emphasized through its repetition in these one-word or one-sentence paragraphs? How does it strengthen the major meanings of the essay?
6. What strength as a writer does Richler demonstrate in the words "Following his last operation for cancer. . . ." (par. 97)?

Ideas:

1. What are the benefits of trying to understand our parents and grandparents? Why do some people research the lives of even their distant ancestors?

2. Why is the "generation gap" often severe in families that have immigrated? Is this the main cause of friction between young Richler and his father and grandfather?

3. Who is young Richler most like — his mother, father or grandfather? With which of these four people do you most identify, and why?

4. Richler writes in paragraph 18, "My father never saw Paris. Never read Yeats. Never stayed out with the boys drinking too much. Never flew to New York on a whim. Nor turned over in bed and slept in, rather than report to work. Never knew a reckless love. What did he hope for? What did he want?" In specifying these acts that his father never performed, what is Richler suggesting about life? Which of these acts, if any, represent the life you would like to lead?

5. "What I'm left with are unresolved mysteries," writes Richler in paragraph 91. Do you think that writing this essay has failed to give Richler new insights into his father's life? Why or why not? How often does writing give you new insights into your own topics?

6. If you have read "Coming of Age in Putnok," compare the relationship of father to son as described by George Gabori and Mordecai Richler.

7. In essay form, *compare and/or contrast* yourself to any one of these persons:
    your mother
    your father
    your brother
    your sister
    your grandmother
    your grandfather

(NOTE: See also the Topics for Writing at the end of this chapter.)

Topics for Writing

Chapter 5: Comparison and Contrast

(Note also the topics for writing that appear after each selection in this chapter.)

Compare and/or contrast one of the following pairs:

1. The pessimist and the optimist
2. The conformist and the nonconformist
3. The introvert and the extrovert
4. The atheist and the religious person
5. The idealist and the realist
6. The pacifist and the militarist
7. The liberated woman and the liberated man
8. Morning people and night people
9. City people and country people
10. Americans and Canadians
11. The metric system and the imperial system
12. My first language and my second language
13. Telephoning and writing a letter
14. Eating at home and eating out
15. Public school and private school
16. French Canada and English Canada
17. Life in a high-rise apartment and in a house
18. Marriage and living common-law
19. Two ways to get rich
20. Two ways to lose weight
21. Two current fads in clothing
22. Two current fads in music
23. Two current fads in dance
24. The fifties and the sixties
25. The seventies and the eighties

"We were all, brothers and sisters alike, born in a long three-storey wooden house, a house as humped and crusty as a loaf of homemade bread, as warm and clean inside as the white of the loaf."

Félix Leclerc, "The Family House"

In a way, it's like ....

ANALOGY and Related Devices

One student wrote this memory of his childhood in Toronto:

> I heard and felt a rumbling from the ground, looked up
> and saw a huge red metallic monster with a tail on the end
> approach us. "Run, run," I said, "before it eats us." My
> mother reassured me that no fear was necessary. The
> monster slowly rolled up beside us, opened its mouth, and
> we went in.

As adults, we know that monsters have not roamed the shores of
Lake Ontario for many millions of years, and that they were not red
but green! We also know that monsters and streetcars have little in
common. Yet who would say that this *analogy* does not clearly
explain the child's first encounter with a streetcar? It may even help
us, as adults, to view with new eyes something that we have taken
for granted.

203

In the last chapter, we discussed how two items from the same category — say, two centres of population — can be explained logically through comparison and contrast. By seeing how the town and the city are alike or unlike, we gain a clearer understanding of both. An *analogy*, though, brings together two apparently unlike items from different categories. And instead of using both items to explain each other, it more often uses one as a device to explain the other. It is not the monster we care about but the monstrous aspects of the streetcar.

In the last chapter, we speculated whether, instead of comparing a city and a town, we could compare a city and an ant hill. To those of us who live in chambers along the corridors of apartment buildings or who each day crowd into holes in the ground to take the subway, the similarities may be all too clear. We see right away that such an argument is hardly logical, for the very good reason that people are not insects. Yet the analogy may be a fresh, thought-provoking way to describe some aspects of life in a city.

As the selections in this chapter demonstrate, an entire essay can be built on one analogy developed with details. The more similarities between the two items, the stronger and more satisfying the analogy. Our account of the city as an ant hill should no doubt include more items than the apartment buildings and subway, and those items should be described and explained in some detail. Yet even a brief statement, "The city is like an ant hill," has value. As a *simile*, it is not much of an argument in itself but is a vivid statement that can be used in support of another argument.

While a *simile* states that one thing is *like* another, a *metaphor* states that one thing *is* another ("The city is an ant hill"). Both devices occur often in poetry and in fiction, and both are effective in essays. The last selection in this chapter, Félix Leclerc's description of his boyhood home, contains a steady stream of similes and metaphors that convey a vividly poetic sense not only of the place but also of the author's feelings about the place. Perhaps nothing objective has been proven, but a message has certainly been given.

Robertson Davies

The Decorums of Stupidity

If any Canadian can be called a Renaissance man, it is Robertson Davies. The breadth of his knowledge, the variety of his interests, and the polish and wit and dramatic flair with which he writes make him one of Canada's most versatile and widely read authors. He was born in 1913 in Thamesville, Ontario. After attending Upper Canada College, he studied at Queen's University and in 1938 earned his B. Litt. at Balliol College, Oxford. For a time he was an actor in the English provinces, then joined the Old Vic Company to act and teach in its drama school. He returned to Canada in 1940 and in 1942 began a distinguished career in journalism as editor of the Peterborough Examiner. *He returned to academia in 1963 as Master of Massey College, University of Toronto, a post which he held until retirement in 1981. Despite his busy schedule, Davies has written numerous plays, books of literary criticism, and the works for which he is best known, his novels.* Tempest-Tost *appeared in 1951,* Leaven of Malice *in 1954,* A Mixture of Frailties *in 1958,* The Rebel Angels *in 1981 and* What's Bred in the Bone *in 1985. But Davies' reputation, both at home and abroad, rests chiefly on his* Deptford Trilogy *of novels:* Fifth Business *(1970),* The Manticore *(1972) and* World of Wonders *(1975). Our selection comes from a collection of Davies' essays,* A Voice from the Attic *(1960).*

Not all rapid reading is to be condemned. Much that is badly 1
written and grossly padded must be read rapidly and
nothing is lost thereby. Much of the reading that has to be
done in the way of business should be done as fast as it can be
understood. The ideal business document is an auditor's report; a
good one is finely edited. But the memoranda, the public-relations
pieces, the business magazines, need not detain us. Every kind of
prose has its own speed, and the experienced reader knows it as a
musician knows Adagio from Allegro. All of us have to read a great
deal of stuff which gives us no pleasure and little information, but
which we cannot wholly neglect; such reading belongs in that
department of life which Goldsmith called "the decorums of
stupidity." Books as works of art are no part of this duty-reading.

Books as works of art? Certainly; it is thus that their writers 2
intend them. But how are these works of art used?

Suppose you hear of a piece of recorded music which you think you 3
might like. Let us say it is an opera of Benjamin Britten's — *The
Turn of the Screw.* You buy it, and after dinner you put it on your
record player. The scene is one of bustling domesticity: your wife is

writing to her mother, on the typewriter, and from time to time she appeals to you for the spelling of a word; the older children are chattering happily over a game, and the baby is building, and toppling, towers of blocks. The records are long-playing ones, designed for 33 revolutions of the turntable per minute; ah, but you have taken a course in rapid listening, and you pride yourself on the speed with which you can hear, so you adjust your machine to play at 78 revolutions a minute. And when you find your attention wandering from the music, you skip the sound arm rapidly from groove to groove until you come to a bit that appeals to you. But look — it is eight o'clock, and if you are to get to your meeting on time, Britten must be choked off. So you speed him up until a musical pause arrives, and then you stop the machine, marking the place so that you can continue your appreciation of *The Turn of the Screw* when next you can spare a few minutes for it.

4   Ridiculous? Of course, but can you say that you have never read a book in that fashion?

5   One of the advantages of reading is that it can be done in short spurts and under imperfect conditions. But how often do we read in conditions which are merely decent, not to speak of perfection? How often do we give a book a fair chance to make its effect with us?

Structure:

1. In discussing "duty-reading" that is best done at high speed, how does paragraph 1 prepare us for the main point?
2. Where is the main point first stated?
3. Paragraph 3 develops the analogy upon which this essay is based: listening to music as reading a book. Books have been discussed in the introduction, but why are they not mentioned in the analogy itself?
4. Davies uses a standard technique in closing his essay: the asking of questions. Are these true questions that are open to debate, or are they rhetorical questions designed to make us agree with the author?

Style:

1. Why is this essay so much shorter than others you have read in this book? Has Davies failed to develop his point fully?
2. Why are paragraphs 1 and 3 so long while paragraphs 2 and 4 are so short?

3. What FIGURE OF SPEECH does Davies use in this sentence from paragraph 1: "Every kind of prose has its own speed, and the experienced reader knows it as a musician knows Adagio from Allegro"?
4. Is Davies entirely serious, as his elevated and dignified style would suggest? Or is humour important to his argument? Give examples.

Ideas:

1. Is a desire to read fast like a desire to eat fast? To drive fast? To work fast? To live fast? Why is speed so highly regarded in our culture? Are you familiar with another culture that encourages a slower pace? If so, which do you prefer, and why?
2. Before writing was invented, all stories and poems were of course spoken aloud. What advantages do you think a listener has over a reader? What advantages do you think a reader has over a listener?
3. If you have read "A Tongue-Lashing for Deaf Ears," by Wendy Dennis, compare the distractions of the modern reader with those of the modern movie-goer.
4. Francis Bacon said, "Some books are to be tasted, others to be swallowed, and some few to be chewed and digested. . . ." Make a list of the five or ten books you have most recently read. Which did you "taste," which did you "swallow" and which did you "chew and digest"? What factors influenced your method in each case?
5. In an essay based on *analogy*, tell how you "taste," "swallow" or "chew and digest" different kinds of music.

(NOTE: See also the Topics for Writing at the end of this chapter.)

Alan Stewart

Cars Make the Man a Boy

Alan Stewart was born in 1943 in Glasgow, Scotland. He immigrated to Canada, earned a B.A. and a M.A., then taught for a time. Now he writes regularly for the Toronto Globe and Mail. *"Cars Make the Man a Boy" appeared in 1981 in the* Globe and Mail *column "Between the Sexes." Like his other contributions to this column, our selection examines an aspect of sex in modern society.*

1   One of the signs of the creeping androgyny that is skulking around everywhere these days, coming on little cat feet to fog up our precious and time-honored sexual distinctions, is the growing lack of masculine absorption in cars. I have met very few women who really cared at all about cars, cared in the same sense that they care about ecology or world peace or bringing home the constitution; traditionally, it was always men who clustered in corners at otherwise boring parties to discuss transmissions or the evolution of the Plymouth tail-light during the 50s. It was men who wrote car magazines and men who read them. It was men who, with the instinctive regularity of swallows homing in on Capistrano, visited the automobile showrooms every fall, not because they needed a car but just to have a look.

2   It seemed the younger the man, the greater the interest and nowhere was the interest more ardent than among boys approaching 16, the magical age at which you could get your driver's licence and hence be able, in theory at least, to drive a Ferrari. I was lucky to be that age during a time when cars were taken very seriously by all right-thinking people, and no one took cars more seriously than I did.

3   It was not odd that I wanted to stop being a pedestrian at about the same stage that I wanted to stop being a virgin; the connection between automobiles and sex, in the masculine mind, has been extensively documented. I remember that someone came up with a theory that when a man was buying a car, he went at it in the same way he chose a woman. What he really wanted, according to the theory, was a convertible, because a convertible represented the glamor and excitement of having a mistress.

4   However, there being a crust of solid citizenship over the seething ooze of his libido, he usually settled for a sedan, which represented the more sensible and socially acceptable wife. Egged on by this

research, the manufacturers came up with the hardtop convertible, a sexy compromise which enabled a man to have a car that he could park in the bedroom as well as in the kitchen.

Almost everything is a sedan these days, which certainly does not   5
say much for the sexual aspirations of modern men. The writer Trevanian, in his novel *Shibumi*, argues that Italian men drive as if the car were an extension of their penis, while Frenchmen drive as if it were a substitute for one. How does this jibe with the current trend of each year's cars seeming smaller than those of the year before? Even the Cadillac, perhaps the Burt Reynolds of the automotive world, proudly offers a smaller edition than it once did.

Some wet blankets claim that sex should be sex and cars should be   6
cars. But if everything from gardening to politics can be appreciated for its sexual overtones, why must sexual equality and the price of gasoline stamp all the raunchiness out of driving a car? Why must a man's attachment to his automobile be considered puerile and silly? If I can manage to hold down a halfway respectable job, pay the rent on time, and refrain from littering our parks, I should be allowed to enjoy a little fantasy as I crawl up the Parkway during rush hour.

As a teenager, I fantasized of one day owning my own car. It would   7
be a brassy convertible with a very loud radio and I would zoom around town in it with my sleeves rolled up, smoking cigarets, wearing sunglasses, and looking out at the world like Steve McQueen. From my current vantage point of incipient middle age, I can see that all this was mindless and juvenile. Nevertheless, a few years ago I did get such a car. It was a sprawling, eight-cylinder Mustang, and I had it painted what the Ford people called Deep Orchid. On summer evenings I would put on my sunglasses, roll up my sleeves, and wheel along Yonge Street, with the top down and the radio way up.

Was it possible to go back and experience an adolescent thrill I   8
had missed the first time around? Could a grown man enjoy making an empty-headed spectacle of himself? Can you go home again?

You bet your life.   9

Structure:

1. Where does the THESIS STATEMENT of this essay appear?
2. What is the analogy upon which this selection is built, and which sentence introduces it?
3. How do paragraphs 7–9 develop the main point?
4. Why does the last paragraph contain only four words?

Style:

1. Alan Stewart uses words normally found in serious writing — "androgyny" (par. 1), "libido" (par. 4), "puerile" (par. 6) and "incipient" (par. 7) — in the same essay with expressions more likely to be heard in casual conversation: "egged on" (par. 4), "jibe" (par. 5), "wet blankets" (par. 6), "raunchiness" (par. 6), "zoom" (par. 7) and "You bet your life" (par. 9). For what sort of reader do you think this mixture of FORMAL and INFORMAL language is intended? How effective do you think it is?
2. Point out at least one passage that deliberately uses repetition to achieve an effect.
3. The emotionally loaded words "creeping" and "skulking," in Stewart's opening sentence, convey bias. Point out other words or phrases like them in the rest of the essay.
4. Use a desk-size dictionary to find the origins of the word "androgynous." Discuss how "androgynous" and "androgyny" are related to the words "androgen," "android," "gynecology," "gynecocracy" and "misogyny."

Ideas:

1. How serious is Stewart in his argument against "creeping androgyny" (par. 1) when he makes an "empty-headed spectacle of himself" (par. 8) in his own male-centred enjoyment of cars? Point out passages that support your interpretation.
2. Point out all the ways in which Stewart's analogy links cars and sex.
3. Does this essay have anything to say to women? If men symbolize their sexuality through driving cars, how do women symbolize theirs?
4. Do we STEREOTYPE people by the vehicles they drive? What kind of person do we think of as driving a "muscle car"? A van? A station wagon? A semitrailer truck? A pickup truck? A Buick? A Volvo? A Volkswagen? A motorcycle? Or no vehicle at all? If you recognize such stereotypes, do you know individuals who are exceptions to the rule? If so, describe them and their vehicles.
5. Many critics see the automobile as a threat to our society. It has killed more North Americans than have all of our wars combined; it consumes large amounts of fossil fuel, making us dependent upon oil imports; it pollutes our cities; and it causes our farmland to disappear under pavement. Yet neither these problems nor the rapidly rising costs of cars, fuel and insurance

have stopped North Americans from driving. Why do we love cars so much? Are there reasons other than the one Stewart has given?

6. Are you familiar with a culture in which most people do not have a car? What advantages and disadvantages do they experience? What are their methods for getting along without a car?

7. Write an essay based on an *analogy* between cars and one of the following:

horses
elephants
dinosaurs
one's clothes
one's own body
loaded guns
houses

(NOTE: See also the Topics for Writing at the end of this chapter.)

Michael Ondaatje

*Tabula Asiae**

In more than one way Michael Ondaatje is the least "Canadian" of our major Canadian writers. He was born in 1943 in Ceylon (now Sri Lanka) to the family of exuberant and eccentric aristocrats he later portrayed in his fictionalized autobiography Running in the Family. *And although he has since become one of Canada's major poets, his works are typically set outside our borders and are written in a richly lyrical, often surreal, often cinematic style that suggests other places and other influences. Ondaatje moved to England in 1954 and to Canada in 1962. Here he took a B.A. and a M.A. and began teaching, first at Western Ontario University, then since 1971 in the English Department of Glendon College, York University, in Toronto. His first book of poetry,* The Dainty Monsters, *appeared in 1967. In 1969 appeared* The Man with Seven Toes, *in 1973* Rat Jelly, *and in 1979 There's a Trick with a Knife I'm Learning to Do: Poems 1973–1978. It won the Governor-General's Award. His book of prose and poetry,* The Collected Works of Billy the Kid *(1970), also won a Governor-General's Award, and in 1976 appeared his richly poetic novel* Coming Through Slaughter. *Ondaatje has also written literary criticism, edited anthologies, made films and edited for Coach House Press. Our selection comes from* Running in the Family *(1982).*

1   On my brother's wall in Toronto are the false maps. Old portraits of Ceylon. The result of sightings, glances from trading vessels, the theories of sextant. The shapes differ so much they seem to be translations — by Ptolemy, Mercator, François Valentyn, Mortier, and Heydt — growing from mythic shapes into eventual accuracy. Amoeba, then stout rectangle, and then the island as we know it now, a pendant off the ear of India. Around it, a blue-combed ocean busy with dolphin and sea-horse, cherub and compass. Ceylon floats on the Indian Ocean and holds its naive mountains, drawings of cassowary and boar who leap without perspective across imagined 'desertum'* and plain.

2   At the edge of the maps the scrolled mantling depicts ferocious slipper-footed elephants, a white queen offering a necklace to natives who carry tusks and a conch, a Moorish king who stands amidst the power of books and armour. On the south-west corner of

---

**Tabula Asiae*: Map of Asia (in Latin; apparently the words Ondaatje sees on his brother's old maps of Ceylon)
**desertum*: empty land

212

some charts are satyrs, hoof deep in foam, listening to the sound of the island, their tails writhing in the waves.

The maps reveal rumours of topography, the routes for invasion and trade, and the dark mad mind of travellers' tales appears throughout Arab and Chinese and medieval records. The island seduced all of Europe. The Portuguese. The Dutch. The English. And so its name changed, as well as its shape, — Serendip, Ratnapida ("island of gems"), Taprobane, Zeloan, Zeilan, Seyllan, Ceilon, and Ceylon — the wife of many marriages, courted by invaders who stepped ashore and claimed everything with the power of their sword or bible or language. 3

This pendant, once its shape stood still, became a mirror. It pretended to reflect each European power till newer ships arrived and spilled their nationalities, some of whom stayed and intermarried — my own ancestor arriving in 1600, a doctor who cured the residing governor's daughter with a strange herb and was rewarded with land, a foreign wife, and a new name which was a Dutch spelling of his own. Ondaatje. A parody of the ruling language. And when his Dutch wife died, marrying a Sinhalese* woman, having nine children, and remaining. Here. At the centre of the rumour. At this point on the map. 4

Structure and Style:

1. Why is "Tabula Asiae" so much shorter than most selections in this book? Because it says less? Because it communicates differently? If the latter, what are some techniques Michael Ondaatje has used that many contributors to this book have not?

2. Michael Ondaatje's usual form of writing is poetry. How CONCISE is most poetry compared to most PROSE? Why? Is there a sharp dividing line between poetry and prose, or can they draw on the same techniques? Can they ever resemble each other so closely that they almost merge? Where would you place "Tabula Asiae" in this respect, and why?

3. In paragraph 1 Ondaatje describes the shape of Ceylon in early "false maps" as an "amoeba" and a "stout rectangle." Would you call these comparisons METAPHORS or analogies? Why?

4. In paragraph 1 Ondaatje goes on to call Ceylon a "pendant off the ear of India." What FIGURE OF SPEECH is this? Does he develop it fully enough to make it an analogy?

*Sinhalese (or Singhalese): the largest population group of Sri Lanka

5. In paragraph 3 Ondaatje calls Ceylon "the wife of many marriages." Explain his meaning. Also tell what FIGURE OF SPEECH he has used.
6. In paragraph 4 the "pendant" becomes a "mirror." In what sense? And again, is this image a METAPHOR or analogy?
7. In what sense do the "false maps" of Ondaatje's brother in Toronto constitute an analogy of Ceylon?
8. "Serendip" is one of Sri Lanka's early names, as we are told in paragraph 3. In a desk-size or reference dictionary, find the connection between this name and the often-used word "serendipity."

Ideas:

1. The Sri Lanka of "Tabula Asiae" — mysterious, romantic and legendary — is not at all the Sri Lanka of the encyclopedia. Name all the reasons you can think of why Michael Ondaatje presents the land of his childhood in the SUBJECTIVE, poetic way he does.
2. "Tabula Asiae" is a chapter of Michael Ondaatje's autobiographical book *Running in the Family.* If you were to write the story of your own childhood and family, how far back in time could you begin? Who are your earliest known ancestors? When and where did they live? Do you think the homeland or personalities of your ancestors before your parents and grandparents had much influence in making you the person you are today?
3. Ondaatje's brother puts old maps of Ceylon on his wall in Toronto. Do those who move to a new country do better to cherish and preserve their past, as the Ondaatjes do, or to forget the past in order to make a new life? If you or your parents immigrated to Canada, which path have you taken, and why? If English is your second language, do you intend to retain your first? If so, how? Will you then teach it to your children? Why or why not?
4. If you have read "Old Year's Night," compare the way colonialism is presented in Barbados by Austin Clarke and in Sri Lanka by Michael Ondaatje.
5. In paragraph 3 Ondaatje describes the early invaders of Ceylon who ". . . stepped ashore and claimed everything with the power of their sword or bible or language." Have these three — sword, Bible and language — all been used as tools of conquest? If so, deliberately or accidentally? If you can, give examples, either from other countries or from Canada.

6. Immigration has occurred at some point in the background of all Canadians, even the native peoples. Choose one of these topics:

   My ancestral homeland
   The arrival of my ancestor(s) in Canada
   My immigration to Canada

   Select the one most appropriate to you. Focus it to fit your circumstances, knowledge and interest. Then as you write, colour and heighten your account with the kinds of poetical devices Michael Ondaatje has used in his account. (See FIGURES OF SPEECH, and especially METAPHOR, in the glossary.)

NOTE: See also the Topics for Writing at the end of this chapter.)

Farley Mowat

The One Perfect House*

Farley Mowat is one of Canada's more flamboyant public figures. Soldier, traveller, writer, anthologist, story teller, conservationist and public gadfly, Mowat has always been more warmly received by the reading public than by the critics, who are only now recognizing him as a serious writer. He was born in 1921 in Belleville, Ontario. From 1940 to 1946 he served in the Canadian army in Europe, then after the war spent two years in the Arctic and in 1949 earned a B.A. at the University of Toronto. Since then Mowat has written or edited more than 25 books; his work has been translated into more than 20 languages and published in more than 40 countries. He is probably Canada's most widely read author. Among his works are children's books (Lost in the Barrens, 1956; The Dog Who Wouldn't Be, 1957; Owls in the Family, 1961), light humour (The Boat Who Wouldn't Float, 1969), accounts of his experiences in the Arctic (People of the Deer, 1952; The Desperate People, 1959; Never Cry Wolf, 1963; Sibir, 1970), numerous anthologies and a highly acclaimed account of his experiences at war (And No Birds Sang, 1979). In 1980 appeared an anthology of his selected works, The World of Farley Mowat. In recent books such as A Whale for the Killing (1972), and Sea of Slaughter (1984), Mowat's attention has turned more and more to the destructiveness of humankind towards nature. Our selection, "The One Perfect House," comes from People of the Deer, Mowat's study of the Ihalmiut among whom he stayed in the Arctic Barrens. These original Canadians, who called themselves "the People," have since vanished.

1   A s I grew to know the People, so my respect for their intelligence and ingenuity increased. Yet it was a long time before I could reconcile my feelings of respect with the poor, shoddy dwelling places that they constructed. As with most Eskimos, the winter homes of the Ihalmiut are the snow-built domes we call igloos. (Igloo in Eskimo means simply "house" and thus an igloo can be built of wood or stone, as well as of snow.) But unlike most other Innuit, the Ihalmiut make snow houses which are cramped, miserable shelters. I think the People acquired the art of igloo construction quite recently in their history and from the coast Eskimos. Certainly they have no love for their igloos, and prefer the skin tents. This preference is related to the problem of fuel.

---

*Editor's title

Any home in the arctic, in winter, requires some fuel if only for 2
cooking. The coast peoples make use of fat lamps, for they have an
abundance of fat from the sea mammals they kill, and so they are
able to cook in the igloo, and to heat it as well. But the Ihalmiut can
ill afford to squander the precious fat of the deer, and they dare to
burn only one tiny lamp for light. Willow must serve as fuel, and
while willow burns well enough in a tent open at the peak to allow
the smoke to escape, when it is burned in a snow igloo, the choking
smoke leaves no place for human occupants.

So snow houses replace the skin tents of the Ihalmiut only when 3
winter has already grown old and the cold has reached the
seemingly unbearable extremes of sixty or even seventy degrees
below zero. Then the tents are grudgingly abandoned and snow
huts built. From that time until spring no fires may burn inside the
homes of the People, and such cooking as is attempted must be done
outside, in the face of the blizzards and gales.

Yet though tents are preferred to igloos, it is still rather hard to 4
understand why. . . . Great, gaping slits outline each hide on the
frame of a tent. Such a home offers hardly more shelter than a
thicket of trees, for on the unbroken sweep of the plains the winds
blow with such violence that they drive the hard snow through the
tents as if the skin walls did not really exist. But the People spend
many days and dark nights in these feeble excuses for houses, while
the wind rises like a demon of hatred and the cold comes as if it
meant to destroy all life in the land.

In these tents there may be a fire; but consider this fire, this 5
smoldering handful of green twigs, dug with infinite labor from
under the drifts. It gives heat only for a few inches out from its
sullen coals so that it barely suffices to boil a pot of water in an hour
or two. The eternal winds pour into the tent and dissipate what
little heat the fire can spare from the cook-pots. The fire gives
comfort to the Ihalmiut only through its appeal to the eyes.

However, the tent with its wan little fire is a more desirable place 6
than the snow house with no fire at all. At least the man in the tent
can have a hot bowl of soup once in a while, but after life in the
igloos begins, almost all food must be eaten while it is frozen to the
hardness of rocks. Men sometimes take skin bags full of ice into the
beds so that they can have water to drink, melted by the heat of
their bodies. It is true that some of the People build cook shelters
outside the igloos but these snow hearths burn very badly, and then
only when it is calm. For the most part the winds prevent any
outside cooking at all, and anyway by late winter the willow supply
is so deeply buried under the drifts, it is almost impossible for men
to procure it.

7   So you see that the homes of the Ihalmiut in winter are hardly models of comfort. Even when spring comes to the land the improvement in housing conditions is not great. After the tents go up in the spring, the rains begin. During daylight it rains with gray fury and the tents soak up the chill water until the hides hang slackly on their poles while rivulets pour through the tent to drench everything inside. At night, very likely, there will be frost and by dawn everything not under the robes with the sleepers will be frozen stiff.

8   With the end of the spring rains, the hot sun dries and shrinks the hides until they are drum-taut, but the ordeal is not yet over. Out of the steaming muskegs come the hordes of bloodsucking and flesh-eating flies and these find that the Ihalmiut tents offer no barrier to their invasion. The tents belong equally to the People and to the flies, until midsummer brings an end to the plague, and the hordes vanish.

9   My high opinion of the People was often clouded when I looked at their homes. I sometimes wondered if the Ihalmiut were as clever and as resourceful as I thought them to be. I had been too long conditioned to think of home as four walls and a roof, and so the obvious solution of the Ihalmiut housing problem escaped me for nearly a year. It took me that long to realize that the People not only have good homes, but that they have devised the one perfect house.

10   The tent and the igloo are really only auxiliary shelters. The real home of the Ihalmio is much like that of the turtle, for it is what he carries about on his back. In truth it is the only house that can enable men to survive on the merciless plains of the Barrens. It has central heating from the fat furnace of the body, its walls are insulated to a degree of perfection that we white men have not been able to surpass, or even emulate. It is complete, light in weight, easy to make and easy to keep in repair. It costs nothing, for it is a gift of the land, through the deer. When I consider that house, my opinion of the astuteness of the Ihalmiut is no longer clouded.

11   Primarily the house consists of two suits of fur, worn one over the other, and each carefully tailored to the owner's dimensions. The inner suit is worn with the hair of the hides facing inward and touching the skin while the outer suit has its hair turned out to the weather. Each suit consists of a pullover parka with a hood, a pair of fur trousers, fur gloves and fur boots. The double motif is extended to the tips of the fingers, to the top of the head, and to the soles of the feet where soft slippers of harehide are worn next to the skin.

12   The high winter boots may be tied just above the knee so that they leave no entry for the cold blasts of the wind. But full ventilation is provided by the design of the parka. Both inner and outer parkas

hang slackly to at least the knees of the wearer, and they are not belted in winter. Cold air does not rise, so that no drafts can move up under the parkas to reach the bare flesh, but the heavy, moistureladen air from close to the body sinks through the gap between parka and trousers and is carried away. Even in times of great physical exertion, when the Ihalmio sweats freely, he is never in any danger of soaking his clothing and so inviting quick death from frost afterwards. The hides are not in contact with the body at all but are held away from the flesh by the soft resiliency of the deer hairs that line them, and in the space between the tips of the hair and the hide of the parka there is a constantly moving layer of warm air which absorbs all the sweat and carries it off.

Dressed for a day in the winter, the Ihalmio has this protection over all parts of his body, except for a narrow oval in front of his face — and even this is well protected by a long silken fringe of wolverine fur, the one fur to which the moisture of breathing will not adhere and freeze. 13

In the summer rain, the hide may grow wet, but the layer of air between deerhide and skin does not conduct the water, and so it runs off and is lost while the body stays dry. Then there is the question of weight. Most white men trying to live in the winter arctic load their bodies with at least twenty-five pounds of clothing, while the complete deerskin home of the Innuit weighs about seven pounds. This, of course, makes a great difference in the mobility of the wearers. A man wearing tight-fitting and too bulky clothes is almost as helpless as a man in a diver's suit. But besides their light weight, the Ihalmiut clothes are tailored so that they are slack wherever muscles must work freely beneath them. There is ample space in this house for the occupant to move and to breathe, for there are no partitions and walls to limit his motions, and the man is almost as free in his movements as if he were naked. If he must sleep out, without shelter, and it is fifty below, he has but to draw his arms into his parka, and he sleeps nearly as well as he would in a double-weight eiderdown bag. 14

This is in winter, but what about summer? I have explained how the porous hide nevertheless acts as a raincoat. Well, it does much more than that. In summer the outer suit is discarded and all clothing pared down to one layer. The house then offers effective insulation against heat entry. It remains surprisingly cool, for it is efficiently ventilated. Also, and not least of its many advantages, it offers the nearest thing to perfect protection against the flies. The hood is pulled up so that it covers the neck and the ears, and the flies find it nearly impossible to get at the skin underneath. But of course the Ihalmiut have long since learned to live with the flies, and they 15 feel none of the hysterical and frustrating rage against them so common with us.

16   In the case of women's clothing, home has two rooms. The back of the parka has an enlargement, as if it were made to fit a hunchback, and in this space, called the *amaut*, lives the unweaned child of the family. A bundle of remarkably absorbent sphagnum moss goes under his backside and the child sits stark naked, in unrestricted delight, where he can look out on the world and very early in life become familiar with the sights and the moods of his land. He needs no clothing of his own, and as for the moss — in that land there is an unlimited supply of soft sphagnum and it can be replaced in an instant.

17   When the child is at length forced to vacate this pleasant apartment, probably by the arrival of competition, he is equipped with a one-piece suit of hides which looks not unlike the snow suits our children wear in the winter. Only it is much lighter, more efficient, and much less restricting. This first home of his own is a fine home for the Ihalmio child, and one that his white relatives would envy if they could appreciate its real worth.

18   This then is the home of the People. It is the gift of the land, but mainly it is the gift of Tuktu.*

Structure:

1. In this selection, where does the analogy begin?
2. To what extent is the analogy developed? Point out all the ways in which the clothes of the Ihalmiut are described in terms of a house.
3. Why is this discussion of Eskimo clothing in terms of a house considered an analogy rather than a comparison and contrast?
4. Paragraphs 1–9 describe the qualities of the igloo and the tent. Is this passage an analogy or a comparison and contrast? Why?
5. In what way does Farley Mowat's discussion of the igloo and tent prepare us for his discussion of Eskimo clothing?

Style:

1. A SIMILE states that one thing is like another, while a METAPHOR states poetically that one thing is another. Which of the following are similes and which are metaphors?

---

*Tuktu: the caribou

A. "... the wind rises like a demon of hatred. ..." (par. 4)
B. "... almost all food must be eaten while it is frozen to the hardness of rocks." (par. 6)
C. "... the hot sun dries and shrinks the hides until they are drum-taut. ..." (par. 8)
D. "The real home of the Ihalmio is much like that of the turtle, for it is what he carries about on his back." (par. 10)
E. "... a long silken fringe of wolverine fur. ..." (par. 13)
F. "A man wearing tight-fitting and too bulky clothes is almost as helpless as a man in a diver's suit." (par. 14)
G. "... the porous hide nevertheless acts as a raincoat." (par. 15)

2. To what extent has Mowat used SENSE IMAGES to make this selection vivid? Give one example each of appeals to sight, hearing, touch, taste and smell.
3. Hold your book at arm's length so that you have an overall view of the selection's appearance. Does Mowat's writing seem to consist mostly of long words or short words? What effect do you think his preference for long or for short words has upon his style?

Ideas:

1. Dying cultures such as those of the Inuit are being recorded by anthropologists, and dead cultures are being reconstructed by archaeologists. Why do we study ways of life that are passing or past? Can such study in any way improve our present lives?
2. Over the last decades, the federal government has provided the Inuit of Canada with houses so that, except on hunting trips, they no longer need the igloos or tents described by Farley Mowat. Do you agree with the government's actions? Did it make more sense to reduce physical hardships among the Inuit, or would it have made more sense to preserve at least some of their stone-age culture? And would such preservation have been possible?
3. A North American Indian once observed that the White Man works in an office fifty weeks of the year so he can live like an Indian the other two weeks. How much truth do you find in this statement? In what ways does a temporary outdoor experience differ from a permanent one?
4. Write an essay based on an extended *analogy* between a house and one of the following:

a nest
the burrow or den of an animal
a car or van
the earth's atmosphere
our government's system of social benefits
a complicated theoretical argument
a person's system of psychological defences

(NOTE: See also the Topics for Writing at the end of this chapter.)

Félix Leclerc

*The Family House**

Translated from the French by Philip Stratford

Félix Leclerc, born in 1914 at La Tuque, Quebec, is a singer and writer. From 1934 to 1942 he was an announcer, actor and writer with Radio-Canada, occasionally singing his own songs as well. For a few years he acted with a theatre company, then from 1951 to 1953 lived in Paris, where his music hall appearances as "le Canadien" won him immense popularity. In Quebec he is now considered the original chansonnier — *as singer Gilles Vigneault puts it, "the father of us all." Yet Leclerc thinks of himself as primarily a writer. He has published more than a dozen books, including poetry, plays, fables, stories and novels. Among his most widely read have been* Adagio *(1943) and* Allegro *(1944), two collections of his fables and stories written for radio;* Pieds nus dans l'aube *(1946), the autobiographical novel from which our selection comes; and his novel* Le fou de l'île *(1958), translated by Philip Stratford in 1976 as* The Madman, the Kite and the Island.

W e were all, brothers and sisters alike, born in a long 1
three-storey wooden house, a house as humped and crusty
as a loaf of homemade bread, as warm and clean inside as
the white of the loaf.

Roofed over with shingles, harbouring robins in its gables, it 2
looked itself like an old nest perched up there in the silence. Taking
the north wind over the left shoulder, beautifully adjusted to nature,
from the roadside one might also have mistaken it for an enormous
boulder stranded on the beach.

In truth it was a stubborn old thing, soaking up storms and 3
twilight, determined not to die of anything less than old age, like the
two elms beside it.

The house turned its back squarely on the rest of town so as not to 4
see the new subdivision with its shiny little boxes as fragile as
mushrooms. Looking out over the valley, highroad for the wild St.
Maurice river, it focused as if in ecstasy on the long caravan of blue
mountains over there, the ones that flocks of clouds and the oldest
seagulls don't seem able to get over.

With its rusty sides, its black roof and its white-trimmed 5
windows, our common cradle crouched over a heavy cement
foundation sunk solidly in the ground like a ship's anchor to hold us

---
*Translator's title

223

firm, for we were eleven children aboard, a turbulent, strident lot, but as timid as baby chicks.

6   A big, robust, rough fieldstone chimney, held together by trowelsmoothed mortar, began in the cellar near the round-bellied furnace just above that drafty little iron door that sticking a mirror into you could see the stars. Like the hub of a wheel it rose through the floors distributing spokes of heat, then broke through to the outside as stiff as a sentinel with a plumed helmet and smoked there with windswept hair, close to a grey ladder lying along the roof. The grey ladder and the sooty little door, we were told, were not for human use, but for an old man in red who in winter jumped from roof to roof behind reindeer harnessed in white.

7   From top to bottom our home was inhabited: by us in the centre like the core of a fruit; at the edges by parents; in the cellars and attics by superb and silent men, lumberjacks by trade. In the walls, under the floors, between the joists, near the carpets, and in the folds of the lampshades lived goblins, gnomes, fairies, snatches of song, silly jokes and the echoes of games; in the veins of our house ran pure poetry.

8   We had a chair for rocking in, a bench for saying prayers, a sofa to cry on, a two-step staircase for playing trains. Also other fine toys that we didn't dare touch, like the two-wired bird with its long beak and the bell in its forehead that talked to the grown-ups. A flower-patterned linoleum was our garden; a hook in the wall, a bollard to tie up our imaginary boats; the staircases were slides; the pipes running up the walls our masts; and armchairs miniature stages where we learnt with the hats, gloves and overcoats of our elders how to make the same faces that we wear today but without finding them funny.

9   A vast corridor divided the ground floor lengthwise. A few rung-backed chairs made a circle in one corner; above them a row of hooks like question marks disappeared beneath the coats of visitors who came to consult Papa, the biggest timber merchant in the valley. The living room and a bedroom for visitors stood side by side. The living room, with its black piano, its net curtains, its big blue armchair, its gold-framed pictures, a few old-style chairs up-holstered in satin (particularly a spring-rocker dressed up like an old lady out of the past with tassels on the hem of her dress) gave our lives a quality of Sunday celebration. Our parents' bedroom closed its door on impenetrable secrets. In its obscurity slumbered an old dresser full of camphor-scented sheets between which my mother hid mysterious notebooks, repositories of the exact hour of our birth, the names of godfathers and godmothers, and very private family events.

To the left of the hall a smoking room served as my father's study
and as library for all of us. A door opened to the dining room —
classroom would be more exact, for we only ate there once or twice a
year. In the sewing room between the sewing machine and an
enormous cupboard stood the sofa, ready to be cried on. At the back
of the house, spreading the full width, was our gay and singing
kitchen: the cast-iron stove with its built-in mirror, the red kitchen
cupboards, the white muslin curtains hanging like fog in the narrow
windows, and the patches of sunlight playing on the left of the long
family table. There shone the ever-burning lamp, known to all
people throughout all time as the soul of the home. There we were
told of good news and bad. There Papa signed our school report
cards. There in the high rocking chair we would often sit in silence
to think of facts of creation discovered that day and ponder on the
strange and marvellous world we had fallen into. 10

The first floor was lined with children's bedrooms. There were
eight, I think, divided between girls and boys. In the girls' rooms it
was cleaner, rosier, airier, more airy than the boys'. On the walls
they pinned up tiny frames, graceful silhouettes and sprigs of
flowers. On ours we stuck huge vulgar calendars, of hunters waiting
for game and old gents smoking rubbed tobacco. 11

Our room, the most spacious on the floor, looked out on the
garden, its black earth full as a cornucopia, and cut through with
straight little paths that we walked down every evening, watering
under the watching eyes of the cottontails. 12

We each had our own bed, a little white bed with a real straw
mattress and iron bedposts ending in brass knobs where we hung
our clothes, our slingshots, and our hands clasped in prayer. 13

On the second floor a screened veranda jutted out in a bow like a
pilot-house. It was a veritable observation post dominating the
waves of the valley like those of the sea: waves of snowstorms, waves
of loggers in springtime, waves of poor families gathering wild fruit,
waves of falling leaves, of showers of sunshine, of the beating of
birds' wings, of paths traced by children, hunters and fishermen. On
hot nights we slept there above the waves on that wooden porch
which was also the children's playroom. Soldiers, teddy bears,
drums, little wooden shoes, dolls seated at table before empty china
plates, all keeping good company together. A tin bridge built long
ago by my eldest brother served as access to this cardboard world. 14

On the floor above, behind a bull's-eye window, stretched the
attic, a long deserted dusty cage, dormitory in winter for several
lumberjacks. Between the three-legged chairs and the family
portraits, these men on their mattresses, devoured by fatigue,
tumbled headlong each night into sleep. 15

16   And like the crew of a happy ship, thinking neither of arrivals nor of departures, but only of the sea that carries them, we sped through childhood all sails set, thrilled with each morning and every night, envying neither distant ports nor far cities, convinced that our ship was flying the best colours and that we carried on board all necessary potions to ward off pirates and bad luck.

17   The house we lived in was number 168, rue Claire-Fontaine.

Structure:

1. This selection is filled with figures of speech — SIMILES, METAPHORS and PERSONIFICATION — but only one is developed extensively enough to be considered an analogy. What is it and which paragraphs develop it?
2. What is the main purpose of this selection, and where does Leclerc most openly state it?

Style:

1. Roughly how many METAPHORS and SIMILES appear in this selection as compared to the other selections in this book? Twice as many? Four times as many? Ten times as many? And what effect does Leclerc achieve through such a concentration of FIGURES OF SPEECH?
2. Among his other achievements, Félix Leclerc is a poet and is one of Quebec's best-loved singers. What relationship, if any, do you find between his experience as poet and singer and the approach he took to writing "The Family House"?
3. Point out at least ten SIMILES in this selection. Point out at least ten METAPHORS. Point out at least five examples of PERSONIFICATION. Do these figures of speech work together to build a dominant impression or do they seem to be used separately for their own sake?
4. Do you suppose "The Family House" was easy or difficult to translate from French to English? Is a perfect translation possible? If you know two languages, how easy or difficult is it to translate words and expressions from one to the other?

Ideas:

1. In paragraph 8, Leclerc describes how he and his brothers and sisters imitated their elders, learning "how to make the same

faces that we wear today but without finding them funny." Do
you sense in this passage (and perhaps in the whole selection) a
regret for lost childhood? Do you ever regret your own lost
childhood? Do most people? If so, what might be the reasons?

2. Almost everything that Félix Leclerc has published expresses
the same happiness and security, the same good will towards
the natural world and the people in it, that we see in "The
Family House." Does a happy childhood such as the one he
describes here lead inevitably to a happy adulthood? Can a
happy adulthood follow an unhappy childhood? Give reasons
and examples to support your answers.

3. "Coming of Age in Putnok" is the opening of George Gabori's
autobiography, while "The Family House" is the opening of
Félix Leclerc's autobiographical novel. If you have read both,
compare them. Which gives more facts? Which gives more
feeling? Which seems to give a greater insight into the author's
background and personality? Do the two openings differ in
TONE? And which would more strongly motivate a reader to
finish the book?

4. If you have read "The One Perfect House," compare the ways in
which Farley Mowat describes that "house" with the ways in
which Leclerc describes the house of his childhood.

5. Using a great many METAPHORS and SIMILES, describe your own
childhood home in such a way as to strongly convey the feelings
you have toward it and toward the life you led there.

(NOTE: See also the Topics for Writing at the end of this chapter.)

Topics for Writing

Chapter 6: ANALOGY and related devices

(Note also the topics for writing that appear after each selection in this chapter.)

Develop one of the following topics into an extended analogy:

1. Manners as a mask
2. A person you know as the pet he or she keeps
3. A large corporation as an octopus
4. A town, city, province or country as the animal it reminds you of
5. A sports team as an army
6. Chess as war
7. Capitalism or communism as a religion
8. Life as a journey
9. Knowledge as light
10. Art as a mirror
11. A library as a brain
12. A computer as a brain
13. A camera as an eye
14. Hockey as life
15. Success as a ladder
16. A motorcycle as a horse
17. A newborn child as an astronaut in space
18. Home as a fortress
19. The city as a jungle
20. Crime as war
21. Crime as a disease
22. An industrial worker as a robot
23. Television as a drug
24. School as a factory
25. The atom as a solar system

*"There isn't a reason in the world to suppose that twenty million
people really enjoy going fishing . . . ."*
    Roderick Haig-Brown, "Articles of Faith for Good Anglers"

There are three kinds of them....

CLASSIFICATION

Our world is so complex that without classification we would be lost. To call a friend we use an alphabetized phone book. To buy a steak we go to the meat section of the supermarket. To buy a used car we open our newspaper to the *classified* section. Putting things into categories is one of our most common methods of thought, both for good and for bad. Who would look through the whole dictionary when the word in question begins with "T"? What school child would enter a grade one *class*room when he has been *class*ified into grade five?

Yet as Hitler and other bigots have demonstrated, classifying people by skin colour, race or religion can lead to stereotypes and stereotypes can lead to violence. Ethnic jokes may seem innocent (*Why does it take two WASPs to change a light bulb? One makes the gin and tonics while the other calls the repairman*). But such a characterization of a group makes it harder for others to view a member of that group as an individual. If all WASPs (or all Newfoundlanders or Torontonians or women or Jews or Indians or bankers or postal workers) are classified as the same, we have dehumanized them. Dislike and even persecution are now possible. Be careful, then, not to let a classification become a stereotype. For example you may have a practical reason to group people by age, but do leave room for individuals: not all teenagers are delinquents, not all forty-year-olds are getting a divorce and not all retired people are ready for the rocking chair.

Whatever its subject, your essay of classification should have at least three categories, because only two would form a comparison and contrast. And it should have no more than you can adequately develop — perhaps six or seven at the most. To be logical your essay will follow these principles:

Classify all items by the same principle. An essay on sources of energy for home heating might include oil, natural gas, hydro, coal, wood and solar heat. But it would not include insulation as a category, for insulation is not a *source* of energy but a means of *retaining* energy.

Do not leave out an obvious category. Would you discuss six artists in an essay about the Group of Seven?

Do not let categories overlap. An essay on the major types of housing might include the detached single-family house, the semi-detached house, the row house and the high-rise apartment. The bungalow has no place in this list, though, because it *is* a detached single-family house. And rental units have no place in the list, because any of the above forms of housing can be rented.

Classifying is not easy; it is a real exercise in logic. But it will become easier when you observe the most important principle of all: *Know your purpose.* Is one form of housing cheaper, more pleasant, more appropriate to the city, more energy efficient, better suited to singles or to families or to retired people? Let that idea, whatever it is, underlie your classification so that your essay will emerge as a clear and unified message.

Roderick Haig-Brown

Articles of Faith for Good Anglers

Since the time of Izaak Walton, enthusiasts of fishing have written eloquently about their sport. The best of these writers in North America, and the man often called Canada's finest essayist, was Roderick Haig-Brown (1908–1976). Born in England to an aristocratic family, he moved at age 17 to the state of Washington and worked as a logger and semi-pro boxer. After a short return to England he settled in British Columbia, where he worked as a guide, logger, trapper, bounty hunter for cougars, and fisherman. Then in 1941 he was appointed magistrate and judge at Campbell River, B.C. Sometimes late to court sessions because of his fishing, Haig-Brown retained a passion for the sport to the end of his life and in flawless prose imparted his experiences, his close observations of nature, his code of sportsmanship and his devotion to conservation. More than a dozen of his books are still in print. The best-loved are A River Never Sleeps *(1946),* Fisherman's Spring *(1951) and* Fisherman's Summer *(1959). A shortened version of our selection, "Articles of Faith for Good Anglers," appeared in* Life Magazine *in 1960; the complete version was collected in* The Master and His Fish *(1981).*

Some twenty million angling licences a year are sold on the   1
North American continent and considerably more than twenty million people go fishing each year. There isn't a reason in the world to suppose that twenty million people really enjoy going fishing; a remarkably high proportion of them contribute vastly to the discomfort of others while finding little joy in the sport for themselves. This is sad but inevitable; it grows directly out of the misconception that anyone with two hands, a hook, and a pole, is equipped to go fishing. After all, the beloved fable has it that the boy with the worm on a bent pin always does far better than the master angler with his flies and intricate gear, so it follows logically that a state of blissful ignorance, combined with youthful clumsiness, is the perfect formula for success. If the formula doesn't prove itself, the trouble is probably the weather.

Fishing is not really a simpleton's sport. It is a sport with a long   2
history, an intricate tradition, and a great literature. These things have not grown by accident. They have developed by the devotion of sensitive and intelligent men and they make not only a foundation for rich and satisfying experience but the charter of a brotherhood that reaches around the world and through both hemispheres.

233

234 CLASSIFICATION

3   It is a brotherhood well worth joining. There are no papers to sign, no fees to pay, no formal initiation rites. All that is required is some little understanding of the sport itself and a decent respect for the several essentials that make it.

4   The first purpose of going fishing is to catch fish. But right there the angler separates himself from the meat fisherman and begins to set conditions. He fishes with a rod and line and hook — not with nets or traps or dynamite. From this point on, man being man, further refinements grow naturally and the sport develops. The fisherman is seeking to catch fish on his own terms, terms that will yield him the greatest sense of achievement and the closest identification with his quarry.

5   This establishes the first unwritten article of the brotherhood. Fishing is a sport, a matter of intimate concern only to fish and fisherman; it is not a competition between man and man. The man's aim is to solve by his own wits and skill the unreasoning reaction of the fish, always within the limits of his self-imposed conditions. Besides this, any sort of outshining one's fellow man becomes completely trivial. The fisherman is his own referee, umpire, steward, and sole judge of his performance. Completely alone, by remote lake or virgin stream, he remains bound by his private conditions and the vagaries of fish and weather. Within those conditions, he may bring all his ingenuity to bear, but if he departs from them or betrays them, though only God and the fish are his witnesses, he inevitably reduces his reward.

6   This total freedom from competitive pressure leads the fisherman directly to the three articles of faith that really govern the brotherhood: respect for the fish, respect for the fish's living space, and respect for other fishermen. All three are interrelated and, under the crowded conditions of today's fishing waters, all three are equally important.

7   Respect for other fishermen is simply a matter of common courtesy and reasonably good manners. The more crowded the waters the more necessary manners become and the more thoroughly they are forgotten. The rule can be expressed in a single golden-rule phrase: "Give the other guy the kind of break you would like to get for yourself." Don't crowd him, don't block him, don't push him. If he is working upstream, don't cut in above him; if he is working downstream, don't pile in directly below him. If you see he is hooking fish along some favourite weed bed, don't force your boat in beside him and spoil it for both. Don't park all day in what you think is a favoured spot so that no one else can get near it — give it a fair try and move on.

On uncrowded waters a self-respecting fisherman always gives 8
the other fellow first chance through the pool or the drift; as often as
not the second time through is just as good. On crowded waters give
whatever room and show whatever consideration you can and still
wet a line; better still, try somewhere else. The crowds are usually
in the wrong places anyway.

If you would be part of the brotherhood, be generous. Don't hide 9
the successful fly or lure or bait; explain every last detail of it and
give or lend a sample if you can. Show the next man along where you
moved and missed the big one, make him aware of whatever little
secret you may have of the river's pools or the lake's shoals or the
sea's tides — but only if the other guy wants it. If he doesn't, be
generous still and keep quiet. If he wants to tell you his secret
instead of listening to yours, reach for your ultimate generosity and
hear him out as long as you can stand it. Good things sometimes
come from unlikely sources.

Respect for the fish is the real base of the whole business. He is not 10
an enemy, merely an adversary, and without him and his progeny
there can be no sport. Whatever his type and species, he has certain
qualities that make for sport and he must be given a chance to show
them to best advantage. He is entitled to the consideration of the
lightest gear and the subtlest method the angler can use with a
reasonable chance of success. Trout deserve to be caught on the fly;
other methods may be necessary at times, but it is difficult to believe
they give much joy to the fisherman. A northern pike or a muskie
taken by casting is worth half a dozen taken by trolling. A black
bass tempted to the surface is a far greater thrill than one hooked in
the depths; an Atlantic salmon or summer steelhead risen to a
floating fly is a memory that will live forever. If it takes a little time
to learn such skills, there is no doubt the fish is worthy of them. And
if the angler is any kind of a man he is unlikely to be satisfied with
less.

Even in the moment of success and triumph, when the hooked fish 11
is safely brought to beach or net, he is still entitled to respect and
consideration: to quick and merciful death if he is wanted, to swift
and gentle release if he is not. Killing fish is not difficult — a sharp
rap on the back of the head settles most species. Releasing fish is a
little, but only a little, more complicated. Fly-caught trout of
moderate size are easy. Slide the hand down the leader with the fish
still in the water, grip the shank of the hook, and twist sharply.
Where it is necessary to handle the fish, a thumb and finger grip on
the lower jaw does the least harm and is usually effective. If not, use
dry hands and a light but firm grip on the body just forward of the

dorsal fin. Wet hands force a heavier grip which is extremely likely to injure vital organs. For heavily toothed fish like northern pike and muskies many fishermen use a grip on the eye sockets or the gill-covers. The first may be all right, but seems dangerous and unnecessarily cruel. The second is destructive. Fish up to ten pounds or so can be gripped securely on the body just behind the gill-covers and should not be harmed.

12 Larger fish that have fought hard are often in distress when released and need to be nursed in the water until they can swim away on their own. Generally little more is needed than to hold them on an even keel, facing upstream, while they take a few gulps of water through their gills. If they lack the strength for this, draw them gently back and forth through the water so that the gills will be forced to work; all but the most exhausted fish will recover under this treatment and swim smoothly away. Fish that have bled heavily or fish that have just swum in from salt water are less likely to recover and should be kept.

13 Respect for the fish's living space should be comprehensive. It includes the water, the bed of the stream or lake, the land on both sides of the water, and all the life that grows there, bird or mammal, plant or fish or insect. There isn't an excuse in the world for litter-leavers, tree-carvers, brush-cutters, flower-pickers, nest-robbers, or any other self-centred vandals on fishing waters. The fisherman comes at best to do some damage — to the fish — and the best he can do is keep it to that. He doesn't need to junk-heap the place with cartons and bottles and tin cans; he need not drop even so much as a leader case or cigarette pack; he can afford to remember that no one else wants to be reminded of him by his leavings.

14 These are elementary and negative points and if parents raised their children properly there would be no need to mention them in this context. A fisherman, any kind of a fisherman, should know better than to spoil the place that makes his sport. But a true share in the brotherhood calls for a little more. The fisherman is under obligation to learn and understand something about the life of his fish and the conditions it needs, if only so that he can take his little part in helping to protect them.

15 All fish need clean waters and all nations, if they know what is good for them, can afford to keep their waters clean. Pollution, whether from sewage or industrial wastes, starts as a little thing scarcely noticed and goes on to destroy all the life of the waters. Its damage can be repaired, slowly, painfully, expensively, but there is no excuse for it in the first place, though many are forthcoming.

16 Besides clean water for their own lives and the many living things they depend on, fish need special conditions for spawning and

hatching and rearing. Migratory fish need free passage upstream and down. These things and many others like them are worth understanding not merely because they suggest protections and improvements, but because knowledge of them brings the fisherman closer to the identification he seeks, makes him more truly a part of the world he is trying to share.

The old days and the old ways, when every stream was full of fish 17 and empty of people, are long gone. They weren't as good as they sounded anyway. It took time and the efforts of good fishermen to learn what could be done and should be done to produce the best possible sport. North American angling has now come close to full development. No one is going to get what he should from the sport by simply buying some gear and going out on the water, nor can he achieve very much by sneering at better men than himself who do take the trouble to learn the delicate skills of the subtler methods. The real world of fishing is open to anyone, through the literature and the generosity of the brotherhood. Once entered upon, the possibilities are limitless. But even the casual, occasional fisherman owes the sport some measure of understanding — enough, shall we say, to protect himself and others from the waste and aggravations of discourtesy and bad manners that are so often based on ignorance.

In Winchester Cathedral, not far from a famous trout stream in 18 Hampshire, England, is the tomb of William of Wykeham, a great fourteenth-century bishop and statesman who left a motto to a school he founded: "Manners makyth man." Within the same cathedral lie the bones of our father, Izaak Walton, who remarked three hundred years ago: "Angling is somewhat like poetry, men are to be born so." Perhaps Izaak's precept is for the inner circle of the brotherhood, but William's is certainly universal. It is just possible that nice guys don't catch the most fish. But they find far more pleasure in those they do get.

Structure:

1. Haig-Brown states four "articles of faith" for anglers, the first one serving as a general introduction to the three that "really govern the brotherhood" (par. 6). Point out all four articles of faith, specifying where each occurs.
2. Point out all the contrasts that you find in the first four paragraphs of the essay.
3. Which paragraphs make fullest use of examples as a means of development?

4. In the last paragraph, what does Haig-Brown achieve by quoting William of Wykeham's motto, "Manners makyth man"?
5. Can you think of a relevant "article of faith for good anglers" that Haig-Brown has omitted from his classification?

Style:

1. How FORMAL or INFORMAL would you judge the style of Haig-Brown's essay to be?
2. Largely because of his prose style, Haig-Brown is sometimes described as Canada's finest essayist. Analyze two especially good examples, paragraphs 5 and 9: In what ways is their STYLE effective?
3. Careful word choice is a central trait of Haig-Brown's style. In paragraph 10, why does Haig-Brown point out that the fish "is not an enemy, merely an adversary. . . ."?
4. In this 1960 essay, Haig-Brown continually uses expressions such as "brotherhood," "fisherman," "competition between man and man," "if the angler is any kind of man" and so on, as if no woman has ever fished. If Haig-Brown were writing today, how do you think he would have phrased these passages?

Ideas:

1. In our modern society, which produces food industrially and scientifically, why do people still hunt and fish?
2. According to a Chinese proverb, the time a person spends fishing is not subtracted from that person's life. Discuss the ways in which this philosophy may be true.
3. Many people consider overtly competitive and even violent sports, such as hockey and football, to be the best ones. Yet according to Haig-Brown, it is an absence of competition between anglers that contributes to the best qualities of fishing as a sport (par. 5). In your opinion, what makes a sport good? Is competition necessary? Is body contact or even violence desirable? Illustrate your answers by referring to sports you have played.
4. Haig-Brown writes, "Pollution, whether from sewage or industrial wastes, starts as a little thing scarcely noticed and goes on to destroy all the life of the waters" (par. 15). By 1980, twenty years after those words were published, acid rain had killed 140 lakes in Ontario. An Ohio state government survey quoted by *Maclean's* (June 30, 1980) warned that "if something is not done quickly, 2,500 lakes a year to the end of the century

will die in Ontario, Quebec and New England." Are there ways in which we as individuals might reduce this damage, caused mainly by the fumes of oil refineries, chemical plants, smelters, coal-fired power plants, paper mills, factories and the private automobile?

5. Write an essay *classifying* the different types of hunters, hikers, boaters, skiers, snowmobilers or campers.

(NOTE: See also the Topics for Writing at the end of this chapter.)

Erika Ritter

Bicycles

Erika Ritter is known to Canadians as a playwright and a radio personality. Born in 1948 in Regina, she studied literature at McGill, then drama at the University of Toronto. After teaching English and drama for three years at Loyola (now Concordia), Montreal, she turned her attention more fully to writing theatre. Her 1978 play The Splits *was a critical success. The next year her historical drama* Winter 1671 *was produced. In 1980 Ritter's comedy* Automatic Pilot, *about a female stand-up comedian whose routines are based on her own unhappiness, was a popular success in Toronto, won the Chalmers Award and went on to performances across the country. And* The Passing Scene, *a play about journalism, was produced in 1982. In 1985 CBC Radio, as part of its effort to attract a younger audience and improve its ratings, hired Ritter to host* Dayshift, *a new afternoon talk show. Our selection comes from Ritter's book* Urban Scrawl *(1984), a collection of comic essays and sketches. She dedicates the volume to her mother, "who made the mistake of encouraging this kind of thing."*

1   It wasn't always like this. There was a time in the life of the world when adults were adults, having firmly put away childish things and thrown away the key.

2   Not any more. The change must have come about innocently enough, I imagine. Modern Man learning to play nicely in the sandbox with the other grown-ups. Very low-tension stuff.

3   Now, in every direction you look, your gaze is met by the risible spectacle of adults postponing adolescence well into senility by means of adult toys: running shoes, baseball bats, roller skates, and — bicycles!

4   But the attitude is no longer the fun-loving approach of a bunch of superannuated kids, and I'm sure you can envision how the evolution occurred. Jogging progressed from a casual encounter with the fresh air to an intensive relationship, attended by sixty-dollar jogging shoes and a designer sweatband. Playing baseball stopped being fun unless you had a Lacoste (as opposed to low-cost) tee-shirt in which to impress your teammates. And where was the thrill in running around a squash court unless it was with a potentially important client?

5   As for bicycles — well, let's not even talk about bicycles. On the other hand, maybe we *should* talk about them, because there's something particularly poignant about how it all went wrong for the

bicycle, by what declension this once proud and carefree vehicle sank into the role of beast of burden, to bear the weight of sobersided grown-ups at their supposed sport.

First, there was the earliest domestication of the North American 6 bicycle (*cyclus pedalis americanus*) in the late Hippie Scene Era of the 1960s. This was the age of the no-nuke whole-grain cyclist, who saw in the bicycle the possibility of Making a Statement while he rode. A statement about pollution, about materialism, about imperialism, about militarism, about — enough already. You get the picture: two wheels good, four wheels bad.

Thus it was that the basic bicycle gradually evolved into a chunky 7 three-speed number from China, bowed down under a plastic kiddie carrier, army surplus knapsacks, and a faded fender-sticker advising Make Tofu, Not War. And a rider clad in a red plaid lumber-jacket, Birkenstock sandals, and an expression of urgent concern for all living things.

Once the very act of bicycle riding had become an act of high 8 moral purpose, it was an easy step to the next phase of the bicycle's journey along the path of post-Meanderthal seriousness.

I'm speaking of the era of the high-strung thoroughbred bicycle, 9 whose rider had also made advances, from pedalling peacenik to a hunched and humorless habitué of the velodrome, clad in leather-seated shorts, white crash helmet, and fingerless gloves, whizzing soundlessly, and with no hint of joy, down city streets and along the shoulders of super-highways, aboard a vehicle sculpted in wisps of silver chrome. A vehicle so overbred, in its final evolutionary stages, that it began to resemble the mere exoskeleton of a conventional cycle, its flesh picked away by birds of carrion.

Having been stripped of any connection with its innocent and 10 leisurely origins, the bicycle now no longer bore the slightest resemblance to the happy creature it once had been. And in the mid-Plastic Scene Era, another crippling blow was struck by the upscale name-brand cyclist, who came along to finish what the fanatical velodromist had refined. Namely, the complete transfor-mation of an ambling and unhurried mode of transit into a fast, nerve-wracking, expensive, and utterly competitive display of high speed, high technology, and high status.

The Upscale Cyclist was looking for a twelve-speed Bottecchia 11 that matches his eyes, something that he'd look trendy upon the seat of, when riding to the office (the office!), and he was ready to pay in four figures for it.

Not only that, he was also prepared to shell out some heavy bread 12 for those status accessories to complete the picture: the backpack designed by the engineers at NASA, the insulated water-bottle to keep his Perrier chilled just right, the sixteen-track Walkman that would virtually assure him the envy of all his friends.

13   So much for the cyclist. What of his poor debased mount?

14   Not surprisingly, amongst the breed of bicycle, morale is currently low, and personal pride all but a thing of the past. And yet ... and yet, there are those who say that *cyclus pedalis americanus* is an indomitable creature, and that it is the bicycle, not its rider, who will make the last evolution of the wheel.

15   In fact, some theorize that the present high incidence of bicycle thievery, far from being evidence of crime, is actually an indication that the modern bicycle has had enough of oppressive exploitation and man's joyless ways, and is in the process of reverting to the wild in greater and greater numbers.

16   There have always remained a few aboriginal undomesticated bicycles — or so the theory goes — and now it is these free-spirited mavericks, down from the hills at night, who visit urban bikeracks, garages, and back porches to lure tame bicycles away with them.

17   Costly Kryptonite locks are wrenched asunder, expensive accoutrements are shrugged off, intricate gear systems are torn away, and lo — look what is revealed! Unadorned, undefiled *cyclus* in all his pristine glory, unfettered and unencumbered once more, and free to roam.

18   A wistful fantasy, you might say? The maundering illusions of someone who's been riding her bicycle too long without a crash helmet? I wonder.

19   Just the other day, there was that piece in the paper about a bicycle that went berserk in a shopping centre, smashing two display windows before it was subdued. And did you hear about the recent sighting of a whole herd of riderless bicycles, all rolling soundlessly across a park in the night?

20   It all kind of gets you to thinking. I mean, do *you* know where your ten-speed is tonight?

Structure:

1. In starting with the words "It wasn't always like this," what is Erika Ritter's opening strategy?
2. Ritter classifies the evolution of *"cyclus pedalis americanus"* into three main stages. Describe these three divisions of her classification and show where each begins and ends.

3. Have any categories of this classification overlapped? Have any obvious categories been left out?
4. Ritter marks each major change of subject with a transitional passage. Point out three of these transitions.
5. In concluding this selection, paragraphs 14–20 exploit the device discussed in our previous chapter, *analogy*. As the bicycle starts "reverting to the wild," to what is it compared? Point out at least ten words or phrases through this section that develop the analogy.
6. In closing, Ritter asks ". . . do *you* know where your ten-speed is tonight?" To what does she allude here? Is the ALLUSION appropriate? Does it work as a closing?

Style:

1. Where did you first recognize the humorous TONE of this selection? Does Ritter's humour work?
2. What device of humour is exploited in paragraph 4, where baseball players wear "Lacoste (as opposed to low-cost)" tee-shirts?
3. What is Ritter doing when she refers to "the late Hippie Scene Era" (par. 6), "post-Meanderthal seriousness" (par. 8) and "the mid-Plastic Scene Era" (par. 10)?
4. Is Ritter's highly COLLOQUIAL style effective in this selection? Point out 5 or 10 of her most strongly colloquial expressions.
5. In a piece that has so many colloquial expressions, why do we also find academic or even learned terms such as "risible" (par. 3), "superannuated" (par. 4) and "exoskeleton" (par. 9)? What is the total effect? Toward what kind of reader do you think Ritter has aimed this selection?
6. Does Ritter use CONCRETE detail effectively? From each of the three divisions of her classification, pick out the two or three details that say the most to you, and explain how they work.
7. In paragraph 9 the "thoroughbred" bicycle is described as so overbred "that it began to resemble the mere exoskeleton of a conventional cycle, its flesh picked away by birds of carrion." What FIGURES OF SPEECH do you find in this passage?

Ideas:

1. Erika Ritter is well known in Canada as both a playwright and a radio host. Do either of these professions seem reflected in the way she has written "Bicycles"?

2. How do you react when the humour of paragraphs 1–12 turns to fantasy in paragraphs 13–20? Has Ritter gone too far? Or is fantasy sometimes a legitimate way to deal with a subject?

3. Is Ritter right: do we sometimes go too far in "improving" products, such as the bicycle? Have we done so to any of the following? If so, describe how.

   automobiles
   motorcycles
   radios, sound systems,
      television, VCRs, computers
   housing
   food
   clothes

4. Do you own a bicycle? Does it fit one of Ritter's categories? If so, how? If not, how does it differ?

5. Paragraphs 10–12 describe the bicycle as status symbol. What are your own major status symbols? Describe the qualities that give them — and therefore you — this status. Does a status symbol have to be an object? If not, what else can it be?

6. Erika Ritter has *classified* the evolutionary stages of the bicycle. In your own essay, either humorous or serious, do the same for any other invention that you use in your daily life.

_____

(NOTE: See also the Topics for Writing at the end of this chapter.)

Edgar Roussel

Letter from Prison*

Translated from the French by Mary Conrad and Jean-Paul Chavy

Edgar Roussel is considered one of Canada's most dangerous convicts. In 1974 he was among the gunmen who entered the Gargantua Bar in Montreal, locked thirteen patrons in a closet and burned the place down. Roussel was found guilty of two of those murders, and in 1978 was sentenced to life imprisonment. That same year he led hostage-taking uprisings at both Dorchester Penitentiary and the St. Jerome provincial jail and as a result was sent to a super-maximum security unit within Laval Institute, the Correctional Development Centre. It is this place that he describes in his long and impassioned letter of April 12, 1980, which was sent to External Affairs Minister Mark MacGuigan and a few months later appeared in the Montreal newspaper Le Devoir. *Three months after he sent the letter, Roussel was transferred from the CDC to Laval Institute. A few weeks after that he tried to escape.*

Since March 29, 1978, I have been detained in the Correctional   1
Development Centre (the CDC) where I am serving a life
sentence with eligibility for parole in twenty years.

Everything has been said about federal penitentiaries. All I can   2
do is retell it — except when it comes to special detention units such
as the CDC, the subject of this letter. The purpose of such centres,
according to Directive 174 of the national commissioner, is to
prepare "dangerous" prisoners for reintegration into the penitentiary.

To do this, the administration has set up a program that I'd like to   3
examine carefully, to discover in what original way the system
works to bring about the desired metamorphosis, so that the
caterpillar might become a butterfly — how, in cutting us off from
life, they claim to reacquaint us with it. They carry out this program
within four boundaries placed like watch towers: a cell, a common
room, an outside courtyard, and on top of all that, a Socialization
Division.

At the CDC the amount of time spent in the cell is even greater   4
than at most Canadian federal penitentiaries. To keep the prisoner

---

*Editor's title

245

from sinking into boredom or even madness, the administration grants what other institutions categorically forbid: a television set. This gift to the prisoner is important in view of his mental state caused by being alone. But it is even more a confession of failure and, worse yet, a flagrant lack of imagination.

5   During the first days it is used all the time, then gradually less, and finally more again but this time to drown out the noises that the prisoners never noticed before.

6   Sometimes the television is an aspirin that relieves suffering and at other times it is a window to the outside world. After months of this routine come nausea and disgust; you turn off the machine only to learn a new phenomenon: noise! Searches, guards' rounds, everything takes second place to noise, which in the cells is louder than anywhere else, with never a lull. Very late at night, when sleep finally comes and re-establishes the equilibrium so dangerously broken during the day, the night rounds begin. Each hour, without fail, the loud steps of the guard making his rounds ring on the ceiling of the cell. At the CDC they've found a new way to count the prisoners — from above. The guard can get a full view of the captive through an opening in the ceiling. It's always possible to make up lost sleep by sacrificing the daily walk. But this is just the time the guards choose to search the cells of prisoners who are outside. They arrive in the cell-block corridors in a mob, their noses in the air, and bang! on the walls to see if there are any holes, bang! on the ceiling to see if the opening has been tampered with and bang! on the air vent. Once their work is done they leave, deliberately slamming all the cell doors shut at once in an infernal din. Good-bye sleep and calm.

7   It would be hard to speak of ventilation because there isn't any; there are no windows, and the doors are solid. The air is so heavy that it hangs over you like a thick fog.

8   In summer it's a furnace and our inactivity makes the heat unbearable; we sweat from doing nothing. In the morning, there is a symphony of throat clearing, of nose blowing, and of hoarse coughing to clear respiratory passages.

9   I've been sleeping right on the floor of my cell for nearly two years, my head at the bottom of the door to catch the smallest breeze, an incomparable luxury.

10   For time spent outside the cell, a common room is available every night from 6:30 to 10:30 but never for more than ten inmates at a time. This is part of the socialization; they want to teach us to get along in small groups, in order to plunge us into a population of three or four hundred other prisoners, with the problems of adjustment which that implies.

Several group games, another television set, and above all, 11
surveillance. Apart from its larger size, this common room is just
another cell like the ones we spend most of our time in.

Outside we use a 75-foot-square courtyard where again never 12
more than ten prisoners are let in; no more, no less — it's an
administrative fixation. In summer, the high walls keep out any
breeze, and from the asphalt pavement rises a stifling heat. No
greenery, no benches, nothing but asphalt, cement and iron.

For exercise we practice boxing on a punching bag that cost $172 13
of our own money. The administration lost a good chance to
demonstrate justice, for in all the other prisons punching bags are
paid for out of the recreation budgets. All physical activity is risky
because of the asphalt surface. Almost all of us suffer from some
muscle problem; it would be interesting to see the medical requests
and to count the inmates who have asked for special shoes.

Our visits are our greatest comfort and only contact with the 14
outside world; these are timed by the administration for the day and
hour that suit them. The privilege of a visit is stingily granted on
Wednesdays and Thursdays. At the CDC, visits are considered
favours and are scrutinized carefully.

There's no contact with parents, wives and children; it's in this 15
way that the administration promotes individual development.

Several years ago some officials of a zoo travelled across the world 16
to find a female elephant so the captive male wouldn't get bored. The
animals' space is constantly being relandscaped so it will be as much
as possible like their natural habitat. In their parks, the animals
actually have more space than we do.

A Socialization Division, staffed by an evaluation officer and a 17
psychologist, completes the program and is without a doubt the
worst problem of all. We get to meet these social science experts
when we're at our wits' end; it's when things are ready to blow up
that we get to benefit from their bright ideas.

Their main concern is determining whether we're so disturbed 18
that we might attack a staff member, or, much less importantly,
whether we might attack fellow prisoners. Once they find this out,
these servants of the administration report their conclusions, and
it's on the basis of their testimony that the National Special
Handling Unit Review Committee will transfer a prisoner. So more
often than not, the decision of the committee, though well
intentioned, will be based on erroneous reports that were warped
from the beginning because they were based on an abnormal
situation in which the prisoner was totally confused.

Experts all agree that a prison term longer than five years creates 19
irreversible problems, not to mention the special problems created

by units like ours. What we undergo only turns us into animals, bringing out our killer instincts. There are several cases of criminals who were kept in isolation, some longer than others, and who are good examples of what I'm saying.

20   I'll name just four I knew personally and whose fate I was able to learn: Jacques Mesrine, Richard Blass, Jean-Paul Mercier and Jean Lachapelle.

21   All have certain things in common: they spent several years in isolation and they are all dead today because they refused to relive, even for one day, what they had known in the past.

22   It might be useful to know just what they did after experiencing this isolation.

23   Jean Lachapelle was imprisoned about six years in one cell. Upon his return behind bars, he pleaded guilty to nine charges of murder, not to mention the fact that during his escape — the last, it goes without saying — he was himself shot full of holes.

24   As for Richard Blass, only his death kept him from being charged with fifteen murders. And as for Jean-Paul Mercier (like Blass, isolated for three years), he confessed to murdering two guards after his escape, to avoid being recognized and getting several more years in solitary. As for Jacques Mesrine, a close reading of his two books clearly reveals the mental state produced by his years of isolation in a cell.

25   None of these four individuals had been found guilty of murder before their time in isolation. Was this a coincidence? You can draw your own conclusions. The system aims to make the criminal feel small, to repress the least initiative, and in a word to assassinate his personality so it will conform to the closed prison world in which they force it to develop. When the inmate has become enough of a cheat, hypocrite and liar that he can fake gratitude to his torturers, then he's eligible for a transfer.

26   The individuals considered "dangerous" cases are the product of a myth perpetuated by rituals meant to remind us of our past crimes.

27   Nothing can erase a criminal act, and to think that punishment causes redemption is a trap. When they intend to change the individual, arbitrarily deciding to make him the same as everyone else — then I claim the right to be different.

28   All the inmates brought here when I was have since been transferred. Only an unchanging thirst for vengeance can explain my presence at the CDC. The last inmate of the group left April 10, 1980 and his honours list speaks for itself; recently this guy was hit with a one-year sentence for assaulting two officers of the CDC with a knife. At first he had been charged with attempted murder, but his

jurors accepted the reduced charge; according to them, the inmate could not judge the nature of his act, because the conditions during his imprisonment had altered his reason.

Some time ago they released a prisoner from the CDC directly into 29 society, although only a few months before he had been considered too dangerous for transfer to a maximum security penitentiary.

In this long and detailed letter I have tried to give you an inside 30 view of the situation that I have endured for too long. These days I talk to myself, laugh without reason or shake from nervous spasms. I sense that something in me is breaking down, and if no one intervenes on my behalf the worst will happen. I've reached a point of saturation where the slightest incident could trigger a desperate act.

For two long, endless years, I have not hugged my wife, my 31 mother or my daughter, and for two long years I have not seen the moon or stars. Even the lowest of animals is not denied this right. Konrad Lorenz maintains that it is dangerous to corner an animal with no chance of escape. Friedrich Nietzche states in his book *Thus Spake Zarathustra* that man has made the wolf into a dog and has made himself into man's best domestic animal. In the introduction to the same book, he also denounces cruelty clothed in justice, saying that it is in tragedies, bullfights and crucifixions that man has felt best on earth; when he invented hell, that was his paradise on earth.

It is in the name of these great men and in the veneration of their 32 thought that I ask you now to intercede on my behalf. Already in 1976 as president of a subcommittee investigating violence in the penitentiaries, you denounced the ineptitude of administrators. Now your new position gives you the influence and power to improve my condition. This is the purpose of my request.

If this document one day serves as a defence before the courts, it 33 will be because the change from caterpillar to butterfly has not taken place.

I dare hope, Honourable Minister, that despite all the responsibil- 34 ity and work that your new position brings, my appeal will not be in vain.

Structure:

1. This selection was written as a letter to an individual, External Affairs Minister Mark MacGuigan. Why, then, has it been made

public in *Le Devoir* and in this book? In what ways might this specific case be of general interest?

2. Where does Edgar Roussel first name the four categories of his classification?

3. In this classification of the CDC environment, paragraphs 4–9 are devoted to the cell, 10 and 11 to the common room, 12 and 13 to the outside courtyard, and 17 and 18 to the Socialization Division. Why does Roussel devote as many paragraphs to the cell as he does to all the other categories combined?

4. Do the four "boundaries" of the CDC program overlap at all, or are they mutually exclusive, as befits the parts of a logical classification?

5. The classification of Roussel's prison environment ends with paragraph 18. In what ways do the classification and the rest of Roussel's letter support each other?

6. Identify and discuss the cause and effect argument upon which "Letter from Prison" is to a large extent based: what are the causes? What are the effects?

Style:

1. Analyze the sources of power in this passage from paragraph 31: "For two long, endless years I have not hugged my wife, my mother or my daughter, and for two long years I have not seen the moon or stars. Even the lowest of animals is not denied this right."

2. Point out two FIGURES OF SPEECH in paragraph 3 and discuss their relevance to the subject.

3. What technique gives life to paragraph 12?

Ideas:

1. Edgar Roussel's letter to Mark MacGuigan apparently made its point: three months after it was sent, Roussel was released from the CDC and returned to the general prison population of Laval Institute. But a few weeks after that, Roussel attempted to escape from the prison altogether. Discuss this act: does it demonstrate that Roussel was insincere in writing his so carefully reasoned letter? Or does it merely prove his own point that the program of the CDC is a failure?

2. Roussel writes, ". . . to think that punishment causes redemption is a trap" (par. 27). Do you agree or disagree? What, if anything, does redeem a criminal? Does the Correctional

Development Centre, as described by Roussel, seem designed for punishment? For redemption? For some other purpose?

3. If you have read "Living with Automation in Winnipeg," what similarities do you find between the lives of industrial workers, as described by Ian Adams, and the lives of CDC inmates, as described by Roussel?

4. Write a letter requesting something that is very important to you, addressed to the person or organization that could grant your request. Include many supporting details, as Roussel does.

5. Write an essay that *classifies* the "boundaries" of your present life (these could include home, school, employment, etc., but should be mutually exclusive as are the "boundaries" that Roussel names in paragraph 3).

(NOTE: See also the Topics for Writing at the end of this chapter.)

W. P. Kinsella

How to Write Fiction

W. P. Kinsella was born in 1935 and raised in a remote area of Alberta. He never attended school until grade five. Before he earned an M.F.A. at the Iowa Writers' Workshop and began teaching fiction writing at the University of Calgary, he held a number of jobs in the business world: selling advertising, running a credit bureau and a pizza restaurant, and selling life insurance. He has published over 50 short stories in literary magazines as well as books of his stories: Dance Me Outside *(1977),* Scars *(1978),* Shoeless Joe Jackson Comes to Iowa *(1980),* Born Indian *(1981) and* The Moccasin Telegraph *(1983). Upon the invitation of an American book editor, Kinsella expanded his short story about baseball, "Shoeless Joe Jackson Comes to Iowa," into a novel.* Shoeless Joe *was published in 1982 and was awarded the Houghton Mifflin Literary Fellowship. Our selection, "How to Write Fiction," appeared in 1985 in the Toronto* Globe and Mail.*

1 The title, of course, is a lie, as fantastical as any of my fictional creations. I cannot teach anyone how to write fiction. No one can teach anyone how to write fiction.

2 What I can do, in my capacity as a professional fiction writer, is to smooth the road for those people I find who show talent as storytellers, to show them a few tricks of the trade — how to market their material, how to deal with publishers, editors, agents and the like.

3 I can never suggest what a would-be fiction writer should write about. If you don't have a few dozen ideas for stories floating around in your head, stories that have to be told, then stick to your other hobbies and forget fiction writing.

4 But if you have your heart set on writing fiction, consider the following: fiction writing, I tell my students, consists of ability, imagination, passion and stamina. Let's consider each individually.

5 By "ability" I mean the ability to write complete sentences in clear, straightforward, standard English.

6 This will not pose a problem for most of the people in the Writers Union, but it is surprising how many university students are unable to write simple sentences. If you can't express yourself clearly, abandon hope unless you are prepared to take a remedial English course. I've been known to suggest to my university students that they get a Grade 5 grammar book and begin their study there.

7 "Imagination" involves the ability to create stories. Little children can create wonderful, uninhibited stories full of fanciful

252

characters. But as the years pass, the regimens of school and community kill the storyteller that lives within each of us. To write fiction you have to dig deep and discover that storyteller.

Some writing instructors tell students to "write of what you 8
know." I disagree with that. In 99 cases out of 100, writing about what you know will fill pages, but fill them with dull and uninteresting material.

Let's face it, for nine out of 10 of us our lives are so dull that no one 9
would care in the least about them. The 10th person has a life so bizarre no one would believe it if it were written down. The secret of a fiction writer is to make the dull interesting by imagination and embellishment, and to tone down the bizarre until it is believable.

I belong to the nine. I live a very quiet life; I have a lovely wife 10
who is a true helpmate and ultrasupportive of my career; we have a nice home on the ocean; we have the freedom to travel. In other words, we are very happy.

If I wrote about that I would soon be back selling life insurance, or 11
something equally vile. People don't want to read about happy people. Conflict is an absolute must in every story or novel.

I think I clipped the following statement from an American 12
Amateur Press Association publication a few years ago: "The master plot of all novels and stories is: 'An appealing character struggles against great odds to attain a worthwhile goal.' "

"Struggles against great odds" are the key words. Something 13
must be at stake, and the character must take some action. What will the conflict be? What action will the appealing character take? That is up to the author. Authors spend half their time writing, and the rest looking at their story and saying, What if? What if? What if? What if I take the story this way? What if I take it that way?

"Passion" is an almost nebulous ingredient. It is what an author 14
does to make you love a character. It takes very hard work to analyze it. When you find a novel or story in which you absolutely loved a character, where you had a sweet tear in your eye at the end of the story, or where you found yourself laughing uncontrollably, read it again for pleasure. Then re-read it 10 more times for business; analyze every line to learn how that author made you laugh or cry. When you learn the secret, use it in your next story.

Never forget that fiction writers are entertainers. Fiction writing 15
comes from the days when the cavemen were gathered around a campfire and Ugh stood up, pounded his chest and said, "Listen to me! I want to tell you a story!" If his story wasn't interesting and suspenseful, his companions soon wandered off to their caves.

Fiction writers are not philosophers, or essayists, or pushers of 16
causes religious or otherwise. And above all they are not navel-

gazers. All of these are types of non-fiction, and should never be confused with storytelling.

17   One important point to remember is called Valgardson's Law (after B.C. writer W. D. Valgardson): Stories or novels are not about events, but about the people that events happen to. The fact that the Titanic is sinking or a skyscraper toppling — or even that the world is ending — is not important unless you have created an appealing character who is going to suffer if the dreaded event happens.

18   If you want to write fiction, cut out that paragraph and paste it on the wall in front of your typewriter. It will save you weeks, months, maybe even years of struggle.

19   The final ingredient is "stamina." Each of the others I have described is about 5 per cent of the writing process. Stamina is the final 85 per cent. Stamina is keeping your buns on the chair and writing even when you don't feel like it. I know it's a cliché, but though inspiration is nice, 98 per cent of writing is accomplished by perspiration.

20   Stamina is doing as I have done — sitting down to write my 50th short story, the previous 49 having been unpublishable, knowing that number 50 will also be unpublishable, but that it will be 2 per cent better than the previous 49.

21   Stamina is getting up at 5 a.m., running water over your fingers, so they will make the typewriter keys work for an hour or two before you go off to your hateful job. I did that for 20 years while I beat my head against the walls of North American literature.

22   If your head is still full of stories and you are still determined to write them down, lots of luck. You'll need that, too.

Structure:

1. "The title, of course, is a lie . . . ," states Kinsella in his first line. Is this confession a good opening? What effects do it and the rest of the introduction achieve?
2. Where does Kinsella first announce the four categories of his classification?
3. Do you see a pattern in the way each division of Kinsella's classification is introduced? If so, what is it?
4. Do you think "ability," "imagination," "passion" and "stamina" appear in random order or in a logical progression? Explain.
5. Do any of Kinsella's categories overlap?
6. Do you find paragraphs 19 through 21 more forceful than most other parts of the essay? If so, why? What techniques give them power?

7. The next chapter of our book examines process analysis: the act of explaining how something is done. Would Kinsella's essay fit into that chapter? How fully, how clearly and how usefully has Kinsella explained how to write fiction?

Style:

1. How FORMAL or INFORMAL is Kinsella's STYLE in this selection? Give evidence to support your answer.
2. In paragraph 19 Kinsella deliberately includes a CLICHÉ: writing as "perspiration" rather than "inspiration." Do you recognize any clichés elsewhere in the essay?

Ideas:

1. In paragraph 6 Kinsella states that ". . . many university students are unable to write simple sentences." Do you believe he is right? If so, what factors have caused the problem? And do people who lack grammar also lack imagination? Is it worthwhile for a writer at the "developmental" level to attempt fiction?
2. Picasso once said that he spent fifty years learning to paint as he could when he was a child. Is Kinsella right that "the regimens of school and community" (par. 7) kill children's imagination? If so, how? Did it happen to you? Is this process inevitable? Or might school and community take steps to preserve children's power of imagination? If so, what steps?
3. In his opening sentence Kinsella implies that fiction can be a "lie." In what ways might this be true? In what ways can an invented plot and invented or embellished characters embody more "truth" than "lie"?
4. Do you agree with Kinsella's view that, since most of us live dull lives, we should avoid writing about what we know (pars. 8-13)? Do any of your favourite authors write about what they know?
5. Write a short story, following as much of Kinsella's advice as you can.
6. Write an essay of *classification*, explaining one by one the main ingredients of success in any of the following activities:

    writing a poem writing a lab report
    writing a love letter writing a business letter
    writing a letter of writing a letter to the editor
    application for a job

(NOTE: See also the Topics for Writing at the end of this chapter.)

Jill Davey

Pumping Iron—à la Femme

Jill Davey writes about her own sport in "Pumping Iron — à la Femme." A first-year social-work student at Ryerson Polytechnical Institute when she wrote the essay in 1985, she says she began as a "Janice" but is now more of a "Cyndi." Davey was born in 1961 in Toronto, but grew up "in a little place called Watsons Corners that made Little House on the Prairie *look luxurious." Her mother was the teacher in a one-room schoolhouse, and her father was the local minister. Davey has travelled extensively in Canada and the United States, has seen Nepal and India and hopes someday to work in a Third-World country.*

1   They've changed! Weight trainers are no longer the freshly primed Charles Atlas impersonators who attempted to conquer the world by kicking sand in the faces of skinnier men. In fact — are you sitting down? — many of them are women.

2   Women are realizing that there are no restrictions on who can get involved in the sport. Weight training has something to offer women of all shapes, sizes and ages. Body-building stereotypes are being shattered in fitness centres all across the country. Women weight trainers are not just a nicer smelling version of their male counterparts.

3   For women, the world of muscle is quickly adapting itself to meet individual needs. Valerie is one example of a growing percentage of women in today's gyms. She was anorexic. Her doctor recommended weight training as a means of gradually gaining back her strength. When she first came to the gym she was unable to squat down once (even without weights) because her muscles had almost completely dissolved. As the months have passed, Valerie has become more and more energetic. The places where bones once protruded have become soft and tender. Now Valerie smiles when she sees her reflection. She sees the body of a woman, not of a child.

4   The largest group of women in the gym is overweight. Janice was one of these women. She had always hated jogging, didn't have enough energy for aerobics, and was too self-conscious to put on a bathing suit for swimming. When Janice started doing floor exercises, the instructor had to help her up when she was finished. It took several months before she would change or shower at the gym.

5   Janice didn't expect weight training to work any more than the "pineapple diet," fasting, or "cassette hypnosis" had. But just before

summer arrived, she found herself shopping for a bathing suit again. She felt like a butterfly that had finally shed its cocoon. Now everyone could see her as the woman she knew she was.

The smallest percentage of women is already physically fit. Cyndi   6
is one of this rare breed; she is truly content with her physique. She has always been athletic and never seems to run out of energy. Whenever she comes to the gym she changes the radio station to Q107 and turns it up two or three notches. Cyndi has the inconceivable ability to look good in grey sweatpants. She looks to higher and higher weights to keep herself from being bored. Recently, Cyndi has begun posing in front of the mirrors after a workout, imitating the photographs of the professionals that line the walls. Each day her mind tentatively reaches further toward a vision of competition.

Weight trainers are not alien beings. They are mothers and   7
sisters and daughters and everything in between. Beware, they are all around you!

Structure:

1. How long is "Pumping Iron — à la Femme" compared to most compositions you write for class? Compared to most selections in this book? Is it long enough to be an essay? What factors determine the length of an essay?
2. What techniques does Davey use in paragraph 1 to interest and prepare her readers? Evaluate each technique: to which do you respond the most? The least? And why?
3. Is Davey's classification logical? Do Valerie, Janice and Cyndi belong to the same category? Do they overlap? Has any other obvious type of woman weight trainer been left out?
4. What logic do you see in the order of the three characters? Would you have described them in a different order? Why or why not?

Style:

1. In representing each group by only one of its members, has Davey increased or decreased the force of her classification? Explain.
2. How FORMAL or INFORMAL are most of your class essays compared to most of the essays you have read so far in this book? Compared to "Pumping Iron — à la Femme"? As a student

writer, do you sense pressure of any kind in either the one
direction or the other? If so, do you believe that pressure to be
justified or unjustified? Explain.

Ideas:

1. Do you view weight training for women as a feminist activity?
Why or why not? If you are a woman, have you tried it? Would
you? Why or why not?
2. Lately great numbers of both men and women in North America
have turned to weight training. How do you account for the
fast-rising popularity of this sport?
3. Do you agree with Davey that the image of "weight trainers"
has changed? If so, give descriptive details to contrast the old
STEREOTYPES to the new image.
4. A look at the self-help section of almost any bookstore can give
the impression that self-improvement, in its many forms, has
become a craze. Name five or ten ways in which large numbers
of us systematically attempt to improve ourselves. Which, if
any, have you tried? Why? Describe the method you followed
and tell the results.
5. If you have read "How to Live to Be 200," by Stephen Leacock,
contrast the weight-training experiences of Jiggins to those of
Valerie, Janice and Cyndi.
6. Write a *classification*, in essay form, of one of the following
groups. Try Jill Davey's approach: use one person, real or
hypothetical, to represent each division of your topic.

runners	downhill skiers
swimmers	cyclists
cross country skiers	squash or tennis players

(NOTE: See also the Topics for Writing at the end of this chapter.)

David Godfrey

No More Teacher's Dirty Looks

For years David Godfrey has been on the leading edge of things, moving regularly from one avant-garde to the next. He has served with CUSO in Ghana, written experimental fiction, been an outspoken socialist and Canadian nationalist, begun three anti-establishment publishing houses, and now that the Information Age is upon us operates a computer software company. SOFTWORDS, owned by Godfrey and his wife, has signed a contract to apply the NATAL system (which he describes in "No More Teacher's Dirty Looks") to an educational project in China: 2000 ground satellite stations will broadcast a first-year computer science course from the University of Shanghai to 200,000 students across the country. Godfrey was born in Winnipeg in 1938 and was educated at the Universities of Toronto and Iowa. He has spent most of his working life as a teacher, writer and publisher. Godfrey co-founded the House of Anansi Press in 1967, New Press in 1969 and Press Porcépic (which he still heads) in 1972, and in 1970 co-founded the Independent Publishers' Association. His own first book was a highly experimental collection of short stories, Death Goes Better with Coca-Cola *(1968). He drew upon his CUSO experience to produce a novel about Africa,* The New Ancestors, *which won the 1970 Governor-General's Award. Godfrey has co-authored books about subjects such as CUSO, economic nationalism and Canadian books, and in 1978 published a second collection of short stories,* Dark Must Yield. *Our selection, drawn from his recent work with computers, comes from the book he co-authored in 1979,* Gutenberg Two. *He was still a teacher when he wrote it.*

**No more pencils, no more books
No more teacher's dirty looks.**

It is generally agreed that perhaps the most startling of changes envisaged in education over the next 10–15 years will be the extent to which technological systems will be employed. For instance, Information Retrieval Television systems (IRTV) would probably be employed in most schools to provide audio-visual television rather than decentralized type systems. There is also considerable discussion in informed circles of the possible diminution of the role of the school itself. Evolving

1

259

concurrently with the implementation of the technological systems for education, audio-visual communications could transform the home into part-
time school. According to a study by Bell Canada,
within a decade a significant number of homes could
be equipped with home terminals capable of utiliz-
ing IRTV and computerized library systems. Con-
sequently, it is quite likely that significant numbers
of post secondary students will spend more time
working at home or in small groups by 1990.
Secondary students could follow by 1993 and primary students by the year 2010 (1).

2   Before you put too much trust in that prediction you might note
that its source was a 1971 document and all that I have done is add
ten years to every date mentioned in the original.

3   Although the media . . . see growth as well as vulnerability in the
new technologies, on the whole the teaching establishment sees,
quite rightly, nothing but danger. Why did this revolution predicted
by Bell not come about? Partly because of the teaching establishment's relatively firm control of both Content and Carrier aspects of
education (can a student bring his own textbook to class?), and
partly because those who became involved in the technology early
were quickly absorbed by the fascinating techniques available and
failed to pose the deeper philosophic questions that will probably
have to be answered before the revolution is actually implemented.

4   Anyone who has taught for a number of years comes to recognize a
set of problems which exist beneath the set of problems that occupy
one's teaching efforts and hours.

5   Because these deeper problems seem insoluble, they tend to
disappear from view. The evolution of the Electronic Highway and
NABU's force one to consider them, however, and once they are
considered as solvable, then major structural changes within the
educational system become almost inevitable. In many instances,
the unhappiness that attends all such structural changes will attach
itself to the mechanisms of solution rather than to the deeper set of
problems, and it would be unwise to underestimate either the
changes or the unhappiness likely to be involved, but in the
beginning at least one can concentrate upon the problems themselves.

6   My personal terms for these problems are a little unusual, but
perhaps useful.

LOCKSTEPS	TRANSCRAPS
MR. GRUNDY	BULL CURVES
STUDENT X	PRE-SOLUTIONS

By LOCKSTEPS, I attempt to summarize those problems generated by the requirement to process a large number of students through the same teaching sequence at the same moment. The result, of course, if the teacher is reasonably honest, is that 90% of the students are bored, lost, or out of phase at least 90% of the time and most actual learning takes place outside of the sequence or on its peripheries while the main talents of the teachers are best described in entertainment terms. The result for students is twofold: a general mistrust of education and the development of individual adaptive techniques to bypass the structure they find themselves enmeshed within. 7

MR. GRUNDY refers to those inevitable disasters that occur as LOCKSTEPS ensures that certain teachers will be notched with certain students for fixed periods. All students have had the experience of a year or course of excitement and stimulation followed by one of extreme boredom, non-comprehension, or personality clashes. Teachers sometimes find themselves turned into MR. GRUNDY simply by the particular chemistry of a group of students. 8

The system and the students still make some attempts to grade teachers, but the MR. GRUNDY factor makes such comparisons more or less useless. It is possible to grade teachers on their effectiveness within a general population, but their effectiveness range with specific groups of students will likely vary far more than the comparative range of their effectiveness measured against that of other teachers. 9

The question of defining effectiveness of teaching is thus shuffled to one side and only random attempts can be made to match teachers and students according to such factors as personality type, cultural backgrounds, teaching modes, degree of authoritarianism, libertarianism, intelligence quotients. 10

STUDENT X represents the other side of the equation. Except at the graduate level, the process of education remains largely exterior to the students. They are processed through a system that must seem almost totally artificial to them and are graded on accomplishment only. Rare indeed are the skylights of a sympathetic and knowledgeable teacher, a well-trained educational counsellor, or a co-op or intern program that demonstrates how the real world goes about its learning. 11

12   At the extremes, something is known of STUDENT X as he or she passes through the kinks of the system: honour students and trouble makers impose their presence on the system; but in general, each new teacher takes on STUDENT X as a fully unknown quantity.

13   After a lecture on *The Heart of Darkness*, I once had a first-year student was enthusiastic over my presentation. I woke up when she said, "That's the first time I ever understood that book." In high school, it turned out, she had studied the text three times. No one had kept track of this fact, nor of her failure to ever understand the book.

14   The list of factors that can affect learning accomplishment is large: social background, personality factors, motivation, right brain/left brain development, aural/visual/conceptual modes of learning, skill mastery, reading habits, etc., but the system cannot afford to record and report on these factors let alone restructure itself to take account of their impact upon actual learning.

15   We all know the student who can recite every Vezina Trophy winner from 1904 on, but can't remember the dates of the War of 1812; none of us really have time to understand why that is so.

16   STUDENT X enters our range of vision, absorbs a vaguely measured quantity of what we push out into his or her domain by methods almost totally unknown to us, and then passes on to the next strange MR. GRUNDY with a duly rewarded B- or 63 or Pass or one-line comment.

17   Cumulatively, these strange little marks make up a very formal and imposing document which may allow or prevent STUDENT X from entering Law School or graduating from Veterinarian College. TRANSCRAPS represent just that, scraps of information of very dubious value carried from step to step of the system and acting as cryptic symbols of STUDENT X's contacts with MR. GRUNDY. In the aggregate, like tribal scars, they do identify the failures and the superstars.

18   The fact that TRANSCRAPS can be produced is a major self-ratification of the system, but as anyone knows who has looked at two or three hundred of them, looking for the one best employee or for the thirty most innovative students, the usefulness of the record is not very high; at the best, it records about 10% of what you really want to know.

19   Looking at the changing ability of certain high schools in Ontario to produce Ontario Scholarship students before and after the elimination of provincial examinations, one can understand the notion of a BULL CURVE as a representation of the system's ability to manipulate its relative grading in order to justify its existence. In B.C., teachers who mark firmly find that their students move to

other classes where high grades are easier to obtain and the "offending" teacher discovers that his or her effectiveness is graded downward. In another variation of the BULL CURVE, B.C. secondary schools whose failure rate exceeds a certain percentage may find themselves in trouble with the certification bodies.

The fundamental problem here is that the system finds it difficult   20
to define mastery and degrees of mastery within its disciplines. How much French does STUDENT X know? Not enough. The causes may be diverse, ranging from mere hesitancy, through conflicting approaches and varied environments, to the real problems of advanced disciplines that are in constant flux.

I recently gave some assistance to a student finishing her MA at   21
the Sorbonne on a West Indian writer. There were gaps in her knowledge of literature that absolutely astounded me. She felt, for example, that the writer was racist because many of his characters made racist remarks about Jews in Toronto. Nonetheless, she passed her MA from the Sorbonne. MR. GRUNDY's law of the BULL CURVE might be expressed as follows:

The knowledge received by any given teacher of any given new student from a TRANSCRAP is always less than 5% of the ideal and the knowledge passed on varies directly with the peculiarities of the institution's grading system but is never greater than the original knowledge.

The cumulative result of many of these factors is one I term   22
PRE-SOLUTIONS. A metaphor that seems applicable is that of the meat-grinder; in goes pork, veal, beef and perhaps a little venison, pony and turtle; out comes hamburger. A few students escape almost completely and most learn to learn despite the system, but all are damaged to some extent and the process itself remains unchanged. The amount of adaptation to the variables of time, innovation and personality is minuscule and the awareness of those involved is but a fraction of what it might be.

All the teacher can do is carry into the classroom a set of   23
pre-solutions, ideas, concepts and methods of presentation which have been used in the past, and hope that they will work as well as they did last time; however well that might be. The dedicated teachers manage to change a small percentage of those PRE-SOLUTIONS every year; the less dedicated don't.

The fascination of computers, databanks and cheap long-distance   24
communications for the innovative teacher is obvious and quite

enormous. One can now begin to deal with all of these deeper problems. Let me start with a small example. During the seventies, the teaching of English in the secondary schools began at last to stress the creative and personal rather than strict rules of composition. This was quite a breakthrough, provided that the teachers were excellent and had the necessary time to devote to this quite difficult task. Many teachers were excellent and made the time to encourage students to write out of their own experience and desires.

25   But the "basics" did suffer, punctuation, grammar, and structure. In fact, of course, these "basics" are much easier to teach than a sense of creativity and provide ideal material for experimental computer-aided courses. I no longer "teach" punctuation in any of my classes. Students who haven't mastered that particular aspect of the discipline receive an 80-page manual covering over 180 rules of punctuation and an introduction to the computer. Then, at their own speed, they master the rules and demonstrate that mastery to the computer/program, which is endlessly patient, keeps track of exactly which rules have been mastered and which not, never asks them anything they already know and politely refers them back to the manual if they miss a test question too many times. In addition, it allows the students to decide if they want me to be able to see the computer's evaluation of their current session.

26   Obviously not all educational material is suitable for this type of CAL (Computer Assisted Learning) presentation, but far more is than is not. There are a number of centres of excellence in the country involved with computer systems and satellites, especially the University of Quebec (2), which has thirteen campuses deliberately linked together by computerized communications to encourage all the segments to function as an Omnibus Network, and the Ontario Institute for Studies in Education (3), which will be one of the primary foci for experiments involving education.

27   The National Research Council has sponsored the development of a new language, designed for educational purposes, which makes the writing of courses far easier. Unlike the PLATO and TICCIT systems, NATAL is not restricted to a single terminal type nor to a single manufacturer's equipment with all the limitations and often unnecessary expense implicit in such a restriction. NATAL currently supports a variety of terminals ranging from basic alphanumeric units to graphics units incorporating local processing and is capable of accommodating new hardware developments such as the Telidon terminal.

28   NATAL now functions on the Digital Equipment Corporation's PDP10 and implementation is underway on other large, general

purpose, time-sharing systems and on a dedicated mini-computer. These efforts will result in a standard specification for NATAL, implementations of which are expected to be available from a wide variety of sources.

One of its many features is that it is bilingual. For every command in the language there is a French and English version, so that programmers can work in the language of their own choice with the same system being capable of running both English and French programs (4). 29

Let us look at my "class" in terms of the six problems: 30

LOCKSTEPS. Bob does not have to listen as I explain comma splices to Peter for the 27th time. In fact, Bob isn't even present while Peter spends the ten minutes (or fifty minutes) necessary to master this particular unit. If a new student enters the "class" and has problems with only five of the 180 units, then graduation may take place within twenty minutes. All the time-oriented functions of education (periods, days, Grades, Years, Majors and Degrees) are unnecessary for those portions of knowledge available in similar CAL courses. On Monday, the student might improve his mastery of punctuation by three percent, of trigonometry by one percent and of French Vocabulary Level Five by six percent. Every student would thus have a completely distinct learning track in all segments of all disciplines. 31

MR. GRUNDY does not completely disappear, but little is left beyond the memory. As students become more aware of the process of learning and more of the routine aspects of teaching are taken over by programs, teachers will be able to be matched with those students with whom they function well rather than those whom the timetable demands. Neither a student nor teacher will have to face a year with a "fink," or a "complete idiot." Most courses will contain a shadow of their originator, of course, but teachers or students will be able to select different courses covering the same material. From the teacher's point of view, dealing with students who have self-selected themselves, with the more theoretical and complex aspects of the subject, all with a minimum of grading, must surely reduce frustration. 32

The STUDENT X problem will be reduced in a number of ways. Primarily, the student will be able, and ought to be encouraged, to examine the process by which a given body of material is being taught. That is, the program itself will be available to the student and the student's suggestions will be part of the continual amendment of the program. Questions that are ambiguous, elements that are unclear, options that should be added, can all be dealt with in discussions, either group or individual. 33

34   Properly constructed programs will also provide a great deal of information to the student about the process of learning so that each student will be able to develop an individual profile of learning skills and difficulties. If some students wish to keep most of this fairly private, they should be allowed to.

35   In other instances, acceptance into certain learning situations might require some documentation of learning skills rather than merely learning accomplishments, but in these instances the student would at least be able to improve the skills before application.

36   In the majority of cases, a student moving to a new learning situation would carry with them a great deal of information which would greatly improve their chances of success.

37   The TRANSCRAP as such would lose most of its functions. Employers would have their own ways of examining in detail for the skills and accomplishments they required and so would graduate schools. Since education would be far less time-bound and place-bound than it is now, one could expect a far greater degree of transfer between the private sector and the formal educational system. The actuality of failure would not disappear, of course, but the recording of it on TRANSCRAPS would. A case can be made that most educational failures represent either inadequate teaching or inadequate self-analysis that draws the student into a particular LOCKSTEPS situation from which the only exit door is marked Failure. Individualized learning should consist of individually established goals as well as individual learning speed, routing and approach.

38   BULL CURVES are not entirely the educational system's responsibility. The society's general fear of the twenty-hour work week has created a hidden demand on the system, which might be expressed in the vernacular as "teach the buggers anything, movies, bowling, science fiction, even sex, but keep them out of the labour market as long as possible."

39   The universities have listened to this message (suitably translated of course) with more care than most of the community colleges who, out of fear or intelligence, have felt that students might like to be employed once they do graduate. As one result, unlike the universities, many of the community colleges have two applicants for every position.

40   But much of the responsibility remains within the system. Faced with declining enrolments and uncertain about its functions because of society's own uncertainty about the future, the system becomes terrified at the thought of a fifty percent "failure" rate and the moment of truth is put off, either until university or until the student enters the real work world.

Let us assume, however, that a university develops a computer- 41
based course in Physics with a reasonable effectiveness ratio. What
is to prevent secondary school teachers from taking the course, from
letting their best students take the course in their senior year, from
revising the course for their other students? Only a few technical
considerations which will soon become quite minor.

As such transfers become more common, fraudulent grades will 42
become obviously fraudulent. At the moment, most university
departments have learned to recognize the schools which prepare
students well and those which don't, but no action can be taken of
any real effectiveness. Being able to send back some detailed
comparative statistics drawn out automatically by the program and
demonstrating that an A in Physics from School Bloat is comparative to a C- from School Honest, will be a start at least.

But it is in the elimination of PRE-SOLUTIONS that the most 43
excitement lies. The creative teacher will be delighted to see 80% of
the rote aspects of any discipline adapted for presentation by this
methodology for many reasons. First of all, it forces one to examine
the content of what is being taught. Since the information presented
is public in ways that a lecture or discussion are not, even this
initial step can be salutary. Secondly, one must seriously examine
one's assumptions about how the material might best be presented.
LOCKSTEPS simplifies presentation in many ways. But suppose
one needn't worry about holding up the entire class for a half hour
while Paul grasps the second law of thermodynamics; suppose it
doesn't matter if he needs fifteen examples instead of two. Do you
have fifteen? Why didn't the first fourteen work? Perhaps what is
needed is more drama, or humour, or a game context?

The program can store data about hundreds of reactions to specific 44
questions and summarize them in patterns that help indicate why
some elements didn't work for certain students; the students
themselves will discuss their reactions and suggest improvements.
Most amendments can be made fairly quickly. In addition, other
teachers can utilize the program and report on it to the originator.
One thus begins to seriously analyse the educational process itself
in addition to participating in it.

Programs should act as a neutral buffer between teacher and 45
student. Both can amend it; both can draw information from it that
is not normally available. Rather than guessing as to whether or not
a particular segment works, one can compare its effectiveness with
other segments of the same course and even with other experiences
of that particular class.

The time saved by this method of presentation of rote portions of 46
the material can be spent not only upon specific difficulties and the
complexities of a particular discipline, but upon the larger questions

of how we acquire and retain knowledge.

47   This is not to say that adaptation of a large proportion of the curriculum to this teaching method will come about overnight. For every program that is complete and functioning, there seem to be a dozen horror stories of disasters, fantasies, meanderings or brave beginnings best forgotten. There are at least three major categories of error: inadequate equipment, over-ambitious plans, and lack of comprehension of what it is that is to be taught.

48   Nonetheless, successful programs do exist and if the educational establishment fails to recognize the innovation it will simply have to watch as the new methodology establishes itself outside of the existing institutions.

49   The establishment of schools as we know them was influenced greatly by Gutenberg's inventions. J. L. Vives was describing a revolution when he wrote in 1531:

> The man desirous of wisdom must make use of books, or of those men who take the place of books . . . . Let a school be established in every township, and let there be received into it as teachers men who are of ascertained learning, uprightness and prudence. Let their salary be paid to them from the public treasury . . . . Let the teacher know the mother-tongue of the boys exactly, so that by means of their vernacular he may make his instruction easier and more pleasant . . .; the teacher should keep in his mind the earlier history of his mother-tongue (5).

50   The innovations we term Gutenberg Two do not have a "schoolroom" as their natural environment: an appendage of a library, a room in which books can be distributed, collected and stored. There is no technical reason why a student in my punctuation "class" couldn't "pass" the course without leaving home. It is inevitable that some . . . entrepreneurs . . . will recognize the possibilities of educational content within the new electronic environment and promote the advantages of home learning via the friendly NABU.

51   Education has existed for a long time without serious competition, partly because of its social function and partly because of its high labour content; competition is about to arrive. As in all instances where a social group faces a threat from mechanical innovation, we

can expect a good deal of protest, intensified in this instance by the prior lack of competition and the articulateness of the threatened group. The educational system at the present is a Carrier whose Content is the accepted and valued knowledge of the society. It is place-bound, time-bound and unused to competition or innovation. No other sector of society is more vulnerable to the new technologies. I will predict, however, that within the system (after an initial period of protest), terror will become the mother of adaptation, and although the formal structures will continue to shrink as the work week shortens, creative teachers will have tasks and opportunities that they had previously never even considered possible.

Vulnerability Coefficient: .75   52
Prognosis: Small craft warnings in the straits at last. High winds. Danger of capsizing for the ill-prepared. Light in distant harbours for the adventurous.

References . . . .

1. *The Film Industry in Canada: Report*, prepared by The Bureau of Management Consulting for the Department of the Secretary of State, Arts and Culture Branch, Ottawa, 1977, p. 107.
2. The address of the Université du Quebec is 2875, boulevard Laurier, Sainte-Foy, Quebec, G1V 2M3, Management of Omnibus Network project.
3. The address of the Ontario Institute for Studies in Education is 252 Bloor St. W., Toronto, Ontario, M5S 1V6.
4. For more information on NATAL write J.W. Brahan, Senior Research Officer, Information Science Section, National Research Council, Montreal Road, Ottawa, K1A 0R8.
5. From Hirsch, Rudolf, *Printing, Selling and Reading: 1450–1550*, Otto Harrassowitz, Wiesbaden, 1967, p. 152.

Structure:

1. In what way does the schoolyard rhyme "No more pencils, no more books/No more teacher's dirty looks" help to introduce the topic?
2. The six problems of traditional schooling are discussed once in paragraphs 6–25 and again in paragraphs 30–48. In what major way does the purpose of the second section differ from that of the first?

3. Are the six categories of David Godfrey's classification mutually exclusive?
4. Why does Godfrey save "PRE-SOLUTIONS" for last?
5. Point out the ways in which examples help to develop paragraph 31.
6. Discuss the comparison that Godfrey makes (in pars. 49 and 50) between Gutenberg's invention of printing and modern technology's invention of computers.

Style:

1. Do you find the METAPHOR of the meat-grinder (par. 22) to be appropriate?
2. In paragraph 36, Godfrey writes, "In the majority of cases, a student moving to a new learning situation would carry with them a great deal of information which would greatly improve their chances of success." In making the plural pronouns "them" and "their" refer to the singular noun "student," has Godfrey committed a grammatical error? Or has Godfrey, in the past known as a highly politicized writer, tried to avoid the sexism of making "he" and "his" refer to "student"? If you think the latter is true, is there a way to make this passage avoid bad grammar and sexism at once?
3. What FIGURE OF SPEECH does Godfrey use in paragraph 51 when he states that ". . . terror will become the mother of adaptation. . . ."?

Ideas:

1. To what extent does your own experience confirm or deny the problems that David Godfrey labels as "LOCKSTEPS," "MR. GRUNDY," "STUDENT X," "TRANSCRAPS," "BULL CURVES" and "PRE-SOLUTIONS"?
2. Godfrey states in paragraph 25, "I no longer 'teach' punctuation in any of my classes." Would you prefer to study punctuation in class or by computer? Why? Is there a way to bypass both of these alternatives and still master punctuation?
3. Do you agree or disagree with Godfrey when he describes universities as trying to keep students out of the labour market while community colleges are trying to get students into it (pars. 38 and 39)? What can universities do for students that community colleges cannot do? And what can community colleges do for students that universities cannot do?

4. Can you imagine your schooling taking place at home, as Godfrey suggests in paragraph 50? What might be the advantages? What might be the disadvantages?
5. Either verbally or in writing, describe a day at college or university as you imagine it in the year 2000.
6. Write an essay based on a *classification* of one of the following:
   Uses of computers
   Types of computers
   Types of computer
      enthusiasts
   Types of computer haters
   Types of English classes
   Types of English
      teachers

(NOTE: See also the Topics for Writing at the end of this chapter.)

Topics for Writing

Chapter 7: Classification

(Note also the topics for writing that appear after each selection in this chapter.)

Develop one of the following topics into an essay of classification:

1. Gamblers
2. Drinkers
3. Writers
4. Sports fans
5. Coaches
6. Drivers
7. Bullies
8. Cowards
9. Garage mechanics
10. Farmers
11. Weather
12. Unidentified flying objects
13. Hair styles
14. Cameras
15. Musical instruments
16. Newspapers
17. Magazines
18. Movies
19. Restaurants
20. Dogs
21. Cats
22. Parents
23. Friends
24. Neighbours
25. Districts of your town or city

"In our early 20s, the lung capacity, the rapidity of motor responses and physical endurance are at their peak. This is the athlete's finest hour."
Judy Stoffman, "The Way of All Flesh"

Here's how it's done. . . .

PROCESS ANALYSIS

In the last quarter century, how-to-do-it books and magazines have flourished. Perhaps we have lost the skills we need to build a garage, grow cabbages or bake bread and need to look them up. Perhaps the increasing cost of labour has driven us to do our own work. Or perhaps increased leisure has led us to new hobbies. Whatever the reason, we are very familiar with the practical writing known as *process analysis*.

It is a sort of narrative, taking us from the beginning to the end of a task, usually in the strict time order required to build the garage, grow the cabbages or make the bread. It includes every step, for each is necessary to the success of the whole project. And if it is written for the amateur, it includes *all* the details right down to the size of the nails, or the spacing and depth of seeds in the ground, or the amount of yeast or salt in the dough. A highly experienced cook might just say "Add some yeast" or "Put in a little salt," but the writer of a recipe tries to save us from failure by giving measurements. The main thing to remember in giving directions is to *keep the reader in mind*. If you are writing in your area of expertise, you'll be tempted to take short cuts, leaving out details the reader will be lost without. And you'll be tempted to load your writing with technical terms. But if you accurately estimate your reader's level of knowledge and write accordingly, your directions will stand a greater chance of working.

Another kind of process analysis satisfies not our practical needs but our curiosity. You may enjoy learning how a space satellite is launched, how stockholders are swindled, how liquor is distilled, how World War II was won or how a heart is transplanted — without ever doing these things yourself. Of course not every detail must be given in armchair reading such as this: only as many as it takes to clearly convey the information and to interest the reader.

Sometimes a writer will use process analysis not to instruct or inform, but for a totally different reason. When Stephen Leacock tells us "How to Live to Be 200," he advises us to eat cement — a strange way to reach the goal — until we see that his goal is not longevity but laughs.

Whether you aim to help the reader accomplish a task, or to satisfy the reader's curiosity, or just to entertain, your process analysis will work only if you observe the most basic principle of writing any essay: know your purpose at the beginning and keep it firmly in mind as you write.

Stephen Leacock

How to Live to Be 200

During his lifetime Stephen Leacock became the world's best-known humorist writing in English, and he remains Canada's favourite writer of all time. Even today, no Canadian author has more books in print. Leacock was born in England in 1869, but at age 6 came with his family to Ontario. He studied at Upper Canada College, the University of Toronto and the University of Chicago where, in 1903, he was awarded a Ph.D. In the same year McGill hired him to teach economics and political science, and from 1908 until his retirement in 1936, he served as head of his department. He died in 1944. Leacock wrote over sixty books, many on academic subjects, but of course it is for his books of humour that he is treasured. The best-loved have been Literary Lapses *(1910),* Nonsense Novels *(1911),* Sunshine Sketches of a Little Town *(1912),* Arcadian Adventures with the Idle Rich *(1914) and* My Remarkable Uncle and Other Sketches *(1942). Our selection, which comes from a later edition of* Literary Lapses, *is vintage Leacock: through exaggeration and incongruities, it reduces to absurdity a topic that many people, today as in Leacock's time, take seriously.*

Twenty years ago I knew a man called Jiggins, who had the   1
Health Habit.
He used to take a cold plunge every morning. He said it   2
opened his pores. After it he took a hot sponge. He said it closed the pores. He got so that he could open and shut his pores at will.

Jiggins used to stand and breathe at an open window for half an   3
hour before dressing. He said it expanded his lungs. He might, of course, have had it done in a shoe-store with a boot stretcher, but after all it cost him nothing this way, and what is half an hour?

After he had got his undershirt on, Jiggins used to hitch himself   4
up like a dog in harness and do Sandow exercises. He did them forwards, backwards, and hind-side up.

He could have got a job as a dog anywhere. He spent all his time at   5
this kind of thing. In his spare time at the office, he used to lie on his stomach on the floor and see if he could lift himself up with his knuckles. If he could, then he tried some other way until he found one that he couldn't do. Then he would spend the rest of his lunch hour on his stomach, perfectly happy.

In the evenings in his room he used to lift iron bars, cannon-balls,   6
heave dumb-bells, and haul himself up to the ceiling with his teeth. You could hear the thumps half a mile.

He liked it.   7

8   He spent half the night slinging himself around his room. He said it made his brain clear. When he got his brain perfectly clear, he went to bed and slept. As soon as he woke, he began clearing it again.

9   Jiggins is dead. He was, of course, a pioneer, but the fact that he dumb-belled himself to death at an early age does not prevent a whole generation of young men from following in his path.

10   They are ridden by the Health Mania.

11   They make themselves a nuisance.

12   They get up at impossible hours. They go out in silly little suits and run Marathon heats before breakfast. They chase around barefoot to get the dew on their feet. They hunt for ozone. They bother about pepsin. They won't eat meat because it has too much nitrogen. They won't eat fruit because it hasn't any. They prefer albumen and starch and nitrogen to huckleberry pie and doughnuts. They won't drink water out of a tap. They won't eat sardines out of a can. They won't use oysters out of a pail. They won't drink milk out of a glass. They are afraid of alcohol in any shape. Yes, sir, afraid. "Cowards."

13   And after all their fuss they presently incur some simple old-fashioned illness and die like anybody else.

14   Now people of this sort have no chance to attain any great age. They are on the wrong track.

15   Listen. Do you want to live to be really old, to enjoy a grand, green, exuberant, boastful old age and to make yourself a nuisance to your whole neighbourhood with your reminiscences?

16   Then cut out all this nonsense. Cut it out. Get up in the morning at a sensible hour. The time to get up is when you have to, not before. If your office opens at eleven, get up at ten-thirty. Take your chance on ozone. There isn't any such thing anyway. Or, if there is, you can buy a Thermos bottle full for five cents, and put it on a shelf in your cupboard. If your work begins at seven in the morning, get up at ten minutes to, but don't be liar enough to say that you like it. It isn't exhilarating, and you know it.

17   Also, drop all that cold-bath business. You never did it when you were a boy. Don't be a fool now. If you must take a bath (you don't really need to), take it warm. The pleasure of getting out of a cold bed and creeping into a hot bath beats a cold plunge to death. In any case, stop gassing about your tub and your "shower," as if you were the only man who ever washed.

18   So much for that point.

19   Next, take the question of germs and bacilli. Don't be scared of them. That's all. That's the whole thing, and if you once get on to that you never need to worry again.

If you see a bacilli, walk right up to it, and look it in the eye. If one [20] flies into your room, strike at it with your hat or with a towel. Hit it as hard as you can between the neck and the thorax. It will soon get sick of that.

But as a matter of fact, a bacilli is perfectly quiet and harmless if [21] you are not afraid of it. Speak to it. Call out to it to "lie down." It will understand. I had a bacilli once, called Fido, that would come and lie at my feet while I was working. I never knew a more affectionate companion, and when it was run over by an automobile, I buried it in the garden with genuine sorrow.

(I admit this is an exaggeration. I don't really remember its name; [22] it may have been Robert.)

Understand that it is only a fad of modern medicine to say that [23] cholera and typhoid and diphtheria are caused by bacilli and germs; nonsense. Cholera is caused by a frightful pain in the stomach, and diphtheria is caused by trying to cure a sore throat.

Now take the question of food. [24]

Eat what you want. Eat lots of it. Yes, eat too much of it. Eat till [25] you can just stagger across the room with it and prop it up against a sofa cushion. Eat everything that you like until you can't eat any more. The only test is, can you pay for it? If you can't pay for it, don't eat it. And listen — don't worry as to whether your food contains starch, or albumen, or gluten, or nitrogen. If you are a damn fool enough to want these things, go and buy them and eat all you want of them. Go to a laundry and get a bag of starch, and eat your fill of it. Eat it, and take a good long drink of glue after it, and a spoonful of Portland cement. That will gluten you, good and solid.

If you like nitrogen, go and get a druggist to give you a canful of it [26] at the soda counter, and let you sip it with a straw. Only don't think that you can mix all these things up with your food. There isn't any nitrogen or phosphorus or albumen in ordinary things to eat. In any decent household all that sort of stuff is washed out in the kitchen sink before the food is put on the table.

And just one word about fresh air and exercise. Don't bother with [27] either of them. Get your room full of good air, then shut up the windows and keep it. It will keep for years. Anyway, don't keep using your lungs all the time. Let them rest. As for exercise, if you have to take it, take it and put up with it. But as long as you have the price of a hack and can hire other people to play baseball for you and run races and do gymnastics when you sit in the shade and smoke and watch them — great heavens, what more do you want?

Structure:

1. This essay is divided into two main parts. How do they differ from one another and where do we pass from one to the other?
2. Is the story of Jiggins explained in any particular order? And what effect is achieved at the end of his case (par. 9)?
3. Are Stephen Leacock's health instructions organized according to the order in which they should be applied?
4. What is our first clue that Leacock's process analysis is meant not to instruct but to entertain?

Style:

1. Leacock uses the word "eat" seven times in this passage from paragraph 25:

> **Eat what you want. Eat lots of it. Yes, eat too much of it. Eat till you can just stagger across the room with it and prop it up against a sofa cushion. Eat everything that you like until you can't eat any more. The only test is, can you pay for it? If you can't pay for it, don't eat it.**

   Is this repetition accidental or deliberate? What effect does it achieve? Where else in the essay does Leacock use repetition?
2. In paragraph 25, Leacock writes: "That will gluten you, good and solid." What is the effect of the word "gluten" as used in this sentence?
3. In paragraph 21, Leacock writes: "I had a bacilli once, called Fido, that would come and lie at my feet while I was working." Analyze the sources of humour in this sentence.
4. Reduction to absurdity is a comic device often used by Leacock. One good example is the analogy of "bacilli" as insects being swatted or as a favourite dog being run over by a car. Where else in this essay is an idea reduced to absurdity?

Ideas:

1. Do you have the "Health Habit," like Jiggins, or do you prefer comfort and luxury, like our narrator? Give reasons to justify your preference.

2. How would you revise Leacock's essay for our times? Which aspects of the "Health Mania" would you drop from the argument, which would you keep, and which might you add?
3. If you are following a serious program of physical fitness, describe in a process analysis exactly how you do it. At the end, describe the effects of the program.
4. Write a serious or humorous *process analysis* on the topic of how to attain old age in good health. Be as specific as possible.

(NOTE: See also the Topics for Writing at the end of this chapter.)

Judy Stoffman

The Way of All Flesh

Judy Stoffman has been a senior editor of Today *magazine and author of articles that have appeared in* Today *and other periodicals. She grew up in Vancouver, studied English literature at the University of British Columbia and at Sussex University, England, where she earned an M.A.; she studied also in France. Her future seemed decided as early as grade two: when a teacher read out to the class her composition on recess, Stoffman knew she wanted to be a writer. At UBC she wrote for the student newspaper. And now, living in Toronto, she writes on a broad variety of subjects. "I love the research and dread the writing," she says. "Before I start writing I have a kind of stage fright and from talking to other writers I know they have it too, but they persist because when the words finally start to flow there is an exhilaration nothing else can give." Our selection, "The Way of All Flesh," appeared in* Weekend Magazine *in 1979. Before writing it Stoffman did extensive research: she read ten books on aging and interviewed three gerontologists, a family doctor and a sex therapist. "Then," she says, "I tried to synthesize what I had learned, while exploring my own deepest fears. But you'll notice that I never used the word 'I'."*

1   When a man of 25 is told that aging is inexorable, inevitable, universal, he will nod somewhat impatiently at being told something so obvious. In fact, he has little idea of the meaning of the words. It has nothing to do with him. Why should it? He has had no tangible evidence yet that his body, as the poet Rilke said, enfolds old age and death as the fruit enfolds a stone.

2   The earliest deposits of fat in the aorta, the trunk artery carrying blood away from the heart, occur in the eighth year of life, but who can peer into his own aorta at this first sign of approaching debility? The young man has seen old people but he secretly believes himself to be the exception on whom the curse will never fall. "Never will the skin of my neck hang loose. My grip will never weaken. I will stand tall and walk with long strides as long as I live." The young girl scarcely pays attention to her clothes; she scorns makeup. Her confidence in her body is boundless; smooth skin and a flat stomach will compensate, she knows, for any lapses in fashion or grooming. She stays up all night, as careless of her energy as of her looks, believing both will last forever.

3   In our early 20s, the lung capacity, the rapidity of motor responses and physical endurance are at their peak. This is the athlete's finest hour. Cindy Nicholas of Toronto was 19 when she first swam the

English Channel in both directions. The tennis star Bjorn Borg was 23 when he triumphed this year at Wimbledon for the fourth time.

It is not only *athletic* prowess that is at its height between 20 and 30. James Boswell, writing in his journal in 1763 after he had finally won the favors of the actress Louisa, has left us this happy description of the sexual prowess of a 23-year-old: "I was in full glow of health and my bounding blood beat quick in high alarms. Five times was I fairly lost in supreme rapture. Louisa was madly fond of me; she declared I was a prodigy, and asked me if this was extraordinary in human nature. I said twice as much might be, but this was not, although in my own mind I was somewhat proud of my performance." 4

In our early 30s we are dumbfounded to discover the first grey hair at the temples. We pull out the strange filament and look at it closely, trying to grasp its meaning. It means simply that the pigment has disappeared from the hair shaft, never to return. It means also — but this thought we push away — that in 20 years or so we'll relinquish our identity as a blonde or a redhead. By 57, one out of four people is completely grey. Of all the changes wrought by time this is the most harmless, except to our vanity. 5

In this decade one also begins to notice the loss of upper register hearing, that is, the responsiveness to high frequency tones, but not all the changes are for the worse, not yet. Women don't reach their sexual prime until about 38, because their sexual response is learned rather than innate. The hand grip of both sexes increases in strength until 35, and intellectual powers are never stronger than at that age. There is a sense in the 30s of hitting your stride, of coming into your own. When Sigmund Freud was 38 an older colleague, Josef Breuer, wrote: "Freud's intellect is soaring at its highest. I gaze after him as a hen at a hawk." 6

Gail Sheehy in her book *Passages* calls the interval between 35 and 45 the Deadline Decade. It is the time we begin to sense danger. The body continually flashes us signals that time is running out. We must perform our quaint deeds, keep our promises, get on with our allotted tasks. 7

Signal: The woman attempts to become pregnant at 40 and finds she cannot. Though she menstruates each month, menstruation being merely the shedding of the inner lining of the womb, she may not be ovulating regularly. 8

Signal: Both men and women discover that, although they have not changed their eating habits over the years, they are much heavier than formerly. The man is paunchy around the waist; the woman no longer has those slim thighs and slender arms. A 120-pound woman needs 2,000 calories daily to maintain her weight 9 when she is 25, 1,700 to maintain the same weight at 45, and only 1,500 calories at 65. A 170-pound man needs 3,100 calories daily at 25, 300 fewer a day at 45 and 450 calories fewer still at 65. This decreasing calorie need signals that the body consumes its fuel ever more slowly; the cellular fires are damped and our sense of energy diminishes.

10   In his mid-40s the man notices he can no longer run up the stairs three at a time. He is more easily winded and his joints are not as flexible as they once were. The strength of his hands has declined somewhat. The man feels humiliated: "I will not let this happen to me. I will turn back the tide and master my body." He starts going to the gym, playing squash, lifting weights. He takes up jogging. Though he may find it neither easy nor pleasant, terror drives him past pain. A regular exercise program can retard some of the symptoms of aging by improving the circulation and increasing the lung capacity, thereby raising our stamina and energy level, but no amount of exercise will make a 48-year-old 26 again. Take John Keeley of Mystic, Connecticut. In 1957, when he was 26, he won the Boston marathon with a time of 2:20. This year he is fit and 48 and says he is as fiercely competitive as ever, yet it took him almost 30 minutes longer to run the same marathon.

11   In the middle of the fourth decade, the man whose eyesight has always been good will pick up a book and notice that he is holding it farther from his face than usual. The condition is presbyopia, a loss of the flexibility of the lens which makes adjustment from distant to near vision increasingly difficult. It's harder now to zoom in for a closeup. It also takes longer for the eyes to recover from glare; between 16 and 90, recovery time from exposure to glare is doubled every 13 years.

12   In our 50s, we notice that food is less and less tasty; our taste buds are starting to lose their acuity. The aged Queen Victoria was wont to complain that strawberries were not as sweet as when she was a girl.

13   Little is known about the causes of aging. We do not know if we are born with a biochemical messenger programed to keep the cells and tissues alive, a messenger that eventually gets lost, or if there is a 'death hormone,' absent from birth but later secreted by the thymus or by the mysterious pineal gland, or if, perhaps, aging results from a fatal flaw in the body's immunity system. The belief that the body is a machine whose parts wear out is erroneous, for the machine does not have the body's capacity for self-repair.

14   "A man is as old as his arteries," observed Sir William Osler. From the 50s on, there's a progressive hardening and narrowing of the arteries due to the gradual lifelong accumulation of calcium and

fats along the arterial walls. Arteriosclerosis eventually affects the majority of the population in the affluent countries of the West. Lucky the man or women who, through a combination of good genes and good nutrition, can escape it, for it is the most evil change of all. As the flow of blood carrying oxygen and nutrients to the muscles, the brain, the kidneys and other organs diminishes, these organs begin to starve. Although all aging organs lose weight, there is less shrinkage of organs such as the liver and kidneys, the cells of which regenerate, than there is shrinkage of the brain and the muscles, the cells of which, once lost, are lost forever.

For the woman it is now an ordeal to be asked her age. There is a 15 fine tracery of lines around her eyes, a furrow in her brow even when she smiles. The bloom is off her cheeks. Around the age of 50 she will buy her last box of sanitary pads. The body's production of estrogen and progesterone, which govern menstruation (and also help to protect her from heart attack and the effects of stress), will have ceased almost completely. She may suffer palpitations, suddenly break into a sweat; her moods may shift abruptly. She looks in the mirror and asks, "Am I still a woman?" Eventually she becomes reconciled to her new self and even acknowledges its advantages: no more fears about pregnancy. "In any case," she laughs, "I still have not bad legs."

The man, too, will undergo a change. One night in his early 50s he 16 has some trouble achieving a complete erection, and his powers of recovery are not what they once were. Whereas at 20 he was ready to make love again less than half an hour after doing so, it may now take two hours or more; he was not previously aware that his level of testosterone, the male hormone, has been gradually declining since the age of 20. He may develop headaches, be unable to sleep, become anxious about his performance, anticipate failure and so bring on what is called secondary impotence — impotence of psychological rather than physical origin. According to Masters and Johnson, 25 percent of all men are impotent by 65 and 50 percent by 75, yet this cannot be called an inevitable feature of aging. A loving, undemanding partner and a sense of confidence can do wonders. "The susceptibility of the human male to the power of suggestion with regard to his sexual prowess," observe Masters and Johnson, "is almost unbelievable."

After the menopause, the woman ages more rapidly. Her bones 17 start to lose calcium, becoming brittle and porous. The walls of the vagina become thinner and drier; sexual intercourse now may be painful unless her partner is slow and gentle. The sweat glands begin to atrophy and the sebaceous glands that lubricate the skin decline; the complexion becomes thinner and drier and wrinkles appear around the mouth. The skin, which in youth varies from about one-fiftieth of an inch on the eyelids to about a third of an inch on the palms and the soles of the feet, loses 50 percent of its thickness between the ages of 20 and 80. The woman no longer buys sleeveless dresses and avoids shorts. The girl who once disdained cosmetics is now a woman whose dressing table is covered with lotions, night creams and makeup.

18   Perhaps no one has written about the sensation of nearing 60 with more brutal honesty than the French novelist Simone de Beauvoir: "While I was able to look at my face without displeasure, I gave it no thought. I loathe my appearance now: the eyebrows slipping down toward the eyes, the bags underneath, the excessive fullness of the cheeks and the air of sadness around the mouth that wrinkles always bring. . . . Death is no longer a brutal event in the far distance; it haunts my sleep."

19   In his early 60s the man's calves are shrunken, his muscles stringy looking. The legs of the woman, too, are no longer shapely. Both start to lose their sense of smell and both lose most of the hair in the pubic area and the underarms. Hair, however, may make its appearance in new places, such as the woman's chin. Liver spots appear on the hands, the arms, the face; they are made of coagulated melanin, the coloring matter of the skin. The acid secretions of the stomach decrease, making digestion slow and more difficult.

20   Halfway through the 60s comes compulsory retirement for most men and working women, forcing upon the superannuated worker the realization that society now views him as useless and unproductive. The man who formerly gave orders to a staff of 20 now finds himself underfoot as his wife attempts to clean the house or get the shopping done. The woman fares a little better since there is a continuity in her pattern of performing a myriad of essential household tasks. Now they must both set new goals or see themselves wither mentally. The unsinkable American journalist I.F. Stone, when he retired in 1971 from editing *I.F. Stone's Weekly*, began to teach himself Greek and is now reading Plato in the original. When Somerset Maugham read that the Roman senator Cato the Elder learned Greek when he was 80, he remarked: "Old age is ready to undertake tasks that youth shirked because they would take too long."

21   However active we are, the fact of old age can no longer be evaded from about 65 onward. Not everyone is as strong minded about this as de Beauvoir. When she made public in her memoirs her horror at her own deterioration, her readers were scandalized. She received hundreds of letters telling her that there is no such thing as old age, that some are just younger than others. Repeatedly she heard the

hollow reassurance, "You're as young as you feel." But she considers this a lie. Our subjective reality, our inner sense of self, is not the only reality. There is also an objective reality, how we are seen by society. We receive our revelation of old age from others. The woman whose figure is still trim may sense that a man is following her in the street; drawing abreast, the man catches sight of her face — and hurries on. The man of 68 may be told by a younger woman to whom he is attracted: "You remind me of my father."

Madame de Sévigné, the 17th-century French writer, struggled to   22
rid herself of the illusion of perpetual youth. At 63 she wrote: "I have been dragged to this inevitable point where old age must be undergone: I see it there before me; I have reached it; and I should at least like so to arrange matters that I do not move on, that I do not travel further along this path of the infirmities, pains, losses of memory and the disfigurement. But I hear a voice saying: 'You must go along, whatever you may say; or indeed if you will not then you must die, which is an extremity from which nature recoils.'"

Now the man and the woman have their 70th birthday party. It is   23
a sad affair because so many of their friends are missing, felled by strokes, heart attacks or cancers. Now the hands of the clock begin to race. The skeleton continues to degenerate from loss of calcium. The spine becomes compressed and there is a slight stoop nothing can prevent. Inches are lost from one's height. The joints may become thickened and creaking; in the morning the woman can't seem to get moving until she's had a hot bath. She has osteoarthritis. This, like the other age-related diseases, arteriosclerosis and diabetes, can and should be treated, but it can never be cured. The nails, particularly the toenails, become thick and lifeless because the circulation in the lower limbs is now poor. The man has difficulty learning new things because of the progressive loss of neurons from the brain. The woman goes to the store and forgets what she has come to buy. The two old people are often constipated because the involuntary muscles are weaker now. To make it worse, their children are always saying, "Sit down, rest, take it easy." Their digestive tract would be toned up if they went for a long walk or even a swim, although they feel a little foolish in bathing suits.

In his late 70s, the man develops glaucoma, pressure in the   24
eyeball caused by the failure of the aqueous humour to drain away; this can now be treated with a steroid related to cortisone. The lenses in the eyes of the woman may thicken and become fibrous, blurring her vision. She has cataracts, but artificial lenses can now be implanted using cryosurgery. There is no reason to lose one's sight just as there's no reason to lose one's teeth; regular, lifelong

dental care can prevent tooth loss. What can't be prevented is the yellowing of teeth, brought about by the shrinking of the living chamber within the tooth which supplies the outer enamel with moisture.

25 Between 75 and 85 the body loses most of its subcutaneous fat. On her 80th birthday the woman's granddaughter embraces her and marvels: "How thin and frail and shrunken she is! Could this narrow, bony chest be the same warm, firm bosom to which she clasped me as a child?" Her children urge her to eat but she has no enjoyment of food now. Her mouth secretes little saliva, so she has difficulty tasting and swallowing. The loss of fat and shrinking muscles in the 80s diminish the body's capacity for homeostasis, that is, righting any physiological imbalance. The old man, if he is cold, can barely shiver (shivering serves to restore body heat). If he lives long enough, the man will have an enlarged prostate, which causes the urinary stream to slow to a trickle. The man and the woman probably both wear hearing aids now; without a hearing aid, they hear vowels clearly but not consonants; if someone says "fat," they think they've heard the word "that."

26 At 80, the speed of nerve impulses is 10 percent less than it was at 25, the kidney filtration rate is down by 30 percent, the pumping efficiency of the heart is only 60 percent of what it was, and the maximum breathing capacity, 40 percent.

27 The old couple is fortunate in still being able to express physically the love they've built up over a lifetime. The old man may be capable of an erection once or twice a week (Charlie Chaplin fathered the last of his many children when he was 81), but he rarely has the urge to climax. When he does, he sometimes has the sensation of seepage rather than a triumphant explosion. Old people who say they are relieved that they are now free of the torments of sexual desire are usually the ones who found sex a troublesome function all their lives; those who found joy and renewal in the act will cling to their libido. Many older writers and artists have expressed the conviction that continued sexuality is linked to continued creativity: "There was a time when I was cruelly tormented, indeed obsessed by desire," wrote the novelist André Gide at the age of 73, "and I prayed, 'Oh let the moment come when my subjugated flesh will allow me to give myself entirely to. . . .' But to what? To art? To pure thought? To God? How ignorant I was! How mad! It was the same as believing that the flame would burn brighter in a lamp with no oil left. Even today it is my carnal self that feeds the flame, and now I pray that I may retain carnal desire until I die."

28 Aging, says an American gerontologist, "is not a simple slope

which everyone slides down at the same speed; it is a flight of irregular stairs down which some journey more quickly than others." Now we arrive at the bottom of the stairs. The old man and the old woman whose progress we have been tracing will die either of a cancer (usually of the lungs, bowel or intestines) or of a stroke, a heart attack or in consequence of a fall. The man slips in the bathroom and breaks his thigh bone. But worse than the fracture is the enforced bed rest in the hospital which will probably bring on bed sores, infections, further weakening of the muscles and finally, what Osler called "an old man's best friend": pneumonia. At 25 we have so much vitality that if a little is sapped by illness, there is still plenty left over. At 85 a little is all we have.

And then the light goes out.   29

The sheet is pulled over the face.   30

In the last book of Marcel Proust's remarkable work *Remembrance of Things Past*, the narrator, returning after a long absence from Paris, attends a party of his friends throughout which he has the impression of being at a masked ball: "I did not understand why I could not immediately recognize the master of the house, and the guests, who seemed to have made themselves up, in a way that completely changed their appearance. The Prince had rigged himself up with a white beard and what looked like leaden soles which made his feet drag heavily. A name was mentioned to me and I was dumbfounded at the thought that it applied to the blonde waltzing girl I had once known and to the stout, white-haired lady now walking just in front of me. We did not see our own appearance, but each like a facing mirror, saw the other's." The narrator is overcome by a simple but powerful truth: the old are not a different species. "It is out of young men who last long enough," wrote Proust, "that life makes its old men."   31

The wrinkled old man who lies with the sheet over his face was once the young man who vowed, "My grip will never weaken. I will walk with long strides and stand tall as long as I live." The young man who believed himself to be the exception.   32

Structure:

1. "The Way of All Flesh" is a striking example of chronological order used to organize a mass of information. Point out at least ten words, phrases or sentences that signal the flow of time.

2. Does Judy Stoffman's process analysis tell the reader how to do something, how something is done by others, or how something happens?
3. How long would this essay be if all its examples were removed? How interesting would it be? How convincing would it be?
4. What device of organization underlies both paragraphs 14 and 16?
5. What effect does Stoffman achieve when, in the last paragraph, she refers to the first paragraph?

Style:

1. Why are paragraphs 29 and 30 so short?
2. To what extent does Stoffman rely on statistics? What do they do for her argument?
3. To what extent does Stoffman rely on quotations? Would you call this selection a research essay? Why or why not?
4. In a desk-size dictionary, look up the origins of the word "gerontologist" (par. 28). How is it related to the words "geriatrics," "Geritol," "gerontocracy," "astrology" and "zoology"?

Ideas:

1. Did this essay frighten or depress you? If so, was this effect a failure or a success on the part of the author?
2. Do you share the attitude of Stoffman's young man who "has seen old people" but who "secretly believes himself to be the exception on whom the curse will never fall" (par. 2)? What are the benefits of such an attitude? What are the dangers?
3. Jonathan Swift said, "Every man desires to live long, but no man would be old." How do you explain the apparent contradiction in this PARADOX?
4. In paragraph 21, Stoffman contrasts our "subjective" and "objective" realities. Which do you think is more important in forming our self-image? Which do you think *should* be more important, and why?
5. Is compulsory retirement at 65 good for the individual? For the company? For society? When would you retire if you had the choice, and why? Would you apply a standard other than age?
6. If you have read "The Firewood Gatherers," compare the description of old age given by Thierry Mallet with that given by Stoffman.

7. Using examples to illustrate your points, write a *process analysis* on one of these topics:

> How to stay physically fit past thirty
> How to retain a feeling of self-worth in old age
> How to help parents and grandparents to be happy in their old age

----

(NOTE: See also the Topics for Writing at the end of this chapter.)

Richard Gossage and Melvin Gunton

Peopleproofing Your Child

Richard C. Gossage lives in Toronto and Melvin J. Gunton lives in Collingwood, Ontario. They are partners in an agency that produces films, manuals and advertising for business and government. At work the two men often discussed the joys and troubles of raising their respective children. Then one day they shared a sense of horror at a news report: in Toronto a six-year-old girl was lured from a park by a stranger and that evening was found brutally murdered. "Shaken to the bone," write Gossage and Gunton, "we realized that it could easily have happened to our own son or daughter." The two fathers set out to learn techniques for safeguarding their children, then, finding little published information, expanded the project into a book of their own. They interviewed police, social workers, teachers and psychologists before producing the work from which our selection comes, A Parent's Guide to Streetproofing Children. *Published in 1982, the book has been widely read in Canada.*

1   As soon as your children are on the street and away from your supervision, they will be faced with the necessity of sizing up people on their own. Peopleproofing your children for the street means providing them with some ground rules for making judgments about the behavior of others. Can I trust this person? Is she being honest with me? Why is he behaving that way?

2   No matter how sophisticated a child appears, it's probably best to assume that he is pretty gullible. His basic criterion for judging other people is whether or not those other people are nice to him. This isn't a bad starting point but, as every adult knows, it's not a good finishing point.

3   We've all made people mistakes. Sometimes we've trusted those we shouldn't have, and other times we've been embarrassed to learn that someone we've been wary of was filled with the purest of motives. Because of our errors, we often shy away from all but the most superficial generalizations.

4   "Johnny, I don't want to see you talking with that man again."

5   "What man, Mother?"

6   "The one who sits in the park and drinks cheap sherry."

7   No parent would disagree with Johnny's mother on this point, but beyond that, where do you go in order to provide your children with useful advice?

When we were talking with the police, they told us a story that 8
crystallized the problem. It seems that a young girl had been
abducted. In an attempt to get background information on the story,
a newspaper reporter had gone to a number of schoolyards to talk to
the children. Of the twenty-five six- and seven-year-olds he spoke to,
only one refused to talk. All the others carefully explained that their
parents had instructed them never to speak to strangers. Having
done this, they proceeded with the interviews. Apparently, a man in
a shirt and tie who says he is a reporter does not qualify as a
stranger. Strangers for youngsters look similar to the bum drinking
sherry. If you watch the papers, you may conclude that he's far more
harmless than the respectable gentleman in the suit.

RECOGNIZING STRANGERS

So, what's a stranger? A young child will tell you that it's a person 9
he's never met. "So when you meet somebody for the first time
they're a stranger, right?"

"That's right." 10

If you pursue this line of questioning, you'll discover that your 11
child probably doesn't consider a person a stranger after two or three
more meetings. If the person seems nice after this many encounters,
then he is to be trusted . . . or is he?

You have to tread a fine line here. While you clearly don't want 12
your children to be suspicious of everybody, you do want them to
develop a healthy skepticism. Developing it will be a process as
unique to your family as your philosophical beliefs. However, we can
give you some ground rules and guidelines; by discussing them, we
hope you will define your own.

Some parents say, "Make sure the people you meet earn your 13
respect and friendship." This is done, they say, by "showing you
respect and friendship." The message is sort of a reversed golden
rule. The next step is to give examples. Capitalize on the
opportunities in which you can say, "The reason we don't trust so
and so is because. . . ." It's important, when attempting this, to
explain your method of judging. While example is a good teacher,
circumstance may cloud the message for your kids. If, on the other
hand, they understand your reasoning, they will be able to apply it
more quickly when they are on the street.

All adults have cues and signals they use to evaluate others. 14
Discuss yours. Provide your children with some guidelines on how to
judge the people they meet. First, try to provide them with a basic
understanding of what is normal or natural behavior. For example,
many people are somewhat ill at ease in their initial contacts with

new people. Tell your kids that this is normal. For someone to appear shy, or possibly a little silly or flippant, is not unusual.

Beware of Flatterers

15 Next, explain what they should be wary of. We've all heard the old expression "Flattery will get you nowhere." Though as an adult, I've changed it to "Flattery may get you everywhere," you should tell your child that if he meets someone who spends too much time telling him what a great person he is, he should be on his guard. Though this may not happen to youngsters often, they're certainly subjected to the reverse. Those are people who spend a great deal of time telling a young person how wonderful they personally are. Children should ask themselves why a person is doing this. It's our opinion that if a person is coming on too strong, then a child can conclude they're trying to sell something. The challenge, then, is to identify what it is.

Information, Please

16 Another type whom we've all met at one time or another is the individual who wishes to know everything about you while providing virtually no background on himself. Kids should be taught that it's inadvisable to tell their life story to total strangers. If, in the long run, the person earns their friendship, there'll be plenty of time for swapping family histories. A person who refuses to give a little for what she gets may well be hiding a past that she is not proud of. It's important to explain to a youngster that someone who is ashamed of her past should have her offer of friendship considered very carefully.

17 Remind your child that friendships, good friendships, take a long time to create: they don't happen overnight. We must be careful not to send our children mixed messages on this matter. We must examine our own use of the word *friend*. We sometimes refer to people we've only met twice as "my friend." We feel you should teach your child the difference between the words *acquaintance* and *friend*, that the people you just meet once or twice are merely acquaintances, while the people you enjoy being with and see regularly are your friends.

18 Children hear and see much more of what parents say and do than we sometimes realize, and they model their actions on the total image, not just the parts we want them to. So we must all be careful not to seem like the people we're trying to teach them to be cautious of. We were told a story by a friend that points up the problem

graphically. Our friend's wife was trying to teach their boy that the policeman was his friend, that he was a friend to the whole family and could be trusted. The only comment the little boy had was "Well, how come he never comes to the house for drinks or dinner?" That started a whole new tack of peopleproofing by explaining the difference between acquaintances, helping friends, and personal friends, a difference we all too often ignore by dumping too many people into the friend category without any explanation or thought as to how it will affect our children.

Pressure Tactics

The next type of individual your child should be wary of doesn't   19
tell your youngster he's wonderful, doesn't go on about himself, and doesn't hide his background. As a matter of fact, he is quite forthright during the initial contact. However, he may want your child to do something that is against his will. It could be a borderline proposition, like going for a nature hike in a ravine. It might even be legitimate. Where the interaction goes off the tracks is when your child feels pressured to make an immediate decision in case he misses "this great opportunity." Kids should understand that good people will respect them even if they're confused about what they should do in a particular situation. Explain that it's normal for people to be provided with an appropriate amount of time to make up their minds. Tell your youngster that if he is having difficulty evaluating the alternatives, you want him to discuss them with you. Kids need to understand that a nice person making a reasonable request will not mind in the slightest if parents are consulted.

Equal Point

The next lesson a youngster should learn is the equal input   20
theorem. Kids should be taught to ask themselves what the relationship means for the other person. The best way to bring the idea out is to ask them if they'd be really interested in playing with someone who is substantially younger than they are. If they look at you as though they think you've lost your mind, then discuss the reverse possibility with them. What would they think if someone substantially older wanted to spend a great deal of time in their company? The general point is that children of similar ages usually have similar interests. If an adult is still fascinated by what kids are up to, there may be something wrong. You can point out that there are, of course, exceptions. An older person may love telling stories to young kids. In this situation the kids learn about someone's life, and

the older person has the pleasure of being valued and needed. But if an older person wants to play with your child, and your youngster can't figure out why, then he should discuss it with you.

21   These, and other rules you will think up, should help a youngster avoid problems. While they may occasionally cut the child off from normal interaction, we believe that, at best, they'll cause the child to slow down and think, and that's not bad.

Structure:

1. How far does the introduction to this selection extend? What are its two major techniques for interesting and preparing the reader? How well have these worked on you?
2. Most process analyses give their instructions in chronological order. Does this one? If so, to what extent?
3. Do you like the subtitles? Do they help clarify the organization? Do they help to interest and motivate you? Or do they distract you by chopping the passage into sections? Have you ever used subtitles in your essays? Why or why not?
4. Are the authors' instructions clear? Are they practical? How easy or difficult would they be for a parent to follow?

Style:

1. The word "peopleproofing" is probably not in your dictionary. Is it still a legitimate term? Do you think NEOLOGISMS help us to communicate, by expressing new ideas? Or do they confuse us and merely contaminate our linguistic heritage?
2. Judging by the STYLE of this selection — its vocabulary, its TONE, its presentation in general — what sort of reader did the authors have in mind as they wrote? Cite examples to illustrate your answer.

Ideas:

1. Did your parents "peopleproof" you? If so, to what extent? Give examples of their rules and advice. Tell the results. Would you use the same approach with your own children? If not, how will your approach be different? How close will it be to the approach suggested by our authors?
2. How do adults "peopleproof" themselves, especially in cities? Describe some common techniques used to avoid robbery, sexual

assault and other crimes. What are your own favourite
techniques? How often do you feel the need to use them?

3. In paragraph 21 Gossage and Gunton admit that their rules
"may occasionally cut the child off from normal interaction." Is
this a reasonable price to pay for making childhood safer? Or
can "peopleproofing" go too far, making children fearful and
mistrustful? Give examples if you can.

4. How great a threat to children is each of the following? Rank all
the items in order of danger, and give reasons for your answer:
communicable diseases
traffic
pollution
the arms race
divorce of the parents
child abuse in the family
strangers

5. If you have read "Coming of Age in Putnok" or "The Iron Road,"
discuss how the childhood of George Gabori or of Al Purdy
would have been changed by "peopleproofing."

6. How do strangers become friends? Write an essay of *process
analysis*, explaining all the main steps in their most reasonable
order and giving as many practical suggestions as you can.

(NOTE: See also the Topics for Writing at the end of this chapter.)

Captain Thomas James

*Our Mansion House**

In May of 1631 Captain Thomas James (1593–1635) sailed with his crew from Bristol, England, in search of the fabled Northwest Passage. Such a route would speed merchant sailors to the Orient, to make their fortunes in trade without the danger and expense of sailing around Cape Horn. James never found the passage, for it did not exist. But in the process of looking, he explored and mapped the west coast of Hudson's Bay. He and his crew also beached their ship, built shelter and spent a harrowing winter encamped on Charlton Island, at the south end of the sea which was later named for him: James Bay. After a desperate struggle against pack ice, the men escaped Hudson's Bay the next summer and arrived home in October, their ship "broken and bruis'd." King Charles I welcomed the captain of this failed but heroic expedition and commanded him to write his story. Our selection comes from The Dangerous Voyage of Capt. Thomas James, in His Intended Discovery of a North West Passage into the South Sea, *published in 1633 (our text follows the spelling, capitalization and punctuation of the revised 1740 edition). In this passage James tells how he and his men built the shelter that saved their lives.*

1   When I first resolv'd to build a House, I chose the warmest and convenientest Place, and the nearest the Ship withal. It was among a Tuft of thick Trees, under a South Bank, about a slight Shot from the Sea Side. True it is, that at that Time we could not dig into the Ground, to make us a Hole, or Cave, in the Earth, which had been the best Way, because we found Water digging within two Foot; and therefore that Project fail'd. It was a white light Sand; so that we could, by no Means, make up a Mud-Wall. As for Stones, there were none near us; moreover, we were all now cover'd with the Snow. We had no Boards for such a Purpose; and therefore we must do the best we could, with such Materials as we had about us.

2   The House was square, about 20 Foot every Way; as much namely, as our Main Course* could well cover: First, we drove strong Stakes into the earth, round about: which we wattel'd* with Boughs, as thick as might be, beating them down very close. This our first Work was six Foot high on both Sides, but at the Ends,

*Editor's title
*Main Course: a large sail, the lowest on a square-rigged mast
*Wattel'd [wattled] with Boughs: Wattling is the process of weaving small branches or twigs into a framework of larger ones to produce a wall, roof or fence.

298

almost up to the very Top. There we left two Holes, for the Light to come in at; and the same Way the Smoke did vent out also. Moreover, I caus'd at both Ends, three Rows of thick Bush Trees, to be stuck up, as close together as possible. Then at a Distance from the House, we cut down Trees; proportioning them into Lengths of 6 Foot, with which we made a Pile on both Sides, 6 Foot thick, and 6 Foot high; but at both Ends, 10 Foot high, and 6 Foot thick. We left a little low Door to creep into, and a Portal before that, made with Piles of Wood, that the Wind might not blow into it. We next fasten'd a rough Tree aloft over all: Upon which we laid our Rafters; and our Main Course over them again, which lying thwartways over all, reach'd down to the very Ground, on either Side. And this was the Fabrick of the Outside of it. On the Inside, we made fast our Bonnet Sails* round about. Then we drove in Stakes, and made us Bedstead Frames; about 3 Sides of the House, which Bedsteads were double, one under another, the lowermost being a Foot from the Ground: These, we first fill'd with Boughs, then we laid our spare Sails on that, and then our Bedding and Cloaths. We made a Hearth, in the Middle of the House, and on it made our Fire: Some Boards we laid round about our Hearth, to stand upon, that the cold Damp should not strike up into us. With our Waste Cloaths, we made us Canopies and Curtains; others did the like with our small Sails. Our second House was not past 20 Foot distant from this, and made for the Wattling much after the same Manner, but it was less,* and cover'd with our Fore-Course*: It had no Piles on the South Side; but in Lieu of that, we pil'd up all our Chests, on the Inside: And indeed the Reflex of the Heat of the Fire against them, did make it warmer than the Mansion House. In this House, we dress'd our Victuals; and the subordinate Crew did refresh themselves all Day in it. A third House, which was our Storehouse, about 29 Paces off from this; for fear of firing. This House was only a rough Tree fasten'd aloft, with Rafters laid from it to the Ground, and cover'd over with our new Suit of Sails. On the Inside, we had laid small Trees, and cover'd them over with Boughs; and so stored up our Bread, and Fish in it, about 2 Foot from the Ground, the better to preserve them. Other Things lay more carelessly.

    Long before *Christmas*, our Mansion House was cover'd thick over with Snow, almost to the very Roof of it. And so likewise was our second House; but our Storehouse all over; by Reason we made no Fire in it. Thus we seem'd to live in a Heap, and Wilderness of Snow; forth of our Doors we could not go, but upon the Snow; in which we

3

---

*Bonnet Sail: an additional strip of canvas laced to the bottom of a foresail or jib
*less: smaller
*Fore-Course: on a square-rigged ship, the bottom sail of the mast nearest the bow

made us Paths middle deep in some Places; and in one special Place, the Length of ten Steps. To do this, we must shovel away the Snow first; and then by treading, make it something hard under Foot: The Snow in this Path, was a full Yard thick under us. And this was our best Gallery for the sick Men; and for mine own ordinary Walking. And both Houses and Walks, we daily accommodated more and more, and made fitter for our Uses.

Structure:

1. In his process analysis, how closely does Captain James seem to follow the chronological order in which his "Mansion House" of Charlton Island would have been built?
2. Point out at least ten time signals (such as "next" or "then") which direct and speed the process analysis.
3. Do you think James left any important steps out of his process analysis? Did he leave any minor steps out?
4. Do you think the short accounts of building the second and third shelters contribute to this process analysis, or do they merely dilute the focus?

Style:

1. It is obvious that our language has changed since the time of Captain James. How do you react to the following aspects of his STYLE? Which aspects seem weaker than their replacements in contemporary English? Which seem stronger?
   A. Very long sentences joined with many commas, semicolons and colons
   B. Much more extensive capitalization, almost always of nouns
   C. Variant spellings
   D. Shortened suffixes (as in "resolv'd," of sentence 1)
   E. Very long paragraphs
   F. A preference for short words (Hold the text at arm's length to judge the "look" of the page. Now do the same with five or ten pages from more recent selections in this book, and compare the proportion of short and long words.)
2. Question 1 discusses some differences between our contemporary language and that of Captain James. Has our language changed radically? To what extent has it changed compared to changes in the following areas of life?

transportation
physics
medicine
business
communications

3. Captain James dedicated his book to King Charles I, saying:
   "Your Majesty will please to consider, That they were rough
   Elements, which I had to do withal; and will vouchsafe to
   pardon, if a Seaman's Stile be like what he most converseth
   with." Do you view James' STYLE as carefully worded and
   crafted? Or is it "like what he most converseth with"? Is James
   merely pretending humility or is he genuinely apologizing? And
   is a speech-like style necessarily bad?

Ideas:

1. By the time Captain James wrote of his voyage, the word
   "mansion" had several meanings. According to the *Oxford
   English Dictionary* it could signify "a place where one stays or
   dwells; a place of abode, an abiding-place" or "a structure or
   edifice serving as a dwelling or lodging place. . . . A house, tent,
   etc." or "the chief residence of a lord; . . . a manor-house. Hence,
   in later use, a large and stately residence." Which of these
   meanings do you think Captain James had in mind when he
   called his structure "our Mansion House" (par. 3)?
2. How easy or difficult do you think it would be to follow James'
   directions? Explain.
3. According to the rest of James' book, several of the crew died of
   scurvy, of drowning, of other accidents or of weakness caused by
   the intense cold of winter on James Bay. And many times they
   all narrowly escaped death in the water, as rocks, pack ice and
   even icebergs ground against their wooden ship. Do you think
   the planners of this expedition were wrong? Did the possible
   gains justify the cost in human misery and life?
4. If you have read "The Western Way" by Donald Creighton,
   compare the winter camp of Captain James and his crew with
   the Viking settlement of L'Anse aux Meadows, Newfoundland.
5. If you have read "The One Perfect House," compare the shelters
   of Thomas James and his crew with those of "the People"
   described by Farley Mowat.
6. Write an essay of *process analysis* explaining how you
   constructed or would construct one of these:

a temporary camping shelter
 (summer or winter)
a snow fort
a tree house
a play house
an igloo
a hunter's blind
a log cabin

(NOTE: See also the Topics for Writing at the end of this chapter.)

Martin Allerdale Grainger

In Vancouver

Born in London, England, and educated at Cambridge, Martin Allerdale Grainger (1874–1941) might have led a conventional life. But a love of action led him to British Columbia where he worked as a backpacker, miner, hunter, logger and writer. He also fought in South Africa and for a time taught jujitsu in London, but it was logging that became the main interest of his life and the subject of his book. Woodsmen of the West, *the semiautobiographical novel from which our selection "In Vancouver" comes, appeared in 1908 and was dedicated by Grainger "TO MY CREDITORS AFFECTIONATELY." Grainger went on to become an influential conservationist, government official and businessman in the forest industry of British Columbia.*

As you walk down Cordova Street in the city of Vancouver you notice a gradual change in the appearance of the shop windows. The shoe stores, drug stores, clothing stores, phonograph stores cease to bother you with their blinding light. You see fewer goods fit for a bank clerk or man in business; you leave "high tone" behind you.   1

You come to shops that show faller's axes, swamper's axes — single-bitted, double-bitted; screw jacks and pump jacks, wedges, sledge-hammers, and great seven-foot saws with enormous shark teeth, and huge augers for boring boomsticks, looking like properties from a pantomime workshop.   2

Leckie calls attention to his logging boot, whose bristling spikes are guaranteed to stay in. Clarke exhibits his Wet Proof Peccary Hogskin gloves, that will save your hands when you work with wire ropes. Dungaree trousers are shown to be copper-riveted at the places where a man strains them in working. Then there are oilskins and blankets and rough suits of frieze for winter wear, and woollen mitts.   3

Outside the shop windows, on the pavement in the street, there is a change in the people too. You see few women. Men look into the windows; men drift up and down the street; men lounge in groups upon the curb. Your eye is struck at once by the unusual proportion of big men in the crowd, men that look powerful even in their town clothes.   4

Many of these fellows are faultlessly dressed: very new boots, new black clothes of quality, superfine black shirt, black felt hat. A few wear collars.   5

6   Others are in rumpled clothes that have been slept in; others, again, in old suits and sweaters; here and there one in dungarees and working boots. You are among loggers.

7   They are passing time, passing the hours of the days of their trip to town. They chew tobacco, and chew and chew and expectorate, and look across the street and watch any moving thing. At intervals they will exchange remarks impassively; or stand grouped, hands in pockets, two or three men together in gentle, long-drawn-out conversations. They seem to feel the day is passing slowly; they have the air of ocean passengers who watch the lagging clock from meal-time to meal-time with weary effort. For comfort it seems they have divided the long day into reasonable short periods; at the end of each 'tis "time to comeanavadrink." You overhear the invitations as you pass.

8   Now, as you walk down street, you see how shops are giving place to saloons and restaurants, and the price of beer decorates each building's front. And you pass the blackboards of employment offices and read chalked thereon: —

"50 axemen wanted at Alberni
  5 rigging slingers $4
  buckers $3½, swampers $3."

And you look into the public room of hotels that are flush with the street as they were shop windows; and men sit there watching the passing crowd, chairs tipped back, feet on window-frame, spittoons handy.

9   You hear a shout or two and noisy laughter, and walk awhile outside the kerb, giving wide berth to a group of men scuffling with one another in alcohol-inspired play. They show activity.

10   Then your eye catches the name-board of a saloon, and you remember a paragraph in the morning's paper —

   "In a row last night at the Terminus Saloon several men . . ."

and it occurs to you that the chucker-out of a loggers' saloon must be a man "highly qualified."

• • • • • • •

11   The *Cassiar* sails from the wharf across the railway yard Mondays and Thursdays 8 P.M. It's only a short step from the Gold House and the Terminus and the other hotels, and a big bunch of the boys generally comes down to see the boat off.

12   You attend a sort of social function. You make a pleasing break in the monotony of drifting up the street to the Terminus and down the

street to the Eureka, and having a drink with the crowd in the Columbia bar, and standing drinks to the girls at number so-and-so Dupont Street — the monotony that makes up your holiday in Vancouver. Besides, if you are a *woodsman* you will see fellow aristocrats who are going north to jobs: you maintain your elaborate knowledge of what is going on in the woods and where every one is; and, further, you know that in many a hotel and logging-camp up the coast new arrivals from town will shortly be mentioning, casual-like: "Jimmy Jones was down to the wharf night before last. Been blowing-her-in in great shape has Jimmy, round them saloons. Guess he'll be broke and hunting a job in about another week, the pace he's goin' now."

You have informed the *Morning Post!*   13

If logging is but the chief among your twenty trades and   14
professions — if you are just the ordinary western *logger* — still the north-going *Cassiar* has great interest for you. Even your friend Tennessee, who would hesitate whether to say telegraph operator or carpenter if you asked him his business suddenly — even he may want to keep watch over the way things are going in the logging world.

So you all hang around on the wharf and see who goes on board,   15
and where they're going to, and what wages they hired on at. And perhaps you'll help a perfect stranger to get himself and two bottles of whisky (by way of baggage) up the gang-plank; and help throw Mike M'Curdy into the cargo-room, and his blankets after him.

Then the *Cassiar* pulls out amid cheers and shouted messages,   16
and you return up town to make a round of the bars, and you laugh once in a while to find some paralysed passenger whom friends had forgotten to put aboard. . . . And so to bed.

● ● ● ● ● ● ●

The first thing a fellow needs when he hits Vancouver is a   17
clean-up: hair cut, shave, and perhaps a bath. Then he'll want a new hat for sure. The suit of town clothes that, stuffed into the bottom of a canvas bag, has travelled around with him for weeks or months — sometimes wetted in rowboats, sometimes crumpled in a seat or pillow — the suit may be too shabby. So a fellow will feel the wad of bills in his pocket and decide whether it's worth getting a new suit or not.

The next thing is to fix on a stopping-place. Some men take a   18
fifty-cent room in a rooming house and feed in the restaurants. The great objection to that is the uncertainty of getting home at night. In boom times I have known men of a romantic disposition who took

lodgings in those houses where champagne is kept on the premises and where there is a certain society. But that means frenzied finance, and this time you and I are not going to play the fool and blow in our little stake same as we did last visit to Vancouver.

19 So a fellow can't do better than go to a good, respectable hotel where he knows the proprietor and the bartenders, and where there are some decent men stopping. Then he knows he will be looked after when he is drunk; and getting drunk, he will not be distressed by spasms of anxiety lest some one should go through his pockets and leave him broke. There are some shady characters in a town like Vancouver, and persons of the under-world.

20 Of course, the first two days in town a man will get good-and-drunk. That is all right, as any doctor will tell you; that is good for a fellow after hard days and weeks of work in the woods.

21 But you and I are no drinking men, and we stop there and sober up. We sit round the stove in the hotel and read the newspapers, and discuss Roosevelt, and the Trusts, and Socialism, and Japanese immigration; and we tell yarns and talk logs. We sit at the window and watch the street. The hotel bar is in the next room, and we rise once in a while and take a party in to "haveadrink." The bar-tender is a good fellow, one of the boys: he puts up the drinks himself, and we feel the hospitality of it. We make a genial group. Conversation will be about loggers and logs, of course, but in light anecdotal vein, with loud bursts of laughter. . . .

22 Now one or two of the friends you meet are on the bust; ceaselessly setting-up the drinks, insisting that everybody drink with them. I am not "drinking" myself: I take a cigar and fade away. But you stay; politeness and good fellowship demand that you should join each wave that goes up to the bar, and when good men are spending money you would be mean not to spend yours too. . . .

23 Pretty soon you feel the sweet reasonableness of it all. A hard-working man should indemnify himself for past hardships. He owes it to himself to have a hobby of some kind. You indulge a hobby for whisky.

24 About this time it is as well to hand over your roll of bills to Jimmy Ross, the proprietor. Then you don't have to bother with money any more: you just wave your hand each time to the bar-tender. *He* will keep track of what you spend. . . .

25 Now you are fairly on the bust: friends all round you, good boys all. Some are hard up, and you tell Jimmy to give them five or ten dollars; and "Gimme ten or twenty," you'll say, "I want to take a look round the saloons" — which you do with a retinue.

26 The great point now is never to let yourself get sober. You'll feel awful sick if you do. By keeping good-and-drunk you keep joyous.

"Look bad but feel good" is sound sentiment. Even suppose you were so drunk last night that Bob Doherty knocked the stuffing out of you in the Eureka bar, and you have a rankling feeling that your reputation as a fighting man has suffered somewhat — still, never mind, line up, boys; whisky for mine: let her whoop, and to hell with care! Yah-hurrup and smash the glass! !

● ● ● ● ● ● ●

If you are "acquainted" with Jimmy Ross — that is to say, if you **27** have blown in one or two cheques before at his place, and if he knows you as a competent woodsman — Jimmy will just reach down in his pocket and lend you fives and tens after your own money is all gone. In this way you can keep on the bust a little longer, and ease off gradually — keeping pace with Jimmy's growing disinclination to lend. But sooner or later you've got to face the fact that the time has come to hunt another job.

There will be some boss loggers in town; you may have been **28** drinking with them. Some of them perhaps will be sobering up and beginning to remember the business that brought them to Vancouver, and to think of their neglected camps up-coast.

Boss loggers generally want men; here are chances for you. Again, **29** Jimmy Ross may be acting as a sort of agent for some of the northern logging-camps: if you're any good Jimmy may send you up to a camp. Employment offices, of course, are below contempt — they are for men strange to the country, incompetents, labourers, farm hands, and the like.

You make inquiries round the saloons. In the Eureka someone **30** introduces you to Wallace Campbell. He wants a riggin' slinger: you are a riggin' slinger. Wallace eyes the bleary wreck you look. Long practice tells him what sort of a man you probably are when you're in health. He stands the drinks, hires you at four and a half, and that night you find yourself, singing drunk, in the *Cassiar's* saloon — on your way north to work.

Structure:

1. Why do you think Grainger begins this selection with a walk down the street?
2. Where does the process analysis begin? What process does it explain? What are its main events?
3. To what extent is "In Vancouver" a narrative? What purpose does this narration serve?

4. What proportion of "In Vancouver" is given to description?
5. Notice the last word of this selection, "work." What qualifies it to occupy that place?

Style:

1. Since saws have metal teeth, Grainger is using a METAPHOR when he writes of "great seven-foot saws with enormous shark teeth" (par. 2). Do other metaphors appear in the selection? If so, point them out.
2. In paragraph 18, Grainger mentions "men of a romantic disposition who took lodgings in those houses where champagne is kept on the premises and where there is a certain society." What is he saying? These polite EUPHEMISMS were published in 1908; restate the passage as it might appear if written today.
3. Look up the word "expectorate" (par. 7) in a desk-size or reference dictionary. Why does Grainger prefer it to the word "spit"? What are its origins in Latin? How is it related to the words "expand," "expatriate" and "pectoral"?
4. What has Grainger achieved by combining words, as in "comeanavadrink" (par. 7), "blowing-her-in" (par. 12), "good-and-drunk" (par. 20) and "haveadrink" (par. 21)?
5. Grainger frequently refers to "you," as in ". . . this time you and I are not going to play the fool and blow in our little stake same as we did last visit to Vancouver" (par. 18). What has he achieved in doing so?

Ideas:

1. What is a holiday for? What benefits do Grainger's loggers derive from their Vancouver holiday?
2. If you have read Pierre Berton's essay "The Dirtiest Job in the World," point out the ways in which the gold miners he describes suffer from lack of time off.
3. Does Grainger glorify the drinking, fighting and whoring that he describes? To what extent does an attitude of machismo underly the philosophy of "In Vancouver"?
4. Choose one section of "In Vancouver" to rewrite from the point of view of a feminist, retaining all the facts but changing the presentation of them.
5. "There are some shady characters in a town like Vancouver, and persons of the under-world" (par. 19), wrote Grainger in

this 1908 description. If you know Vancouver, discuss the extent to which his statement is true today. Give specific examples. If you live elsewhere, give examples of "shady characters" and "persons of the under-world" in your town or city.

6. Write a *process analysis* of any one of these activities:
   Enjoying a party
   Enjoying a concert
   Enjoying a holiday (specify
      where)
   Enjoying a night out on the
      town

(NOTE: See also the Topics for Writing at the end of this chapter.)

Topics for Writing

Chapter 8: Process Analysis

(Note also the topics for writing that appear after each selection in this chapter.)

Tell your reader how to perform one of these processes:

1. Flirt
2. Break off a romance
3. Make friends in a new city
4. Update your wardrobe
5. Produce a block print, silk screen, lithograph or photographic print
6. Make wine or beer
7. Win at the race track
8. Save money
9. Select a career
10. Learn a second language
11. Select a pet
12. Select a bicycle, motorcycle or car
13. Stop smoking, drinking, overeating or taking drugs
14. Cure insomnia
15. Enjoy winter

Explain how one of these processes is performed or occurs:

1. The making of paper
2. The making of glass
3. The making of cement
4. The evolution of a species
5. The extinction of a species
6. The formation of mountains
7. The formation of soil
8. The formation of sand
9. Desertification
10. The formation of rain
11. The formation and release of lightning
12. The eruption of a volcano
13. The migration of birds
14. The rise and fall of the tides
15. The changing of the seasons

"Sartorially, Johnny Canuck was a cross between a retired forest ranger and a sloppy Mountie in brown. He was supposed to be to Canada what John Bull was to England and Uncle Sam to the States and indeed, in political cartoons, he stood around chatting with John and Sam for decades. He was a nice chap, a follower rather than a leader."

Harry Bruce, "Johnny Canuck Is a Yuk"

Here's exactly what it is....

EXTENDED DEFINITION

We are all familiar with the kind of essay introduction that goes something like this:

> **A Canuck, according to the** *Acme Collegiate Dictionary,* **is "a Canadian, especially a French Canadian."**

We recognize the brief and businesslike wording of the dictionary, which tells us what something is. But after a few well-chosen words the definition is over. We have read only a beginning, an introduction to an idea but not an exploration of a subject.

In the hands of the essayist, though, a definition can expand into more and more detail until the whole essay functions to define the subject. In "Johnny Canuck Is a Yuk," Harry Bruce tells us probably all we ever wanted to know about the term "Canuck": its origin, its meanings in different times and different places, the shades of disapproval that it implies, its personification of Canada as Johnny Canuck, other words derived from "Canuck," and — his main point — the relationship of this dubious word to our self-concept as a nation. By the time we read Bruce's many examples, quotations and comparisons, leading to his suggestion that we discard the word altogether, we have amassed a much clearer and more detailed idea of "Canuck" than the dictionary could ever give us.

The purpose of an *extended definition* is usually to educate. It can also persuade or entertain, as in Harry Bruce's tongue-in-cheek argument, but whatever its tone or purpose, an extended definition *explains* a topic. How do we explain? In "Profile of the Rapist as an Ordinary Man," Myrna Kostash uses the power of facts: the average rapist is 15 to 24 years old; in 82% of rapes in one study, both victim and rapist came from the same neighbourhood; 71% of these rapes were planned. No vague generalization will provide the authority of specific information such as this. One way to define is to tell what the subject is *not*: Kostash develops her "profile" in part by showing that a typical rapist is not an easily recognizable "weirdo," is not insane and does not even consider himself a rapist. And David Suzuki, in his essay, condemns futurism mainly by showing how it is *not* a science.

An extended definition can be organized in almost any way or combination of ways. The writers in this chapter use all the major techniques we have explored in other chapters: *narration, example, description, cause and effect, comparison and contrast, analogy, classification* and *process analysis*. While essays in other chapters of this book have done the same thing, drawing upon a variety of methods, their basic structure usually depends on one organizational form — such as comparison and contrast. But definition is not a *form*, it is a *function*. In constructing your extended definition, you may want to think consciously of forms we have studied — or you may allow these forms to emerge naturally as you write. The process is completely open.

The Last Refuge of the Entrepreneur*

Paul Rush is editor and publisher of The Financial Post Magazine. *Born in Toronto in 1934, he earned a B.A. at the University of Western Ontario, then did graduate studies at the University of Toronto. From 1968 to 1973 he was managing editor of* Weekend Magazine, *then for several years worked at CBC Radio and did public affairs broadcasting for CBC TV. Since 1978 he has been on the staff of* The Financial Post Magazine. *Rush does not limit his writing to sober analysis of the business world. He unleashed his sense of humour in the chapter he contributed to* A Toronto Lampoon *(1984), and he regularly writes columns filled with human interest and wit for* The Financial Post Magazine. *Our selection, published in July 1985, is one of these.*

1   The garage sale is the last refuge of the entrepreneur.
2   No computer controls the inventory of outgrown skates, no director of marketing targets the sale of decade-old lawn tools and warped patio furniture. No executive committee sets the date by which all the paperbacks from the big box in the basement must be sold.

3   No, the motivating force behind the garage sale — or lawn sale or yard sale — is the householder, and his/her rallying cry is "Let's move some of this junk out of here." The staffing is done by available children who are forced to part with *The Hardy Boys In Peace and War* and the fish tank that's been gathering dust in the garage since the newt went west in the summer of '83. The day picked is a Saturday (rain date, Sunday) in spring after the sap has risen and while the scent of lilac pervades the land. The premise is that (a) you will get rid of some junk, and that (b) you might make a few dollars.

4   First you put an ad in the local paper, on the local radio station and then you stick up signs within a two-block radius. That's all the advertising you need — there is an entire culture of sale-goers out there, and they are tightly networked and eager. So eager that you will get some door-knocking Thursday and Friday as veteran buyers try to get the jump on the opposition. "I won't be able to make your sale," they say, "but I was in the neighbourhood and was wondering if you had any majolica creamers?"

5   The action on the day of the sale starts early, especially if there are other sales nearby. (There are *always* other sales nearby.) First

*Editor's title

315

come the vans, cruising slowly along the street, the drivers able to tell with one glance if your offerings are worth a stop. At a sale we had recently, I was just setting up shop in the middle of the driveway when I caught the eye of a van driver who was easing by.

6   "Come on in," I yelled. "Be my first customer."

7   He shook his head. "Nothing there for me."

8   "The garage is full of pine furniture," I called back. "I'm just getting ready to bring it out."

9   That got him — briefly. The brake lights went on and he craned his neck and caught my eye. Then he sighed and rolled on to the sale two houses away. He knew the garage wasn't full of pine furniture; no garage is. But what he might have got were three dark green wooden shutters that were put on our house in Montreal (before my time) in 1927, and have been travelling with us for years; an old window that might be pine and might have come from a corner cupboard; six sash weights; and three aluminum windows of a style that isn't made anymore.

10   After the vans, come the women (mostly) in station wagons. They stop, get out, march briskly up the drive or over the lawn and ask, "Any jewellry?" "Any majolica?" "Any carnival glass?" I shake my head and offer them a French mustard pot and they walk away and I feel guilty. It's barely 9 a.m., opening time, and I've already missed out on the big buyers. And then the real action starts.

11   Now you get the hobbyists and the strollers and the neighbors. The hobbyists like to hit eight or 10 garage sales on a Saturday, looking perhaps for clothes that will fit grandchildren or for dishes that will do for a cottage. Usually they are women, and often if you look down the street, you will see their husbands (one assumes, although these days you never can tell) sitting in family cars tapping fingers on the steering wheel. Hobbyists are hard bargainers:

12   "How much for that suit?"

13   "Twenty-five dollars."

14   "Twenty-five dollars!? For a secondhand suit?"

15   "It cost $110 and was worn once for graduation before the graduate grew six inches in the next week."

16   "Twenty-five dollars (a slow shake of the head and a slow turning back down the drive); imagine that. . . ."

17   And so I chalk up another no sale.

18   Which leaves a lot for the strollers and neighbors. One garage sale theory holds that the movement of junk is circular through a neighborhood. The incredible bargains you offer can't be resisted by the people from one street over. But the acquisition of your junk then forces them to begin unloading their excess. As their neighbors

buy that excess, so they in turn have their own sales. And you, as a prime seller, then become a prime buyer, and as you visit garage sales, you acquire the clones of your own junk. Einstein touched on this when he talked about space being curved.

What has been the outcome of my garage sales? Basically, I have 19 sold cheaply items that once cost me a lot and were used very little. A kitchen cabinet that cost me $85 went for $15 and I practically had to force it on the buyer. A bike that cost more than $100 and was only ridden around the block (admittedly, a very rough block) went for $20 and we threw in an extra tire. A jacket that cost $35 went for $2. But no one bought the pole lamp that had looked so good in 1967 and the lace-up ski boots just drew snickers. Maybe I'll have another sale in September.

Structure:

1. The organization of this extended definition is based on chronological order. Point out its main steps in time.
2. To what extent is this selection supported by examples? Point out at least three that attract your attention, and tell what they achieve.
3. Almost all of us have been to a garage sale. Why, then, does Paul Rush bother to "define" garage sales for us? What does he do for us in addition to "defining"?
4. Rush begins by stating, "The garage sale is the last refuge of the entrepreneur." How fully does this opening reflect what follows? In what ways is the statement shown to be true?

Style:

1. Is this selection CONCISE or wordy? Do Rush's many examples tend to prevent conciseness? Why or why not?
2. How carefully or carelessly has Rush chosen his words and expressions? For example, do you see any special significance in "after the sap has risen" (par. 3), "hit eight or 10 garage sales on a Saturday" (par. 11) or "clones of your own junk" (par. 18)? Explain.
3. When did you first realize that Paul Rush is poking fun at his subject? Is he right in his choice of TONE? Would this selection have been better as a serious argument? Why or why not?
4. Why does Rush cite Einstein (par. 18) in explaining garage sales? What effect is achieved?

Ideas:

1. As editor and publisher of *The Financial Post Magazine*, Paul Rush is a businessman. In his humorous essay has he made any serious points about business? If so, name them.
2. Some government officials are alarmed by the fast-growing popularity of garage sales, of barter and of other branches of the "underground economy" which generate no tax revenue. Is their alarm justified? Why do you think these activities are growing so rapidly? Could they or should they be controlled? Give reasons.
3. How much opportunity does the true entrepreneur have in Canada? More or less than in previous times? More or less than in other countries? Why? Give examples.
4. Make a list of the five or ten most useless objects you own. How did you acquire each? Why have you kept each? Does this information suggest to you any principles of human nature?
5. Write a description of a garage sale that you, your family, or a friend or neighbour gave. Use many carefully chosen examples, as Paul Rush does.
6. Write an *extended definition*, in essay form, of one of the following:
   a rummage sale
   a computer "software club"
   a church bazaar
   a "skills exchange"
   an auction

(NOTE: See also the Topics for Writing at the end of this chapter.)

Harry Bruce

Johnny Canuck Is a Yuk

If any one quality distinguishes the writings of Harry Bruce, it is a sense of place. Born in 1934 in Toronto, he celebrated his city in the 1960s by writing a series of columns for The Toronto Star, *which reported the walks he took through the streets and alleys and neighbourhoods and ravines and waterfront that he had known since childhood. In 1968 these were published in a book as* The Short Happy Walks of Max MacPherson. *In 1971 Bruce moved to Nova Scotia, drawn by old family roots and the prospect of salt-water sailing. Since then he has written lovingly of his adopted province in many articles, in the text for a book of colour photographs,* Nova Scotia *(1975), in* Lifeline: The Story of the Atlantic Ferries and Coastal Boats *(1977) and in* A Basket of Apples: Recollections of Historic Nova Scotia *(1982). Many of his magazine articles, on a prodigious variety of topics, have been collected in* Each Moment as It Flies *(1984), and* Movin' East *(1985). Bruce has worked for the Ottawa* Journal, *the Toronto* Globe and Mail, Maclean's, Saturday Night, The Canadian Magazine, The Star Weekly, The Toronto Star *and* Atlantic Insight, *while also writing on a freelance basis. "Johnny Canuck Is a Yuk" appeared in 1976 in* Saturday Night.

The temperature in Ontario and Québec hung around 100°F,   1
almost enough to boil the blood of your most icy-veined Upper
Canadian, and the front page of the Halifax *Mail-Star*
happily announced, "Canucks Swelter in Heat." Perhaps I only
imagined ill will. Perhaps the deskman who wrote that strange head
did not whisper to himself, "And it serves the bastards right."

But something else about the head bothered me, and it wasn't just   2
the redundancy of "swelter in heat." I wondered, why "Canucks"?
Surely Canadians don't call one another Canucks. Surely it's only
British and American veterans who still use that funny old word.
(*Soldier and Sailor Words and Phrases*, 1925, a British dictionary,
lists "Canuck: A Canadian" just after "Canteen Eggs: A gas
attack.")

But why was a Nova Scotian calling central Canadians "Canucks"   3
unless, deep down somewhere, he regarded all Canucks, Canadians,
or whatever you called "them" up there, as foreigners? The headline
suggested that, in the mind of one bluenose newspaperman at least,
the ancient chasm of Confederation was still too wide for bridges.
Not only that, "Canucks" was musty, like a hand-cranked gramo-
phone machine, a photograph of George V, or coy references to Dan
Cupid on Valentine's Day. Reading that head was like picking up a

newspaper in Memphis or Mobile and finding denunciations of "Yankee carpetbaggers."

4   But perhaps "Canuck" is not so dated as I want it to be. There's a comic book published for nationalists in short pants and it's called *Captain Canuck*. He's a masked muscle man with a maple leaf on his forehead and colourful long johns; and, although I hate to say this, he bears a suspicious resemblance to American comic-book heroes. Maybe his long johns are Stanfields. He doesn't look at all like Johnny Canuck, who wore a boy-scout hat and a vaguely military tunic. Sartorially, Johnny Canuck was a cross between a retired forest ranger and a sloppy Mountie in brown. He was supposed to be to Canada what John Bull was to England and Uncle Sam to the States and indeed, in political cartoons, he stood around chatting with John and Sam for decades. He was a nice chap, a follower rather than a leader. "I like to walk with a man who can set the pace for me," he told Sir Wilfrid Laurier as they strolled through a cartoon in the Toronto *Globe* in 1908. About all Johnny Canuck and Captain Canuck have in common is their surname and the fact they're both a trifle goody-goody. And, oh yes, a country!

5   U.S. presidential politics gave "Canucks" a deplorable shot of importance in 1972. I want the word to disappear in the quicksand of stale slang but now, dammit, it's a footnote to American history. It helped defeat Senator Edmund Muskie of Maine in his effort to win the Democratic nomination for the presidency of the United States. Muskie's enemies published a letter in which he apparently described New Englanders of French-Canadian descent as "Canucks"; and this evidence of his bigotry, which later turned out to have been a forgery by a Republican dirty-trick artist, was a factor in the sudden collapse of his campaign.

6   The baffling thing, for Canadians, was why anyone would mind being called a Canuck. "In spite of the definition given in many dictionaries still," says *A Dictionary of Canadianisms on Historical Principles* (1967), "the term Canuck, as applied by Canadians to themselves, is not at all derogatory, quite the contrary." Canucks think Canucks are good guys. What they don't know is that many Americans use "Canucks" the way bigots use hunky, bohunk, wop, etc. "Polacks and Canucks," the New York *Evening Post* reported in 1907, "have taken the places of most of the old-time American woodsmen in the Adirondacks."

7   The bias is more ancient than that. As far back as 1840, the Boston *Transcript* reported, "The French Canadian — or Conuck, as Her Majesty's provincial subjects of English and American extraction sometimes call him — can never by any means be induced to lay aside the abominable practice [of smoking and chewing in church]."

A character in *Field and Forest* allowed in 1870 that, "I hadn't no 'fection for them pesky half-breeds, nor them French Kanucks nuther. They are thick enough all along the [Arkansas] River."

In 1899 a book called *Trooper and Redskin* gave a prime example 8 of U.S. snottiness with regard to Canucks: "But for pure and unadulterated brag I will back the lower-class Canuck against the world." When the insults were not direct, they lurked in descriptions. In *Whispering Hills* (1912) there was "weary contempt" on the face of "the swarthy Canuck guide." In *Second Base Sloan* (1917), "La Croix was a thickset, hook-nosed Canuck" and, as astute readers of popular fiction have always known, people with hooked noses and thicksets are seldom up to any good.

Sometimes the American opinion that Canucks were an inferior 9 breed revealed itself in contempt and defiance. "Thar ain't no Johnny Canuck kin arrest me," said a rider of the plains in *Riders of the Plains* (1910). More often, the attitude was one of condescension. In 1846, for instance, a W.G. Stewart wrote, "The Cannakers, as they were commonly called, set themselves quietly about reviving their fire." Sturdy primitives they were, with bovine patience. In 1855, another outdoors writer said, "Giving our donkey into the keeping of a lively Canuck . . . we commenced the slow ascent [of Mount Holyoke]." And in 1888, in *Century Magazine:* "One was a short, square-built, good-humoured Kanuck . . . who interlarded his conversation with a mixture of French and English profanity." The *Dictionary of American Slang* (1965 reprint) advises, "Since 1855 the reference is often to a strong, rough woodsman or logger."

Strong, yes, but also kind of dumb and smelly. Look what progress 10 had done to the proud *voyageur*! Turned him into a Canuck, by gar. The guy left holding the donkey while better men climb mountains. He's handy enough in a canoe, all right, but hardly the sort you'd invite to opening night at the opera. Good man to have around when you want wood hewed or water drawn but he talks funny and he's got spruce needles growing out of his ears. "What's that?" someone asked in *Landlord at Lion's Head* (1908), and the reply came: "It's that Canuck, chopping in Whitwell's clearing."

In *Modern Instances* (1882) a character confides to another, 11 "Fridays I make up a sort of chowder for the Kanucks; they're Catholics, you know." (A "sort of chowder"? One imagines the speaker dumping fishgut stew into a huge trough, and letting the Kanucks go at it in the manner to which they were accustomed.) Anyway, this raises the strange matter of Canucks as all Canadians, and Canucks as French Canadians. The origin of the word may have been a corruption of "Connaughts." That's what French Canadians used to call the Irish in Canada. Somehow, it came out sounding like "Canucks" and English-speaking North Americans then nicknamed the French with the French nickname for the Irish. That's the story anyway.

12   The odd thing is, however, that American authorities are virtually unanimous that, as *A Dictionary of American English* (1936) explains the word, it is "in Canada the nickname of French Canadians; in the U.S. a nickname for all Canadians." Moreover, the 1970 reprint of Eric Partridge's *A Dictionary of Slang and Unconventional English* states under "Canuck": "Originally (1855) a Canadian and American term for a French Canadian which, inside Canada, it still means. Etymology obscure."

13   Time has made lies out of these definitions. It is chiefly in the United States, especially in New England, that "Canuck" still means someone of French-Canadian descent; and there, as we've seen, it's often about as friendly a word as "wetback" is in California. Moreover, though English-speaking Canadians have plenty of nasty words for the French, "Canucks" is certainly not one of them. And Johnny Canuck, who began to appear in English-Canadian political cartoons long before 1900, was about as Gallic as Lord Baden-Powell.

14   I am pleased to report that among all the dictionaries I consulted in this matter, so vital to our national identity, the only one that made any contemporary sense was Canadian. It was *A Dictionary of Canadianisms on Historical Principles* (University of Victoria, 1967) and it specifically denied that, in modern Canadian use, "Canuck" had any French-Canadian association. It conceded the term probably *first* designated a French Canadian but only because, in the early nineteenth century, "the term 'Canadian' itself most often referred to a French Canadian." Whatever other Canadians existed in those days, they were so inconspicuous a bunch they didn't deserve even an insulting nickname.

15   Not only did the Americans perpetuate "Canucks" as an insulting label for people of French-Canadian descent, they also went so far as to suggest Canucks were not even human. They were animals. Horses to be exact. From a piece in the *Congressional Globe* of 1867: "They went from St. Louis to Canada to buy the little Canuck ponies at $130 apiece." And C.D. Ferguson, a U.S. adventure novelist, was talking about horses, not some hombres from Québec City, when he declared in 1888 that "no frontier town ever saw a grander sight than those four Canucks."

16   In American slang, Canuck is also a language. The *American Thesaurus of Slang* (1945) lists it right up there with "Blemish: a mixture of Belgian and Flemish . . . Bohunk: the language of any

Slavonic race" . . . "Hunky" for Hungarian . . . and "spick, spic, spig, spigoty" for "the language of any foreigner of dark complexion." The thesaurus also lists, as expressions for Canada, Canuckland, Kanuckland, and Jack Canuck's Country. The best that can be said for them is that they're preferable to "Godamland" for England.

We are fortunate that, although a U.S. magazine called *Outing*   17
once carried "Snowshoeing in Canuckia" as a heading, "Canuckia" never really caught on. (Possibly because, "Oh Canuckia, We stand on guard for thee" was hard to sing.) In 1888, *Dominion Illustrated* used "Canuckiana" as a heading and, though I can't swear there isn't a "Canuckiana" sign in at least one of the bookstores that stretch *a mari usque ad mare*, our escape from an epidemic of that word strikes me as both miraculous and kind.

Canuck has popped up as Canack, Canuk, Conuck, Kanuk,   18
K'Nuck, and Cannaker. In *Leaves of Grass*, Walt Whitman preferred Kanuck. I prefer none of them. They're all repulsive. As French Canadians, "Canucks" were backwoods slobs. As an English Canadian, Johnny Canuck had less character than Mr. Clean without the muscles. Worst of all, "Canuck" is an essentially silly word.

Say it slowly. Listen to it. Can-uck. It has not one but two K   19
sounds, and K sounds have a mysterious quality of the ludicrous. That's why people get it right in the kisser and fall right on their keisters. That's why it is that, when supposedly hilarious violence occurs in comic books, people and animals and things all go kerbam, kerchunk, kerflooey, kerflop, kerflunk, kerslosh, kersmack, and kerspang. The huge metal spring that shoots a comic-book baddie headfirst into a brick wall (kersplat!) should not merely go boi-i-i-i-n-g-g; it must go *ker*boi-i-i-i-n-g-g.

Stand-up comedians have always known the secret of the K.   20
Desperate for a laugh, a cheer, any sign of life from groggy, hostile audiences, they'd mention Saskatoon, Kalamazoo, Hoboken, Albuquerque, Brooklyn. The result? Instant guffaws, titters, whistles. Har, har. Hoo, boy, they're warming up now. Time to hit them with something about Kokomo, the Kootenays, Kirkland Lake, Kelowna:

"Hey, listen folks, the other night I met this meathead, said he   21
was from Kamsack, Saskatchewan, Canader. Or maybe it was Kenogami, Kweebec, Canader. Nope, now I remember, it was Keewatin. Key *what* in? Look fella', you think maybe I should know about the sex life of the Keewatians? You think maybe I'm the Margaret Mead of the aurora borealis or something? Anyway, this fruitcake, he was from Lake Couchiching actually, he sez his name's

Canuck. That's right, Johnny Canuck. Johnny, as in the little boys' room; and Canuck, as in shmuck, shnook, and jerk. Anyway, so this Canucklehead from Kitchener, he sez to me. . . ."

22   Johnny Canuck is a yuk. That's why I wish Canadians would just leave him where he lay: back there in the time before inflatable tires. He's one symbol of our past we can afford to let stay there. Who wants a dink like that as the personification of nationhood?

Structure:

1. This extended definition has a purpose in addition to informing or entertaining the reader. What is that other purpose and where is it most clearly stated?
2. In what ways do the first three paragraphs provide a background for this essay?
3. This investigation into the word "Canuck" appears in sections. In what different ways is the word explained in paragraph 4? In paragraph 5? In paragraphs 6–10? In paragraphs 11–14? In paragraphs 15–17? And in paragraphs 18–21?

Style:

1. Can an essay with a light TONE have a serious purpose? Is the purpose of this essay serious?
2. In paragraph 4, what is the effect of the phrase "colourful long johns" and the statement "Maybe his long johns are Stanfields"?
3. In paragraph 9, where and how is repetition used deliberately as a device of humour?
4. Point out all the sources of humour in paragraph 10.
5. Contrast the style of paragraph 21 to that of the rest of the essay. Why is it different?

Ideas:

1. What does the word "Canuck" mean to you? Where in the essay does Harry Bruce come closest to defining the word as you know it?
2. If the "k" sounds funny, as Bruce says, do other sounds also have particular effects? As an example, look at all the words in your dictionary that begin with "sl" (as in "slippery"). Do a large number of these words create the same feeling? Give examples.

3. In paragraph 18, Bruce sums up the STEREOTYPES he has
   exposed: "As French Canadians, 'Canucks' were backwoods
   slobs. As an English Canadian, Johnny Canuck had less
   character than Mr. Clean without the muscles." How often do
   we think in stereotypes? Do you and the other class members
   agree on a common stereotype of Quebeckers? English
   Canadians? Germans? Russians? Americans? Chinese?
   Italians? Males? Females? Artists? Hockey players? Bankers?
   Teachers? Do you know of individuals in these groups who do
   not conform to the common stereotype? If so, give examples.
4. Discuss the dangers of stereotyping.
5. In an essay, develop an *extended definition* of the word
   "Yankee," and show the similarities, if any, between this word
   and "Canuck."

(NOTE: See also the Topics for Writing at the end of this chapter.)

Pauline Harvey

My Ideal Reader[*]

Translated from the French by Mary Conrad

Virtually unknown in English Canada, Pauline Harvey has emerged in the last few years as one of the most provocative of Quebec's younger writers. She was born in 1950 in Chicoutimi. Harvey attended university at Laval and Vincennes, studying journalism, literature and philosophy, and has worked in Ottawa as a reporter for Radio-Canada and as a translator for the federal government. Her literary career was launched in 1978 with the publication of Ta dactylo va taper, *a book of poems; her public performances of sound poetry also began to attract attention. Three novels followed in quick succession:* Le deuxième monopoly des précieux *(1981),* La ville aux gueux *(1982) and* Encore une parti pour Berri *(1985). In 1982 Harvey won the Prix des Jeunes Écrivains du Journal de Montréal and in 1985, for her third novel, the Prix Molson. Her feminist play* La nuit des braves *(1985) has been produced in Quebec, and numerous journals such as* Hobo/Québec, Mainmise, La Barre du Jour *and* Lèvres urbaines *have published her shorter writings. None of Harvey's books has yet been translated into English; her essay "My Ideal Reader," published November 16, 1985, in the Montreal newspaper* Le Devoir, *is given here in English as a sample of her philosophy and her style.*

1 Writing alone in a room, in the heat of creation, an author has no reader who could tell the truth about the book. There couldn't be one. Only later does the reader come, interfering and struggling with the text. The ideal reader would be the Devil — not because he's evil or sly, but because only he can interpret the fine points right down to the last comma. We always write for the demon or for the god deep down inside us who splits his guts laughing, for the animal in us that yearns to live, and — beyond success and failure, anger and fear, vanity and ideologies — for that slight bit of power we hope to create.

2 Dear ideal reader, soon you'll have to study me in school. This lady will have written very serious, crazy and elegant books, with answers to all kinds of questions no one ever asks. The real question to ask isn't "Where is literature headed?" but "Where are writers headed?" Are they doomed to make consumer goods and sell them through advertising campaigns? *"Get my book — put a tiger in your tank."* Or, "In class today you'll learn to *put lead in your head: study*

---

[*]Editor's title

Hubert Aquin."* Pardon this farce, but formulas almost as bad as these are inflicted on our students.

Dear ideal reader, I write in silence and I don't give a damn   3
whether you exist or not. Is there anything at all between you and me but a long fight? In the corner to your right, weighing 124 pounds, your writer of the evening; in the corner to your left, weighing . . . yourselves. Are you sure you've made the weight, that you can defend yourselves, that you've read everything necessary to do the job, that I won't roar and bite you on the face with my new-style ultra-perfect tiger? Telling long love stories for the reading public is all too easy. Swallow one with the last pastry of the meal, as a digestive cordial, a few pages to make you sleepy before you go to bed, your rest assured, everything fine. Why, it's like selling sleeping pills, a good job in a profitable and solid business: silence, discretion, quality.

The ideal reader would be aggressive and sincere, passionate, a   4
fighter — or else wouldn't be a reader at all. That's the only way to fall in love with books. Even hating books is better than fearing them. A writer's job is not to chat about obscure truths and ignore the others, but to make truth cry out. Why keep your mouth shut, sell supermarket music and become a pillar of salt?* I've begun my novels in the midst of angry women's screams, in the howls of my own rock generation. I know people's frailties and their failures, the empty mornings when life goes nowhere, the anguish in the eyes of those who are pressed for time, and the hunger, the frightening hunger, for love. I want to involve my reader and get a reaction.

"Peaceable and bucolic reader . . . if you haven't learned life from   5
*the Devil . . . throw that book out . . . you won't understand a thing. . . ."**

Ba . . . ba . . . ba . . . the first real word surges up in a private   6
babbling of the tongue, the first childish mumbling of a horrible scribbling — the empty cry of grief and of love, the innocent voice of the starving, the only possible rhetoric, the eloquence of tenderness. And all the rest of language follows, carnival-like, demonic, insane, dizzy, to search out in us our own power and our own reality.

"But if . . . your view is on the depths . . . read me so you will learn   7
to love me."

---

*Hubert Aquin: one of Quebec's major novelists, author of *Prochain episode*. In 1977 he committed suicide by shooting himself in the head.

*Pillar of salt: In *Genesis* 19, Lot and his wife flee the evil cities of Sodom and Gomorrah, which God is destroying. When Lot's wife looks back, against orders, she is transformed into a pillar of salt.

*"Peaceable and bucolic reader" . . .: from *Les Fleurs du mal (The Flowers of Evil)*, published in 1857 by Charles Baudelaire

Structure:

1. Where in Pauline Harvey's *extended definition* of her "ideal reader" do we see the following organizational forms used? Point out at least one passage for each:

    narration

    example

    description

    cause and effect

    comparison and contrast

    analogy

    process analysis

2. Compare the opening sentences of paragraphs 2, 3, 4 and 5. What pattern do you find? What effect does this pattern have on the organization of the essay as a whole?

Style:

1. When Pauline Harvey writes, "I don't give a damn whether you exist or not" (par. 3), she exhibits a highly SUBJECTIVE approach to her topic and her reader. What other passages seem highly subjective? Do you find such a TONE effective for this topic? Would it be effective for any topic or reader? How do you select your tone when you write?

2. Read the second half of paragraph 4 aloud. What effect does it achieve? What causes the effect?

Ideas:

1. Do many people use books as "sleeping pills" (par. 3)? Have you? If so, name the title, specify the dosage and tell the effects of this medication.

2. What are books for? Name five to ten basic uses that we make of them. Rank these uses from best to worst. Tell which use you most often experience in reading a book, and describe its benefits or drawbacks.

3. Do you agree that "even hating books is better than fearing them" (par. 4)? What does Harvey mean by "fearing" books? Have you ever "feared" a book? If so, what book and why? Have you ever "hated" a book? If so, what book and why? Have you ever "fallen in love" with a book? If so, what book and why?

4. Harvey describes her "ideal reader" as an opponent in a boxing match (par. 3). Is she right? In what ways is it good for writer and reader to "fight" each other? Are there ways in which they

should cooperate rather than "fight"? Or would cooperation lead to books as "sleeping pills" or as "supermarket music" (par. 4)? Do you view your own readers as opponents or as partners? Why?

5. In this essay Pauline Harvey seems excited, even angry. Do you ever write under the influence of strong emotion? If so, what are the advantages? What are the disadvantages?

6. In "The Decorums of Stupidity," Robertson Davies develops an analogy of books to music. Expanding on paragraph 3 of "My Ideal Reader," write your own analogy of books as drugs.

7. Write your own *extended definition* entitled "My Ideal Writer."

(NOTE: See also the Topics for Writing at the end of this chapter.)

Joanne Kates

Real Foods and Cold Comfort

Joanne Kates is a restaurant critic for the Toronto Globe and Mail. *"I have been in training for this job all my life," she writes, "and I can eat anybody under the table." Kates confesses that when she was growing up in the 1950s she ate "a lot of grilled cheese (so-called) sandwiches with Kraft Canadian slices and Wonder Bread" and that she was "heavily into red Jell-O with a small mountain of Reddi-Wip on top." It wasn't until later that she experienced gourmet food — "a moment far more exciting than losing my virginity" (quotations from her "Confessions of a Restaurant Critic" in the October 1983* Chatelaine*). At age 19 Kates enrolled in the prestigious Cordon Bleu school of cooking in Paris. Upon her return to Toronto in 1970 she briefly ran a food catering service, then worked as a cook in a French restaurant before becoming a restaurant critic. Although she has published* The Joanne Kates Cookbook *(1984),* The Joanne Kates Toronto Restaurant Guide *(1986) and even* Exploring Algonquin Park *(1983), most of her writing is restaurant reviews. Kates is tough and outspoken, feared by restauranteurs. She loves good food but hates anything overcooked, frozen, canned or smothered by half a pound of butter. She hates arrogant waiters, especially those who seat women near the kitchen door or thank the man after the woman has paid the cheque. And as we see in our selection, from the April 13, 1985,* Globe and Mail, *she hates being told what to eat.*

1   There are certain occasions when I feel unqualified to do my job. Turn me loose on anything from sea urchin to sweetbreads and I'm happy; but I admit that putting brown rice on centre stage makes me nervous and unadulterated tofu is a pain in the taste buds. If someone mentions sea vegetables, in a pious tone, I hunger for a big hamburger. And the very thought of macrobiotics makes me think of catechism. Why? It's not brown rice and tofu per se that I fear. Brown rice is great — as a side order under sweet and sour meatballs. I eat tofu salad readily, as long as it has enough chives and sesame seeds.

2   Food systems make me nervous. Macrobiotics is just another country, gastronomically speaking, and yet walking into Real Foods Café, the new macrobiotic restaurant, I felt none of the anticipatory pleasure that normally greets the introduction to an unfamiliar cuisine. The reason is simple: I rebel against being told what to eat.

Any dogma that systematizes my major source of regular entertainment is unlikely to succeed. If you told me that a daily dose of
hollandaise sauce was essential for human well-being and ar-
tichokes vinaigrette twice a day would prevent cancer, I'd still rebel.

The contradiction is that the macrobiotic fringe is probably   3
correct about what's good for us to eat. Their central notions are
several. First, they believe that food in its most natural, least-
processed state is the healthiest, offers the most nutrients, for
example brown rice, with its bran (rah rah fibre) intact vs. white
rice and whole wheat flour vs. white flour.

Their second notion is that eating locally produced foods in their   4
seasons is important because the body has more adjusting to do
when the food fails to match the environment.

Their third notion is that animal protein is dangerous. In this   5
they are certainly not alone, for it's common knowledge that
hardening of the arteries and various cancers owe a lot to a diet high
in meat. They eat grains and beans instead of animal protein.

And finally, they hold dear a notion of balancing their foods. From   6
the Orient they borrow the idea of a harmony of opposites, the
eternal balancing of yin and yang. In terms of foods, they see yang
as active, hot, male and contractive. Yin is passive, female, cold and
expansive. They've classified all foods as either yin or yang, and
they believe it's necessary to balance the diet in terms of yin and
yang.

Some foods are near the centre of the balance, that is, neither very   7
yin nor very yang. Beans and whole grains are nearest the centre
and thus also nearest to the macrobiotic heart. Way out on the
edges, sugar is as yin as you can get; meat, eggs and salt are as yang
as you can get. Eating out there on the yin/yang extremes is
supposed to make you feel unbalanced, unlike the beans and grains,
which help you feel "centred," a favored macrobiotic word.

Can you now picture the menu at Real Foods Café? You have to   8
like beans and grains. Sea vegetables, which the uninitiated would
call seaweed, also get star billing because they're next to beans on
the yin side. Almost all the ingredients are organically grown. Meat
and dairy do not darken the Real Foods door.

Enter the restaurant and you're in a small passageway bounded   9
on the left by a display of macrobiotic propaganda (ever considered
going to Macrobiotic Summer Camp?) and on the right by a phalanx
of steam tables. Is it a contradiction to serve natural foods from a
steam table? Far be it from your cretinous correspondent to
pronounce. But one thing I do know for sure: any restaurant that
serves its food cafeteria style and fails to tell you so, either verbally

or with a posted sign, is giving off the nasty smell of catering to those in the know.

10   As for the menu, think of brown rice. Plain brown rice. Bulgur rice patty. The chief virtue of the vegetable miso and lentil soups is their rectitude. This can also be said for almost everything else. Stewed daikon (Japanese white radish) comes with a bland ginger parsley sauce made from kuzu, a root vegetable that does a really terrific imitation of cornstarch. Garlic lima beans (très balanced, just a tad yin) would be nice if they'd remembered the garlic. Wakame with carrot is, believe it or not, the best tasting item on the menu. Wakame, a.k.a. sea vegetable a.k.a. seaweed, has a delicate scent of the sea and combines nicely with carrot.

11   At dessert time we return to the counter. There's couscous cake (think grain mush) with a sauce. "What's in the sauce?" I ask. "Tofu and tahini," says the counterman. I press him for other ingredients. "Lemon." I press harder. "Well," he says looking very guilty, "we do put in a little maple syrup." Enough to feel macrobiotically guilty but not enough to make it taste like anything. Mind you, it would take more than crème anglaise to rescue couscous cake from the cold oatmeal school. It is almost as unpleasant as the carob tofu brownie, which tastes rather like garden sand.

12   Dinner for two is very cheap — less than $15 — no charge for the piety.

Real Foods Café. 807 Bloor St. W., 530-1571. No smoking. Not accessible to people in wheelchairs. Not licenced.

Structure:

1. Joanne Kates sometimes feels "unqualified" to do her job, she confesses in the opening sentence. Is this confession sincere? Why or why not? And in what way does it prepare us for the restaurant review that follows?
2. How far does the introduction to this selection extend? Is it too long, or does its function justify its length? What does it accomplish?
3. Kates' extended definition of macrobiotics begins with paragraph 3. Where does it end?
4. Do you like the closing (par. 12)? Why or why not? What does it accomplish?

Style:

1. Kates seems to delight in satirizing "the macrobiotic fringe" and its Real Foods Café. Should she have been more OBJECTIVE? Does the one-sidedness of the SATIRE diminish her argument? Or does it dramatize and therefore heighten her argument?
2. The Real Foods Café calls seaweed "sea vegetables" (par. 8). Why? What rhetorical device is at work here?
3. In paragraph 10 Kates writes that the kuzu "does a really terrific imitation of cornstarch." Explain the IRONY of this statement and its effect. Point out and explain one prominent irony in each of these paragraphs: 1, 2, 3 and 11.

Ideas:

1. What qualities do you think it takes to be a restaurant critic? Judging by this review, do you think Joanne Kates is a good one? Would you trust her recommendations?
2. Which food do you love the most? Why? Which food do you hate the most? Why?
3. Some people hardly care what they eat, while others love or hate certain foods or "food systems." What forms people's attitudes toward food? What formed yours?
4. How do you choose your food? Rank these criteria in importance, and justify your choices:
   taste
   nutrition
   cost
   convenience
   emotional fulfillment (as in
     "soul foods")
   other (specify)
5. Over the last two or three decades Canadians have eaten out much more often than in the past. Why? Is this trend negative or positive? Why?
6. If you have read "Outharbor Menu," compare and contrast the "food system" of Ray Guy with that of the "macrobiotic fringe."
7. If you have read "How to Live to Be 200," compare Stephen Leacock's attitude toward food with that of Joanne Kates.
8. You are the manager of the Real Foods Café. Write a letter to the editor defending your establishment against Joanne Kates' attack.

9. Write an *extended definition* of one of the "food systems" below. If you wish, do it in the form of a restaurant review, after eating at the appropriate restaurant. Like Joanne Kates, use many concrete examples and maintain a consistent TONE (for example, humorous or serious).
   fast food
   junk food
   haute cuisine
   nouvelle cuisine
   organic food
   vegetarian food

(NOTE: See also the Topics for Writing at the end of this chapter.)

Myrna Kostash

Profile of the Rapist as an Ordinary Man

Myrna Kostash is a freelance writer whose subjects range from feminism to ethnicity, regionalism, radical politics and Canadian literature. Born in Edmonton in 1944 to a family of Ukrainian background, she has lived in Europe, Toronto, Montreal and now Edmonton again. In 1968 Kostash earned an M.A. in Russian literature at the University of Toronto and in 1970 published her first magazine article. Since then she has written a great many articles for Saturday Night, Maclean's, Chatelaine, The Canadian Forum *and other magazines, has published short stories and has written scripts for film and television. Her book about Ukrainians in Canada,* All of Baba's Children, *appeared in 1977 and* Long Way from Home: The Story of the Sixties Generation in Canada *in 1980. Our selection, "Profile of the Rapist as an Ordinary Man," illustrates her feminism. It appeared in 1975 in* Maclean's. *Although the word "rape" has now been removed from the Criminal Code, the psychological interest of this essay remains.*

I was hitchhiking from my parents' place to the city and got a ride with a man. When I first got into his car, he looked like a nice, gentle, innocuous guy who wouldn't bother me. He said he was 25 years old and had been out of school for a couple of years. We got to talking and he seemed okay but after about an hour he said he wanted to pull over to the side of the road and rest. I told him I was kind of in a hurry to get home. I had begun to get strange vibes from him — everything we talked about ended up in a discussion about sex. He told me all about his sexual experiences and wanted me to talk about mine. I was wearing jeans and an old top; when I hitchhike I dress as asexually as possible. So there was no way I was indicating my availability by the way I was dressed. Then he said we were going to stop whether I liked it or not and he was going to "make love" to me. I said, "I don't particularly want to make love to you." He pulled over to the side of the road and reached over me and put his elbow on the lock of the door and wouldn't let me out. He jumped on me. He ripped my clothes.*

And then he raped her. Forced her into this act he called "making love," and made believe that what he was recreating in the cramped

335

space of the car's front seat was a lover's pleasure. She went to the police but never pressed charges. Instead she has spent the last year wrestling with her fears and her anger. She finally talked it all out into a tape recorder, partly as therapy and partly so that others would know and understand just what the experience of being raped is like.

3   He was no weirdo. He didn't prowl around neighborhoods and drool at passing women from behind bushes. He didn't have the kind of grizzled face and unfocused gaze of the dirty old men you see in subway cars and buses staring at women's thighs.

4   If you asked him about himself he would tell you he was just an ordinary guy. He had a good job, loved his mum, took girls to the movies and to bars, slept with the ones who let him. Hell, he'd say, most girls are *easy* these days. They all pretend at first that they are virgins or something and waiting for Mr. Right but, in the end, if you put a little pressure on them, and maybe get a little threatening, they almost always give in. Women want to be *persuaded*, roughed up a bit. You certainly don't have to take "no" as their final answer.

5   And if you asked him for his version of what went on in his car that night, this is what he might say: what do you expect a guy to think when he sees a chick all alone on the highway, hitchhiking? And when she turns out to be real friendly and dressed up like a hippie? I mean, come *on*, you'd have to be pretty dense not to figure out that she's on the make. So you can imagine how I felt when she suddenly got on her high horse and said, no, no!

6   No one, neither psychologists nor the police, rape counselors nor judges, seems to know just what pushes an "ordinary guy" over the line between courtship and rape. There is research available and theories have been formulated which attempt a description of *who* the rapist is, what his personal history is likely to be, what might go on in his mind during the attack and how he justifies himself. But precisely what it is that distinguishes a rapist from the rest of men who don't, in spite of frustration, humiliation, guilt or outrage, force sexual intercourse on a woman without her freely given consent, is a mystery. The rapist doesn't understand himself any better than we do. In fact, a rapist may not even be conscious he's done anything wrong. According to a recent study in Denver, Colorado, "most rapists can neither admit nor express the fact that they are a menace to society."

7   *I couldn't believe it was happening and that I could be so completely trapped. He was so much stronger than I was. When he was finished, I threw up and he got mad at me for messing up the*

interior of his car. I begged him to let me go. He said he couldn't because I would have to hitchhike home and suppose somebody picked me up and raped me! I thought, oh my God, he's insane.

But, in all probability, he is *not* clinically insane. According to the Philadelphia criminologist, Menachim Amir, "studies indicate that sex offenders do not constitute a unique or psychopathological type; nor are they as a group invariably more disturbed than the control groups to which they are compared." Most of us share the popular misconception that all rapists are "sexual psychopaths." And the average rapist shares this misconception with us. Since he knows he isn't a Jack the Ripper lurking in dark corners ready to pounce on an unsuspecting female and drag her away, he doesn't think of *himself* as a rapist. He sees rapes committed by others in the same way we do, as the behavior of perverted, *sick* individuals and not something that he, a normal, virile and assertive male does when he "makes love" to the protesting and revolted body of his victim.

He wouldn't, then, recognize himself in most of the psychological accounts of a rapist's motivations: "incestuous desires," "symbolic matricide," "latent homosexuality," "castration anxieties," etc. Even if he did, the information would not be very useful to him or to us: rape is an *act*, not a state of mind. The rapist has imposed his sexuality and his fantasies on someone who doesn't want to participate; he has violated another human being's right to self-determination and he has terrorized her through a show of power. For him to see this as lovemaking is the real sickness. And yet the rapist does operate within the spectrum of normal masculinity and male sexuality. Within that spectrum he is the extremist.

Amir's study (the only comprehensive one to date in North America) showed that the majority of rapists are between 15 to 24 years of age — the period of a man's life when he is most anxiously flexing his muscles in the new role of adult masculinity. Since the social messages he receives about manhood celebrate the mystique of aggressiveness and toughness, a young man who rapes may be covering up for his feelings of weakness, sexual inadequacy and dependence — feelings which he, as a man, is not supposed to have — and taking them out on a handy victim. Almost half of the rapists Amir studied had a previous criminal record and more than half were either unskilled laborers or unemployed. Debra Lewis, University of Toronto criminology student, points out that if you are angry, frustrated, humiliated and a man, you can often deflect your misery safely onto a woman. She's less likely to fight back than a man.

11   Other rapists Amir studied were employed or middle-class. The
only theory that seems to explain their behavior is the psychological
one — "shaky defenses." As one psychologist put it, "Rapists show
strong elements of misogyny and distrust toward the women they
place in the position of sexual objects."

12   In 82% of the rapes studied, the victim and the rapist came from
the same neighborhood and half the rapes originated in a meeting at
the victim's or the rapist's house or at a party or a bar. Chances are
the rapist knows his victim and moves in the same social circles.
Chances are the rape will take place at the end of a social encounter.
This makes it easier for him to see his behavior as "seduction" or
"making love." That 71% of the rapes were planned demolishes the
myth that rape is the impulsive act of a loony who can't help
himself. Eighty-five percent involved the use of force and the most
excessive degrees of violence occurred in group rapes, suggesting
that group rapists perform for each other to prove how "manly" they
really are. It seems that the overpowering and humiliation of
another person is as important as having sexual intercourse with
her; that the event promises more than physical gratification for the
rapist. Debra Lewis sees it in power terms. "If you're a person who
doesn't feel very powerful or important, you're going to have the
same attitude toward your body. The more degraded you can make
your victim feel, the more you feed your own need. There is a large
frequency of the rapist demanding the woman tell him she likes it,
that she loves him, that she will go out with him after. It's a
situation in which he has perfect control at last."

13   So, when a man rapes a woman, a lot more is going on than just
nonconsensual intercourse, more even than a "sexual power
struggle," although that is certainly at the heart of it, as far as the
victim is concerned. In the course of my research, it was pointed out
time and again that rape is about *violence* and *power*. It is a measure
of our social malaise that we group these things with sex.

14   *He said, "Give me one good reason why you should live because I*
want to kill you." I was terrified. I didn't want to die. I gave him what
I considered to be a pretty good reason, that I was a human being and
had as much right to live as anybody else. He said that wasn't good
enough. He put his hands around my neck and told me to come up
with something else. He told me I had no right to be alive.

15   On the one hand, men are taught that women, being supposedly
the softer and weaker sex, are in need of their gentlemanly
protection; on the other hand, there are pervasive social messages in
films, literature, music, television, that women are, in fact, venal,

lascivious and masochistic. The rapist, as a product of this *generalized* hostility toward femaleness *and* the sentimentality around femininity, often makes what can be called the compromise of singling out certain *kinds* of women as rape victims. His mother and sister he'd defend to the death but that broad down the street in the tight sweater who went to bed with his buddy is fair game. Better still if she's non-white, unmarried, living on her own and working class. Amir writes that rapists are "more apt to view certain females as appropriate victims and certain situations as suggestive of, even opportune for, rape." This is not only because these women have low social status and therefore aren't considered "worth" so much, but also because forcible intercourse with them isn't even *perceived* as rape.

I thought about my parents and what a drag it was going to be for 16 *them when my body was found. I got really angry about hurting them. I said, "Look, if you don't get off me, I'm going to kill you." He looked at me and said, "You're crazy, aren't you?" I was playing his game, and it worked. He drove me back to the city. As we were driving, he said he thought we could become good friends and he told me his address three or four times. I think he was probably as scared as I was.*

Although the police advise women *not* to resist an attack for fear 17 of provoking even more violence, the Denver study shows that a woman can stop a rape (at the hands of a stranger) at stage one by refusing to be intimidated. "Above all, the rapist needs ordered and controlled behavior from his victim." As women become more self-confident and aware of their own strength, the incidence of rape may begin to decrease: the Denver study pointed out that "resisters [of rape attempts] scored higher on measures of dominance and sociability . . . were more self-accepting and had a greater sense of well-being [than those who did not resist]."

And maybe fighting back is the only real deterrent there is. It is 18 pretty obvious to everyone that our legal system is no deterrent at all. It's estimated that only one third to one tenth of all rapes committed are reported to the police. Many women who do report attacks never even get into a courtroom. They find the interrogation by the police to be such a brutal process that they don't press charges.

The first thing the police detective said to me was, "What's the 19 *matter, didn't he pay you enough money?" I couldn't believe it. He asked me if I had enjoyed it, he said I must have enjoyed it, look at the*

*way I dress, I must be promiscuous. Then he told me that if I couldn't
take this kind of questioning now, I wouldn't be able to take it later in
court. Did I really want to press charges?*

20 So the percentage of cases actually brought to court is small and
only a few of them actually result in conviction. In many cases, the
conviction that is finally obtained may not be for rape, but for a
reduced charge of indecent assault. It is important to note that the
charge of rape (which can be punished by a life sentence) applies
only to forcible penetration of the vagina (less than 50% of the cases
examined in the Denver study involved vaginal rape).

21 For the victim, any kind of assault and sexual humiliation is
horrible and destructive. But it seems that to jurists and legislators,
to police and to the community at large, it is an attack on the
vagina, the sacred highroad of marriage and maternity, that is the
profoundest affront. Ontario Crown Attorney John Kerr says he has
been involved in cases "in which the girl had been assaulted in a
horrible manner but because no actual vaginal intercourse took
place the accused was liable only to a charge of indecent assault."
Even though vaginal rape is obviously considered, in the eyes of the
law, to be a most serious crime, Sergeant Robert Lynn of the Toronto
police says he hasn't heard of a rapist in the last two years who's
been sentenced even to 10 years. "The average is four to five. If he
had never been in trouble before, and if he's going to be getting
psychiatric help, sometimes he'll only get two to three. Sometimes it
makes you wonder."

22 Kerr isn't encouraged by this trend to leniency among judges and
juries. While no one is suggesting that we should go back to the old
days and in a fury of vengeance castrate a rapist, or even whip him,
Kerr worries that "with our changing standards of morality, maybe
juries aren't treating rape so seriously anymore."

23 We know that rape statistics are rising drastically throughout
North America. In part, this is because greater numbers of women
are actually willing to press charges. But there are more pervasive
reasons. The so-called Sexual Revolution of the Sixties "liberated"
both men and women from the inhibiting restraints of a more
puritanical sexual ethic. Then, with the women's movement of the
Seventies, with the publicized struggle of women for independent
status, many of the protective, Victorian devices surrounding
women were withdrawn. A woman who insists on taking care of
herself can no longer be an object of male solicitude. It was only
when a woman was seen as fluffy, delicate and helpless that male
protective "instincts" toward her seemed sensible. A woman on her
own is fair game.

What, then, is to be done? How do we make our legal system a real   24
deterrent to rapists? How do we make it capable of protecting the
civil rights of women without resorting to extreme "law and order"
measures? The prosecution of rape charges might be made easier by
legislating different degrees of rape carrying different maximum
sentences. Police departments should establish units such as New
York's Sex Crimes Analysis Unit which is run by female detectives.
The New York Unit, besides receiving and processing all cases of
rape and attempted rape, also tries to reeducate male officers in
their attitudes to sex crimes. As of this writing, no police
department in Canada has tried to set up anything like it.

The legal profession has to realize that whatever the psycho-   25
sexual transactions between a man and a woman during a rape, the
physical intimidation involved in the crime is a serious matter.
Barbara Betcherman of Toronto's Rape Crisis Centre thinks that
the way rape cases are handled now, particularly because of Section
142 of the Criminal Code (which requires a judge to instruct a jury
that it is not safe to believe a woman on her word alone), they are
ipso facto prejudicial.

Obviously, there is no single remedy that is going to eradicate   26
sexual assaults on women. Legislative changes are required; so are
"rape squads" in police departments. So are rape crisis centres and
rap groups and pamphlets. But these kinds of changes only deal
with the aftermath of a rape. If we want to *stop* rape, we have to
figure out how to grow up as human beings.

Structure:

1. Why does Myrna Kostash split the rape victim's tape-recorded
   story into five parts instead of presenting it all at once?
2. Point out at least five facts or opinions given by Kostash that
   develop her extended definition of what a rapist is or is not.
3. Kostash admits that in one important sense we are still unable
   to define a rapist. Describe the problem and point out where it
   appears in the essay.
4. Although this essay is an extended definition of a rapist, it also
   defines something else. What does the second definition explain
   and where does it occur?
5. Upon what form of argument is paragraph 23 based?
6. Upon what form of argument is the closing of this essay,
   paragraphs 24–26, based? Why is this topic saved for last?

Style:

1. Why are paragraphs 3 to 5 so INFORMAL and even slangy, while most of the essay is more FORMAL in tone?
2. Discuss the IRONY of the rapist's warning to his victim: if he let her out of the car to hitchhike home, someone might pick her up and rape her (par. 7).

Ideas:

1. Paragraphs 18 and 19 illustrate the blame that society tends to put on the *victim* of a rape. What are the motivations behind this blame?
2. If you have read "The 51-Per-Cent Minority," compare Doris Anderson's description of economic injustices against women with Kostash's description of sexual injustices against women. Do you think these problems are unrelated or do they stem from common causes?
3. Some anti-abortion groups want abortion to be illegal even after a rape. Do you agree or disagree with this point of view? Why?
4. Paragraph 18 describes how few rapes are reported and brought to court, and paragraph 21 describes the light sentences usually given for this crime that, by law, can bring life imprisonment. How great a punishment do *you* think rapists deserve, and why? Might some rapes be worse than others and thus be cause for harsher punishment? Give reasons to support your answers.
5. Paragraph 17 states that it is self-confident women who are best at resisting rape. Has our society failed to encourage that confidence? If so, in what ways? As women gain power in society, will rape diminish?
6. Write a process analysis of what a woman can do to stop an attempted rape.
7. In essay form, write a profile of one of the following, giving enough examples and details to form an *extended definition:*

a vandal	a shoplifter
a burglar	a prostitute
a bully	an arsonist
an embezzler	a drug pusher
a child molester	a tax evader
a terrorist	an extortionist

(NOTE: See also the Topics for Writing at the end of this chapter.)

David Suzuki

Futurism *

Like Joy Kogawa, David Suzuki was born in Vancouver (1936) of Japanese ancestry and during the Second World War was interned as an "enemy alien." Since then, like Kogawa, he has made a major contribution to the life of the country that once persecuted him. Suzuki earned a Ph.D. at the University of Chicago (1961), specializing in genetics, then began to teach at the University of British Columbia. By 1971 he had become involved in TV broadcasting. Today he is one of Canada's best-known media personalities, host of one of the CBC's most popular and long-lived series, The Nature of Things. Though respected as a scientist, Suzuki is sometimes criticized for diluting his subject. But he believes that research alone is not enough: science is so vast, so pervasive, so full of both hope and danger for all of us, that it must be explained to the average person. Suzuki does this every week on television. He also does it in our selection, which appeared in 1985 in The Toronto Star.

A nyone who has spent some time in Ottawa recognizes very quickly that there are a lot of very bright, articulate people who make a good living as futurists.   1

With an indispensable tool, namely the computer, to provide all of the appearance of technological legitimacy, futurists call their profession a science. But I'll let you in on a secret. Futurism has its roots in the ancient practice of reading the entrails of birds for some sign of future events and has scarcely advanced beyond that ritual.   2

Futurism is no more a science than my grandparents telling the weather by the way their bunions felt. And there's a fundamental reason — which I'll let you in on in a moment — why futurism will always be a big swiz if anyone claims or believes that it is a science of prediction.   3

Of course, no major corporation or government organization can afford to be without its prognosticators, else how could one possibly plan ahead for the coming bulge of the elderly or the decline in school enrolments?   4

But this is not prediction; it is extrapolation. There's nothing magic about this. Futurists essentially follow trends (and the more indicators they have, the better their performance) and by plotting a curve from the past through the present, they can project the curve ahead. That's not a science, at least not in my book. Even I could do that, and I never liked statistics.   5

---

*Editor's title

6   Try reading the leading guru of futurism, the late Herman Kahn, who is best known for coining the term "megadeaths" in projecting the consequences of nuclear war and concluding that there are winnable battles. Kahn wrote a book predicting what the world would be like at the turn of the century and completely overlooked or missed the oil crisis that happened a few years later. He also foresaw Japan as an ever increasing giant.

7   But I have made a statement about futurism that is sure to raise the ire of its practitioners, and now is the time to deliver my reason.

8   The basis for the explosive changes occurring around the world today is science. Ideas and techniques discovered by scientists when applied by industry, medicine and the military are changing the planet in ways that transcend today's politicians, military leaders or movie stars.

9   Just reflect on a few of the things that have happened in my lifetime (and I'm not that old): nuclear weapons, jets, computers, satellites, oral contraceptives, plastics, lasers, transistors, organ transplants, tranquilizers, xerography, genetic engineering, embryo transplants, amniocentesis. The list could go on.

10   Each invention has changed the structure of society and the idea of our place in it.

11   If futurism really were a science, then all a company or political party would have to do would be to hire the best futurist available and win every time.

12   But the nature of scientific discovery and application is that they are unpredictable, else we would no longer call them discoveries.

13   Let me show you what I mean. I remember being electrified in the early years of Pierre Trudeau's reign when he talked about cloning as an important new area of concern. I did wonder whether he was thinking about it personally, but felt he was a rare politician who was informed about science and looked ahead. (But he certainly ignored my letters calling for a commitment to the support of a first-class scientific community in Canada.)

14   Let's suppose that 20 years ago a politician had the vision to realize that genetic engineering would be a hot area of research in the 1980s and that Canada should get in on it. He could have set out to establish a leading group in genetics by hiring the best. How would his futurists have advised him?

15   They would probably have told him to hire biochemists, microbiologists, human geneticists, perhaps even a fruitfly expert or two. But no amount of foresight would have suggested that they hire a zoologist who was interested in the toxic components of snake venom, another looking at the digestive enzymes of a snail's gut or a microbiologist investigating how bacteria avoid viral infection.

Yet it was research in these areas that led to the totally 16 unanticipated discovery of tools that have been vital in making genetic engineering possible. No amount of computer analysis could foresee that.

Structure:

1. Where does Suzuki first state his main point?
2. To explain what futurism *is*, Suzuki explains in some detail what it is *not*: a science. What basic device of organization, discussed in an earlier chapter of our book, underlies this approach to extended definition?
3. What proportion of this extended definition would you say consists of *examples*? Do you think these examples are too few, about right or too many? Which is the most effective example and why?
4. If you watch David Suzuki's CBC television series *The Nature of Things*, what similarities do you note between the techniques of explanation Suzuki uses in it and the techniques he uses in his essay?
5. What technique does Suzuki use to close his essay? Do you find the closing strong or weak? Why?

Style:

1. How FORMAL or INFORMAL is Suzuki's STYLE in this essay? (Cite specific passages to support your answer.) In what ways and to what extent do you imagine Suzuki's long experience in television has influenced his writing style?
2. In this essay Suzuki's paragraphs average two sentences each. Should they be longer? How long are they compared to yours? To what extent does paragraph length vary according to the purpose of an essay?
3. As the introduction to this selection states, one of David Suzuki's main goals is to explain large or difficult concepts clearly to the average person. To what extent has he done so here? And what techniques has he applied to this purpose? Cite examples to support your answers.

Ideas:

1. Having told us that futurism is not a science, does Suzuki go on to tell us what it *is*?

2. As professor of genetics at the University of British Columbia, David Suzuki is a scientist. Do you think this has made him biased against futurists? Is his criticism one-sided or fair? Can you think of any arguments in favour of futurism that have been ignored by Suzuki?

3. According to Suzuki, what is the main fact that sets science apart from futurism?

4. In North America the prediction of scientific advances has long been a favourite activity. According to the Toronto *Globe and Mail* of April 27, 1985, these predictions were made by the American Chemical Society fifty years before, in 1935:

   — ". . . colds, influenza, tuberculosis, possibly cancer and many other ills would be vanquished."
   — In the bedroom "you will throw off your bedclothes by snapping your fingers, warm the room instantly by pushing a button, then throw your pyjamas into the wastebasket, for cellulose goods will be so inexpensive it will be cheaper to throw them away than to launder them."
   — "Indigestion will be unknown . . ., for, with the discovery of certain hormones in the stomach of the boa constrictor, it will no longer be necessary to stay up after eating to digest one's dinner — just a boa pill and right to bed."
   — "Dream tablets" will contain chemicals "inducing only pleasant dreams. . . ."
   — ". . . by the use of hormones, chickens would be the size of pigs . . ., pigs the size of cattle and cows as big as mastodons."

   To what extent has each of these predictions come true? What impression do these examples give you of prediction in general? Do you consider these predictions the work of futurists or of scientists? The persons who made these predictions obviously looked forward to the future; do you look forward to the future, are you neutral towards it, or do you dread it? Give reasons.

5. Make five of your own predictions about the future 50 years from now, being as realistic and objective as you can. Give reasons to support each.

6. In essay form, write an *extended definition* of the professional role you plan to perform (for example, being a chemist, urban planner, actor, business administrator, fashion designer, mechanical engineer, etc.).

(NOTE: See also the Topics for Writing at the end of this chapter.)

Topics for Writing

Chapter 9: Extended Definition

(Note also the topics for writing that appear after each selection in this chapter.)

Write an extended definition of one of these:

1. Extrasensory perception
2. Burn-out
3. Epilepsy
4. An education
5. Feminism
6. Machismo
7. Health
8. Death
9. Continentalism
10. Patriotism
11. A Canadian
12. Success
13. Courage
14. Good taste in clothes
15. Gravity
16. Electricity
17. Wood
18. Snow
19. A great book
20. Good sportsmanship
21. Planned obsolescence
22. Organic gardening
23. "Appropriate technology"
24. Conservation
25. Infinity

Glossary

Abstract Theoretical, relying more on generalities than on specific facts. Abstract writing tends to lack interest and force because it is difficult to understand and difficult to apply. *See also* the opposite of abstract, CONCRETE.

Allegory In poetry or PROSE, a passage or an entire work that has two levels of meaning: literal and symbolic (*see* SYMBOL). Like a parable but longer and more complex, an allegory draws such numerous or striking parallels between its literal subject and its implied subject that, without ever stating "the moral of the story," it leads us to perceive a moral or philosophical truth. An analogy differs from an allegory in openly identifying and comparing both subjects.

Allusion An indirect reference to a passage in literature or scripture, to an event, a person, or anything else with which the reader is thought to be familiar. An allusion is a device of compression in language, for in a few words it summons up the meaning of the thing to which it refers, and applies that meaning to the subject at hand. Critics of big government, for example, will often allude to Big Brother, the personification of governmental tyranny in George Orwell's novel *1984*.

Anecdote A short account of an interesting and amusing incident. An anecdote can be a joke or a true story about others or oneself and is often used as an example to introduce an essay, close an essay or illustrate points within an essay.

Bias words Terms which, either subtly or openly, encourage strong value judgments. SUBJECTIVE language is a vital ingredient of much good writing, especially in description; to avoid it altogether would be both impossible and undesirable. The important thing is to avoid blatantly loaded language in an essay: words like "Commie," "slob," "cretin," "Newfie," "ex-con" or "broad" will inflame an uncritical reader and offend a critical one. Note that many bias words are also SLANG.

Cliché A worn-out expression that takes the place of original thought: "to make a long story short," "sadder but wiser," "bite the bullet," "hustle and bustle," "by hook or by crook," "as different as night and day" and "hit the nail on the head." Most clichés were once effective, but like last year's fad in clothing or music, have lost their appeal and may even annoy.

Climax In an essay, the point at which the argument reaches its culmination, its point of greatest intensity or importance. The closing of an essay tends to be most effective if it is a climax; if it is not, it may give the impression of trailing feebly off into nothingness.

Colloquial Speech-like. Colloquial expressions like "cop," "guy," "kid," "nitty gritty" and "okay" are often used in conversation but are best avoided in essays, especially FORMAL essays. Although they are lively, colloquialisms are often inexact: "guy," for example, can refer to a person or a rope, and "kid" can refer to a child or a goat. *See also* SLANG.

Conciseness The art of conveying the most meaning in the fewest words. A concise essay does not explain its topic less fully than a wordy one; it just uses words more efficiently. Concise writers get straight to the point and stay on topic. They are well enough organized to avoid repeating themselves. They give CONCRETE examples rather than pages of ABSTRACT argument. They use a short word unless a long one is more exact. And most concise writers, to achieve these goals, revise extensively.

Concrete Factual and specific, relying more on particular examples than on abstract theory. Concrete language makes writing more forceful, interesting and convincing by recreating vividly for the reader what the writer has experienced or thought. SENSE IMAGES, ANECDOTES, FIGURES OF SPEECH and CONCISENESS all play a part in concrete language and are generally lacking in its opposite, ABSTRACT language.

Dialogue The quoted conversation of two or more people. Normally a new paragraph begins with each change of speaker, to avoid confusion as to who says what. A certain amount of dialogue can lend colour to an essay, but heavy use of it is normally reserved for fiction and drama.

Economy *See* **Conciseness.**

Epigram A short, clever and often wise saying. The best-known epigrams are proverbs, such as, "What can't be cured must be endured" and, "To know all is to forgive all."

Essay Derived from the French term *essai*, meaning a "try" or "attempt," the word "essay" refers to a short composition in which a point is made, usually through analysis and example. While most essays are alike in being limited to one topic, they may vary widely in other ways. The *formal essay*, for example, is objective and stylistically dignified, while the *familiar essay* is subjective, anecdotal and colloquial.

Euphemism A polite expression that softens or even conceals the truth: "pass away" for "die," "senior citizens" for "old people," "low-income neighbourhood" for "slum," "gosh darn" for "God damn," "perspire" for "sweat," "eliminate" for "kill," and "de-hire" or "select out" for "fire." Euphemisms are becoming more and more common in uses ranging from personal kindness to advertising to political repression.

Fiction Imaginative literature written in PROSE. Consisting mainly of novels and short stories, fiction uses invented characters and plots to create a dramatic story; most essays, by contrast, rely on literal fact and analysis to create an argument. There is of course an area of overlap: some fiction is very factual and some essays are very imaginative.

Figures of speech Descriptive and often poetic devices in which meaning is concentrated and heightened, usually through comparisons.
A. SIMILE: A figure of speech in which one thing is said to be like another. ("With its high buildings on all sides, Bay Street is like a canyon.")
B. METAPHOR: A figure of speech, literally false but poetically true, in which one thing is said to *be* another. ("Bay Street is a canyon walled by cliffs of concrete.")
C. HYPERBOLE: Exaggeration. ("The office buildings rise miles above the city.")
D. PERSONIFICATION: A figure of speech in which a non-human object is described as human. ("At night the empty buildings stare from their windows at the street.")

Formal Formal writing is deliberate and dignified. It avoids partial sentences, most contractions, colloquial expressions and slang. Instead its vocabulary is standard and its sentences are often long and qualified with dependent clauses. In general it follows the accepted rules of grammar and principles of style. *See also* INFORMAL.

Hyperbole *See* **Figures of speech.**

Image In literature, a mental picture triggered by words. Because they strongly stimulate thought and feeling, yet take little space, well-chosen images are vital ingredients of writing that is CONCRETE and CONCISE. *See also* SENSE IMAGES.

Informal Informal writing resembles speech and, in fact, is often a representation of speech in writing. It may contain partial sentences, many short sentences, contractions, COLLOQUIAL expressions and sometimes SLANG. *See also* FORMAL.

Irony A manner of expression in which a statement that seems literally to mean one thing in fact means another. "That's just great!" is a literal statement when said by a dinner guest enjoying the fondue but is an ironic complaint when said by a driver who has backed into a tree. In a larger sense, *irony of situation* is a contrast between what is expected to happen and what does happen. It is this that creates our interest in the national leader who is impeached, the orphan who becomes a millionaire or the preacher convicted of tax fraud. Irony is a powerful tool of argument and especially of SATIRE.

Jargon Technical language or language that seeks to impress by appearing difficult or technical. Specialized terms can hardly be avoided in technical explanations: how could two electricians discuss a radio without words like "capacitor," "diode" and "transistor"? But these same words may need definition when used in an essay for the general reader. Other jargon uses technical-sounding or otherwise difficult words to seem important. An honest essayist will try to avoid "input," "output," "feedback," "interface," "knowledgeable," "parameters" and other ugly words of this sort when writing for the general reader.

Juxtaposition The deliberate placing together of two or more thoughts, IMAGES or other elements that emphasize each other, usually by contrast.

Metaphor *See* **Figures of speech.**

Neologism A newly invented word. Some new terms are accepted into our standard vocabulary. For example, a word like "laser" tends to become standard because it is needed to label a new and important invention. Most newly minted words are nuisances, though, for they are meaningless to the great majority of readers who do not know them.

Objective The opposite of SUBJECTIVE. In objective writing the author relies more on hard evidence and logical proof than on intuitions, prejudices or interpretations.

Onomatopoeia A poetical device in which language sounds like what it means. Some onomatopoetic words, such as "boom," "bang" and "crash," are out-and-out sound effects; others, such as "slither," "ooze" and "clatter," are more subtle. Onomatopoeia can be achieved not only through word choice but also through larger aspects of style. A series of short sentences, for example, gives an impression of tenseness and rapidity.

Paradox A statement that seems illogical but that in some unexpected way may be true. The Bible is full of paradoxes, as in "Blessed are the meek, for they shall inherit the earth."

Personification *See* **Figures of speech.**

Prose Spoken or written language without the metrical structure that characterizes poetry. Conversations, letters, short stories, novels and essays are all prose.

Pun A play on words. A pun is based either on two meanings of one word or on two words that sound alike but have different meanings. Often called the lowest form of humour, the pun is the basis of many jokes. (Why did the fly fly? Because the spider spider.)

Quotation The words of one person reproduced exactly in the writing or speech of another person. A well-chosen quotation can add force to an argument by conveying the opinion of an authority or by presenting an idea in words so exact or memorable that they could hardly be improved upon. Quotations should be reproduced exactly, and of course should be placed in quotation marks and attributed to their source.

Satire Humorous criticism meant to improve an individual or society by exposing abuses. In TONE, satire can range from light humour to bitter criticism. Its chief tools are wit, IRONY, exaggeration, and sometimes sarcasm and ridicule.

Sense images Descriptive appeals to one or more of the reader's five senses: sight, hearing, touch, taste and smell. Sense images are vital in helping the reader to experience, at second-hand, what the writer has experienced in person. CONCRETE language has many sense images; ABSTRACT language does not.

Simile *See* **Figures of speech.**

Slang Racy, unconventional language often limited to a certain time, place or group. Slang is the extreme of colloquial language, terminology used in conversation but hardly ever in an essay except for dialogue or special effects. One reason to avoid a slang term is that not everyone will know it: expressions like "swell," "square" and "far out" have gone out of use, while expressions like "bug juice," "croaker," "jointman" and "rounder" are known to only one group — in this case, convicts. *See also* COLLOQUIAL.

Stereotype An established mental image of something. Most stereotypes are of people and are based on their sex, race, colour, size or shape, economic or social class, or profession. Jokes about mothers-in-law, "Newfies," absent-minded professors, women drivers or short people are all examples of stereotyping. While they may provoke humour, stereotypes are anything but harmless: they hinder recognition of people's individuality and they encourage prejudices which, at their extreme, can result in persecution like that of the Jews in Nazi Germany.

Style In general, the way something is written, as opposed to what it is written about. Style is to some extent a matter of TONE — light or serious, INFORMAL or FORMAL, ironic or literal. It is also a matter of technique. Word choice, FIGURES OF SPEECH, level of CONCISENESS, and characteristics of sentence structure and paragraphing are all ingredients of style. Although a writer should pay close attention to these matters, the idea that one deliberately seeks out "a style" is a mistake that only encourages imitation. An individual style emerges naturally as the sum of the writer's temperament, skills and experience.

Subjective The opposite of OBJECTIVE. In subjective writing the author relies more on intuitions, prejudices or interpretations than on hard evidence and logical proof.

Symbol One thing that stands for another, as in a flag representing a country, the cross representing Christianity, or a logo representing a company. Symbols appear frequently in poetry, drama, fiction and also essays. For example the wall, in Austin Clarke's "Old Year's Night," physically separates the islanders from the tourists; at the same time it symbolizes the separation of the two groups by race, culture and economic class. Many symbols, like the wall, are tangible things that represent intangible things.

Thesis statement The sentence or sentences, usually in the introduction, which first state the main point and restrict the focus of an essay.

Tone The manner of a writer toward the subject and reader. The tone of an essay can be light or serious, INFORMAL or FORMAL, ironic or literal. Tone is often determined by subject matter; for example, an essay about cocktail parties is likely to be lighter and less formal than one about funerals. An innovative writer, though, could reverse these treatments to give each of the essays an ironic tone. The identity of the reader also influences tone. An essay for specialists to read in a technical journal will tend to be more OBJECTIVE and serious than one written for the general reader. The main point for the writer is to choose the tone most appropriate to a particular essay, then maintain it throughout.